T. J. Lang
Mystery and the Making of a Christian Historical Consciousness

Beihefte zur Zeitschrift
für die neutestamentliche
Wissenschaft

Edited by
Carl R. Holladay, Matthias Konradt,
Hermann Lichtenberger, Judith Lieu,
Jens Schröter and Gregory E. Sterling

Volume 219

T. J. Lang

Mystery and the Making of a Christian Historical Consciousness

---

From Paul to the Second Century

DE GRUYTER

ISBN 978-3-11-057811-9
e-ISBN (PDF) 978-3-11-043686-0
e-ISBN (EPUB) 978-3-11-043547-4
ISSN 0171-6441

Library of Congress Cataloging-in-Publication Data
A CIP catalog record for this book has been applied for at the Library of Congress.

Bibliographic information published by the Deutsche Nationalbibliothek
The Deutsche Nationalbibliothek lists this publication in the Deutsche Nationalbibliografie;
detailed bibliographic data are available on the Internet at http://dnb.dnb.de.

© 2015 Walter de Gruyter GmbH, Berlin/Boston
This volume is text- and page-identical with the hardback published in 2015.
Printing and binding: CPI books GmbH, Leck

♾ Printed on acid-free paper
Printed in Germany

www.degruyter.com

For Penelope, Henry, Theo, and Jessica

Contents

Acknowledgements — XI

1 Introduction — 1
1.1 Origins — 1
1.2 Thesis — 6
1.3 The History of Μυστήριον — 9
1.4 Μυστήριον in the New Testament — 17
1.5 Μυστήριον in Modern Research — 20
1.6 Structure of the Book — 24

2 Μυστήριον in the Undisputed Pauline Letters — 31
2.1 Introduction — 31
2.2 The Pauline Data — 33
2.2.1 1 Corinthians 4:1; 13:2; 14:2 — 33
2.2.2 2 Thessalonians 2:7 — 40
2.2.3 Romans 11:25 — 43
2.2.4 1 Corinthians 15:51 — 46
2.2.5 1 Corinthians 2:1 — 48
2.2.6 1 Corinthians 2:6–16 — 53
2.3 Conclusion — 67

3 Μυστήριον and the Deuteropauline Mystery Schema of Revelation. Part 1: Ephesians and Colossians — 69
3.1 Introduction — 69
3.2 Colossians — 70
3.2.1 Colossians 1:24–2:5 — 70
3.2.2 Colossians 4:3–4 — 81
3.2.3 Conclusion — 83
3.3 Ephesians — 85
3.3.1 Ephesians 1:9 — 86
3.3.2 Ephesians 3:2–13 — 90
3.3.3 Ephesians 5:32 — 103
3.3.4 Ephesians 6:19 — 106
3.4 Conclusion — 107

4 Μυστήριον and the Deuteropauline Mystery Schema of Revelation. Part 2: The Pastoral Epistles and the Romans 16:25–27 Doxology —— 110
4.1 Introduction —— 110
4.2 Romans 16:25–27 —— 110
4.3 The Pastoral Epistles —— 117
4.3.1 1 Timothy —— 118
4.3.2 2 Timothy and Titus —— 125
4.4 Conclusion —— 128

5 Mystery and History in the Letters of Ignatius and the *Epistle to Diognetus* —— 130
5.1 Introduction —— 130
5.2 Ignatius of Antioch —— 131
5.2.1 Ignatius and Paul —— 132
5.2.2 Μυστήριον in the Ignatian Letters —— 134
5.2.3 Revelation in Ignatius —— 145
5.3 Epistle to Diognetus —— 147
5.3.1 Literary Structure and Content —— 149
5.3.2 Diognetus and Paul —— 151
5.3.3 Mystery and Revelation in Diognetus —— 152
5.3.4 Conclusion: Christian Revelation and the Question of Judaism —— 161

6 Mystery, Scriptural Meaning, and the "Grace to Understand" in Justin Martyr's *Dialogue with Trypho* —— 163
6.1 Introduction —— 163
6.2 Justin Martyr —— 164
6.3 Justin and Paul —— 166
6.4 Μυστήριον in Justin —— 170
6.5 Μυστήριον and Justin's Hermeneutical Vocabulary —— 178
6.6 Prophecy and "the Grace to Understand" —— 183
6.7 Conclusion: The Mystery of Christ, Scripture, and the Question of Judaism —— 190

7 Mystery, Scriptural Meaning, and Ritual Performance in Melito's *Peri Pascha* —— 192
7.1 Introduction —— 192
7.2 Melito and his Peri Pascha —— 194
7.3 Melito and Paul —— 198
7.4 Μυστήριον in Peri Pascha 1–65 —— 199
7.4.1 Μυστήριον in Peri Pascha 1–10 —— 200

7.4.2 Μυστήριον in Peri Pascha 11–45 —— **205**
7.4.3 Μυστήριον in Peri Pascha 46–65 —— **213**
7.5 The Old Model and the Question of Judaism in Peri Pascha 66–105 —— **217**
7.6 Conclusion: Mystery Exegesis, Ritual Practice, and Synkrisis —— **218**

8 Mystery, Scriptural Meaning, and the Unity of God in Tertullian and his *Against Marcion* —— 221
8.1 Introduction —— **221**
8.2 Tertullian and His Treatise Against Marcion —— **222**
8.3 Tertullian and Paul —— **225**
8.4 *Sacramentum* in Tertullian —— **226**
8.4.1 *Sacramentum* and Oaths —— **227**
8.4.2 *Sacramentum* and Ritual Objects, Practices, or Liturgical Observances —— **227**
8.4.3 *Sacramentum* and Hidden Reality or Hidden Scriptural Meaning —— **228**
8.5 *Sacramentum* in Against Marcion —— **230**
8.5.1 *Sacramentum* in Books 1–4 of Against Marcion —— **231**
8.5.2 *Sacramentum* in Book 5 of Against Marcion —— **235**
8.6 Conclusion: Mystery, Paul, and Tertullian's Against Marcion —— **247**

Conclusion —— 249

Bibliography —— 253

Index of names —— 273

Index of Ancient Sources —— 277

Acknowledgements

"Acknowledgements" hardly seems like the right word for this space in which I express my deep appreciation for the many people, institutions, and sources of funding that have made this book and the life required to write it possible. It seems most fitting to begin my thanks with the person who has put more effort into this project – and indeed my entire career – than anyone else other than me. This would be my adviser, Douglas Campbell. "Adviser" is a horribly impersonal word for describing our relationship, which is to say our friendship. The thanks I offer here is an insufficient gesture of appreciation for his dedication to me, my family, and my work. More than a *Doktorvater*, he is my *Vorbild*.

My entire committee has also been a pleasure to work with and a source of unceasing support. Liz Clark exemplifies scholarly precision and creativity. Richard Hays has pressed me to open up my work to more ambitious claims, and he has given me the courage to do so. Kavin Rowe has been a constant conversation partner. I have worked out many problems on his front porch – or at least I have come to figure out just what the problems are. Although alphabetical order places him last in this list, Warren Smith has had a massive influence on my thinking. Our time together in Uganda is something I shall never forget, which is a promise I also made to the so-often forgotten pastors of South Sudan.

After my committee, Nathan Eubank deserves special mention. Nathan read every word of my first drafts, as he has of almost everything I write, and his comments are always meticulous and, in their most helpful instances, critical. Thanks are also due to the many others who have contributed in specific ways to this project: Hans Arneson, Stephen Carlson, Carl-Magnus Carlstein, Pete Jordan, Greg Lee, Joel Marcus, Lou Martyn, Tom McGlothlin, Sebastian Moll, Jason Staples, Matthew Theissen, Matthew Whelan, and Ben White. Many other names could be added to this list.

I should also acknowledge the institutions and people associated with them that have made this work possible. Duke University is a remarkable place to research and write. Funding from Duke's Graduate School and two Summer Research Fellowships provided the finances enabling me to devote myself unburdened to this book. Thanks are also due to the Fulbright Commission, which provided funding in 2009–10 for a year of research as a "Fulbrighter" in Germany at the University of Heidelberg. I express gratitude to my host in Heidelberg, Peter Lampe. Robert Jewett was also a tremendous source of support while in Heidelberg, helping me better formulate some of my early thinking on this project. Last but not least, I acknowledge the Dolores Zohrab Liebmann Fund, which supplied critical financing during the final years of writing.

And finally there is my family. My parents, Tim and Debbie Lang, have always given of everything they have to me and enthusiastically supported my work, even when it is mostly a mystery to them. But it is my wife, Jessica, and our three children, Penelope, Henry, and Theo, who have most patiently endured my daily (and often nightly) labor. As anyone who knows us would attest, little I have done is imaginable without Jessica. To try to indicate my appreciation for her is where words alone fail.

1 Introduction

1.1 Origins

The story of this book (or the initial spark) begins with a lucky literary crossing of wires made possible by the arrangement of the theological library at the University of Heidelberg. While on a Fulbright in Heidelberg in 2009–10 I began research on what I thought would be an exploration of the reception and development of Pauline hermeneutics up to Origen, who is often considered to be the first self-consciously systematic Christian exegete and is certainly a self-conscious claimant of the Pauline exegetical legacy. I intended to trace the influence of Paul upon Origen and his predecessors, hoping to define with greater precision the apostle's importance in the formation of early Christian exegesis. At the time I had also become enamored with the work of the great Jesuit theologian and historian Henri de Lubac, particularly his magisterial four-volume study, *Medieval Exegesis*,[1] as well as his influential monograph on Origen, *History and Spirit: The Understanding of Scripture According to Origen*.[2] In the course of my research I began to share de Lubac's sentiments on Origen's exegetical approach:

> But as I looked in those works for the necessary information, the subject I had at first envisioned assumed a broader scope in my eyes. It was no longer a matter of measuring, in any given exegesis, the part allotted to the "letter" or to history. It was no longer even a matter solely of exegesis. It was a whole manner of thinking, a whole world view that loomed before me.[3]

Aware that a full investigation (a "complete synthesis" as de Lubac called it) of this "whole world view" would include careful scrutiny of New Testament material, particularly the Pauline corpus,[4] de Lubac declined the task, professing,

---

[1] Published as *Exégèse médiévale* between 1959–64.
[2] Available in English as *History and Spirit: The Understanding of Scripture According to Origen* (trans. Anne Englund Nash; San Francisco: Ignatius Press, 2007). The original *Histoire et esprit: L'Intelligence de l'Écriture d'après Origène* appeared in 1950.
[3] De Lubac, *History and Spirit*, 11.
[4] De Lubac was committed to the preeminence of Paul in the formation of Christian exegesis. As he states at the outset of his second volume, *Medieval Exegesis: Volume 2 The Four Senses of Scripture* (trans. E.M. Macierowski; Grand Rapids: Eerdmans, 2000), "Nevertheless, it is sufficient to read a certain number of texts from the two originators, which here are Tertullian and Origen, to guarantee that, in word and deed, Christian allegory comes from Saint Paul" (4). Peter Martens, "Revisiting the Allegory/Typology Distinction: The Case of Origen," *JECS*

"Rather than consider the question in all its breadth, which would have required a rather adventurous foray into the biblical field, I have therefore stayed with my original plan. Origen remains the center of my perspective."[5] I too was becoming impressed by what seemed to me to be much more than just a particular mode of reading. And so, not yet beholden to an original plan, I determined to attempt something akin to what de Lubac had left undone, namely, to undertake an "adventurous foray" into Pauline material and to commence a sketch of that "whole manner of thinking" de Lubac observed in Origen. But where would one possibly begin? What exactly was this thinking, and how could one possibly presume to name and to explore it?

At least with respect to exegesis, I realized that to examine this larger manner of thinking would involve more than merely a catalogue of various formal features that recurred in Christian exegetical approaches. What was needed was an understanding of the fundamental intellectual structure that made revisionary Christian claims possible in the first place.[6] That is, what sort of mental framework could produce and sustain the approaches to scriptural reading found in the likes of Paul, Justin, Melito, or Tertullian? Furthermore, to what other new or creative theological ends might this manner of thinking have been applied? One possible way of getting at these questions came to me one

---

16 (2008): 283–317, has also recently emphasized the importance of Paul for Origen. Martens submits that scholarship on Origen has not "sufficiently highlighted how authoritative the allegorical interpretations offered by Paul were for Origen" (314).

5 De Lubac, *History and Spirit*, 11.

6 Neglect of the question "what makes it work in the first place?" is noted by de Lubac, *Medieval Exegesis: Volume 1 The Four Senses of Scripture* (trans. Mark Sebanc; Grand Rapids: Eerdmans, 1998): "Whether it be to denounce their arbitrariness and archaic character, or, more rarely, to justify them, there is almost always an interest in the methods of ancient exegesis. Its machinery is taken to pieces and its sources are catalogued, but there are no precise questions about the establishment of its methods and what service these methods are meant to perform" (261). Despite acknowledging the importance of the question, de Lubac by and large himself neglects to address it. As Hans Boersma, *Heavenly Participation: The Weaving of a Sacramental Tapestry* (Grand Rapids: Eerdmans, 2011), notes, "Both in his book on Origen and in his other writings on spiritual interpretation, it would have been good to read more about what allowed both Origen and the later Christian tradition to allegorize particular details of the biblical text…. What was it, for example, that allowed the church fathers to see the lamb and the sheep mentioned in Isaiah 53:7 as a reference to Christ? What was it that enabled them to see Christ in the wisdom of Proverbs 8? These questions do have some urgency if spiritual interpretation is to avoid the common charge that it renders interpretation arbitrary and subject to the whims of individual interpreters. We might wish that de Lubac had touched on these kinds of questions" (147).

morning as I went to track down an essay by Nils Dahl in the Bultmann *Festschrift* that seemed worth consulting.[7]

I was interested in Dahl's classification of what he termed a *Revelations-Schema* in early Christian preaching, the central feature of which was the proclamation that some reality, usually a christological reality, had been established before the ages but only recently revealed. The key texts marked out by Dahl include Rom 16:25–26; 1 Cor 2:6–16; Eph 3:4–7, 8–11; Col 1:26; 2 Tim 1:9–11; Titus 1:2–3 (all of which I treat at length in the following chapters).[8] Because of my chosen trail within the Heidelberg library I returned on the errand to retrieve the Dahl essay and, for reasons I cannot remember, had also glimpsed and decided to collect Markus Bockmuehl's *Revelation and Mystery in Ancient Judaism and Pauline Christianity* along with it.[9] Bockmuehl's book explores mystery terminology in early Judaism broadly, but his observations about the use of mystery within the interplay of hiddenness and revelation in much early Jewish exegetical literature had impressed me. As I began to read these two works together something previously embryonic in my mind began to take definable form. In text after text in my research on early Christian exegesis I encountered declarations of new hermeneutical revelation alongside appeals to mystery in order to substantiate exegetical claims about the Christian interpretive referent now manifest in Israel's scriptures. And so I began to recognize that routinely emerging alongside one another in the Christian exegetical texts I was reading was Dahl's "once hidden, now revealed" schema and then data comparable to what Bockmuehl had studied concerning μυστήριον in certain forms of Jewish exegetical practice. Thus these two modern works helped me to perceive an important and recurrent pattern of speech and vocabulary—and indeed a whole structure of thought—undergirding many early Christian exegetical claims. In examining this more extensively I began to notice it was applied to much more than just exegesis. In reply to any number of issues that were provoked by the apocalyptic newness of Christ, the "once hidden, now revealed" schema provided the hermeutical scaffolding for integrating what was now seen as the old and the new.

---

[7] Nils Alstrup Dahl, "Formgeschichtliche Beobachtungen zur Christusverkündigung in der Gemeindepredigt," in *Neutestamentliche Studien für Rudolf Bultmann* (BZNW 21; Berlin: Alfred Töpelmann, 1957), 3–9.
[8] He also includes 1 Peter 1:18–21; 1 John 1:1–3; Ign. *Magn.* 6.1; and Herm. *Sim.* 9.12.
[9] Markus N.A. Bockmuehl, *Revelation and Mystery in Ancient Judaism and Pauline Christianity* (WUNT 2/36; Tübingen: Mohr Siebeck, 1990).

As I began to press on in my investigation and follow up on the reception of Dahl's work and the history of research on μυστήριον, however, I became dissatisfied with what I found in two regards.

First, the response to Dahl's delimitation of the "once hidden, now revealed" schema had for the most part remained preoccupied with the red herring of his modest form-critical claims. While Dahl did offer the schema as one example of "einige feste Schemata die zur Einführung von christologischen Aussagen" and then propose that these schemata had their "ursprünglichen 'Sitz im Leben' innerhalb der Gemeindepredigt," the legitimacy of these particular contentions does not affect the more general observation that Christians, beginning with Paul, did indeed make repeated appeals to divine revelation as having occurred in a particular "once hidden, now revealed" temporal pattern. Hence to use and appreciate Dahl's observations need not entail an endorsement of any particular form-critical conjecture. The potential existence of a traditional, liturgical, or pre-established setting for this discourse is immaterial to its theological and interpretive function, which is to say, to the ways it is applied for theological work.[10] And as for the form-critical claims, it seems to me that in this instance hypotheses are simply unsustainable.[11] The data culled by Dahl, while indeed marked by linguistic overlap and thus appropriately correlated, is still on the whole too varied to be demarcated with strict precision. I concur with Bockmuehl's measured assessment:

> Thus, more helpful than the forced definition of a distinct form-critical unit will be the recognition that Paul views the Christ event and its revelation to the apostles as the decisive historical implementation of God's hidden, age-old plan of salvation.... This theme was developed in a number of ways, though obviously the use of motifs like "mystery," fulfillment, revelation, and the turn of the ages would be likely. We are dealing, therefore, not with a clearly defined liturgical "schema," but with recurring traditional terms and phrases used to express the patterns of realized eschatology.[12]

---

10 Among the more detailed and sophisticated attempts to better define the schema in form-critical terms is Dieter Lührmann, *Das Offenbarungsverständnis bei Paulus und in paulinischen Gemeinden* (WMANT 16; Neukirchen-Vluyn: Neukirchener Verlag, 1965), 124–33.
11 In the case of Lührmann, *Das Offenbarungsverständnis*, for instance, to arrive at a precise definition of the schema, he limits it to texts involving the combination of a verb for revelation with μυστήριον and νῦν, thus reducing the primary occurrences to three: Col 1:26; Eph 3:4–5, 9–10; Rom 16:25–26. As Bockmuehl, *Revelation and Mystery*, points out, "a *Gattung* of only three texts is not a particularly meaningful proposition" (209).
12 Bockmuehl, *Revelation and Mystery*, 210.

Although I continue to use the word "schema"—preferring the description "mystery schema" to "revelation schema"—I am not referring to a fixed kerygmatic tradition or liturgical formula. I mean something more along the lines of an intellectual or discursive framework within which reality is restructured around Christ's advent and then history is renarrated in accordance with the apocalyptic unveiling of God's previously hidden but eternal plan.[13] While this historical hidden/revealed schema certainly attracts a common assemblage of terminology and motifs that then repeatedly materialize according to a sort of rule-governed variation (the rule being the temporal setting of the hidden/revealed binary), it need not be circumscribed in any more precise form-critical sense.

A second shortcoming was the absence of any major study of μυστήριον in early Christianity. This omission seemed all the more astounding given what, on the one hand, appeared to be the widespread importance of the term in second-century Christian literature and yet what, on the other hand, I found to be the excess of scholarly interest in the pre-Christian use of this term (a subject I shall turn to below). The only thing approximating a sustained analysis of the Pauline and post-Pauline data is a 1911 article by Hans von Soden,[14] but von Soden's work, while informative, is more an index of evidence than an analysis of it, and now an incomplete index at that.[15] Hence Bockmuehl remarks on the insufficient analysis of second-century material: "The field here is vast; and in light of the topic's importance in early Judaism and Paul it most certainly merits a full-scale treatment in its own right."[16] I have determined to do just this, but still with an eye toward glimpsing something of that "whole manner of thinking" noticed by de Lubac—or at least one partial but fundamental component of it.

---

13 My use of the term is actually closer to how it is used in philosophy and, more recently, in cognitive psychology. For further discussion see Mary B. McVee, Kailonnie Dunsmore, and James R. Gavelek, "Schema Theory Revisited," *Review of Educational Research* 75 (2005): 531–66.

14 Hans von Soden, "ΜΥΣΤΗΡΙΟΝ und *sacramentum* in den ersten zwei Jahrhunderten der Kirche," *ZNW* 12 (1911): 188–227. At times instructive, but even less detailed (and also occasionally incorrect) is J.D.B. Hamilton, "The Church and the Language of Mystery: The First Four Centuries," *ETL* 53 (1977): 479–94. Even briefer is K. Prümm, "'Mysterion' von Paulus bis Origenes," *ZKT* 61 (1937): 391–425.

15 I am referring to the absence of data from Melito, which was not known until the middle portions of the twentieth century and so not available to von Soden.

16 Bockmuehl, *Revelation and Mystery*, 214. Bockmuehl, to his credit, does offer a useful if "superficial 'spot check'" of some of the data, but it comprises less than seven pages (214–20).

1.2 Thesis

To state the thesis of this book more plainly, I begin with an influential quotation from Adolf von Harnack's *The Mission and Expansion of Christianity in the First Three Centuries* that concisely names the social and intellectual consequences of the dual Christian commitment to apocalyptic newness and the ancient pedigree of Israel's history:

> Convinced that Jesus, the teacher and prophet, was also the Messiah who was to return ere long to finish off his work, people passed from the consciousness of being his disciples into that of being his people, the people of God...and in so far as they felt themselves to be a people, Christians knew they were the true Israel, at once the new people and the old. This conviction that they were a people...at once furnished adherents of the new faith with a political and historical self-consciousness (*politisch-historisches Bewusstsein*). Nothing more comprehensive or complete or impressive than this consciousness can be conceived.[17]

On the most general, theological level this book explores the origins, ensuing articulations, and intellectual implications of what Harnack, in the above quotation, identifies as that distinctly Christian *politisch-historisches Bewusstsein*—that totalizing reconception of history and ecclesial identity that enabled early Christians to imagine themselves as simultaneously new to the world in terms of revelation and yet also ancient with respect to God's eternal plan. On the more specific and descriptive level, I propose that a key to mapping the early development of this new historical consciousness comes via detailed analysis of a single term introduced by the apostle Paul into the Christian theological lexicon, the noun μυστήριον, and the particular understanding of history and revelation that is commonly coupled with it, an understanding I refer to in varying ways as the "once hidden, now revealed" mystery schema.[18] It is, I claim, the historical

---

17 Adolf von Harnack, *The Mission and Expansion of Christianity in the First Three Centuries*. Vol. 1 (trans. James Moffatt; 2d ed; London: Williams and Norgate, 1908), 240–41.
18 While I cannot speak certainly for Harnack's use of *Bewusstsein*, I use the term "consciousness" loosely and as more or less synonymous with words like perception or understanding, and so untethered from the ways in which "historical consciousness" might be associated with Hegelians and other German idealists. According to my usage, a historical consciousness is nothing more than the particular way in which an individual or community conceives history. For a more precise definition, I would endorse Paul Minear's classification in "Historical Consciousness vs. Historical Knowledge," *JBR* 8 (1940): 72–76. "Historical consciousness," Minear writes, "involves not only a curiosity about what has happened but an intense interest that is nourished by the compelling conviction that 'something has happened in what happened'.... It expresses the faith that the meaning of what happened in the past transcends the time and place of its

arrangement of the once hidden/now revealed discourse,[19] and thus the comprehensive division of time into adjacent eras of concealment and revelation, that provided Christians of the first two centuries with the intellectual architecture and accompanying discursive schema to formulate and legitimize some of the most original claims of Christian theology.[20] Among these claims are ecclesiological propositions regarding the status of the Gentiles among the people of God, hermeneutical propositions related to the revisionary Christian readings of Israel's scriptures, and christological propositions about the fact of God's revelation in Christ and the unified identity of the newly revealed Christ and the creator God of Israel.

This particular conjunction of previous concealment and present manifestation is not the only way in which conceptions of past and present are configured by Christians. Identity is also frequently conceptualized in terms of other fundamentally determinative coordinates involving the once and the now—"you who were once slaves to sin...have been set free from sin" (Rom 6:17–18) or "before faith came we were confined under the Law...but now that faith has come..." (Gal 3:23–25). As important and theologically generative as such construals of identity are, however, they do not amount to new ways of comprehending history *per se*. The "once hidden, now revealed" mystery schema reimagines time in a totalizing sense with history itself being conceived in terms of contrasting eras of concealment and revelation, both of which are then knit together by an eternal divine plan. Insofar as the realities belonging to this plan were named mysteries, and so realities newly revealed but eternally known by the God of Israel,

---

happening and that this meaning has decisive relevance to present concerns. It assumes as real the identification of one's own interests and existence with the past, the solidarity of a personal present with a personal past. In its more unconditioned form, it gives rise to the sense that 'we were there'" (72).

19 Given the disparate understandings of the term "discourse" and the complicated specificity given to it by Foucault, I use the word reluctantly but, lacking a better alternative, with some frequency. I find the description of Laura Nasrallah, *An Ecstasy of Folly: Prophecy and Authority in Early Christianity* (HTS 52; Cambridge: Harvard University Press, 2003), to be helpful: "By participating in a given discourse, a text constructs through rhetoric a vision of the world as it should be, and seeks to exercise language in order to convince its audience of the power and reality of that vision" (5). This gives some clarity to Foucault's own claim that discourses are linguistic "practices that systematically form the objects of which they speak" (*Archaeology of Knowledge and the Discourse on Language* [trans. A.M. Sheridan Smith; New York: Pantheon, 1972], 49).

20 In this sense the discourse I am interested in could be viewed as an earlier, perhaps more fundamental, expression of the "totalizing discourse" Averil Cameron finds at work in the Christianization of the Roman empire in *Christianity and the Rhetoric of Empire: The Development of Christian Discourse* (Sather Classical Lectures 55; Berkeley: University of California Press, 1991).

and yet were argued independently of (if not in contradiction of) Torah and other authoritative Jewish writings (see chapters two, three, four, and five), or on the basis of Jewish scriptures but without any obvious presence in their "plain sense" (see chapters six and seven), or by appeal to what had become a textual field of authoritative Christian writings (see chapter eight), some sort of new intellectual apparatus was needed to articulate these novel claims. The notion of an eternal μυστήριον, previously hidden but recently disclosed to the world, provided just such an apparatus. A detailed lexical analysis of μυστήριον in Paul and other early Christian authors should thus provide a helpful constraint for analyzing these larger and less tangible subjects of early Christian thinking about divine revelation and the structures of time.

To be clear, in training my attention on the word μυστήριον and the "once hidden, now revealed" discourse, I am not presuming some sort of idealized concept-in-word equation (or, in this case, a discourse-in-word equation), the error of nomenclaturism as de Saussure termed it.[21] Nor am I suggesting that μυστήριον had any sort of fixed meaning, much less a totality of meanings to be smuggled into every occurrence.[22] The linguistic axioms that words and things share no inviolable, one-to-one correspondence, and that sentences (or other complex syntactical structures), and not individual lexemes, are to be regarded as the fundamental units determining meaning should be truisms. My focus on μυστήριον is simply motivated, first, by the observation that when this signifier is used by early Christian authors it most frequently refers to some theological or hermeneutical claim that was previously hidden but is now currently disclosed and thus, second, by the practicality of treating this word as a limiting heuristic for analyzing the more nebulous hidden/revealed discursive formation. This is not to confuse the word for the discourse.[23] It is to use this particular word,

---

21 De Saussure discusses this at the very outset of the first part of his *Course in General Linguistics*.
22 With respect to biblical studies, the most damning and influential diagnosis of these errors is James Barr, *The Semantics of Biblical Language* (London: Oxford University Press, 1961).
23 The confusion of words and concepts is reckoned among the major theoretical flaws in Kittel's *ThWNT/TDNT*, and it has been trenchantly, if at times uncharitably, documented by Barr, *The Semantics of Biblical Language*. Moisés Silva, *Biblical Words and Their Meaning: An Introduction to Lexical Semantics* (Grand Rapids: Zondervan, 1983), illustrates the issue clearly: "Surely if we wanted to study Kant's epistemology, it would not occur to us to examine Kant's use of the word *wissen*, for we would encounter many passages where a theory of knowledge was the last thing in the philosopher's mind. But further, examining Kant's use of *wissen*, and then concluding our investigation, would leave us with a distorted picture. In fact, it is not hard to imagine the possibility that a relevant chapter from one of his *Critiques* may not contain the word at all; missing that chapter, however, might be disastrous for our conclusions" (27). This point is cru-

which so often appears to approximate a technical term for the discourse, as an entry point into it.²⁴

1.3 The History of Μυστήριον

Before turning to the recent history of research on μυστήριον, it will first prove helpful to explore the ancient history of this word and related vocabulary.²⁵ The noun enters the Greek language as early as the 7ᵗʰ century B.C.E. as a technical term (almost always in the plural) for the assorted ancient religious groups and phenomena identified collectively as "the Mysteries."²⁶ While often part of the title for these various groups—such as the Eleusinian Mysteries or the Mysteries of Dionysius, which are usually identified as classical, and then the Mysteries of Isis, or Cybele, or Mithras, which are among those classified as Hellenistic—the term was also commonly used more specifically for the secretive rites observed by the initiates of these cults, particularly their rites of initiation. Hence Walter Burkert's oft-cited definition of the mysteries as "initiation rituals of a voluntary,

---

cial, and it might appear that my own approach risks committing just this error. My reply is that while my analysis of μυστήριον is close to comprehensive (within the rough confines of the first two centuries, that is), I do not limit it to μυστήριον alone. Other relevant passages in which hiddenness and revelation are in play will also be discussed. Nonetheless, it is the case in this particular instance that the majority of the relevant passages do in fact involve this word. If this qualification were not enough, I would also appeal to the later work of Ludwig Wittgenstein, *Philosophical Investigations: The German Text with a Revised English Translation* (trans. G.E.M. Anscombe; 3d ed.; Oxford: Blackwell, 2001 [1953]): "We are not analysing a phenomenon (e.g. thought) but a concept (e.g. that of thinking), *and therefore the use of a word*. So it may look as if what we were doing were Nominalism. Nominalists make the mistake of interpreting all words as names, and so of not really describing their use, but only, so to speak, giving a paper draft on such a description" (I.383) (italics mine).

24 As David E. Aune, *Prophecy in Early Christianity and the Ancient Mediterranean World* (Grand Rapids: Eerdmans, 1983), notes, μυστήριον was "virtually a technical term in prophetic and apocalyptic contexts in early Judaism and early Christianity" (250). Aune refers to this technical aspect as the "mystery formula" (*Prophecy in Early Christianity*, 333), which seems to be equivalent to what I mean by "mystery schema."

25 What I offer here is in no way comprehensive or even especially detailed. It is merely a sketch for introductory purposes. The best general introduction to the term is still Günther Bornkamm, "μυστήριον, μυέω," *TDNT* 4:802–28. The classic study on the religious phenomena associated with the term is Walter Burkert, *Ancient Mystery Cults* (Cambridge: Harvard University Press, 1987). An accessible entrance into the primary sources is Marvin W. Meyer, *The Ancient Mysteries: A Sourcebook of Sacred Texts* (Philadelphia: University of Pennsylvania Press, 1999).

26 See Heraclitus, fragment 14 (DK).

personal, and secret character that aimed at a change of mind through experience of the sacred."²⁷

Alongside the cultic usage, which remains the default setting of the word throughout antiquity, an important semantic extension occurs in the dialogues of Plato, where the term is for the first time broadened beyond the formal religious sphere and transferred to the field of philosophy. We should, however, be cautious in presuming that the transfer from religion to philosophy entailed any major linguistic overhaul, or that the fields we designate as "religion" and "philosophy" would have been sharply delineated in antiquity.²⁸ As Bornkamm notes, "There is a considerable analogy between the mysteries and philosophy inasmuch as the vision of the divine is the goal of both, and a specific divinely appointed way leads in both to this end and fulfillment."²⁹ And so while the context of usage is expanded by ancient philosophers, and thus its connotations are analogically widened, this does not amount to an erasure of its more basic cultic connotations.³⁰

Although the term actually only occurs twice in the Platonic corpus, imagery and terminology associated with the mysteries appear on multiple occasions throughout the dialogues.³¹ In *Meno* 76E Socrates evokes the practice of initiation into cultic mysteries when he and Meno reach an impasse in their conversation.

---

27 Burkert, *Ancient Mystery Cults*, 11. If not specifically for initiation, the term could also be used for the larger ritual performance, which is how Herodotus appears to employ it: "On this lake they enact by night the story of the god's sufferings, a rite which the Egyptians call the Mysteries (τὰ καλέουσι μυστήρια Αἰγύπτιοι)" (*Hist.* 2.171).
28 That the category "religion" is especially problematic when applied to antiquity should be well known. See now especially Brent Nongbri, *Before Religion: A History of a Modern Concept* (New Haven: Yale University Press, 2013). I still use the word, but cautiously. See also Édouard des Places, "Platon et la Langue des Mystères," *Annales de la Faculté des Lettres d'Aix* 38 (1964): 9–23.
29 Bornkamm, *TDNT* 4:808. See also Hamilton, "The Church and the Language of Mystery," 479–81; and Erwin R. Goodenough, "Literal Mystery in Hellenistic Judaism," in *Quantulacumque: Studies Presented to Kirsopp Lake* (ed. Robert P. Casey, Silva Lake, and Agnes K. Lake; London: Christophers, 1937), 227–41.
30 It would be better to view Plato and those after him as making creative philosophical use of these cultic images. As Christoph Riedweg, *Mysterienterminologie bei Platon, Philon und Klemens von Alexandrien* (Untersuchungen Zur Antiken Literatur Und Geschichte 26; Berlin/New York: de Gruyter, 1987), writes, "Die Mysterienterminologie…ist ganz von der genialen Eigenart des Dichter-Philosophen Platon geprägt, der es versteht, gerade religiöse Elemente in spielerischem Ernst umzuformen und völlig in den Dienst seiner Aussage zu stellen…. Vielmehr verwendet [Platon] Mysterientermini und die damit gegebene Atmosphäre sozusagen in eigener Sache, webt Dichtung und kultische Realität so eng ineinander, dass das eine vom anderen nicht immer leicht zu trennen ist" (1).
31 See *Euthyd.* 277D; *Gorg.* 497C; *Phaedr.* 249C-250C; *Symp.* 209E–210A.

Eager to win over his young interlocutor, Socrates urges him not to depart "before the mysteries" (πρὸ τῶν μυστηρίων) but to stay and "be initiated" (μυηθείη), thereby remaining under Socrates' intellectual tutelage so as to realize the veracity of his claims. A similar appropriation of cultic imagery occurs in *Theaetetus*. At an early point in the dialogue, Socrates' disciple expresses wonder at the ideas Socrates is voicing (155C). Socrates in turn offers to help Theaetetus search out the "hidden truth" (τὴν ἀλήθειαν ἀποκεκρυμμένην) of the matter under discussion, but first Socrates warns that they must look around to ensure that none of the uninitiated (τῶν ἀμυήτων) are listening (155E) because, as they concur, such individuals are unfit for τὰ μυστήρια (156A). Following Plato the depiction of philosophy as an induction into sacred mysteries becomes commonplace in Greco-Roman philosophical traditions and, as in Plato, this depiction continues to insinuate experiences of cultic belonging into pictures of the philosophical life.[32] As Goodenough, following the work of Jeanne Croissant,[33] notes, "Aristotle similarly began with the view that the goal of philosophy is initiation, a mystic vision which was explicitly made the true initiation and mystery," and "Aristotle's successors in Hellenistic and Roman times did not lose sight of the fact that he, like Plato, had presented the goal of philosophy as an initiation into Truth…. To them Aristotle was like Plato in making Philosophy into the true mystery."[34]

As for Jewish literature, the word appears relatively infrequently in texts of the postexilic period and with some variation.[35] Included in this is the use of μυστήριον in Greek Daniel, where it translates רז (a word only found in the Aramaic portions of Daniel and nowhere else in the Hebrew Bible),[36] and then its

---

[32] An especially elaborate philosophical appropriation of the cultic realm is Plutarch's *On Isis and Osiris*.
[33] Jeanne Croissant, *Aristote et les Mystères* (Liège: Faculté de philosophie et lettres; Paris: E. Droz, 1932).
[34] Goodenough, "Literal Mystery in Hellenistic Judaism," 234.
[35] The observations of Jonathan Z. Smith, *Drudgery Divine: On the Comparison of Early Christianities and the Religions of Late Antiquity* (Chicago: University of Chicago Press, 1990), are worth reiterating: "That *mystērion* is a relatively rare term in the Septuagint is well-known. What has not been sufficiently reflected on is the limited range of the six documents in which it occurs—Daniel, Judith, Tobit, Sirach, Wisdom, and 2 Maccabees. None are from archaic Israel; each was composed, at the earliest, during the hellenistic period and thus reflect a Late Antique situation from their origin, not just in their translation. Indeed, their status as translation documents is scarcely homogenous…. In no case are we treating with an archaic indigenous Israelite document later clothed in hellenistic form. We are reading six documents representative, in their very composition, of different modes of Hellenized Judaisms" (72).
[36] It is also possible to read רז in Isa 24:16, but this is disputed. The Hebrew term otherwise most associated with רז is סוד ("council"), which occurs 21 times in the MT and is translated

sporadic use in a few other early Jewish documents. In these texts μυστήριον is often used simply for personal secrets—a "purely secular" usage as it has been problematically characterized.³⁷ In Sirach, for instance, μυστήρια is used four times in proverbs that warn against betraying the secrets of a friend: "the one who reveals secrets (μυστήρια) destroys loyalty" (27:16; cf. vv. 17, 21 and 22:22).³⁸ Similar to this is the μυστήριον in Judith 2:2, which refers to "the secret plan" (τὸ μυστήριον τῆς βουλῆς) that Nebuchadnezzar sets before his ministers (cf. 2 Macc 13:21). Similar again is Tobit 12:11, in which the angel Raphael prepares to disclose his identity: "The whole truth I will make clear to you, and I will not hide from you any word. Already I have made it clear to you in the saying, 'The secret (μυστήριον) of a king is good to hide and the works of God honorable to unveil'."³⁹

The term also appears on occasion in Jewish sources in its conventional cultic sense. Thus in Wis 14:15, amid a lengthy censure of idolatry, the text describes a father worshipping an image of his deceased child and then handing on to his dependents the new "mysteries and initiations" (μυστήρια καὶ τελετάς) for this cult. Again in 14:23 the text denounces those who engage in rites involving the murder of children (τεκνοφόνους τελετάς), secret mysteries (κρύφια μυστήρια), and other frenzied rituals involving exotic customs.⁴⁰ Elsewhere in Wisdom, however, the term is used positively and in ways that better anticipate the con-

---

in a variety of ways, but only occasionally by μυστήριον in some variant readings. See, for instance, Greek variants in Job 15:8.

37 Thus Raymond E. Brown, *The Semitic Background of the Term "Mystery" in the New Testament* (Philadelphia: Fortress Press, 1968), 7. Because this usage lacks "religious connotations," Brown elects to "pass over" these instances. As Smith, *Drudgery Divine*, points out, such a decision skews the linguistic data (see esp. 73–76). Proper consideration of these "secular" instances in the Jewish evidence further undermines the dubious proposition that there is some singular biblical (or Semitic) sense for the term.

38 Many manuscripts also have an occurrence of μυστήρια (סוד) at 3:19. For a detailed analysis of this passage, see Angelo Passaro, "The secrets of God. Investigation into Sir 3:21–24," in *The Wisdom of Ben Sira: Studies in Tradition, Redaction, and Theology* (ed. Angelo Passaro and Giuseppe Bellia; DCLS 1; Berlin/New York: Walter de Gruyter, 2008), 155–71. Sirach uses the language of κρυπτός similarly to his usage of μυστήρια (1:30; 8:18). In 3:22, 4:18, and 11:4, however, κρυπτός refers to divine secrets, including the secrets of Wisdom that are revealed to those who seek her (4:11–19). Sirach also employs the language of ἀπόκρυφος for divine secrets (16:21; 42:19; 43:32) and the secrets of Wisdom (14:21). In 39:3, however, the ἀπόκρυφα are hidden meanings in the scriptures that are discovered by the spiritually gifted scribe (39:6–7), and in 48:25, the prophet Isaiah is extoled for secretly setting forth hidden things (ἀπόκρυφα) concerning the coming ages.

39 This saying occurs earlier, though in an altered from, in 12:7.

40 Cf. the similar indictment in 12:4–5.

structive theological use of the term by Paul and ensuing Christian authors. Thus in 2:22, the first occurrence in the document, the anarthrous μυστήρια θεοῦ appears to refer to the realities of the afterlife,[41] which the ungodly do not perceive because they have been blinded by their own wickedness (2:21).[42] In 6:22 μυστήρια is again used in a positive theological sense: "What Wisdom is and how she came to be, I will explain to you and I will not hide from you mysteries (οὐκ ἀποκρύψω ὑμῖν μυστήρια), but from the beginning of creation I will investigate and I will make manifest the knowledge of her and I will not pass by the truth." The author further develops the image of Wisdom's "mysteries" in the course of the narration, particularly in 8:4, where Wisdom is described as "an initiate (μύστις) of the knowledge of God," and then again in 7:21, where she is acclaimed as a teacher of both "hidden (κρυπτά) and manifest (ἐμφανῆ) things."[43] Far from mundane secrets, then, the μυστήρια in 6:22 have strong theological and cultic connotations.

Of particular importance is the use of μυστήριον in Daniel, where the word occurs eight times in ch. 2 of both the Old Greek (OG) and Theodotian (Th) versions (2:18, 19, 27–30, 47) and one additional time in ch. 4 of the latter (4:9 [Th]).[44] These are all in the account of Nebuchadnezzar's cryptic dreams and

---

41 Events of the afterlife are also related to μυστήριον in 1 Cor 15:51.

42 It is worth pointing out that this construal of the mystery image differs from the standard cultic and philosophical usage, where the knowledge of mysteries is mediated by other initiates. Here the mysteries are apparently exoteric realities and, hence, ascertainable by anyone. As Giuseppe Scarpat, *Libro della Sapienza. Vol. 1* (Brescia: Paideia, 1989), writes, "Naturalmente il termine era connesso ai culti misterici ai quali si fa esplicito riferimento in 6,22 e 14,15.23 (cfr. anche 8,4 e 12,5) e non figura nei LXX se non negli scritti del period ellenistico (Tobia, Giuditta, Sir., Daniele), ma nel nostro passo μυστήρια denota solo 'i segreti' genericamente, e non I 'misteri' collegati a riti gnostici allora in voga" (197).

43 According to Wis 8:8, Wisdom also has important hermeneutical abilities: "She knows the things of old and infers things to come; she understands tricks of language and undoes riddles; she foreknows signs and portents and the outcomes of times and seasons." The one who posseses Wisdom also has access to her interpretive prowess (cf. 8:17–22; 9:9–18).

44 It should be pointed out that the question of Greek Daniel's influence on Paul is still very much an open one – a fact all the more significant given the prominence afforded to Daniel in many examinations of μυστήριον in Paul. For one, Daniel is a text Paul never cites, and potential allusions to Daniel are rare if not non-existent. Such matters are also complicated by the tortuous compositional and translational history of the document. The data is notoriously complex, and so also are the theories to account for it, but this much is certain: the Greek versions of Daniel available in the first-century C.E. were far from fixed, and even the existence of Greek translations appears to have been a recent development (as in no earlier than the second-century B.C.E. but perhaps as late as the first-century C.E.; for an especially clear discussion of these issues, see John J. Collins, *Daniel* [Hermeneia; Minneapolis: Fortress Press, 1993], 2–12). Therefore, as Smith, *Drudgery Divine*, cautions, we must bear in mind that "when we compare the use

his challenge to the renowned mantics of Babylon to divine both the dream and its meaning.[45] The mantics can do neither and so, enraged by the incompetence of "all the wise men of Babylon" (2:12), Nebuchadnezzar orders their execution, Daniel included. At this point Daniel intervenes and requests that the king give him an opportunity to disclose (δηλώσῃ) the dream and its interpretation (2:16).[46] Each of the ensuing occurrences of μυστήριον in 2:18–47 appear to refer to both aspects of the king's request, that is, to the literal contents of the dream (2:31–35) and to their decoded meaning (2:36–45).[47] Therefore, when Nebuchadnezzar exclaims in 2:47, "Truly your God is God of gods and Lord of kings, the only one disclosing hidden mysteries (ὁ ἐκφαίνων μυστήρια κρυπτὰ μόνος), because you were able to interpret this mystery (ἐδυνάσθης δηλῶσαι τὸ μυστήριον τοῦτο)," he is celebrating Daniel's ability to discern and decipher the whole complex. Simply defined, then, a μυστήριον in Dan 2 is something previously concealed, whether absolutely or in coded figures, which can only be disclosed through God or a divinely empowered mediator. Thus the μυστήριον in this instance is both Nebuchadnezzar's cryptic dream of a great statue of metals and the final establishment of a great mountain and also the decoding of this dream as a political allegory auguring the demise of successive empires and the ultimate triumph of God's eternal kingdom.

As for other Jewish evidence, the term mostly appears in literature postdating Paul (or at least probably postdating Paul).[48] The semantic diversity endures in these documents, which is in no way surprising, and the relevant data has

---

of *mystērion* in Paul to that of Greek Daniel, we are comparing roughly contemporaneous usages, not comparing the authoritative usage of an ancestor or a teacher to his pupil" (73). While such cautions do not diminish the importance of Daniel for filling out the use of μυστήριον in early Jewish literature, they should check any uncritical overestimation of Greek Daniel on Paul's usage.

45 The same scenario is repeated in ch. 4.
46 For a discussion of Daniel as the supreme mantic artist and master of Mesopotamian divinatory practices, see Jack N. Lawson, "'The God Who Reveals Secrets': The Mesopotamian Background to Daniel 2.47," *JSOT* 74 (1997): 61–76.
47 The two are repeatedly mentioned together. See 2:4, 5, 6, 7, 9, 26, 36, 45. So also Brown, *The Semitic Background*, explains that the μυστήριον in Dan 2 refers "both to the dream and to its contents; for the dream itself is a series of complicated symbols which envelop a further mystery: the future of the kingdom" (7).
48 See, for instance, *1En.* 8.3 (Syncellum); 9.6; 10.7; 16.3; 96.2 [103.2]; 97.12 [104.12]; *T. Ab.* 3.4, 12; 6.13; *T. Gad* 6.5; *T. Jud.* 12.6; 16.3–4; *T. Levi* 2.10; *T. Zeb.* 1.6. It also occurs quite frequently in both Philo and Josephus as well. See esp. Bockmuehl, *Revelation and Mystery*, 69–92. For the comparable data in rabbinic literature, see again Bockmuehl, *Revelation and Mystery*, 104–23.

been ably documented in other studies.⁴⁹ What is worth adding at this point, however, is the relatively widespread use of the term רז in material from Qumran which, with well over one hundred occurrences in the Scrolls, is conspicuously prominent.⁵⁰ While in a few instances the term is used in the ordinary sense of human secrets, the vast majority are related to divine realities. These realities are frequently described as having been previously hidden and only recently revealed.⁵¹ As Samuel Thomas concludes, רז in the Scrolls "typically denotes something that falls within the domain of esoteric knowledge—something that is known to the elect and hidden to those outside the group—and reflects the dynamic interaction of revelation, knowledge and concealment."⁵² As we shall observe time and again in early Christian material, the interplay of hiddenness and revelation, as well as the various ways in which the hidden/revealed binary can be creatively applied, proves to be a vital conceptual resource for Christianity's social and theological formation, much as it was in Qumran.

One feature in the Scrolls especially worth underscoring is the widespread interpretive use of רז and the hidden/revealed discourse, a usage that in important ways anticipates Christian exegetical developments.⁵³ The hermeneutical application of this terminology often centers on the Teacher of Righteousness, who is portrayed as a uniquely enabled interpreter of eschatological mysteries that have been hidden in the prophetic scriptures.⁵⁴ The most important document in this regard is the so-called Habakkuk Pesher, particularly 1QpHab 7:1–8:

> And God told Habakkuk to write what was going to happen to the last generation, but he did not let him know the end of the age.... Its interpretation concerns the Teacher of Righteousness, to whom God has disclosed all the mysteries of the words of his servants, the prophets [אשר הודיעו אל את כול רזי דברי עבדיו הנבאים]. For the vision has an appointed

---

49 For further analysis, see Benjamin L. Gladd, *Revealing the* Mysterion: *The Use of* Mystery *in Daniel and Second Temple Judaism with Its Bearing on First Corinthians* (BZNW 160; Berlin/New York: Walter de Gruyter, 2008), 85–107; Brown, *The Semitic Background*, 12–22.
50 See the study by Samuel I. Thomas, *The "Mysteries" of Qumran: Mystery, Secrecy, and Esotericism in the Dead Sea Scrolls* (SBLEJL 25; Leiden/Boston: Brill, 2009). Also helpful are Gladd, *Revealing the* Mysterion, 51–84; Bockmuehl, *Revelation and Mystery*, 42–56; and Brown, *The Semitic Background*, 22–30.
51 Gladd, *Revealing the* Mysterion, 52, provides a helpful synopsis of the data.
52 Thomas, *The "Mysteries" of Qumran*, 186.
53 Particularly insightful regarding this overlap is David E. Aune, "Charismatic Exegesis in Early Judaism and Early Christianity," in *The Pseudepigrapha and Early Biblical Interpretation* (ed. James H. Charlesworth and Craig A. Evans; JSOTSup 14; Sheffield: JSOT Press, 1993), 126–50.
54 See Steven D. Fraade, "Interpretive Authority in the Studying Community at Qumran," *JJS* 44 (1993): 46–69.

time, it will have an end and not fail. Its interpretation: the final age will be extended and go beyond all that the prophets say, because the mysteries of God are wonderful.[55]

The idea here is that God commanded Habbakuk to write things that he was himself prevented from fully comprehending.[56] Concealed from the prophet were the mysteries of his prophecy, which is to say, certain key eschatological facts that remained hidden in his words. These mysteries, however, were recently revealed by the Teacher, "the interpreter *par excallance*."[57] As Samuel Thomas characterizes the hermeneutical dynamic here, "This is an extraordinary statement that makes a rather strong claim not only about the unfolding eschatological drama, but also about the capacity of the Teacher of Righteousness (and his group) to have *even greater* insight into God's 'mysteries' than the earlier prophets themselves had."[58] As we shall see, particularly in chapters six, seven, and eight, this redefinition of scriptural prophecy as a communicative event that is only retrospectively perceived, and hence not as an activity of straightforward foretelling, is standard fare in early Christian "mystery exegesis" as well. Much like the Jewish sectarians of Qumran, early Christian exegetes also maintained that the words of the biblical prophets only yield their ultimate, superordinate prophetic meaning when interpreted from the location of eschatological fulfill-

---

[55] Translations of the Scrolls are from Florentino García Martínez, *The Dead Sea Scrolls Translated: The Qumran Texts in English* (trans. Wilfred G.E. Watson; Leiden: Brill; Grand Rapids: Eerdmans, 1996).

[56] As Fraade, "Interpretive Authority," explains, "God's prophetic revelation comes in two parts: first to the biblical prophets, here represented by Habakkuk, who recorded God's words relating the events that would befall the last historical generation, now understood as that of the commentary's audience. But the true significance of that prophetic message, that is, its fuller and more specific redemptive meaning, was hidden from the prophets and their audience and only revealed to the Teacher of Righteousness. But that fuller meaning was revealed to the Teacher not by the previous prophetic medium of direct divine communication, but by his inspired *interpretation* of the earlier words of the prophets as continuous texts" (50).

[57] Bockmuehl, *Revelation and Mystery*, 47. Bockmuehl also notes structural similarities with Daniel's dream interpretation: "the pattern of this so-called *midrash pesher* exegesis...is in some ways closely akin to the interpretation of dreams.... The two basic ingredients of the *pesher* type of 'revelation', then, are the ר(often plural) and its corresponding פשר: the former is supplied by the prophets, the latter by the Teacher of Righteousness (or his subsequent agents)" (48). Cf. also Shani Berrin, "Qumran Pesharim," in *Biblical Interpretation at Qumran* (ed. Matthias Henze; Grand Rapids: Eerdmans, 2005), 110–33, who writes, "The community understood the figure of the prophet as analogous to that of a dreamer, reporting a dream. The agency of an additional select individual was required for the unraveling of the coded predictions" (124).

[58] Thomas, *The "Mysteries" of Qumran*, 204.

ment, which for Christians was inaugurated by Christ's death and resurrection. Whether you are a Qumranite or a Christian, an historical consciousness in which time is divided into eras of hiddenness and revelation is necessary to sustain such claims.

1.4 Μυστήριον in the New Testament

To be included among the evidence for μυστήριον in antiquity are the occurrences of the term in the non-Pauline portions of the New Testament. While twenty-one of the twenty-eight New Testament occurrences of μυστήριον are in the Pauline letters, the additional seven instances are limited to a single Synoptic pericope (Matt 13:10–13//Mark 4:10–12//Luke 8:9–10) and to the book of Revelation (1:20; 10:7; 17:5, 7). In the course of this investigation we shall see that just as the Pauline usage of the term dominates the canonical New Testament numerically, so also key particulars of Pauline usage come to dominate much subsequent Christian usage – the eternal division of history into epochs of concealment and disclosure being the key Pauline contribution. It is, however, still important to consider these other New Testament instances.

In the Synoptic tradition the term appears immediately after the parable of the sower and just prior to its explanation.[59] Despite noteworthy variations among the three versions of this logion, what is common to each is the interpersonal division between Jesus' immediate followers ("those around him" [Mark 4:10]) and all other associates ("those outside" [Mark 4:11]). It is to insiders alone that the mystery of the kingdom of God is imparted, and so it is by insiders alone that the concealed meaning of the parables is perceived. To all other hearers, Jesus' words remain inscrutable puzzles, and so although they are understood in terms of their literal sense ("a sower went out to sow…"), they yet veil the deeper mystery of the kingdom of God. To be given knowledge of such a mystery is then to be divinely empowered with a certain hermeneutical aptitude to perceive kingdom-related realities in Jesus' parabolic words, much like the experience of Daniel in his interpretation of Nebuchadnezzar's dream.[60] The emphasis in this Synoptic tradition is thus more on the immediate interpersonal implications of the hidden/revealed dynamic than on any sort of comprehensive bifurcation of history.

---

[59] For a detailed consideration of the epistemological implications of this passage, see esp. Joel Marcus's treatment in "Mark 4:10–12 and Marcan Epistemology," *JBL* 103 (1984): 557–74.
[60] On the theme of knowledge as a gift of God in Mark, see Marcus, "Mark 4:10–12 and Marcan Epistemology," 558–59.

Moving on to Revelation, with the exception of 10:7 the instances of μυστήριον are fairly straightforward and, like the above instance, simply identify the presence of some coded or symbolic meaning in some otherwise literal object or statement. Thus in 1:20 the term is used to identify literal objects as having figurative significations. The mystery of the seven stars and the seven lampstands is the seven stars represent the seven angels of the seven churches and the seven lampstands represent the churches themselves. The use of μυστήριον simply identifies the existence of the symbolic correspondences. Similar to this is 17:5 where the term signals that the name inscribed on the woman's forehead has a symbolic signification.[61] Although the coded sense of the name is not explicitly identified in the immediate context, in v. 7 the angel announces that he will reveal the μυστήριον of this woman and the beast she rides upon, and then in vv. 8–18 he provides a point by point exposition of their various symoblic details: the seven heads are seven mountains and also seven kings, the ten horns are ten kings, the waters are the nations, and so on. This culminates in v. 18 where the angel identifies the woman as "the great city that rules over the kings of the earth." The reader here infers Rome, which is perhaps also to be applied to the μυστήριον of her name in v. 5. That is, the tattooed "Babylon" on her forehead stands not for that erstwhile empire but for the existing one.[62]

The use of μυστήριον in 10:7 is a important outlier. Here an angel swears an oath to heaven, saying: "But rather in the days of the sound of the seventh angel, when he blows the trumpet, the mystery of God should be completed (ἐτελέσθη τὸ μυστήριον τοῦ θεοῦ), as he announced to his servants the prophets (ὡς εὐηγγέλισεν τοὺς ἑαυτοῦ δούλους τοὺς προφήτας)."[63] The content of the mystery is nowhere explicitly defined, but since the "mystery of God"[64] is something that is fulfilled, it presumably refers to a preestablished divine plan.[65] Its association with the prophets suggests some sort of scriptural antecedent, and hence that the prophets also somehow announced this mystery. Furthermore, the expression "his servants, the prophets" may allude to Amos 3:7 ("For the Lord God does nothing without revealing the instruction to his servants, the prophets" [ἐὰν μὴ ἀποκα-

---

[61] Note that the function of μυστήριον here is not affected by the syntactical question of whether μυστήριον is actually part of the name on the woman's forehead or is an editorial comment on that name.
[62] Cf. the names of Balaam (2:14), Jezebel (8:20), and especially "the city that is spiritually called (ἥτις καλεῖται πνευματικῶς) Sodom and Egypt" (11:8), which unequivocally indicates that these names are symbolic for Jerusalem.
[63] The performance of this oath appears to echo or to be modeled on Dan 12:7.
[64] This same phrase appears in 1 Cor 2:1; Col 2:2. For the association of μυστήριον and prophetic scriptures, see Rom 16:25–26.
[65] Cf. τελέω in 11:7; 15:1, 8; 17:17; 20:3, 5, 7.

λύψῃ παιδείαν αὐτοῦ πρὸς τοὺς δούλους αὐτοῦ τοὺς προφήτας]), a text whose context again suggests that the mystery made known to the prophets was also communicated by the prophets.⁶⁶ This supposition that the prophets somehow conveyed this mystery, perhaps in veiled form, is supported by the distinct parallels with 1QpHab 7:1–8. Particularly outstanding is the fact that both passages combine references to "the mystery of God" with a potential allusion to Amos 3:7 and specific details about the end of time. If pressed further, this comparison might suggest that the mystery of God in Rev 10:7 is, as in 1QpHab 7:1–8, a reference to "the eschatological plan of God concealed in prophetic books of the OT," and hence reflects what would become the widespread Christian view—that "God communicated to the prophets mysteries that are not fully understood until the time of their fulfillment."⁶⁷ This passage would then be an important witness to the "once hidden, now revealed" schema in the Pauline letters, and one analogous to the hermeneutical use of that schema among other early Christian authors.⁶⁸

In the course of this study we shall consider these Christian authors, beginning with Paul and then running up through the second century to the first great Latin theologian, Tertullian.⁶⁹ The only potentially glaring omission in the analysis is Irenaeus, who does use μυστήριον nearly twenty times in *Against Heresies*. But since Irenaeus primarily associates the term with various "heretical" groups, he only occasionally uses it in constructive ways, and even then not necessarily in ways that differ from the figures I do treat. The decision to limit my analysis to the second century, and to these particular authors, is mostly a matter of manageablity. To venture much further would take us into Alexandrian Christianity and the immense literary archives of the likes of Clement and Origen. It is also the case, however, that after Tertullian there are no significant developments in the Christian use of this terminology of which I am aware.⁷⁰ Before taking a

---

66 The MT has סוד in the place of παιδείαν, which is the Hebrew term most often associated with רז. If known by the author of Revelation, the use of סוד may have influenced this choice of allusion.
67 David E. Aune, *Revelation 17–22* (WBC 52C; Nashville: Thomas Nelson, 1998), 569.
68 For the possibility that this text is an interpolation, see Aune, *Revelation 17–22*, 568.
69 Whether or not Tertullian is properly classified as a second-century figure is an arbitrary matter. Nothing ontological changed in the world when time advanced from 199 to 200 C.E. according to the reckoning of our decimal system and the Gregorian calendar. I have included Tertullian in the conventional second-century classification because his use of the hidden/revealed mystery schema in his dispute with Marcion involves him directly in a major second-century development, and it is another important example of the theological potency of this discourse.
70 One potential exception is the use of this terminology in the Nag Hammadi literature. See esp. the collection of essays in *Mystery and Secrecy in the Nag Hammadi Collection and Other Ancient Literature: Ideas and Practices: Studies for Einar Thomassen at Sixty* (ed. Christian H.

summary glance at these developments, however, we should first briefly consider the long history of μυστήριον in modern research.

1.5 Μυστήριον in Modern Research

At least since Isaac Casaubon's seventeenth-century Protestant assault on Roman Catholic sacramentology, *De rebus sacris et ecclesiasticis exercitationes XVI* (1614), Paul's use of the word μυστήριον has remained a recurrent subject in modern scholarship and, in the legacy of Casaubon, one of ongoing polemical controversy as well.[71] In more recent years scholars have primarily disputed the proper "background" for Paul's use of mystery terminology, the contest being between the two supposedly oppositional cultural spheres of Judaism and Hellenism. The makings of this debate begin in large part with the so-called *religionsgeschichtliche Schule*, as well as with earlier research anticipating it, which made the case in varying ways in a host of studies during the first half of the 20th century that the Greco-Roman mystery religions, or pagan religion in general, contributed the necessary milieu for rightly comprehending the meaning of early Christian mystery speech and sacramental practices.[72] Precursors of this research tendency include Edwin Hatch[73] and Georg Wobbermin,[74] but the most well-

---

Bull, Liv Ingeborg Lied, and John D. Turner; NHMS 76; Leiden/Boston: Brill, 2012). The most noteworthy development is the interest in protological secrets. As John D. Turner, "I Tell You a Mystery: From Hidden to Revealed in Sethian Revelation, Ritual, and Protology," 161–201, in the abovementioned volume points out, the idea of hidden and revealed mysteries provided "a fundamental ontogenetic concept in the protological metaphysics and mystical epistemology of Sethian and related literature" (161). A very similar treatment of concealment, revelation, and protology can also be found in Turner's "From hidden to revealed in Sethian revelation, ritual, and protology," in *Histories of the Hidden God: Concealment and Revelation in Western Gnostic, Esoteric, and Mystical Traditions* (ed. April D. DeConick and Grant Adamson; Gnostica; Durham: Acumen, 2013), 149–74.

[71] The key work on this history of polemics is Smith's *Drudgery Divine*, which we shall discuss in further detail below.

[72] Some early scholars – such as Gustav Anrich, *Das antike Mysterienwesen in seinem Einfluss auf das Christentum* (Göttingen: Vandenhoeck & Ruprecht, 1894) and Samuel Cheetham, *The Mysteries, Pagan and Christian* (London: Macmillan, 1897) – examined pagan parallels but were less optimistic about their influence on Christian origins.

[73] Edwin Hatch, *The Influence of Greek Ideas and Usages upon the Christian Church* (ed. A.M. Fairbairn; London/Edinburgh: Williams and Norgate, 1891). This is the posthumously published version of Hatch's 1888 Hibbert Lectures. A German translation soon followed.

[74] Georg Wobbermin, *Religionsgeschichtliche Studien zur Frage der Beeinflussung des Urchristentums durch das antike Mysterienwesen* (Berlin: E. Ebering, 1896).

known studies are by early 20th century scholars such as Richard Reitzenstein,[75] Alfred Loisy,[76] Wilhelm Bousset,[77] and Percy Gardner,[78] to name just a few.[79] The guiding assumption for most of these scholars is that, as Reitzenstein puts it, although Paul might appear "innerlich doch wieder ganz als Jude," it is also the case that "er ernstlich darum gerungen hat, auch den Hellenen Hellene zu werden."[80] Hence for the scholar of Paul, "Die Wichtigkeit, die für das volle Verständnis der an hellenistische Gemeinden gerichteten Briefe diese Sprache und Anschauungswelt haben, wird man von vornherein zugeben müssen."[81]

Although Greco-Roman analogues to Pauline thought often proved impressive, and the idea that early Christianity was confected in the religious cauldrons of Hellenism was in many ways provocative, the prominence given to Greco-Roman sources quickly drew detractors, and by the middle part of the 20th century Judaism was increasingly promoted as the indispensable, and for some the exclusive, domain for interpreting μυστήριον in Paul. As Raymond Brown, in his influential and widely available monograph, confidently states, "We believe it no exaggeration to say that, considering the variety and currency of the concept of divine mysteries in Jewish thought, Paul and the NT writers could have written everything they did about *mystērion* whether or not they ever encountered the

---

[75] Richard Reitzenstein, *Die Hellenistischen Mysterienreligionen nach ihren Grundgedanken und Wirkungen* (Leipzig: Tübner, 1910).
[76] Alfred Loisy, "The Christian Mystery," *Hibbert Journal* 10 (1911): 45–64; and especially his *Les mystères païens et le mystère Chrétien* (Paris: Nourry, 1914).
[77] Wilhelm Bousset, "Christentum und Mysterienreligionen," *Theologische Rundschau* 15 (1912): 41–61; "Die Religionsgeschichte und das Neue Testament," *Theologische Rundschau* 15 (1912): 251–78; *Kyrios Christos: Geschichte des Christusglaubens von den Anfängen des Christentums bis Irenaeus* (Göttingen: Vandenhoeck & Ruprecht, 1916).
[78] Percy Gardner, *The Religious Experience of St. Paul* (London: Williams & Norgate, 1911); see also his *The Growth of Christianity* (London: Adam and Charles Black, 1907), which is based on a series of lectures given to a London parish beginning in 1903.
[79] A still helpful and more detailed summary of this body of scholarship is Bruce M. Metzger, "Considerations of Methodology in the Study of the Mystery Religions and Early Christianity," *HTR* 48 (1955): 1–20. As Metzger observes, this interest in the contribution of pagan religion to Christian origins was perhaps aroused by the boon of archaeological finds during this period, which "made quite significant additions to our knowledge of the beliefs and practices of devotees of the Mysteries" (2). For important criticism of other aspects of Metzger's article, see Smith, *Drudgery Divine*, 43, 48–49.
[80] Reitzenstein, *Die Hellenistischen Mysterienreligionen*, 533. Reitzenstein even suggests that Paul was intiated into two or three mystery religions, or at least was well acquainted with their language and procedures.
[81] Reitzenstein, *Die Hellenistischen Mysterienreligionen*, 419–20.

pagan mystery religions."[82] Besides Brown, the most important representatives of this movement include D. Deden,[83] K. Prümm,[84] Günther Bornkamm,[85] Arthur Darby Nock,[86] Markus Bockmuehl,[87] and most recently Benjamin Gladd.[88]

Despite the often impressive historical contributions of studies on both sides of the Jewish/Greco-Roman debate, in the end the matter cannot and in fact should not be decided in favor of either term of the binary – and certainly not in *a priori* terms.[89] To reify "Judaism" and "Hellenism" as established and discrete domains, and thus contextual choices one must choose between for the study of Christian origins, is a methodological, as well as historical, distortion.[90] On the historical front, Christianity, like Judaism, was a Greco-Roman religion and, as such, was ineluctably shaped in varying measures by the pervasive influences of Hellenization – as well as by Romanization. A person such as Paul, who for nearly two decades nomadically encamped among assorted Mediterranean inhabitants as a missionary to the nations, is irreducible to either a Jewish or Greco-Roman "context," and attempts to define him in this way misrepresent the fact that he belonged to that broader and multilayered Mediterranean milieu.[91] On the methodological front, as Jonathan Z. Smith has trenchantly demonstrated, the preoccupation with "backgrounds" to μυστήριον in Paul has all too rarely been motivated by anything approaching sincere scholarly inquiry.

---

[82] Brown, *The Semitic Background*, 69. This smaller work is based on Brown's 1958 Johns Hopkins dissertation. See also his "The Pre-Christian Semitic Concept of 'Mystery'," *CBQ* 20 (1958): 417–43; "The Semitic Background of the New Testament *Mystêrion* (I)," *Bib* 39 (1958): 426–48; "The Semitic Background of the New Testament *Mystêrion* (II)," *Bib* 40 (1959): 70–87.
[83] D. Deden, "Le 'Mystère' Paulinien," *ETL* 13 (1936): 405–42.
[84] K. Prümm, "Mystères," *DBSup* 6 (1960): 10–225; "Zur Phänomenologie des paulinischen Mysterion und dessen seelischer Aufnahme: Eine Übersicht," *Bib* 37 (1956): 135–61.
[85] Günther Bornkamm, "Μυστήριον κτλ.," *TWNT* 4 (1942): 809–34.
[86] See esp. Arthur Darby Nock, *Early Gentile Christianity and Its Hellenistic Background* (New York: Harper & Row, 1964); "Hellenistic Mysteries and Christian Sacraments," *Mnemosyne* 5 (1952): 177–213; "Mysterion," *HSCP* 60 (1951): 201–4; "The Vocabulary of the New Testament," *JBL* 52 (1933): 131–39. For an extended and instructive critique of Nock, see Smith, *Drudgery Divine*, 66–71.
[87] Bockmuehl, *Revelation and Mystery*.
[88] Gladd, *Revealing the* Mysterion.
[89] Bockmuehl, *Revelation and Mystery*, is one important exception to the abovementioned polemics. Even given the focus of his study on Ancient Judaism, he nonetheless remains committed to not "losing sight of the influence of the Hellenistic religious milieu" (2).
[90] See the excellent studies in *Paul Beyond the Judaism/Hellenism Divide* (ed. Troels Engberg-Pedersen; Louisville: Westminster/John Knox Press, 2001).
[91] This is not to mention his self-professed resolve to accommodate himself to all peoples, including the lawless (1 Cor 9:19–22).

Particularly in defenses of the Jewish background to Christian mystery language, "[p]hilology has served as a stratagem," explains Smith, and "[t]he central task has been the protection of the uniqueness of early Christianity, its *sui generis*, or non-derivative nature."[92] Thus scholars have frequently constructed "the image of an insular and insulated Judaism in relation to its larger environment to claim that early Christianity, as an originally inner-Jewish phenomenon, fell, likewise, within Judaism's *cordon sanitaire*."[93] Hence "the appeal to lexicographical studies of the presumed Semitic background of the notion of 'mystery' has simply enabled [scholars] to sweep from view the spectre of Hellenistic influence to such a degree that it disappears entirely from the scene."[94]

The disavowal of apologetic agendas does not imply that all sources are of equal value when it comes to Paul's cultural and theological formation, nor that Paul's use of μυστήριον in this particular instance is most helpfully illuminated by comparison with Jewish precursors, which I think it is. It is simply to point out the need to take full account of the Greco-Roman data, to which Judaism and Christianity contribute critical parts. I propose that one way of changing the terms of these older, now hackneyed debates is to avoid retreading old material and instead to travel along the important and mostly unexplored trajectories of μυστήριον through early Christian literature, beginning with Paul himself.

It is also worth noting that the comprehensive survey of μυστήριον in Paul I offer in this book is not a mere rehearsal of data already examined *ad nauseam* in other studies. An additional consequence of the scholarly fixation with the ostensible "backgrounds" to μυστήριον in Paul has been the relative neglect of Paul's own use of the term. The Pauline mystery passages have without question often been assembled and commented on, but the extent of interaction with them has been comparatively meager—the focus remaining not on how the term is used across the Pauline corpus but on the context from which Paul's usage derives. In terms of recent comprehensive analyses, Bockmuehl's is probably the most the substantial, but even he devotes just 57 pages specifically to the Pauline passages in what is a 230 page book.[95] Also lacking is a sustained

---

92 Smith, *Drudgery Divine*, 79.
93 Smith, *Drudgery Divine*, 81.
94 Smith, *Drudgery Divine*, 79–80. Smith also contends that there has been a triumphalist agenda at work in these polemics: "Judaism has served a double (or, a duplicitous) function. On the one hand it has provided apologetic scholars with an insulation for early Christianity, guarding it against 'influence' from its 'environment'. On the other hand, it has been presented by the very same scholars as an object to be transcended by early Christianity" (83).
95 Bockmehl, *Revelation and Mystery*, 157–214. Representative of the neglect of the full range of Pauline data is Gladd, *Revealing the* Mysterion. Gladd's book is of course specifically on "The

analysis of what I shall argue is a noticeable shift in the use of μυστήριον between the so-called disputed and undisputed (or deuteropauline) letters. I maintain that this shift is not only significant for thinking about the "Pauline" use of the term and the authorship of this corpus. It also came to have substantial consequences for the ensuing Christian use of the hidden/revealed mystery discourse.

1.6 Structure of the Book

This study begins with the Pauline data, investigating the twenty-one occurrences of μυστήριον in Paul's letters, first in the purportedly undisputed letters of Romans, 1 Corinthians, and 2 Thessalonians[96] (chapter two), then in the so-called deuteropauline letters of Ephesians and Colossians (chapter three), and finally in the Pastoral Epistles and Romans 16:25–27, which I take to be a later addendum to an earlier letter form (chapter four). For a study that is in many respects concerned with the early reception of the Pauline corpus, this division of the letters according to conventions of modern scholarship may appear anachronistic. While it is certainly the case that early Christians sometimes disputed the legacy of Paul, and this sometimes involved arguments over which documents in which form rightly witnessed to it, they knew no authentic, canonical Paul contraposed to a putative deutero- or pseudo-Paul. Although his letters were variously collected and esteemed, known or unknown, and refracted through accompanying traditions (Acts and other literary traditions being most prominent), they were not read as epistolary deceits addressed to contrived audiences and personages. Whether dismissed or revered, they were treated collectively, in whatever number or textual forms they existed, and invariably as authentic and complementary witnesses to the life and thinking of the apostle to the Gentiles. So why, given the nature of this investigation, continue to segregate Paul's corpus in this modern historical-critical fashion?

Use of *Mystery* in Daniel and Second Temple Judaism with Its Bearing on First Corinthians" (as the subtitle announces), but it includes very little on Pauline mystery passages outside of 1 Corinthians. A similar limitedness of scope is to be found in Chrys C. Caragounis, *The Ephesian Mysterion: Meaning and Content* (ConBNT 8: Lund: CWK Gleerup, 1977), which I again point out not as a fault but as further illustrating the neglect of all the Pauline data.

96 While it is true that 2 Thessalonians is classed among the deuteropaulines, its use of μυστήριον does not adhere to what is found in Ephesians, Colossians, and the Pastorals, and so it belongs in this grouping.

I argue in these chapters that, irrespective of the historical-critical consensus, there remains an observable distinction between the undisputed and deuteropauline letters in their use of μυστήριον. That is, in contrast to Romans, 1 Corinthians, and 2 Thessalonians, where μυστήριον appears in varying ways (and sometimes in the plural), in the purportedly deuteropauline letters of Ephesians, Colossians, 1 Timothy, and the Romans 16:25–27 interpolation, the term is used in a consistent manner (and always in the singular) to denote a specific understanding of divine revelation in history.[97] According to this deuteropauline mystery schema, the plan for Gentile salvation, which has been eternally known but hidden by God, is now revealed through Christ's advent and Christian proclamation of this fact. Besides the repeated focus on the new social inclusion of the Gentiles, what most distinguishes the deuteropauline schema is the repeated historical arrangement of the hidden/revealed binary. As Michael Wolter has pointed out, while in the undisputed letters the hidden/revealed binary is primarily arranged "*als zeitgleiches Nebeneinander*," and so spatially or interpersonally, in the deuteropauline letters it is consistently presented "*als zeitliches Nacheinander*," or chronologically.[98] And so whereas in the undisputed letters the binary of disclosure and concealment is primarily what divides contemporaneous individuals ("Menschengruppen") into those who do and do not perceive the mystery, in the deuteropauline tradition it is time itself ("Zeiträume") that is partitioned into contrasting eras of hiddenness and revelation. Building on these

---

97 Particularly attentive to some of the differences at work here is Joseph Coppens, "'Mystery' in the Theology of Saint Paul and its Parallels at Qumran," in *Paul and Qumran: Studies in New Testament Exegesis* (ed. Jerome Murphy-O'Connor; Chicago: Priory Press, 1968), 132–58.
98 Michael Wolter, "Verborgene Weisheit und Heil für die Heiden: Zur Traditionsgeschichte und Intention des 'Revelationsschema'," *ZTK* 84 (1987): 297–319, 298. It should be pointed out straightaway that these distinctions are really matters of emphasis and not absolute divisions. Insofar as revelation involves making someone aware of something the person did not previously know, there is always a temporal element. The issue is whether the emphasis is on that temporal element ("once hidden, now revealed"), or whether it is on the interpersonal distinction ("revealed to some, hidden from others"), or on creative combinations of both (for examples of some of these possibilities, see Wolter, "Verborgene Weisheit und Heil für die Heiden," 300–3). I should note that Wolter's article focues on what he identifies as a displacement of Torah in the deuteropauline usage of the schema. He writes, "Seine massgebliche Voraussetzung findet das Revelationsschema in der paulinischen Abrogation des Gesetzes als Heilsweg." Salvation is thus now grounded "nicht auf das Gesetz, sondern auf Christus." Therefore, "Dieser Heilsweg, den Gott in seinem freien, an keine menschlichen Voraussetzungen gebundenen Gnadenhandeln ermöglicht hat…, hebt den im Besitz der Torah gründenden Privilegansspruch Israels gegenüber den Heiden auf…und eröffnet den Weg des Heils zu den Heiden, den Paulus in seiner missionarischen Praxis beschritten hat" (317–18). Wolter's observations interestingly anticipate developments in the subsequent Christian usage of the schema.

observations, I argue that this particular historical formulation of the deuteropauline mystery schema codifies a "Pauline" theology of revelation that, in the context of the Pauline corpus, is mobilized primarily in order to explain the origins of the Gentile mission but in due course becomes fundamental to early Christian thinking on other christological, hermeneutical, and historical matters.

Chapter four begins the exploration of this early Christian thinking about history, particularly as it relates to the problems generated by Christian claims of newness. I turn to the letters of Ignatius and the anonymously authored *Epistle to Diognetus*. Although Ignatius' use of μυστήριον is limited to three occurrences, we find in two of these instances clear expressions of the historically arranged hidden/revealed schema. In *Eph.* 19.1 the mysteries of Christ's incarnation, birth, and death – "three mysteries of a cry" – are described as divine shouts interjected into "the silence of God." These mysteries are thus events of new proclamation shattering that silence, inaugurating the overthrow of the old kingdom, and making manifest the newness of eternal life (19.2–3). In *Magn.* 8.2–9.1 Ignatius again similarly describes the μυστήριον of Christ's advent and death as "a Word proceeding from silence." Christ is thus presented as the λόγος of God whose advent represents a new utterance in the world and, as such, the instantiation of a new era of divine disclosure. While Ignatius does allow for some form of prophetic anticipation of this new revelation (see esp. *Magn.* 8.1–9.2), and so exhibits at least some concern for integrating the more recent past with the new, his particular understanding of this anticipation entails a quite negative, if not categorically hostile, construal of Judaism.[99] His superficial interest in Israel's history and scriptures seems to be symptomatic of this antagonistic posture toward Judaism as well.

The same sort of historically ordered hidden/revealed structure undergirds many of the key arguments in the *Epistle to Diognetus*. The author of this letter sets out to address, among other things, questions regarding the recent appearance of Christianity in the world – "why did this new race enter the world now and not earlier?" (*Diogn.* 1.1). To answer such questions the author first encourages his pagan addressee to set aside any prejudice and to become, as it were, a "new man" capable of hearing this "new story" (2.1). The idea of newness is then a key refrain throughout the letter, along with the concurrent claim that Christianity is necessarily beyond human discovery. As the author writes in 4.6, which is also the first occurrence of μυστήριον in the document, "Do not suppose that

---

[99] Ignatius' negative approach to Judaism should not, however, be confused with Marcionism. By at least claiming that the prophets had some form of anticipatory relationship with Christian realities, Ignatius is far from bifurcating a creator God of Israel and the newly revealed Christ.

you are able to learn from a human the mystery of the Christians' own religion." The mysteries of Christianity are repeatedly characterized as beyond any human administration or earthly apprehension because they are carefully guarded heavenly secrets only knowable by divine initiative (7.1–2). The principal mystery in this letter is God's eternally established plan for human salvation. As the author explains in 8.9–11, this "great and inexpressible design" was previously "concealed in a mystery," being known only by the Father and the Son, but then, at the proper time, the Father sent his Son who revealed to humanity these things that had been prepared from the beginning.

As with Ignatius, then, the notion that God established but concealed this plan for human salvation until the advent of Christ provokes serious questions about the role of Israel within God's eternal designs. Some have argued that the theology in this letter tends toward, if not exemplifies, a Marcionite exclusion of Israel and thus that the "distance of Christians from Judaism is so great that they are too estranged for a relationship to have ever existed."[100] I argue that although this is an untenable reading of the text, there are indeed still severe implications in the author's portrayal of Judaism and its history. And so, as with Ignatius, while the author of this document presents a clear vision of how to reconcile the eternal past with the new Christian present, still largely unaddressed (or crudely addressed) is the question of what a Christian juxtaposition of old and new means for Christian thinking about historical Israel.

In the next two chapters (six and seven) we finally encounter two explicit examples of the potential forms that Christian thinking about Israel can take. These come in the detailed exegetical engagements with Jewish scripture on display in Justin Martyr's *Dialogue with Trypho* and Melito of Sardis' *Peri Pascha*. Chapter six takes an in-depth look at the exegetical machinery at work in Justin's *Dialogue*, first, by examining its lexical parts and then by considering what the entire system means for Justin's claims regarding how biblical prophecy works. I focus the investigation on the thirty-seven occurrences of μυστήριον in the *Dialogue*. Besides the occasional reference to cultic mystery practices, the term is used in this document in two primary ways. The first is in reference to some aspect of Christ himself, particularly the salvation that has been secured for humanity through his suffering and death. This usage places emphasis on the interpersonal aspects of the hidden/revealed binary – the *Nebeneinander* dynamic in Wolter's terminology: to some the mystery of Christ's death is comprehended as the securing of salvation, but to others the mystery is missed and the death is

---

[100] Horacio E. Lona, "Diognetus," in *The Apostolic Fathers: An Introduction* (ed. Wilhelm Pratscher; Waco: Baylor University Press, 2010), 197–213, 204.

seen only for what it literally is, a criminal execution. The second type of usage refers to scripture as a mystery. By designating it as such Justin is claiming that scripture prophetically prefigures a newly revealed Christian reality, usually the mystery of Christ's saving death. Such a claim does not deny scripture's original (or "literal") sense, the sense in which Trypho reads it. It rather alleges that the previously concealed Christian sense has been newly revealed. As Justin himself puts it, "For if it has been proclaimed in a concealed manner through the prophets that Christ would suffer first and after these things be Lord of all, it was then not possible to be understood by anyone until he convinced the apostles that these things were explicitly proclaimed in the scriptures" (*Dial.* 76.6). Therefore, while the mystery of Christ was indeed announced beforehand by the prophets, it was announced in such a way that it could not be known until after the advent of Christ and his own exegetical demonstration. So although the mystery of Christ has been witnessed to by the mystery of scripture, the antecedent mystery is only perceivable by those who have come to know the new mystery. That Jews or the people of Israel from any time did not or still have not understood that the facts of Christ were foretold by their own scriptures is not, then, so much a function of their own incapacity as it is a function of scripture itself and its capacity to veil Christian mysteries. By redefining the function of prophecy in accordance with the hidden/revealed schema, I argue that Justin has actually altered the true subject of the debate, though without ever clearly acknowledging this fact. More fundamental to the separation of Justin and Trypho is not so much the question of what scripture means as it is whether or not one has come to recognize Christ's revelation as true. The pretense of exegetical debate only masks this deeper, more determinative divide.

In chapter eight I examine Melito's *Peri Pascha*, a lengthy homily on Exod 12 and the account of Israel's original paschal celebration. Similar to Justin, Melito applies the term μυστήριον in a strict twofold manner, referring either to the "mystery of the Lord," which he exclusively associates with Christ's crucifixion, or to some earlier mystery previously concealed in scripture and, given the subject of the homily, most frequently the "mystery of Pascha." In naming Christ and Pascha mysteries Melito, like Justin, names their dynamic capacity to conceal and reveal new meaning. The mystery of Pascha is its prefiguration of Christ's own mystery, which is his salvific suffering and death. And so Pascha is a mystery because it about more than Pascha; it is about Christ. As Melito puts it, "For although as a sheep it was led to slaughter, yet it was not a sheep; although as a lamb speechless, yet neither was it a lamb. For the model indeed existed, but then the reality appeared. For instead of the lamb there was a Son, and instead of the sheep a man, and in the man is Christ who has comprised all things."[101] According to Melito's reading, then, the historical events of Pascha extend beyond themselves to Christ, and in so doing they come to acquire a new, christological significance. Thus insofar as the old is drawn into the reality of the new, the old is transformed by the new, and even becomes the new. So he states, "Understand then, O beloved, how it is new and old, eternal and temporary, perishable and imperishable, mortal and immortal – this mystery of the Pascha."[102] It is again critical to point out that the new christological significance Melito ascribes to Pascha is only possible when those events are refracted through the new and hermeneutically determinative events of Christ's death – the newly revealed mystery. Thus once again it is only from the *a posteriori* vantage point of Christian salvation that the otherwise latent mysteries hidden in scripture become unveiled.

While much of this agrees with Justin and other early Christian authors, there are important innovations in Melito's use of the mystery discourse. For one, he is perhaps the first Christian author to evoke explicitly the cultic connotations of mystery terminology by reading the ceremonial details in Exod 12 as akin to mystery rites performed among Israel's initiates. More significant, however, is his creative deployment of the rhetorical figure of *synkrisis*, a comparative trope that juxtaposes two entities for either praise or deprecation. But rather than straightforward *synkrisis*, Melito fuses a model/reality comparison with the hermeneutical mystery discourse. Since Melito's mystery hermeneutic essentially merges the old model of Israel with the new reality of Christ, he is precluded from abandoning the old, which would otherwise have become defunct in the model/reality construal. Instead, by reincorporating the old model into the new and totalizing reality of Christ, Melito reinvests the old with the eternal significance of the new. What would otherwise have become obsolete is therefore retained, albeit on exclusively christological terms. In the end, Melito's particular hermeneutical juxtaposition of old and new entails rather different but no less considerable implications for his understanding of historical Israel and her Jewish heirs.

The final chapter examines the expansive corpus of the North African theologian Tertullian. Although the language is now Latin and the key term now *sacramentum*, many features of Tertullian's usage agree with what precedes him.[103]

---

101 *Peri Pascha* 4–5.
102 *Peri Pascha* 2.
103 Tertullian does use the cognate *mysterium* when referring to mystery cults, but *sacramentum* is his term for translating μυστήριον in Paul and for discussing "mystery" as we have become familiar with it as well.

In his scriptural exegesis, for instance, Tertullian frequently presents his readings as disclosing the previously hidden *sacramentum* of various biblical passages, and in many specific instances his exegetical offerings are identical with those of his predecessors. But Tertullian is distinctive in the particular argumentative ends to which he applies the historical hidden/revealed mystery discourse in his contest with Marcion over the apostle Paul. Tertullian's appeals to mystery gather with conspicuous frequency in Book 5 of *Against Marcion*, which is Tertullian's letter-by-letter attempt to read Marcion's Pauline corpus against Marcion's own theology. This is in part because Paul is the primary Christian source for the language of mystery but also in the main because the conjunction of a previously hidden but presently revealed scriptural mystery presents Tertullian with decisive evidence against Marcion's uncoupling of Christ and the creator God of Israel. That is, insofar as Christ and the Creator can be shown to work in concert, they cannot be severed as Marcion contends. The historical arrangement of the hidden/revealed mystery schema is thus not simply of service for Christian exegetical claims. It also supplies a framework within which the juxtaposition of old and new entails unity between the newly revealed Christ and the God of ancient Israel. And so again the comprehensive historical consciousness provided by the mystery schema enables Christian theologians to articulate unity in what would otherwise appear to be an irreducible contradiction.

The conclusion briefly discusses some of the major implications of this study and then briefly considers its contribution to scholarship on the expansion and eventual domination of Christianity in the Mediterranean landscape.

2 Μυστήριον in the Undisputed Pauline Letters

2.1 Introduction

For a study interested in the early reception and development of Paul's language and theology, the division of the Pauline corpus into "undisputed" and "disputed" (or deuteropauline) letters risks committing to an arbitrary, and likely distortive, taxonomy. However many Pauline letters various early Christian readers possessed, and whatever other traditions affected their impression of the apostle, there is scant evidence of any inclination to question the authenticity of the letters that now comprise the canonical Pauline corpus,[1] whereas there is widespread data indicating that each of the thirteen canonical letters were widely known and revered throughout the second century, and perhaps even earlier.[2] Therefore, the historical-critical reflex to segregate Paul's corpus and, in so doing, to give disproportionate attention to the undisputed letters, particularly the *Hauptbriefe*,[3] potentially confuses an analysis of the subsequent history of

---

[1] The potential absence of the Pastorals in P46, their apparent nonappearance in Marcion (Tertullian, *Marc.* 5.21), and their alleged rejection by Basilides (Jerome, *Preface to the Commentary on Titus*), some Gnostics (Clement of Alexandria, *Strom.* 2.11), and Tatian (who, for theological/ethical reasons, rejected just 1 Timothy; Jerome, *Preface to the Commentary on Titus*) is potential evidence of an occasional openness to questioning the authenticity or theological integrity of select Pauline letters – unless the above mentioned manuscript and authors simply did not know the Pastorals as we now know them, which is quite possible.

[2] General reverence for Paul is observable as early as Acts, 2 Peter (3:15–16), *1 Clement* (5.5; 47.1), Ignatius, Marcion, and perhaps even in texts such as the Gospel of Mark (see Joel Marcus, "Mark – Interpreter of Paul," *NTS* 46 [2000]: 473–87). The early existence and dissemination of the Pauline letter collection is also indicative of Paul's rapid literary popularity. On this see now Andreas Lindemann, "Die Sammlung der Paulusbriefe im 1. und 2. Jahrhundert," in *The Biblical Canons* (ed. J.-M. Auwers and H.J. DeJonge; Lueven: University Press, 2003), 321–51. Occasional hostility to Paul must be admitted, but such opposition confirms his prominence. On such hostility, see Richard I. Pervo, *The Making of Paul: Constructions of the Apostle in Early Christianity* (Minneapolis: Fortress Press, 2010), 187–98.

[3] Among the earliest and most influential exemplars of this tendency is F.C. Baur's threefold classification of the Pauline Epistles, wherein the so-called *Hauptbriefe* are given pride of place in terms of historical importance because of their purportedly more credible claims to authenticity. See Baur's *Paulus, der Apostel Jesu Christi, sein Leben und Wirken, seine Briefe und seine Lehre* (Stuttgart: Becher und Müller, 1845). See also the trenchant analysis of these modern developments in Pauline scholarship offered by Benjamin L. White, *Remembering Paul: Ancient and Modern Contests over the Image of the Apostle* (Oxford: Oxford University Press, 2014), and my review essay on it, T.J. Lang, "Spectres of the Real Paul and the Prospect of Pauline Scholarship." On Benjamin L. White's, *Remembering Paul: Ancient and Modern Contests over*

his letters, a history in which they circulated and were appropriated as a cohesive entity. Consequently, any approach to the reception history of the Pauline corpus that fails to treat the thirteen canonical letters with some degree of equality will, at best, yield a partial portrait of Paul's literary legacy and, at worst, a disfigured one. Mindful of this risk of distortion, I nonetheless contend that when it comes to the subject of the Pauline use of μυστήριον there is practical and, indeed, historical value in approaching this topic in light of what modern critics have come to recognize as the undisputed and disputed letters. In agreement with the predominant historical-critical hypothesis, there is an observable distinction between the disputed and undisputed letters in their use of μυστήριον.[4] In the undisputed letters (among which I include 2 Thessalonians, against the convention, because its usage fits best here) μυστήριον is used in a heterogeneous fashion (and in both the singular and the plural), being applied to matters as varied as the historical and eschatological destinies of Israel and the Gentiles (Rom 11:25–26a), the future somatic transformation of the living and the dead (1 Cor 15:51–52), the content of Paul's missionary proclamation (1 Cor 2:1, 7; 4:1), the inscrutable utterances of those who speak in tongues (1 Cor 14:2), and the cryptic account of the "mystery of lawlessness" (2 Thess 2:7). In the so-called deuteropauline letters (among which I include the Rom 16:25–27 doxology), however, the term begins to be used in a more consistent manner, and always in the singular, to express a specific understanding of divine revelation in history. According to this deuteropauline schema, the plan for Gentile salvation, which has been eternally known but hidden by God, is now revealed through Christ's advent and in apostolic proclamation of that fact. This schema thus asserts a division of history into a previous era of hiddenness and a current era of revelation. Such a chronological arrangement of the hidden/revealed mystery is never a matter of emphasis in the undisputed letters, and aspects of it are perhaps even contradicted in those texts.

Even though observing this distinct pattern of usage in Paul's canonical corpus by no means incontrovertibly validates the historical-critical consensus, it does lead to certain potential implications for the chronology and authenticity of the Pauline letters. If the current critical partitioning of Paul's corpus is deemed historically probable, then the uses of μυστήριον in Ephesians, Colossians, 1 Timothy, and the Romans 16:25–27 doxology represent the earliest instances of the reception and development of Paul's mystery speech and should be

---

the Image of the Apostle. Marginalia Review of Books, 26 May 2015: http://marginalia.lareviewofbooks.org/spectres-of-the-real-paul-and-the-prospect-of-pauline-scholarship-by-t-j-lang/.

4 It should be noted that the existence of this distinction does not confirm the regnant critical consensus, though it does further reinforce it.

analyzed accordingly. The primary purpose of this chapter, however, is to map the assorted occurrences of μυστήριον in what most modern scholars regard as undisputed Pauline letters. We shall turn to larger questions of the history of the Pauline corpus at the conclusion of chapter three.

2.2 The Pauline Data

2.2.1 1 Corinthians 4:1; 13:2; 14:2

Although these three passages are the least specific of all the Pauline mystery texts and the only occurrences of the plural form of the noun in the entire Pauline corpus, I begin with them because they exhibit three fundamental associations of μυστήριον in Paul: divine revelation, the Holy Spirit, and Paul's apostolic commission:[5]

1 Cor 4:1
οὕτως ἡμᾶς λογιζέσθω ἄνθρωπος ὡς ὑπηρέτας Χριστοῦ καὶ οἰκονόμους **μυστηρίων θεοῦ**.

Let a person consider us in this way: as servants of Christ and administrators of the mysteries of God.

1 Cor 13:2
καὶ ἐὰν ἔχω προφητείαν καὶ εἰδῶ **τὰ μυστήρια** πάντα καὶ πᾶσαν τὴν γνῶσιν καὶ ἐὰν ἔχω πᾶσαν τὴν πίστιν ὥστε ὄρη μεθιστάναι, ἀγάπην δὲ μὴ ἔχω, οὐθέν εἰμι.

And if I should possess prophetic powers and should know all mysteries and all knowledge and if I should have all faith so as to remove mountains, but I should not have love, I am nothing.

1 Cor 14:2
ὁ γὰρ λαλῶν γλώσσῃ οὐκ ἀνθρώποις λαλεῖ ἀλλὰ θεῷ· οὐδεὶς γὰρ ἀκούει, πνεύματι δὲ λαλεῖ **μυστήρια**.

The person who speaks in a tongue does not speak to people but to God, for no one understands, even though he speaks mysteries in the Spirit.

4:1. In 4:1 the apostles' standing as "administrators of the mysteries of God" is correlated with their identity as "servants of Christ."[6] Both ὑπηρέτης and οἰκονόμος[7] are administrative terms, implying some degree of subordination,

---

[5] The use of the plural in these instances likely reflects their generality.
[6] Cf. 1 Cor 3:5.
[7] Cf. the use of this term in Rom 16:23; 1 Cor 4:2; Gal 4:2; Titus 1:7. The closely related οἰκονομία is found in 1 Cor 9:17; Eph 1:10; 3:2, 9; Col 1:25; 1 Tim 1:4. For an excellent summary of

and are used in an array of domestic, commercial, and civic contexts. An οἰκονόμος could perform a wide variety of duties in the ancient world, ranging from tasks related to household management (see Luke 12:42; 16:1–8; Gal 4:2) to larger municipal responsibilities such as a city treasurer (see Rom 16:23; Ἔραστος ὁ οἰκονόμος τῆς πόλεως).[8] The association in 4:1 with Christ and God's mysteries, however, would seem connote a form of sacred employment.[9] John Reumann has shown that an οἰκονόμος often served in what he terms "religious" (or, perhaps better, cultic) capacities, including in private societies and Mysteries such as those of Sarapis, Asclepius, and Hermes-Trismegistos.[10] Therefore, whatever (if anything very specific) Paul meant by the expression "administrators of the mysteries of God," "this extension of *oikonomoi* to the religious sphere is not novel,"[11] and the expression certainly could have been understood by Corinthian readers as generally commensurate with Greco-Roman cultic practices and terminology.[12]

---

this terminology see C. Spicq, "οἰκονομέω, οἰκονομία, οἰκονόμος," *TLNT* 2:568–75. The most detailed study of this term with respect to Paul is now John K. Goodrich, *Paul as an Administrator of God in 1 Corinthians* (SNTMS 152; Cambridge: Cambridge University Press, 2012). For a much more expansive analysis, see Gerhard Richter, *Oikonomia: Der Gebrauch des Wortes Oikonomia im Neuen Testament, bei den Kirchenvätern und in der theologischen Literatur bis ins 20. Jahrhundert* (AKG 90; Berlin/New York: de Gruyter, 2005).

8 As Peter Landvogt, *Epigraphische Untersuchung über den Oikonomos: Ein Beitrag zum hellenistischen Beamtenwesen* (Strasbourg: M. Dumont Schauberg, 1908), has shown, the term has a range of uses, but it usually connotes servile status. See also the discussion of "managerial slaves" in Dale B. Martin, *Slavery as Salvation: The Metaphor of Slavery in Pauline Christianity* (New Haven: Yale University Press, 1990), 15–22, 174–76.

9 Cf. Titus 1:7; 1 Peter 4:10. As we shall see in chapter 5, the phrase "administration of the mysteries" is taken up again in *Diogn.* 7.1 (using the feminine form of the noun) to emphasize that Christians have not been entrusted with "the administration of merely human mysteries" (ἀνθρωπίνων οἰκονομίαν μυστηρίων). The Christian mysteries, the reader infers, are divine mysteries.

10 John Reumann, "'Stewards of God' – Pre-Christian Religious Application of *OIKONOMOS* in Greek," *JBL* 77 (1958): 339–49. For the "religious" use of this terminology, see the evidence cited by Reumann, "'Stewards of God'," esp. 342–49. Cf. also C. Spicq, "οἰκονομέω, οἰκονομία, οἰκονόμος," *TLNT* 2:574–75. Goodrich, *Paul as an Administrator of God*, 52–54, also points to places where an οἰκονόμος serves within the sphere of the sacred.

11 C. Spicq, "οἰκονομέω, οἰκονομία, οἰκονόμος," *TLNT* 2:574.

12 Benjamin L. Gladd, *Revealing the* Mysterion: *The Use of* Mystery *in Daniel and Second Temple Judaism with Its Bearing on First Corinthians* (BZNW 160; Berlin/New York: Walter de Gruyter, 2008), reports that scholars are divided on the question of whether or not "the content…behind the phrase [οἰκονόμους μυστηρίων θεοῦ] lies either in a Greco-Roman or a Jewish background" or perhaps "a bit of both" (171). He then remarks that "[t]he accentuation of the Greco-Roman background strikes at the heart of one's perception of Paul and Christianity at this point in the

One additional feature of οἰκονόμος language that illumines Paul's use of the word is the financial – or, exploiting the cognate, the economical – associations of such terminology. As John Goodrich has thoroughly demonstrated, throughout Greco-Roman history and across multiple circumstances of employment, an οἰκονόμος was almost always primarily engaged with the management and expenditure of finances, whether regal, civic, or private.[13] Even within cultic domains οἰκονόμοι "were not in such contexts only, or even primarily, acting as 'religious' officials, since the religious responsibilities of *oikonomoi* were always accompanied by administrative tasks."[14] Hence "while a handful of inscriptions mention the cultic duties occasionally delegated to municipal *oikonomoi*, it is apparent in each case that religious oversight only accompanied the administrative responsibilities normally entrusted to them."[15] Recognizing the economic resonances in Paul's collocation of οἰκονόμος and μυστήριον is important because, as we shall see in the next chapter, in Colossians and Ephesians μυστήριον also appears alongside language of economy, wealth, and benefaction. Therefore, the detailed descriptions of "the economy of the mystery" (ἡ οἰκονομία τοῦ μυστηρίου)[16] and "the wealth of the glory of this mystery" (ὁ πλοῦτος τῆς δόξης τοῦ μυστηρίου τούτου)[17] that are developed in Ephesians and Colossians are potentially dependent on (or developments of) the image of the οἰκονόμος μυστηρίων θεοῦ in 1 Cor 4:1.

As for the content of the mysteries in this verse, Paul provides no additional detail beyond the mention of an οἰκονομία entrusted to him in 1 Cor 9:17, which is related to his apostolic charge to proclaim the gospel. Since 1 Cor 3 is primarily about Paul's founding work in Corinth and since he has already claimed in 1 Cor 2:1–2 that when he first came to them he proclaimed the mystery of God exclu-

---

first century" and then proceeds to argue that the expression is "primarily a Semitic metaphor" (171–72). This type of reasoning is conceptually misguided, especially insofar as it reifies a Jewish/Hellenistic divide. Whatever Gladd means by "backgrounds," the fact is that first-century Christianity, like first-century Judaism, was a Greco-Roman religion, and therefore the importance of the Greco-Roman context for understanding Paul cannot be ignored.

13 See Goodrich, *Paul as an Administrator of God*, 25–102. "Regal," "Civic," and "Private" are the three contexts within which Goodrich observes οἰκονόμοι serving.
14 Goodrich, *Paul as an Administrator of God*, 53.
15 Goodrich, *Paul as an Administrator of God*, 54. Goodrich cites Reumann, "'Stewards of God'," as in agreement with him on this matter: "At best we can say that these governmental *oikonomoi* at times had cultic duties along with financial ones" (344).
16 Eph 3:9. Cf. Eph 3:2 (οἰκονομίαν τῆς χάριτος τοῦ θεοῦ τῆς δοθείσης μοι εἰς ὑμᾶς); Col 1:25 (ἐγενόμην ἐγὼ διάκονος κατὰ τὴν οἰκονομίαν τοῦ θεοῦ τὴν δοθεῖσάν μοι).
17 Col 1:27. Cf. Col 2:2 (πᾶν πλοῦτος τῆς πληροφορίας τῆς συνέσεως); Eph 3:8 (τὸ ἀνεξιχνίαστον πλοῦτος τοῦ Χριστοῦ).

sively in the plain declaration of the crucified Christ, we can infer that however extravagant and unexpected some of the mysteries entrusted to Paul might have been (such as the mystery disclosed in 15:51), they also included the most basic confessions of the gospel, such as those outlined in 1 Cor 1:18–25.[18] But it is important to keep in mind that, rather than on the content of the mysteries, the emphasis in 4:1–2 is on the identities of apostles as subordinates of God who have been charged with remaining trustworthy superintendents of divine mysteries.

13:2. Turning to 13:2 we again find the plural μυστήρια being used in an unspecified sense, but here it is coupled with exalted charismatic phenomena like prophecy (προφητείαν),[19] extraordinary knowledge (πᾶσαν τὴν γνῶσιν),[20] and supernatural faith (πᾶσαν τὴν πίστιν ὥστε ὄρη μεθιστάναι).[21] The phrase "all mysteries"[22] in this verse is specifically linked with knowledge, since the subjunctive εἰδῶ governs both τὰ μυστήρια πάντα and πᾶσαν τὴν γνῶσιν.[23] The irony in this passage, presented hyperbolically,[24] is that even the possession of the most extraordinary charismatic and cognitive capacities is, in the end, "nothing" (οὐθέν) if it is unaccompanied by love.[25]

Although the content of the "all mysteries" in 13:2 is unstated, there is a noteworthy parallel in 12:8 where Paul refers to the λόγος σοφίας given through the Spirit. This λόγος σοφίας expression is then juxtaposed with λόγος γνώσεως, much like the μυστήρια/γνῶσις juxtaposition in 13:2:

---

[18] In this sense Richard B. Hays, *First Corinthians* (IBC; Louisville: John Knox Press, 1997), is probably incorrect in stating that the stewardship of the mysteries in 4:1 "refers to nothing other than the gospel message itself (cf. 2:1, 7), the secret wisdom of God that has decreed salvation for the world through the death and resurrection of Jesus" (65). There is no reason why other mysteries like those disclosed in Rom 11:25 and 1 Cor 15:51, and hinted at in 1 Cor 13:2 and 14:2, are not also under Paul's stewardship. This would seem to be the point of the plural, as opposed to the singular in 1 Cor 2:1, 7.
[19] Cf. 12:10.
[20] Cf. 12:8.
[21] Cf. 12:9. For the idea of faith moving mountains, recall Mark 11:22–23 and its Synoptic parallels.
[22] Cf. Dan (Th) 4:9 (καὶ πᾶν μυστήριον οὐκ ἀδυνατεῖ σε).
[23] Notice also the simple chiasm linking these expressions: τὰ μυστήρια πάντα καὶ πᾶσαν τὴν γνῶσιν.
[24] That it is hyperbole is confirmed by 13:9–12, where Paul describes the unavoidable partiality and imperfection of human knowledge.
[25] As Hans Conzelmann, *1 Corinthians* (trans. James W. Leitch; Hemeneia; Philadelphia: Fortress Press, 1975), observes, "Compared with the overstrained protasis, the apodosis comes with cutting brevity: οὐθέν εἰμι, 'I am nothing'" (222).

ᾧ μὲν γὰρ διὰ τοῦ πνεύματος δίδοται λόγος σοφίας, ἄλλῳ δὲ λόγος γνώσεως κατὰ τὸ αὐτὸ πνεῦμα.

For to one person the word of wisdom has been given through the Spirit, but to the other person is the word of knowledge according to the same Spirit.

Placed in parallel, the λόγος σοφίας "given through the Spirit" in 12:8 would correspond to the mysteries in 13:2, and the λόγος γνώσεως that is "according to the same Spirit" in 12:8 would correspond to the "all knowledge" in 13:2. Mystery, wisdom, and knowledge are already closely associated by Paul in 1 Cor 2:6–16, along with the Spirit's revelatory function in these matters (2:10–16). The pneumatological emphasis in 12:8 is then perhaps significant for 13:2. Although the Spirit is not explicitly mentioned in 13:2, given the parallel with 12:8 and the fact that the Spirit's role in revealing mysteries and knowledge is stated in other passages, most notably 1 Cor 2:6–16, the Spirit's agency can be inferred in 13:2 as well.[26] Also possible is the suggestion of Johannes Weiss, who proposes that "all mysteries" "ist doch wohl eine Entfaltung von ἔχω προφητείαν."[27] Whether or not this is the case here, in passages like Rom 11:25 and 1 Cor 15:51 mysteries do involve predictive statements that could be characterized as prophetic revelations.

14:2. In 14:2 the content of the plural μυστήρια is again undefined, and again it is related to a charismatic phenomenon, in this instance Spirit-inspired glossolalia.[28] Multiple ancillary issues accompany this text: the nature of glossolalia, its place in early Christian worship, and examples of parallel phenomena. Most important is the fact that although elsewhere in the New Testament the discussion of tongues refers to a spiritually enabled capacity to speak intelligibly in other known languages (the "tongues of humans" in 13:1; cf. Acts 2; 10:46; 19:6), throughout 1 Cor 12–14 the Corinthian glossolalia appears to be of a different sort, namely, the "tongues of angels" (13:1),[29] which are unintelligible apart from an interpreter who is empowered by the Spirit to translate them (12:10–

---

26 Cf. also Dan 4:9; 1 Cor 14:2; Eph 3:5.
27 Johannes Weiss, *Der erste Korintherbrief* (MKNT; Göttingen: Vandenhoeck & Ruprecht, 1910), 314, Andreas Lindemann, *Der Erste Korintherbrief* (HNT 9/1; Tübingen: Mohr Siebeck, 2000), similarly states, "Gegenstand der προφητεία wäre dann das Wissen um τὰ μυστήρια πάντα..." (284).
28 For general studies on this phenomenon, see Clint Tibbs, *Religious Experience of the Pneuma: Communication with the Spirit World in 1 Corinthians 12 and 14* (WUNT 2/230; Tübingen: Mohr Siebeck, 2007); Christopher Forbes, *Prophecy and Inspired Speech in Early Christianity and its Hellenistic Environment* (WUNT 2/75; Tübingen: Mohr Siebeck, 1995).
29 T. Job 38–40 presents important parallels for this enigmatic form of glossolalia.

11, 30; 14:13, 26–28).³⁰ The tongues under discussion in 14:2 are of this second, celestial type.

Paul's aim in much of the rest of the chapter, as stated in 14:2, is to clarify the appropriate place of πνευματικά such as glossolalia within the context of communal worship. Far from prohibiting these spiritual practices (see esp. 14:5, 18), Paul insists they be properly submitted to communal love and thereby oriented toward edifying the assembly as a whole, not just solitary individuals. As Paul explains, the problem with uninterpreted tongues is that the one who speaks in them "speaks not to other humans, but to God alone, for no one else understands (ἀκούει)." To this private experience of human and divine communication Paul contrasts prophecy, which he recommends as more appropriate for communal worship because it is comprehensible to all and thus enables all to participate equally in the edification of the church (14:1, 4). Difficult questions now arise, however, concerning the expression πνεύματι δὲ λαλεῖ μυστήρια and its relation to the preceding material. While the dative πνεύματι could be taken in reference to the human spirit (as in 2:11; 4:21; 5:3–4; 7:34; 14:14–15),³¹ Paul routinely describes the Christian as "in the Spirit" with the dative πνεύματι in the sense of being inspired by the Holy Spirit (6:11; 12:3, 9, 13). Especially indicative is the instance of πνεύματι in 12:3, which describes the Christian as speaking (λαλῶν) "in the Spirit of God" (ἐν πνεύματι θεοῦ). Moreover, according to 12:8–9, all gifts, including "a message of wisdom" (λόγος σοφίας), are given "according to the same Spirit" (κατὰ τὸ αὐτὸ πνεῦμα) and "by the one Spirit" (ἐν τῷ ἑνὶ πνεύματι). Since the topic in 14:2 is a charismatic form of speech that is addressed to and only intelligible to God, the πνεῦμα here is almost certainly the Holy Spirit.³² This is then additional confirmation of the Spirit's instrumental role in making known mysteries.

Even more pressing is the question of the relationship between speech spoken to God alone in 14:2a and the mysteries spoken in the Spirit in 14:2b, a question complicated by the inconveniently unspecific conjunction δέ. A common approach is to take δέ here as explanatory, thus linking the preceding

---

30 For a more detailed summary of the approaches to tongues in 1 Cor 12–14, see esp. Anthony C. Thiselton, *The First Epistle to the Corinthians* (NIGTC; Grand Rapids: Eerdmans, 2000), who lists no fewer than six different descriptions of the phenomenon (972–88).
31 For such a reading, see Joseph A. Fitzmyer, *First Corinthians: A New Translation with Introduction and Commentary* (AB 32; New Haven: Yale University Press, 2008), 511; Jean Héring, *The First Epistle of Saint Paul to the Corinthians* (trans. A. W. Heathcote, and P. J. Allcock; London: Epworth Press, 1962), 146; Frédéric Godet, *Commentaire sur la première épître aux Corinthiens*, t. 2 (Neuchâtel: l'Imprimerie Nouvelle L.-A. Monnier, 1965 [1865]), 270–71.
32 Cf. also the role of the Spirit in 2:10–13.

characterization of private glossolalia with the following statement regarding mysteries so that the latter expression provides a rationale for the former: the person speaking in tongues speaks only to God *because* that person speaks mysteries in the Spirit. Read this way, the mysteries here are often described as "what transcends normal human understanding."[33] This assumes then that "[s]i Paul les qualifie de 'mystères', c'est plutôt à cause de la forme inaccessible du langue que pour le contenu des exclamations."[34] The main problem with this reading is that it contradicts Paul's usual use of μυστήριον, which in every other instance does not refer to "mysterious realities"[35] or to "undurchdringliche Geheimnisse"[36] but to declarations that, while perhaps controversial or surprising, are nonetheless quite evident. Since μυστήρια throughout the Pauline letters are always otherwise comprehensible pronouncements, should we expect mysteries spoken in the Spirit to be impenetrable speech here? While Thiselton is correct that "every writer uses terminology in context dependent ways that may modify a more usual meaning," it is not the case, as he claims, that "Paul's usual meaning [of μυστήριον] cannot make sense [in 14:2] without undermining his own argument."[37] There is another option, and it is to take the δέ as contrastive: the person speaking in indecipherable tongues speaks only to God *even though* she speaks mysteries in the Spirit. Taken this way, Paul is lamenting that private interaction between the believer and God in incomprehensible tongues obscures what would otherwise be profitable for the whole community. As Robertson and Plummer put it, "Mysteries must be revealed to be profitable; but in the case of Tongues without an interpreter there was no revelation, and therefore no advantage to the hearers."[38] Hence the mysteries being spoken in the Spirit in 14:2 are genuine mysteries, which is to say, previously hidden but now knowable Christian truths that would be of benefit to the entire assembly. But because what is supposed to be stated plainly is being stated unintelligibly, in a language of private devotion, Paul advises his readers to reconsider the practice of individual

---

33 Fitzmyer, *First Corinthians*, 510–11. So also Gordon D. Fee, *The First Epistle to the Corinthians* (NICNT; Grand Rapids: Eerdmans, 1987), 656.
34 E.-B. Allo, *Saint Paul. Première Épître aux Corinthiens* (Paris: Gabalda, 1934), 356. For a similar reading, see Lindemann, *Der Erste Korintherbrief*, 297.
35 Raymond F. Collins, *First Corinthians* (SP 7; Collegeville, MN: The Liturgical Press, 1991), 492.
36 Weiss, *Der erste Korintherbrief*, 322.
37 Thiselton, *The First Epistle*, 1085.
38 Archibald Robertson and Alfred Plummer, *A Critical and Exegetical Commentary on the First Epistle of St. Paul to the Corinthians* (ICC; 2d ed.; Edinburgh: T&T Clark, 1929), 306.

glossolalia without interpretation within the communal context.³⁹ Such a reading of the μυστήρια in 14:2 accords exactly with Paul's other uses of the signifier,⁴⁰ as well as with the fact that glossolalia is apparently not in itself problematic for Paul. The problem is instead, as Barrett states, that "the speaker and God are sharing hidden truths that others are not permitted to share,"⁴¹ a circumstance that undermines ecclesial οἰκοδομή (14:3–5).

2.2.2 2 Thessalonians 2:7

The remainder of the occurrences of μυστήριον in the undisputed letters utilizes the singular form of the noun and always specifies the precise referent of the mystery. Importantly, in each of these instances, that which is designated a mystery is some newly revealed and plainly stated eschatological or christological fact. In contrast to the common use of "mystery" in ordinary English, the Greek μυστήριον, at least as Paul applies it, does not indicate obscurity or inscrutability. Rather the term designates some important truth of Christian theology or eschatology that was previously hidden and has now been made known. This is not to deny that these truths are profound. It is rather to emphasize that they are straightforwardly communicated and readily accessible to the Christian mind.

I first consider the mysteries in 2 Thess 2:7, Rom 11:25, and 1 Cor 15:51 because of several similarities that they share. I treat 1 Cor 2:1 and 2:7 last because of their particular importance for the deuteropauline Pauline mystery passages that will be the focus of the following chapter.

---

39 For a similar reading, see Wolfgang Schrage, *Der erste Brief an die Korinther (1 Kor 11,17–14:40)* (EKK VII/3; Zürich: Benziger and Neukirchen-Vluyn: Neukirchener Verlag, 1999), 385; Gerhard Dautzenberg, *Urchristliche Prophetie: Ihre Erforschung, ihre Voraussetzung im Judentum und ihre Struktur im ersten Korintherbrief* (BWANT 6/4; Stuttgart: W. Kohlhammer, 1975), 234–37.
40 Cf. Christopher Forbes, *Prophecy and Inspired Speech*, who writes, "With the exceptions of 2 Thessalonians 2.7 and Ephesians 5.32, the term μυστήριον is uniformly a term of revelation in Paul. It would take considerable evidence to show that a revelatory sense is not applicable here, yet again scholars have tried to avoid the force of the term…. If we grant that Paul views glossolalia as inspired, it is hard to make any sense of the gift of interpretation of tongues unless tongues contain matter to be communicated. If they do, and edify in the same way as prophecy, on what basis are we to rule out (contrary to the normal meaning of the term μυστήρια in Paul) the concept of divine revelation?" (96–97).
41 C.K. Barrett, *A Commentary on the First Epistle to the Corinthians* (London: Black, 1968), 316.

The first text, 2 Thess 2:7, is not especially representative of the larger Pauline usage, but, if authentic, it is in all likelihood the earliest extant occurrence of μυστήριον in the thirteen-letter canonical corpus. It is also the most unusual of all the Pauline applications of the term and so a noticeable outlier in an already diverse data set:

τὸ γὰρ **μυστήριον** ἤδη ἐνεργεῖται τῆς ἀνομίας· μόνον ὁ κατέχων ἄρτι ἕως ἐκ μέσου γένηται.

This verse is notoriously enigmatic, both in terms of syntax and sense, but it is perhaps best translated as follows: "for the mystery of lawlessness is already at work—[but will] only [be so] until the one who restrains is [removed] from our midst."[42] Translated as so, this is a statement about the temporal limits within which the mystery of lawlessness will be active and then an explanation of the reason for this restricted time frame.[43]

The context is a discussion regarding Jesus' impending Parousia (2:1) ("the day of the Lord" [2:2]) and the specific events that must precede it (2:3–12). Paul warns his readers not to be deceived by any message or letter claiming that the day of the Lord has already occurred (2:2) because, as he explains, this day will not appear until the prior occurrence of a certain rebellion (ἀποστασία) and then concurrent revelation (ἀποκαλυφθῇ) of "the man of lawlessness, the son of destruction" (2:3).[44] Paul reminds his readers of what he told them when he was with them (2:5), namely, that there is at present something "restraining" (τὸ κατέχον) the man of lawlessness, ensuring that his revelation occurs at the proper time (2:6). However, although the man of lawlessness is barred from revealing himself, "the mystery of lawlessness is already at work" and will continue to be so until "the restrainer" (ὁ κατέχων) is removed (2:6–7).[45] Once this latter event occurs, the man of lawlessness will be revealed, although only to be destroyed by the Lord at his Parousia (2:8).

---

42 This translation follows Gordon D. Fee, *The First and Second Letters to the Thessalonians* (NICNT; Grand Rapids: Eerdmans, 2009), 288. The brackets helpfully illustrate just how much must be inserted in order to make any sense in English of the clause and its ellipses.
43 The adverb μόνος is thus indicating temporal limitation.
44 This man will also "make his seat in the temple of God, declaring that he is God" (2:4).
45 Literature on the "restrainer" (τὸ κατέχον/ὁ κατέχων) in 2:6–7 is vast. See most recently Paul Metzger, *Katechon: II Thess 2,1–12 im Horizont apokalyptischen Denkens* (BZNW 135; Berlin/New York: de Gruyter, 2005).

Conjectures about the identities of "the man of lawlessness" and "the restrainer" abound and need not be multiplied.[46] The key point in 2:7 is the temporal declaration that even though "the man of lawlessness" is yet to be revealed, "the mystery of lawlessness" (τὸ μυστήριον τῆς ἀνομίας) is nonetheless already at work in the world (2:7a). The principal questions are then: (1) what is meant by τὸ μυστήριον τῆς ἀνομίας? (2) why is the current lawlessness termed a mystery? and (3) what is the relationship between this mystery of lawlessness and the man himself?

There are ancient parallels to the expression τὸ μυστήριον τῆς ἀνομίας, but no exact equivalent. Josephus once refers to the behavior of Antipater as "a mystery of wickedness" (κακίας μυστήριον) (J.W. 1.470), but it is unclear just what Josephus means by the phrase.[47] What is clear is that it has nothing to do with eschatological events and timetables. Intriguing parallels also appear in material from Qumran, particularly in the phrase "mysteries of iniquity" (רזי פשע).[48] What the רזי פשע expression appears to describe is, in Bockmuehl's description, "a fundamentally dualistic cosmology" in which "the workings and devices of the evil one are equally real, and equally inscrutable to man, as the mysteries of God."[49] A similar sort of dualism seems implicit in the Pauline expression as well. Insofar as the man of lawlessness is an impostor for God (2:4) and agent of Satan (2:9), his designs are fundamentally opposed to God's. By extension, the mystery of lawlessness, which must somehow be associated with the man, likely refers to something akin to "Satan's economy of damnation"[50] or "the Satanic plan to oppose the redemptive work of Christ."[51] It is then any rebellious enterprise that intends to controvert the plans of God. Despite the fact

---

[46] For a concise summary of past proposals, see Colin Nicholl, "Michael, the Restrainer Removed (2 Thess. 2:6–7)," *JTS* 51 (2000): 27–53, esp. 30–35. As Fee, *The First and Second Letters*, correctly notes, "It is precisely because [the Thessalonians] know what Paul meant that we do not" (288).

[47] According to Markus N.A. Bockmuehl, *Revelation and Mystery in Ancient Judaism and Pauline Christianity* (WUNT 2/36; Tübingen: Mohr Siebeck, 1990), the expression "seems to be taken from the Hellenistic mystery rites – i.e.: Antipater's life was a continual orgy of secret wickedness" (196 n. 12).

[48] See 1Q 27 1:2–4; 1QH 5:36 and frg. 50:5; cf. also 1QapGen 1:2. As Raymond E. Brown, *The Semitic Background of the Term "Mystery" in the New Testament* (Philadelphia: Fortress Press, 1968), points out, on some twenty occasions the LXX translates the Hebrew פשע with the Greek ἀνομία and, therefore, the phrase רזי פשע appears to be a plural Hebrew equivalent for the singular τὸ μυστήριον τῆς ἀνομίας (40).

[49] Bockmuehl, *Revelation and Mystery*, 56.

[50] Brown, *The Semitic Background*, 40.

[51] Paul Hanly Furfey, "'The Mystery of Lawlessness'," *CBQ* 8 (1946): 179–91, 191.

that the man of lawlessness has not yet been revealed, to the extent that the satanic forces associated with him are presently active in the world, the mystery of lawlessness is at work, even if imperceptibly to those not privy to the mystery.

Although Paul speaks of the mystery of lawlessness as a plainly known fact, it remains unclear to what extent it is generally knowable and observable, or how Paul himself came to know it. Given the emphasis on pneumatic illumination in other Pauline mystery passages, we can reasonably suppose that a similar sort of revelation occurred in this case. The designation μυστήριον presumably also indicates, as it does elsewhere in Paul, that the mystery of lawlessness is something perceived exclusively by Christians. By virtue of possessing the Spirit, Christians recognize that the ἀνομία surrounding them is in fact a critical precursor to the forthcoming rebellion and apocalypse of the man of lawlessness. Others may still witness this same ἀνομία, even perhaps acknowledging it as such, but they remain ignorant of its specific eschatological significance. Also unclear is the precise relationship between the mystery and the man. Is the present existence of the mystery of lawlessness (ἤδη ἐνεργεῖται) an indicator that Paul (or the author) believed the man to be alive and soon to be revealed? On this matter we can only speculate, but it does seem likely in light of the attention Paul gives it and the eschatological urgency elsewhere in the Pauline corpus.

2.2.3 Romans 11:25

Rom 11:25–26a comes at the conclusion to the intricate argument of Rom 9–11. One common element in both Rom 11:25–26a and 2 Thess 2:7 is that the term μυστήριον is used to correlate a current historical situation with an impending eschatological event:[52]

> οὐ γὰρ θέλω ὑμᾶς ἀγνοεῖν, ἀδελφοί, **τὸ μυστήριον** τοῦτο, ἵνα μὴ ἦτε [παρ'] ἑαυτοῖς φρόνιμοι, ὅτι πώρωσις ἀπὸ μέρους τῷ Ἰσραὴλ γέγονεν ἄχρι οὗ τὸ πλήρωμα τῶν ἐθνῶν εἰσέλθῃ, καὶ οὕτως πᾶς Ἰσραὴλ σωθήσεται...

> For I do not want you to be ignorant, brothers, about this mystery, lest you should be wise in your own conceits: a hardening has come upon a portion in Israel until the fullness of the Gentiles should come in, and so all Israel will be saved...

---

52 The γάρ links it to the olive tree image in 11:16–24 and, more specifically, to the claim that God can and will again graft severed Israel onto the tree (11:23–24).

The introductory formula (οὐ θέλω ὑμᾶς ἀγνοεῖν)[53] marks the object of the disclosure (τὸ μυστήριον τοῦτο) as being of special significance to the Roman auditors, and the ensuing purpose clause (ἵνα μὴ ἦτε [παρ'] ἑαυτοῖς φρόνιμοι)[54] explains why. Paul introduces the content of the μυστήριον with a ὅτι clause.[55] Although grammatically singular, the mystery involves three interrelated circumstances: (1) the current (γέγονεν) hardening of a portion of Israel; (2) the future (ἄχρι οὗ) inclusion of the "fullness of the Gentiles"; and (3) the consequent (καὶ οὕτως)[56] salvation of "all Israel."[57] The mystery in 11:25 is God's design to save Israel along with the nations in this surprising sequence. Paul's use of the singular μυστήριον is therefore potentially misleading. It is not any individual element that makes the mystery; it is their surprising logical and temporal interconnectedness that constitutes the new revelation.[58]

This is not the place for an exhaustive analysis of every fine detail in these verses, and there are many.[59] The two most important questions are: (1) why does Paul designate this specific prediction regarding Israel and the Gentiles a mystery? and (2) how did Paul himself come to know it? As for the first question, the impending historical equation in which Israel's hardening plus Gentile inclusion equals all of Israel's salvation is a μυστήριον insofar as it is a newly revealed prophetic announcement (or "new doctrine").[60] It is important to emphasize, therefore, that while each individual element of the schema could

---

53 Cf. Rom 1:13; 1 Cor 10:1; 12:1; 2 Cor 1:8; 1 Thess 4:13.
54 Cf. Prov 3:7.
55 Cf. 1 Thess 4:13–16, where Paul also uses the οὐ θέλω ὑμᾶς ἀγνοεῖν formula (v. 13a), followed by a purpose clause introduced by ἵνα (v. 13b), and then a ὅτι clause (v. 15b) that supplies the information that Paul wishes his readers to know.
56 I say "consequent," but the logical relationship suggested by καὶ οὕτως is not necessarily temporally posterior or causative. The salvation of all Israel might very well coincide with the inclusion of the Gentiles. For such a reading see Jason A. Staples, "What Do the Gentiles Have to Do with 'All Israel'? A Fresh Look at Romans 11:25–27," *JBL* 130 (2011): 371–90. For the causative reading of καὶ οὕτως, see E.P. Sanders, *Paul, the Law, and the Jewish People* (Minneapolis: Fortress, 1983), 193.
57 Some scholars deny that the third element in v. 26a is part of the mystery proper, but even if not it is still logically linked to what is disclosed in v. 25 and must be considered in relation to it.
58 Notice that once again there is nothing necessarily "mysterious" or cryptic about the mystery. It is a mystery strictly in the sense that it is a previously unknown divine secret that Paul is now sharing with the Roman Christians.
59 Most challenging is the question of what is meant by πᾶς Ἰσραήλ. On this topic see esp. the recent analysis of Staples, "What Do the Gentiles Have to Do with 'All Israel'?," and 371–74 for previous interpretations.
60 So Bockmuehl, *Revelation and Mystery*, 170–75.

conceivably be derived independently from scripture,[61] there is no scriptural or traditional source for the particular sequence that Paul offers,[62] which is why he does not cite one.[63] Just because that particular historical construal has not been explicitly prophesied in scripture need not entail that it controverts scripture. It is instead the case that portions of scripture, such as those cited in 11:26b–27 (Isa 59:20–21; Isa 27:9), become differently appreciated when reread retrospectively in light of the new eschatological mystery.[64] The newly revealed mystery thus functions as a hermeneutical catalyst, transforming the prior revelation of scripture and rendering it freshly prophetic for new eschatological circumstances.

So when and how did Paul come to know this mystery? It is unwise to be too precise here. While other Pauline mystery passages specify the agents by which a mystery is made known (such as God [Eph 1:9] or the Holy Spirit [1 Cor 2:10]) and the means (such as direct revelation [Eph 3:3] or – arguably – the prophetic writings [Rom 16:26]), Rom 11:25 provides no such details. Some scholars contend that the revelation came to Paul through the study of scripture, perhaps in a moment of charismatic illumination,[65] and the results of this oracular-like exegetical endeavor were then labeled a mystery.[66] While this is possible, the fact still remains that the key particular of the mystery – that is, the correlation of Gentile

---

[61] For the scriptural analogues to the three elements of the mystery, see Seyoon Kim, "The 'Mystery' of Rom 11.25–6 Once More," NTS 43 (1997): 412–29, esp. 415–20.

[62] Thus Pablo T. Gadenz, Called from the Jews and from the Gentiles, (WUNT 2/267; Tübingen: Mohr Siebeck, 2009), writes, "[T]here are no texts which support the three clauses of the mystery together; i.e., there are no texts which speak of Israel's salvation following upon a period of hardening which ends when the fullness of the nations comes in. The mystery is thus not revealed *as such* in the Scriptures" (210 n. 149).

[63] Cf. Kim, "The 'Mystery'," who asks, "Is it not strange that Paul explicitly substantiates the inference from the 'mystery' proper with the Scriptures but does not do the same for the 'mystery' proper itself? Had he obtained the 'mystery' from the exegesis of the Scriptures, is it not to be expected of him to substantiate it with reference to those Scriptures?" (416–17).

[64] Thus Gadenz, Called from the Jews, writes, "Since it is something new, the mystery in 11,25b-26a is not contained *as such* in the (OT) Scriptures. The mystery itself goes beyond the Scriptures (but not against them), and indeed, the Scriptures can be *re-read* in light of the revealed mystery" (210–11).... "In other words, the function of the citation in vv. 26b-27 is not that of a proof from authority in support of v. 26a; rather, the cited texts, *re-read* in light of the mystery, take on a new meaning which serves to further illustrate the mystery" (211 n. 150).

[65] So Richard H. Bell, Provoked to Jealousy: The Origin and Purpose of the Jealousy Motif in Romans 9–11 (WUNT 2/63; Tübingen: Mohr Siebeck, 1994), 126–27; F. Mussner, "'Ganz Israel wird gerettet werden' (Rom 11,26)," Kairos 18 (1976): 241–55, esp. 254–55.

[66] Cf. the conclusion of Bockmuehl, Revelation and Mystery, 174–75.

inclusion with Israel's hardening and salvation – is not derivable from scripture as such and would therefore still require some sort of divine elucidation. This caveat does not exclude the possibility that Paul came to perceive the mystery while querying scripture for immediate answers to his current questions as apostle to the Gentiles, but it does mean that this still would have been an event of personal revelation.[67]

2.2.4 1 Corinthians 15:51

The mystery passage most similar to Rom 11:25 is that of 1 Cor 15:51–52:[68]

> ἰδοὺ **μυστήριον** ὑμῖν λέγω· πάντες οὐ κοιμηθησόμεθα, πάντες δὲ ἀλλαγησόμεθα, ἐν ἀτόμῳ, ἐν ῥιπῇ ὀφθαλμοῦ, ἐν τῇ ἐσχάτῃ σάλπιγγι· σαλπίσει γὰρ καὶ οἱ νεκροὶ ἐγερθήσονται ἄφθαρτοι καὶ ἡμεῖς ἀλλαγησόμεθα.[69]
>
> Behold, I tell you a mystery: we shall not all sleep, but we shall all be transformed, in a moment, in the blink of an eye, at the last trumpet. For the trumpet will sound and the dead will be raised imperishable and we shall be transformed.

What 1 Cor 15:51–52 and Rom 11:25 have in common (and 2 Thess 2:7 to some degree as well) is the use of μυστήριον to designate some newly disclosed teaching that concerns an event immediately penultimate to the eschaton. In 1 Cor 15:51 the new mystery that Paul reveals to the Corinthians appears to be that at the inauguration of the Parousia those who are still living, like those who

---

[67] So Karl Olav Sandnes, *Paul – One of the Prophets?: A Contribution to the Apostle's Self-Understanding* (WUNT 2/43; Tübingen: Mohr Siebeck, 1991), writes, "The mystery and its immediate context are deeply influenced by scriptural quotations and ancient traditions. We conclude that the prophetic oracle was dependent upon scriptural material. This does not mean, however, that the mystery is simply a conclusion drawn from different OT texts. A revelatory response made Paul able to re-read the Scriptures with respect to the problem raised in Rom 9–11" (182). As mentioned in the introduction, perhaps the best comparanda for this sort of hermeneutical interaction with scripture are *pesharim* like 1QpHab 7:1–8, where the exegete of Habakkuk emphasizes that Habakkuk himself was prevented from knowing the mysteries concerning the end of the age that Habakkuk was writing about. Those mysteries are only discerned retrospectively through the disclosure of the Teacher of Righteousness.

[68] Cf. the synopsis of these two passages and the discussion in Bockmuehl, *Revelation and Mystery*, 170–73. As Bockmuehl notes, there are also important parallels with 1 Thess 4:13–17.

[69] The textual variation in the manuscript history of this verse is extreme and theologically significant. Cf., for instance, the very different reading found in the Vulgate: *Ecce mysterium vobis dico, omnes quidem resurgemus, sed non omnes immutabimur.* For a fuller discussion of these matters see Thiselton, *The First Epistle*, 1293.

are dead, will be somatically transformed.⁷⁰ The announcement of this mystery comes near the end of a section that started in 15:35 with the questions: "How are the dead raised and in what sort of body do they come?"⁷¹ Paul addresses those matters in vv. 36–50, first by variously illustrating the differences between heavenly and earthly bodies (vv. 36–44), and then by particularizing those differences via an extended figural contrast of the first man, Adam, and the last man, Christ (vv. 45–50). The mystery spoken of 15:51 addresses a different but closely related subject. Perhaps anticipating a Corinthian retort, Paul explains in 15:51–54 how those who are still alive at the Parousia will, just like the dead, undergo a somatic metamorphosis and obtain an imperishable body. The ἰδού preceding μυστήριον in 15:51 strikes a revelatory and prophetic chord. This demonstrative particle is rare in Paul but quite common in contexts of prophecy, visionary experience, and oracular revelation.⁷² To preface μυστήριον with ἰδού is therefore quite appropriate, as it intensifies what is about to be disclosed, as well as the necessity (or, perhaps, difficulty) of comprehension.

To the question of how Paul came to know this mystery about bodily resurrection, again little can be said. There is new information regarding the Parousia in 1 Thess 4:15–18 that Paul alleges is "by the word of the Lord" (ἐν λόγῳ κυρίου), which could be taken as a claim to personal revelation.⁷³ As was the case in Rom 11:25, Paul has no precise scriptural proof text for this vision of the somatic transformation of the living at the time of Parousia.⁷⁴ In 15:54b–55 he does freely combine Isa 25:8 and Hos 13:14 as scriptural supplements – presented as fulfillment claims – to the preceding announcement, just as he appends scriptural texts in Rom 11:26b–27. The original prophetic fulfillment that these scriptural passages portend, however, is not the transformed bodies of the living but

---

70 It is initially unclear whether the accent is on the declaration that "we" (as in Paul and his Corinthian auditors) will not all die (κοιμηθησόμεθα) or the declaration that "we" (as in both the living and the dead) will all be changed (ἀλλαγησόμεθα). Given the surrounding context, however, it seems that the stress is on the fact that even living bodies, like dead bodies, will be transfigured in the eschaton. Thus it is not necessarily a statement regarding an imminent Parousia.
71 For the idea of a future resurrection involving some sort of human transformation, see esp. 2 Bar. 50.1–51.6. Also relevant are Dan 12:2–3; 1 En. 62.15–16.
72 Examples of ἰδού in the prophets are too numerous to cite. The only other Pauline uses of ἰδού are 2 Cor 6:2; 6:9; 7:11; 12:4; Gal 1:20 (Rom 9:33 is a scriptural citation).
73 For a comprehensive analysis of this passage and presentation of additional exegetical options, see Michael W. Pahl, *Discerning the 'Word of the Lord': The 'Word of the Lord' in 1 Thessalonians 4:15* (LNTS 389; London/New York: T&T Clark, 2009).
74 As Weiss, *Der erste Korintherbrief*, glosses Paul's use of μυστήριον here, it is "etwas, das weder den Lesern noch ihm vorher bekannt war, sondern durch besondere Erleuchtung ihm klar geworden ist" (378).

God's ultimate power over death.⁷⁵ But, when applied to the mystery of 15:51, the prophetic declarations of Isaiah and Hosea are themselves transformed, acquiring a new specificity in the light of the newly revealed insight. Once again, therefore, a new mystery effects a hermeneutical renovation of the antecedent revelation of Israel's scriptures, refracting their prophetic claims through the prism of some recent disclosure. The hermeneutical movement here is again critical. The motion is not from scripture to eschatological solution. Rather, the newly revealed solution is extended retroactively to scripture, which is then perceived as newly and more immediately prophetic.

2.2.5 1 Corinthians 2:1

The first occurrence of μυστήριον in 1 Corinthians comes at 2:1:

> κἀγὼ ἐλθὼν πρὸς ὑμᾶς, ἀδελφοί, ἦλθον οὐ καθ' ὑπεροχὴν λόγου ἢ σοφίας καταγγέλλων ὑμῖν **τὸ μυστήριον** τοῦ θεοῦ.
>
> And I, when I came to you, brothers, did not come proclaiming to you the mystery of God according to the superiority of reason or wisdom.

The first matter to consider is the textual uncertainty of μυστήριον in this verse. Although it is corroborated by important early witnesses (P⁴⁶ᵛⁱᵈ ℵ* A C 88 436 ar r syᵖ bo Hipp BasA Ambst),⁷⁶ it is outnumbered by the more widely attested and orthographically similar μαρτύριον (ℵ² B D F G Ψ 33 81 614 1739 1881 Maj b vg syʰ sa).⁷⁷ At present a majority of scholars favors the reading of μυστήριον, but the matter is far from straightforward.⁷⁸ When considered on internal grounds, there are two questions to be addressed: (1) Did Paul use μυστήριον in 2:1 in anticipation of 2:7, or was he again associating μαρτύριον with preaching as he did in 1:6? And (2) did scribes alter μυστήριον to μαρτύριον because of 1:6, or did they change μαρτύριον to μυστήριον, whether inadvertently or not, in anticipation

---

75 For a more detailed analysis of Paul's use of these passages, see Hays, *First Corinthians*, 275–76.
76 Notice, however, the preponderance of Egyptian witnesses.
77 The noun μαρτύριον only otherwise appears in the Pauline corpus in 1 Cor 1:6; 2 Thess 1:10; 1 Tim 2:6; 2 Tim 1:8.
78 See the lengthy inventory of scholars on both sides of the question provided by Gladd, *Revealing the* Mysterion, 123 n. 41.

of 2:7?⁷⁹ The difficulty is that these questions can be answered in favor of either reading. Perhaps Paul is indeed resuming the phrase τὸ μαρτύριον τοῦ Χριστοῦ from 1:6. Or perhaps he is anticipating the phrase ἐν μυστηρίῳ in 2:7. Perhaps a scribe thought back to 1:6. Or perhaps a scribe inadvertently glanced ahead to 2:7. How are we to decide? While Fee points to the relative rarity of μαρτύριον in favor of its originality (thus reckoning it as the *lectio difficilior*),⁸⁰ the prominence of μυστήριον in 1 Corinthians could favor its suitability here. A further point that has not been considered is the apparent awkwardness of the expression "announcing the witness" (καταγγέλλων τὸ μαρτύριον). If Paul wished to communicate a μαρτύριον, why would he not just adapt his expression and use μαρτυρέω?⁸¹ Outside of texts that attest to μαρτύριον in 2:1, there are no other instances in the *TLG* database where μαρτύριον is coordinated with either καταγγέλλω or ἀγγέλλω. By contrast, it would be entirely appropriate for Paul to refer to his earlier missionary work in Corinth as a time in which he was "announcing τὸ μυστήριον τοῦ θεοῦ." While mysteries are verbally communicated elsewhere in 1 Corinthians (1 Cor 2:7; 14:2; 15:51), and in other Pauline letters as well (Eph 6:19; Col 4:3), the noun μαρτύριον is never so described.⁸² It is also worth pointing out that other early Christian authors do freely coordinate καταγγέλλω and μυστήριον outside of citations of 2:1 which, as mentioned above, is not the case for μαρτύριον. However the matter is decided on text-critical terms, μυστήριον remains the earliest extant reading and one that continues to be accepted by most readers of 1 Corinthians (as the decision of the NA²⁷/NA²⁸ has ensured).⁸³

Again, the first thing to note about Paul's claim that he arrived in Corinth "announcing the mystery of God" (καταγγέλλων...τὸ μυστήριον τοῦ θεοῦ) is that it is not unusual for Paul to refer to mysteries as things that are spoken. I shall contend 2:7 is best read as a reference by Paul to "speaking in a mystery" (λαλοῦμεν...ἐν μυστηρίῳ) about the hidden wisdom of God. Paul likewise describes mysteries as being orally communicated on two other occasions in 1 Cor-

---

79 On these questions see Gordon D. Fee, "Textual-Exegetical Observations on 1 Corinthians 1:2, 2:1, and 2:10," in *Scribes and Scriptures: New Testament Essays in Honor of J. Harold Greenlee* (ed. David Alan Black; Winona Lake, IN: Eisenbrauns, 1992), 1–15, 6.
80 Fee, "Textual-Exegetical Observations," 6–8.
81 This verb usually implies verbal communication: "testify," "bear witness," "declare," "speak well of," etc. See the numerous examples in BDAG.
82 See, e.g., Origen, *Hom. Luc.* 10; Hippolytus, *Comm. Dan.* 4.48.1; Gregory of Nyssa, *De anima* (PG 46:132a).
83 For a more recent defense of μυστήριον and a more thorough presentation of the data, see V. Koperski, "'Mystery of God' or 'Testimony of God' in 1 Cor 2,1: Textual and Exegetical Considerations," in *New Testament Textual Criticism and Exegesis* (ed. A. Denaux; BETL 161; Leuven: Leuven University Press, 2002), 305–15.

inthians, which were discussed above (14:2; 15:51). Similar expressions involving verbal communication appear in Ephesians and Colossians:

Eph 6:19

...καὶ ὑπὲρ ἐμοῦ, ἵνα μοι δοθῇ λόγος **ἐν ἀνοίξει τοῦ στόματός μου**, ἐν παρρησίᾳ **γνωρίσαι τὸ μυστήριον** τοῦ εὐαγγελίου.

...and also for me, so that in opening my mouth a message should be given to me, with boldness to make known the mystery of the gospel.

Col 4:3

...προσευχόμενοι ἅμα καὶ περὶ ἡμῶν, ἵνα ὁ θεὸς ἀνοίξῃ ἡμῖν θύραν τοῦ λόγου **λαλῆσαι τὸ μυστήριον** τοῦ Χριστοῦ, δι' ὃ καὶ δέδεμαι.

...praying at the same time for us, that a door for the word should be opened for us, to speak the mystery of Christ, on account of which also I have been bound.

It is, therefore, quite fitting that Paul would characterize τὸ μυστήριον τοῦ θεοῦ in 2:1 as the subject of his missionary proclamation.

While the style of Paul's initial preaching is recalled in 2:1 ("not according to the superiority of reason or wisdom"), the content of "the mystery of God" that Paul first announced to the Corinthians is underscored in 2:2: "for I decided to know nothing else while among you except Jesus Christ, this man who has been crucified." Paul already stressed in 1:18–31 that though the "word of the cross" is a stumbling block to Jews and foolishness to Greeks, it is power and wisdom to the Corinthian believers. This is precisely what makes it a mystery: Jews and Greeks view it as it appears to their unspiritual minds – a criminal execution – whereas belivers perceive it for what it truly is – "the power of God for those who are being saved" (1:18). Having now identified the content of his mystery proclamation as the crucified Christ, in 2:3 Paul refers again to his disposition when he first appeared before the Corinthians announcing his gospel: "and I appeared to you in weakness and in fear and much trembling (ἐν ἀσθενείᾳ καὶ ἐν φόβῳ καὶ ἐν τρόμῳ πολλῷ)." These pictures of the apostle as weak and fearful mirror the content of his proclamation, which is publically perceived as foolishness.

The language of "fear and trembling" occurs elsewhere in Paul,[84] as does the motif of personal weakness.[85] "Fear and trembling" is in fact a stock phrase commonly found in Jewish literature, where it usually depicts a human response to

---

[84] The usages range from how Titus was greeted (2 Cor 7:15), to how salvation should be "worked out" (Phil 2:12), to the proper demeanor of a slave (Eph 6:5).
[85] Rom 8:26; 1 Cor 15:43; 2 Cor 11:30; 12:5, 9, 10; 13:4; Gal 4:3. Cf. also Rom 6:19; 1 Tim 5:23.

some vision, action, or appearance of God.⁸⁶ Fear and trembling is also a conventional description of the behavior of an apocalyptic visionary. As Gary Selby has observed, the rhetorical persona Paul dons as a man in weakness and fear and much trembling "bears a striking resemblance to the manner in which the traditional apocalypticist would describe his reaction to the experience of divine revelation."⁸⁷ Consider the descriptions of the following apocalyptic visionaries who were struck by bouts of fear, paroxysm, and weakness as a result of divine revelations:

Dan 4:19
But Daniel was greatly amazed as a deeper sense (ὑπόνοια) oppressed him and, being afraid (φοβηθείς), trembling seized him (τρόμου λαβόντος αὐτόν) and his appearance changed (ἀλλοιωθείσης τῆς ὁράσεως αὐτοῦ)...

Dan 7:15 (Th)
And as for me, Daniel, my spirit shuddered (ἔφριξεν τὸ πνεῦμά μου) involuntarily, and the visions in my head were distressing me (αἱ ὁράσεις τῆς κεφαλῆς μου ἐτάρασσόν με).

Dan 10:7–9
And I, Daniel, saw this great vision, and the men who were with me did not see this vision, as a strong fear (φόβος ἰσχυρός) fell upon them and they fled in haste. And I was left alone, and I saw this great vision. And there was no strength left in me (οὐκ ἐγκατελείφθη ἐν ἐμοὶ ἰσχύς) and a spirit turned against me for destruction, and I did not prevail...and I fell on my face to the ground.⁸⁸

1 En. 14.13–14
...fear covered me and trembling seized me (φόβος με ἐκάλυψεν καὶ τρόμος με ἔλαβεν). And I was shaking and trembling (καὶ ἤμην σειόμενος καὶ τρέμων) and I fell and beheld my vision.⁸⁹

1 En. 60.3–4
(Then) a great trembling and fear seized me and my loins and kidneys lost control. So I fell upon my face. Then Michael sent another angel from among the holy ones and he raised me up. And when he raised me up, my spirit returned; for (I had fainted) because I could not withstand the sight of these forces...⁹⁰

4 Ezra 5:13–15
These are the signs which I am permitted to tell you, and if you pray again and weep as now and fast for seven days, you will hear even greater things than these. Then I awoke, and my

---

86 See, i.a., Exod 15:16; Deut 11:25; Ps 2:11; Isa 19:16.
87 Gary S. Selby, "Paul, the Seer: The Rhetorical Persona in 1 Corinthians 2.1–16," in *The Rhetorical Analysis of Scripture: Essays from the 1995 London Conference* (ed. Stanley E. Porter and Thomas H. Olbricht; JSNTSup 146; Sheffield: Sheffield Academic Press, 1997), 351–73, 368.
88 Cf. also Dan 8:27 and 10:17, which describe Daniel as "weak" (ἀσθενήσας, ἠσθένησα) following his visionary experiences.
89 The context of this passage is Enoch's heavenly journey and vision.
90 Trans. E. Isaac, *OTP*.

body trembled violently (*et corpus meum horruit valde*), and my soul was so troubled it fainted (*et anima mea laboravit ut deficeret*). But the angel who had come and talked with me held me and strengthened me and set me on my feet.

Reading Paul's words as evoking the image of an inspired visionary makes even more sense when they are related to his subsequent statement in 2:4: "And my speech and my proclamation were not with persuasive words of wisdom but with a demonstration of the Spirit and of power."[91] At first glance, this verse seems to contradict what immediately precedes it. If Paul's preaching to the Corinthians amounted to a powerful display of the Spirit, then how was his appearance also one of weakness, fear, and trembling? How could Paul have appeared so weak if he preached so powerfully? The best solution is to take Paul's self-characterization in 2:3 as evoking the image of a pneumatic seer. Paul's self-described weakness, fear, and trembling are then not pitiable ailments. They are the afflictions of an inspired visionary with a divine mystery to announce.[92] There is therefore no need to posit some specific physical malady,[93] or "shyness in venturing unaccompanied into strange surroundings,"[94] or disappointment about his failure in Athens,[95] or to suppose that he was "overwhelmed by the task of evangelizing in this great city."[96] While any or all of these circumstances might have been true, such speculation misses the rhetorical persona of the apocalyptic visionary that Paul is adopting.[97] And note that in his transvaluative

---

[91] Cf. 1 Thess 1:5.
[92] As Selby, "Paul, the Seer," concludes: "[S]ituated as it is within a discourse which employs apocalyptic categories to characterize his message as the 'mystery of God', Paul's language reflects a deliberate attempt to place himself in the apocalyptic tradition. He has assumed the *persona* of the 'inspired seer' who receives a divine revelation and who faithfully – yet also in weakness, fear and trembling – transmits the mysterious, secret wisdom of God to God's people" (369–70). Collins, *First Corinthians*, comes close to this reading: "Paul's use of the traditional binomial [fear and trembling] is consistent with the apocalyptic atmosphere that characterizes his discourse.... The word group is used in a variety of ways, one of which is to suggest that weakness is the locus of the revelation of God's power" (119). Cf. also Gladd, *Revealing the* Mysterion, who, following Selby, characterizes fear and trembling as "apocalyptic behavior" (120–23).
[93] Fee, *First Epistle*, 93.
[94] Robertson and Plummer, *First Epistle of St. Paul to the Corinthians*, 31.
[95] Weiss, *Der erste Korintherbrief*, 47.
[96] Fee, *First Epistle*, 94.
[97] By assuming this role, Paul captures important rhetorical advantages. Even if he was in fact suffering under some obvious malaise (as appears to be the case in Gal 4:13–14), by remaking it into a consequence of a visionary experience, he potentially neutralizes critiques of his unimpressive personality or physical appearance (recall 2 Cor 10:10). Otherwise, the self-deprecating recollections of his weaknesses would be just that and, as Selby wonders, "[H]ow can such self-

reworking of δύναμις in 2:4–5 Paul is not unwittingly trading in worldly Corinthian social currency. He is instead deconstructing that form of cultural capital, subverting it from the inside and, at the same time, reconfiguring his own appearance in order to authenticate his ministry (2:4) and the divine foundation of the Corinthians' faith (2:5). Taken together, then, Paul's remarks on his mystery proclamation in 2:1–5, especially when read in light of his previous remarks on the "word of the cross" in 1:18–31, illustrate how the form and content of Paul's preaching coincide: what may appear externally as weak and foolish is in reality someone in the grip of God's power. The medium (or in this case the man) is also the message as the mystery is as much performed as it is proclaimed.[98]

2.2.6 1 Corinthians 2:6–16

Although μυστήριον only appears in 2:7, vv. 6–16 comprise a discernible unit with several key terms and propositions that will be important for our analysis in the next chapter, and so it should be treated here as a whole. These verses also comprise one of the most contested stretches of text in the Pauline corpus, so much so that its integrity has occasionally been questioned.[99]

A common assumption is that the style of 2:6–16 is un-Pauline and that the arguments deviate from Paul's preceding claims in 1:18–2:5. What these flat readings of 1 Cor 1–2 fail to recognize, however, is the subtle and in fact insurrectionary character of Paul's argumentative strategy.[100] Far from departing from his previous propositions, in 2:6–16 Paul continues to advance them, now by cap-

---

deprecating language possibly help the cause of one who seeks to earn the right to speak?" (Selby, "Paul, the Seer," 352–53).
98 As other passages indicate, the idea that Paul's own body depicts the sufferings of the crucified Christ is not figurative speech. See Gal 4:13–14; 6:17; 2 Cor 4:7–10; 6:4–6. The balance between physical disfigurement and weakness, on the one hand, and apocalyptic enthusiasm on the other is most aggressively developed in 2 Cor 11:23–12:12.
99 So William O. Walker, Jr., "1 Corinthians 2.6–16: A Non-Pauline Interpolation?," *JSNT* 47 (1992): 75–94; Martin Widmann, "1 Kor 2 6–16: Ein Einspruch gegen Paulus," *ZNW* 70 (1979): 44–53. E. Earle Ellis, "Traditions in 1 Corinthians," *NTS* 32 (1986): 481–502, proposes that the passage is from pre-Pauline midrashic material that Paul adapted for a new context.
100 Hays, *First Corinthians*, in commenting on this passage, notes, "Irony is the most dangerous of rhetorical devices, because it employs semantic misdirection; the author relies upon the audience to pick up the clues that what is meant is not exactly what is said. Thus, the risk of misunderstanding is great: Readers who are not tuned in to the situation of author and audience may miss the clues and drastically misread the text" (40).

turing potential detractors' territory – in this case, their terminology. Paul here redefines what are likely key categories of Corinthian thought – wisdom, mystery, perfection, knowledge, pneumatic experience – in new apocalyptic and cruciform registers. As Thiselton describes it, "Paul takes up the major catchwords which had become embedded in the life of the church at Corinth, and his most urgent task at this point is neither to reject their validity nor to bypass what was important for his readers, but to reclaim the terms for the gospel by redefining them in the light of the nature of God and of the gospel."[101] Therefore, just as he redefined power and weakness in 1:18–2:5, so Paul works here to upend conventional human estimations of wisdom, cognition, and communication style.

The sabotage begins in 2:6 as Paul returns to the subject of σοφία. In 1:18–31 he denounced the vanity of human quests for worldly wisdom, starting with the futility of human attempts to apprehend God. In 2:6, however, Paul invokes σοφία not for further criticism but in order to define its proper place in Christian proclamation. The importance of wisdom is highlighted syntactically by its placement in an emphatic first position: **σοφίαν** δὲ λαλοῦμεν ἐν τοῖς τελείοις, **σοφίαν** δὲ οὐ τοῦ αἰῶνος τούτου οὐδὲ τῶν ἀρχόντων τοῦ αἰῶνος τούτου τῶν καταργουμένων ("but *wisdom* we do speak among the mature, but a wisdom not of this age nor of the rulers of this age who are passing away").[102] Paul's point is that the Corinthians must take care not to mistake "wisdom" for wisdom. That is, they must not confuse the wisdom claimed and achieved by human minds with the wisdom of God that transcends every simulacra of the current age. This other-worldly σοφία is the wisdom about which Paul and his colleagues speak, and eagerly so. In 2:7–8a Paul provides more information about the provenance of this heavenly wisdom:

> ἀλλὰ λαλοῦμεν θεοῦ σοφίαν **ἐν μυστηρίῳ** τὴν ἀποκεκρυμμένην, ἣν προώρισεν ὁ θεὸς πρὸ τῶν αἰώνων εἰς δόξαν ἡμῶν, ἣν οὐδεὶς τῶν ἀρχόντων τοῦ αἰῶνος τούτου ἔγνωκεν.
>
> But rather we speak in a mystery about the wisdom of God, which has been hidden, which God ordained before the ages for our glory, which none of the rulers of this age has known.

Before commenting on this passage in more detail, it is first necessary to address the grammatical ambiguity of the phrase ἐν μυστηρίῳ, which is a matter of long-

---

101 Thiselton, *The First Epistle*, 224.
102 Thus Hays, *First Corinthians*, writes, "At 2:6, Paul pivots sharply on the word 'wisdom,' which is highlighted by the word order of Paul's Greek: '*Sophia*, however, we do speak among the mature....' Is it wisdom you want? All right, he says, let's talk wisdom. This strategy of ironic reversal, abruptly coopting a term which has been previously the opposition's keynote, is a characteristic Pauline argumentative move" (42).

standing dispute. The phrase can be syntactically coordinated in three ways: (1) It can be read adjectivally as modifying the noun phrase θεοῦ σοφίαν (NIV [1984]: "We speak of God's secret wisdom"; NRSV: "But we speak God's wisdom, secret and hidden"). (2) It can be taken with the following participle ἀποκεκρυμμένην (NET: "Instead we speak the wisdom of God, hidden in a mystery"). And (3) it can be read adverbially in relation to the main verb λαλοῦμεν ("We speak in a mystery about the wisdom of God").

None of these options is without difficulties. The problem for taking ἐν μυστηρίῳ adjectivally in relation to σοφίαν is the absence of a preceding τὴν, which would unambiguously mark its attributive position.[103] The same problem exists for coordinating ἐν μυστηρίῳ with τὴν ἀποκεκρυμμένην. If Paul intended to describe God's wisdom as "hidden in a mystery," he could have plainly written τὴν ἐν μυστηρίῳ ἀποκεκρυμμένην or even τὴν ἀποκεκρυμμένην ἐν μυστηρίῳ. Finally, the problem for reading ἐν μυστηρίῳ adverbially in relation to λαλοῦμεν is its syntactical separation from the verb. If Paul wished to describe God's wisdom as being spoken "in a mystery," then why did he not clearly write λαλοῦμεν ἐν μυστηρίῳ?

When considered solely on the internal grounds of 1 Cor 2:7 the matter is ultimately indeterminable. A majority of modern commentators (particularly more recent commentators), however, favors the adjectival arrangement of ἐν μυστηρίῳ with σοφίαν.[104] The reason for this judgment is primarily theological, as interpreters have assumed that Paul could not have claimed to speak "in a mystery" because he would never "intend to imply that he imparted esoteric ideas

---

103 So H.A.W. Meyer, *Critical and Exegetical Handbook to the Epistles to the Corinthians* (trans. W.P. Dickson; New York: Funk & Wagnalls, 1884 [1870]), contends, "But the article, although after the anarthrous σοφίαν not in itself absolutely necessary, would be omitted here at the expense of clearness. Paul would have expressed himself with ambiguity, while he might clearly have avoided it by τὴν ἐν μυστηρίῳ" (49).
104 Proponents of this position include Roy E. Ciampa and Brian S. Rosner, *The First Letter to the Corinthians* (Pillar; Grand Rapids: Eerdmans, 2010), 125–26; Dieter Zeller, *Der erste Brief an die Korinther* (KEK 5; Göttingen: Vandenhoeck & Ruprecht, 2010), 135–36; David E. Garland, *1 Corinthians* (BECNT; Grand Rapids: Baker, 2003), 95; Thiselton, *The First Epistle*, 241; Lindemann, *Der Erste Korintherbrief*, 63–64; Helmut Merklein, *Der erste Brief an die Korinther: Kapitel 1–4* (ÖTNT; Gütersloh: Gütersloher Verlaghaus Mohn and Würzburg: Echter, 1992), 227–29; Wolfgang Schrage, *Der erste Brief*, 251; Fee, *The First Epistle*, 104–5; C.K. Barrett, *A Commentary on the First Epistle*, 70–71; E.-B. Allo, *Saint Paul. Première Épître*, 41; Robertson and Plummer, *First Epistle of St. Paul to the Corinthians*, 37–38. Conzelmann, *1 Corinthians*, after initially admitting that a decision on the syntax is "impossible" (56 n. 1), proceeds to assume the adjectival reading in his exegesis (62).

only to a small circle of clever students and kept it from the immature,"¹⁰⁵ or because "God's wisdom is not some inaccessible teaching, spoken in secret."¹⁰⁶

There are two problems with this reasoning. The first is that it begs the question of what it might mean to speak "in a mystery." While such an expression might imply something like private communication, such an understanding is not prima facie evident. It is also not how most ancient and modern commentators who have read ἐν μυστηρίῳ with λαλοῦμεν have understood the phrase "we speak in a mystery."¹⁰⁷ Second, there is almost no evidence that any ancient Greek reader of Paul ever took ἐν μυστηρίῳ to modify σοφίαν. Having searched every instance of ἐν μυστηρίῳ in the *TLG* database, I have found only one explicit case where a Greek author clearly coordinates ἐν μυστηρίῳ with σοφίαν.¹⁰⁸ There are, however, occasional instances where ἐν μυστηρίῳ is unambiguously arranged with the participle ἀποκεκρυμμένην and numerous cases in which ἐν μυστηρίῳ modifies λαλοῦμεν or some other verb for speaking or otherwise somehow communicating: such as shouting, proclaiming, signifying, and so on.¹⁰⁹

As for these latter two options—ἐν μυστηρίῳ with either λαλοῦμεν or ἀποκεκρυμμένην—there are two factors that strongly support arranging ἐν μυστηρίῳ with λαλοῦμεν. The first is again the ancient Greek evidence. Paul is probably the earliest extant Greek author to use the dative singular

---

105 Garland, *1 Corinthians*, 95.
106 Fee, *The First Epistle*, 105. It is important to point out that scholars have generally assumed that there are just two syntactical options: taking ἐν μυστηρίῳ with either λαλοῦμεν or σοφίαν. It is, however, entirely possible to read ἐν μυστηρίῳ with the participle ἀποκεκρυμμένην. Taken in this way, Paul would be explaining the means by which God's wisdom has been hidden: "...the wisdom of God, which has been hidden in a mystery." Importantly, several ancient Greek authors understood the syntax in this way (see below). Modern commentators who appear to prefer the arrangement of ἐν μυστηρίῳ with ἀποκεκρυμμένην include Fitzmyer, *First Corinthians*, 168–70, 176; and Collins, *First Corinthians*, 129–30.
107 One modern example is Joseph Agar Beet, *A Commentary on St. Paul's Epistles to the Corinthians* (New York: Thomas Whittaker, 1883), who writes, "Paul and his colleagues *speak in* the form of *a mystery*...i.e. in words which contain (under a guise which the world calls foolishness) a secret of infinite worth known only to those to whom God reveals it, viz. to mature Christians" (52).
108 Origen, *Comm. Matt.* 17.2.12: καὶ εἴ τίς ἐστιν ἀξιωθεὶς εἰδέναι τὰ ἄρρητα ῥήματα, ἃ οὐκ ἔξεστιν ἀνθρώπῳ λαλῆσαι, εἰδείη ἂν **τὴν ἐν μυστηρίῳ σοφίαν**, τὴν ἀποκεκρυμμένην…. Even this passage, however, appears to be an anomaly in Origen's corpus, for on multiple other occasion he clearly arranges ἐν μυστηρίῳ to modify ἀποκρύπτω. See, i.a., *Comm. Matt.* 13.3; 15.28; *Comm. Jo.* 10.41.286; 10.15.85; *Comm. Rom.* Fragment 11, Line 7.
109 For a full accounting of this data, see my forthcoming article in *CBQ*, "We Speak in a Mystery: Neglected Greek Evidence for the Syntax and Sense of 1 Corinthians 2:7."

μυστηρίῳ.[110] Moreover, in the two centuries after Paul, the dative singular μυστηρίῳ appears almost exclusively in Christian sources (Justin Martyr, the *Epistle to Diognetus*, Irenaeus, Clement of Alexandria, Origen, the *Acts of Peter*, et al.) and always with the preposition ἐν. Furthermore, in nearly every occurrence of this distinctly Christian phrase in the 150 years following Paul's initial coinage, ἐν μυστηρίῳ is unambiguously arranged in relation to a verb for speaking or communicating. Just a few examples of this usage should suffice:

Acts of Pet. 38
Τὸ πᾶν τοῦτο τῆς διακοσμήσεως συνεστήσατο...ἐν ᾗ τὰ δεξιὰ ἀριστερὰ ἔδειξεν καὶ τὰ ἀριστερὰ δεξιά, καὶ πάντα ἐνήλλαξεν τῆς φύσεως αὐτοῦ σημεῖα, ὡς καλὰ τὰ μὴ καλὰ νοῆσαι καὶ ἀγαθὰ τὰ ὄντως κακά· περὶ ὧν ὁ κύριος **ἐν μυστηρίῳ λέγει**· Ἐὰν μὴ ποιήσητε τὰ δεξιὰ ὡς τὰ ἀριστερὰ καὶ τὰ ἀριστερὰ ὡς τὰ δεξιὰ καὶ τὰ ἄνω ὡς τὰ κάτω καὶ τὰ ὀπίσω ὡς τὰ ἔμπροσθεν, οὐ μὴ ἐπιγνῶτε τὴν βασιλείαν.

[The first man] established the entirety of the ordered world...in which he displayed right things as left things and left things as right things, and he exchanged all the signs of his nature, so that he regarded as noble the ignoble and as good what is actually evil. Concerning which the Lord **says in a mystery:** "If you do not put the right things as left things and the left things as right things and the above as the below and the behind as the in front, surely you do not know the Kingdom."[111]

Justin Martyr, *Dial.* 75.1
Ἐν δὲ τῷ βιβλίῳ τῆς Ἐξόδου, ὅτι αὐτοῦ τὸ ὄνομα τοῦ θεοῦ καὶ Ἰησοῦς ἦν (ὃ λέγει τῷ Ἀβραὰμ μὴ δεδηλῶσθαι μηδὲ τῷ Ἰακώβ), διὰ Μωυσέως **ἐν μυστηρίῳ** ὁμοίως **ἐξηγγέλθη.**

[We know] that in the Book of Exodus the name of God was also Jesus, **which was proclaimed** likewise through Moses **in a mystery** (he says it was not to be revealed to Abraham, nor to Jacob).

Dial. 76.1
...καὶ τὸ λίθον τοῦτον εἰπεῖν ἄνευ χειρῶν τμηθέντα, **ἐν μυστηρίῳ** τὸ αὐτὸ **κέκραγε.**

...and to say "this stone cut without hands,"[112] **he [Daniel] has shouted the same thing in a mystery.**

---

110 The only sources that might predate him are 1 Enoch (10.7; 16.3), which is difficult to date, but quite possibly postdates Paul (see George W.E. Nickelsburg, *1 Enoch 1: A Commentary on the Book of 1 Enoch, Chapters 1–36; 81–108* [Hermeneia; Minneapolis: Fortress Press, 2001], 12–14), and the *Testaments of the Twelve Patriarchs* (*T. Jud.* 12.6), which is likely a second- or third-century C.E. Jewish-Christian composition (see Joel Marcus, "The *Testaments of the Twelve Patriarchs* and the *Didascalia Apostolorum:* A Common Jewish Christian Milieu?," *JTS* 61 [2010]: 596–626).
111 Unless otherwise indicated, all translations are my own.
112 Dan 2:34.

Dial. 100.1

Ὅτι γὰρ καὶ Ἰακὼβ καὶ Ἰσραὴλ καλεῖται ὁ Χριστός, ἀπέδειξα· αἱ οὐ μόνον ἐν τῇ εὐλογίᾳ καὶ Ἰωσὴφ καὶ Ἰούδα τὰ περὶ αὐτοῦ **κεκηρύχθαι ἐν μυστηρίῳ** ἀπέδειξα.

For I demonstrated that Christ is called both Jacob and Israel; and not only in the blessing of Joseph and Judah, I demonstrated that the things concerning him [Christ] **have been proclaimed in a mystery.**

Clement of Alexandria, *Strom.* 5.12.80.7

Ὑμῖν δέδοται γνῶναι τὸ μυστήριον τῆς βασιλείας τῶν οὐρανῶν· καὶ πάλιν φησὶ τὸ εὐαγγέλιον, ὡς ὁ σωτὴρ ἡμῶν **ἔλεγεν** τοῖς ἀποστόλοις τὸν λόγον **ἐν μυστηρίῳ**· καὶ γὰρ ἡ προφητεία περὶ αὐτοῦ φησιν· **ἀνοίξει ἐν παραβολαῖς τὸ στόμα αὐτοῦ** καὶ ἐξερεύξεται τὰ ἀπὸ καταβολῆς κόσμου κεκρυμμένα.

"To you it has been given to know the mystery of the Kingdom of the heavens."[113] And again the Gospel says, "As our savior was **speaking** to the apostles the word **in a mystery**."[114] For, indeed, the prophecy says concerning him, "He will **open his mouth in parables** and will utter things which have been hidden from the foundation of the world."[115]

Strom. 6.15.124.5–6

Ὃ δὲ ἀκούετε εἰς τὸ οὖς (ἐπικεκρυμμένως, δηλονότι, καὶ **ἐν μυστηρίῳ**, τὰ τοιαῦτα γὰρ εἰς τὸ οὖς λέγεσθαι ἀλληγορεῖται) ἐπὶ τῶν δωμάτων, φησί, κηρύξατε.... Οὔτε γὰρ ἡ προφητεία οὔτε ὁ σωτὴρ αὐτὸς ἁπλῶς οὕτως, ὡς τοῖς ἐπιτυχοῦσιν εὐάλωτα εἶναι, τὰ θεῖα μυστήρια ἀπεφθέγξατο, ἀλλ' **ἐν παραβολαῖς διελέξατο**.

"**What you hear** in your ear" (in a hidden manner, that is to say, also **in a mystery**, for such things are allegorically said to be "in the ear") he says "proclaim on the housetops"....[116] For neither prophecy nor the savior himself declared the divine mysteries plainly, so as for them to be easily grasped, but rather **he conversed in parables.**

Admittedly, while the usage of ἐν μυστηρίῳ in subsequent centuries becomes less regular, there remain many indisputable instances where Greek interpreters read the ἐν μυστηρίῳ of 1 Cor 2:7 with λαλοῦμεν.[117] This usually becomes clear when an author rearranges Paul's syntax or freely comments on the expression. Therefore, the ancient Greek data and, in particular, the data from native speak-

---

113 Matt 13:11. Clement appears to have harmonized Matthew's τὰ μυστήρια with Mark's τὸ μυστήριον. Cf. Mark 4:11; Luke 8:10.
114 It is unclear what Gospel Clement has in mind.
115 Ps 78:2; Matt 13:35.
116 This parenthesis interrupts a citation of Matt 10:27.
117 Especially noteworthy is Chrysostom's extended treatment in *Homiliae in epistulum i ad Corinthios*, Homily 7 (PG 61:55–56). Also important is Theodoret who, while acknowledging the syntactical possibility of taking ἐν μυστηρίῳ with λαλοῦμεν, is explicit that it should not be read with the verb, and instead appears to recommend taking it with ἀποκεκρυμμένην (*Interpretation of 1 and 2 Corinthians* [PG 82:241b]). He does not even consider reading ἐν μυστηρίῳ with σοφία a possibility.

ers in closest chronological proximity to Paul, clearly supports the construal of ἐν μυστηρίῳ with λαλοῦμεν.

The second factor supporting this grammatical arrangement is data internal to 1 Corinthians. As was observed above, in 1 Cor 2:1 (καταγγέλλω), 14:2 (λαλέω), and 15:51 (λέγω), mysteries are described as things that are communicated. This data suggests that speaking "in a mystery" about the wisdom of God is synonymous with speaking a mystery (and so λαλοῦμεν ἐν μυστηρίῳ would be tantamount to λαλοῦμεν μυστήριον, or the accusative form of the noun).[118]

Also quite significant, although often overlooked by interpreters, are the parallel λαλέω + ἐν constructions in 2:6 (σοφίαν δὲ λαλοῦμεν ἐν τοῖς τελείοις) and 2:13 (ἃ καὶ λαλοῦμεν οὐκ ἐν διδακτοῖς ἀνθρωπίνης σοφίας λόγοις ἀλλ' ἐν διδακτοῖς πνεύματος). The λαλέω + ἐν construction only otherwise appears in Paul in 1 Cor 14:35, 2 Cor 2:17, 12:19, and potentially Eph 5:19.[119] In 1 Cor 2, however, this construction possibly occurs three times, with the λαλέω + ἐν in 2:7 parallel to 2:6, both of which then anticipate 2:13. Paul's statement in 2:13 also develops the character of the wisdom that Paul and his associates speak "in a mystery." As opposed to teaching in mere human words of wisdom, Paul and his comrades speak (λαλοῦμεν) "in the instruction of the Spirit" (ἐν διδακτοῖς πνεύματος), a phrase that should be taken as parallel to speaking "in a mystery." Thus to speak about wisdom "in a mystery" is not to speak about a wisdom of this age (2:6), nor is it to speak "in the instructed words of human wisdom" (2:13); it is to speak "in the instruction of the Spirit."

As for the syntactical arrangement in 2:7, Paul again appears to be exploiting word order for rhetorical effect. Whereas in 2:6 Paul apparently situates σοφίαν before λαλοῦμεν for emphasis, in 2:7 he shifts the stress to the latter term: λαλοῦμεν θεοῦ σοφίαν. The emphasis in 2:7 is thus less on what the apostles speak about (as in 2:6) as it is on the fact that they do indeed speak about it. Moreover, Paul's syntax also underscores that the σοφία about which he and others speak is not just any σοφία. It is θεοῦ σοφία.[120] The priority given to

---

118 So Weiss, *Der erste Korintherbrief*, writes, "Wenn nun λαλεῖν ἐν mehr auf die Form geht...der akkusativ[isch] Ausdruck mehr auf den Inhalt, so würde es doch zweifellos möglich sein, zu sagen: λαλεῖν ἐν μυστηρίῳ d. h. in der Form eines Geheimnisses; das geht leicht über in die Nuance: 'als ein Geheimnis'" (55). Adalbert Maier, *Commentar über den ersten Brief Pauli an die Korinther* (Freiburg im Breisgau: Friedrich Wagner, 1857), also submits that ἐν μυστηρίῳ modifies λαλοῦμεν as an "Objectsbezeichnung" and that the accusative μυστήριον is equivalent to the prepositional phrase (61).
119 The ἐν in this latter passage is textually uncertain.
120 Thus Robertson and Plummer, *First Epistle of St. Paul to the Corinthians*, write, "The θεοῦ is very emphatic, as the context demands, and nearly every uncial has the words in this order. To read σοφίαν θεοῦ (L) mars the sense" (37).

the genitive is far from incidental.¹²¹ Finally, after emphasizing that he and his coworkers indeed speak about wisdom – God's wisdom, in fact – Paul then characterizes the form in which that wisdom is proclaimed: ἐν μυστηρίῳ. As for what it means to speak "in a mystery," the most likely solution is not that Paul is referring to the manner of his and his colleagues' proclamation but rather, as elsewhere, to its content.¹²² Paul and his associates speak about the wisdom of God "in a mystery" because it is a mystery. That is, insofar as the crucified Christ epitomizes God's wisdom (1:24, 30), to speak about God's wisdom is to speak about the paradoxical wisdom of the cross.¹²³

This correlation of mystery, the wisdom of God, and the cross is further defined in 2:7b–8 with a series of three adjectival clauses, all of which have σοφία as their antecedent. First, God's σοφία is described as "having been hidden" (τὴν ἀποκεκρυμμένην). The association of hiddenness with mystery is also found in Col 1:26 (τὸ μυστήριον τὸ ἀποκεκρυμμένον) and Eph 3:9 (ἡ οἰκονομία τοῦ μυστηρίου τοῦ ἀποκεκρυμμένου), both of which likewise use the perfect passive participle and relate μυστήριον to redemption.¹²⁴ No more details are supplied regarding the nature of the hiddenness. Was it hidden in an absolute sense? Was it hidden from some but not from others? Was it hidden in some specific location and so potentially accessible or knowable?¹²⁵ Irrespective of these ques-

---

121 Cf. Bo Frid, "The Enigmatic ΑΛΛΑ in 1 Corinthians 2.9," *NTS* 31 (1985): 603–11, who suggests that "for reasons of style and thought [Paul] writes ἀλλὰ λαλοῦμεν θεοῦ σοφίαν ἐν μυστηρίῳ τὴν ἀποκεκρυμμένην, stressing that it is θεοῦ σοφίαν that he and other preachers speak. This fact would not have been so strongly emphasized as it now is, if Paul had written ἐν μυστηρίῳ λαλοῦμεν (λαλοῦμεν ἐν μυστηρίῳ) θεοῦ σοφίαν. Therefore he keeps back the adjuncts (to λαλοῦμεν and θεοῦ σοφίαν) until the main statement is made, but then he produces these adjuncts – in due order so to speak –, first ἐν μυστηρίῳ to λαλοῦμεν, and so τὴν ἀποκεκρυμμένην to θεοῦ σοφίαν" (605).
122 Thus the ἐν is functioning, as it often does, just like a "dative proper" and so is signaling "the more remotely concerned" object. See BDF §187, 220, which glosses ἐν μυστηρίῳ as "in the form of a mystery."
123 Interestingly, the Glossa Ordinaria (Migne edition; PL 114) also appears to take the ablative phrase *in mysterio* with the main verb *loquimur*, but it interprets the expression as indicating Paul's exposition of Old Testament prefigurations of Christ's death: *In mysterio:exponendo mysteria Veteris Testamenti in quibus Christus significatus est, ut in hostia Abel, vel Abrahae.*
124 Cf. also Rom 16:25 (κατὰ ἀποκάλυψιν μυστηρίου...σεσιγημένου). Also relevant is Wis 6:22 (ἀπαγγελῶ καὶ οὐκ ἀποκρύψω ὑμῖν μυστήρια). The verb ἀποκρύπτω only otherwise appears in the New Testament in Luke 10:21.
125 For a discussion of these possibilities and presentation of ancient parallels, see Michael Wolter, "Verborgene Weisheit und Heil für die Heiden: Zur Traditionsgeschichte und Intention des 'Revelationsschema'," *ZTK* 84 (1987): 297–319. Wolter discusses three possibilities, preferring the third: (1) "Die Weisheit ist allen Menschen verborgen, und nur Gott kennt sie";

tions, the perfect aspect of the verb accents the prior hiddenness of God's wisdom in contrast to its current disclosure by Paul.¹²⁶ The proposition that it "has been hidden" indicates that it is not entirely *ex nihilo*; rather it had a pre-existence prior to its revelation, and in the final clause of 2:7 Paul spells this out: ἣν προώρισεν ὁ θεὸς πρὸ τῶν αἰώνων εἰς δόξαν ἡμῶν.¹²⁷ God foreordained this divine σοφία before creation itself, intending it for the glory of Christians. That the wisdom of God is described as something predetermined indicates that Paul is not referring to a general attribute of God but instead to some specific plan that was intended for the benefit of humanity. In 1:30 Paul describes Christ as having "become wisdom for us from God" (ὃς ἐγενήθη σοφία ἡμῖν ἀπὸ θεου), and then he defines this wisdom as entailing all the benefits of salvation: "righteousness and also sanctification and redemption" (δικαιοσύνη τε καὶ ἁγιασμὸς καὶ ἀπολύτρωσις). Similarly in 1:24 the crucified Christ is designated as "God's power and God's wisdom" (θεοῦ δύναμιν καὶ θεοῦ σοφίαν)¹²⁸ for those who are called.¹²⁹ The full and powerful economy of Christ's saving work on behalf of humanity is again to be applied here in 2:7.¹³⁰ Therefore, the σοφία that is proclaimed in a mystery and was predestined before the ages by God is, as in 1:18–2:5, none other than the crucified Christ.¹³¹ Whatever preconceived appraisals of σοφία existed in Corinth, Paul is here once again continuing his christological transvaluation of those values.

In 2:8a Paul offers a final qualifying clause for the σοφία of 2:7: ἣν οὐδεὶς τῶν ἀρχόντων τοῦ αἰῶνος τούτου ἔγνωκεν. Here Paul specifically applies the hiddenness of God's wisdom to the rulers of the current age, whom he has al-

---

(2) "Die Weisheit ist außerhalb Israels verborgen und nur dem erwählten Gottesvolk zugänglich gemacht worden, und zwar im Gesetz"; and (3) "Aufgrund ihres transzendenten Charakters bildet die Weisheit für den natürlichen Menschen ein prinzipiell verschlossenes Geheimnis. Sie ist pneumatisch vermitteltes himmlisches Offenbarungsgeschenk, das Gott auserwählten Einzelpersonen gnadenhaft zueignet" (300–3).

126 The chronological orientation of the hidden/revealed binary is made explicit in 2:9.

127 The verb προορίζω is rare, occurring only four other times in the Pauline corpus (Rom 8:29, 30; Eph 1:5, 11), once in Acts (4:28), and never in the rest of the New Testament or the LXX.

128 The priority given to the genitive in these phrases is again significant.

129 When considered in light of these parallels in 1:24 and 1:30, it is perhaps best to translate θεοῦ σοφία as "wisdom from God," thus reading the genitive as expressing source as opposed to possession.

130 Cf. Conzelmann, *1 Corinthians*, who notes that "σοφία is not merely a formal statement of the fact of God's being wise, but that Paul is already thinking of the content, God's plan of salvation" (62 n. 56).

131 For a clear and concise case for this reading of σοφία and an evaluation of alternative construals, see esp. William Baird, "Among the Mature: The Idea of Wisdom in I Corinthians 2:6," *Int* 13 (1959): 425–32.

ready described as passing away (2:6). In 2:8b he explains why the rulers remained blind to God's salvific designs: εἰ γὰρ ἔγνωσαν, οὐκ ἂν τὸν κύριον τῆς δόξης ἐσταύρωσαν. The identity of the "rulers of this age" is a matter of great dispute, but since they are directly implicated in Christ's death, we can at least conclude that some sort of earthy power is in view, even if supernatural ἄρχοντες were involved or ultimately responsible.[132] With respect to the cross, the rationale for rulers' incomprehension in 2:8 is intriguing. Paul's point seems to be that had the rulers of this age understood God's wisdom in the cross, they would not have allowed it to occur, much less directly facilitated it. And so by unsuspectingly enabling Christ's crucifixion they were acting contrary to their own interests.

In 2:9 Paul introduces a scriptural citation in order to reinforce each of the three preceding adjectival clauses and thus further elucidate the mystery that is God's wisdom:

ἃ ὀφθαλμὸς οὐκ εἶδεν
   καὶ οὖς οὐκ ἤκουσεν
   καὶ ἐπὶ καρδίαν ἀνθρώπου οὐκ ἀνέβη,
ἃ ἡτοίμασεν ὁ θεὸς τοῖς ἀγαπῶσιν αὐτόν.

What things an eye did not see
and an ear did not hear
and a human heart did not entertain,
what things God prepared for those who love him.

The first three lines confirm the previous hiddenness of the mystery of God's wisdom (cf. 2:7b), providing prophetic corroboration for the rulers' ignorance (cf. 2:8a), and the final line supports the idea that God's salvific plans had been predetermined (cf. 2:7b). While the source of this quotation is uncertain[133] and its precise grammatical role unclear,[134] the purpose and function of the ap-

---

[132] For a helpful summary of approaches to this question, see Thiselton, *The First Epistle*, 233–39.
[133] Lindemann, *Der Erste Korintherbrief*, 66–67, succinctly summarizes the options. Origen (*Comm. Matt.* 27.9) attributes the quotation to a lost *Apocalypse of Elijah*. The words are also quite similar to those of Jesus in *Gos. Thom.* 17. The most similar antecedent analogues are Isa 64:3 (LXX) and 52:15 (LXX), but these are far from exact. While it is possible that Paul has freely formulated the expression – perhaps creatively recombining scriptural language – its grammatical awkwardness within the sentence suggests an actual *Vorlage* or at least an attempt at recitation.
[134] The grammatical irregularities in this verse are well known. See esp. the description of Frid, "The Enigmatic ΑΛΛΑ," 603–5. My preference is to read the introductory ἀλλά in parallel with the ἀλλὰ λαλοῦμεν of 2:7 and, therefore, the relative ἅ as also the object of that verb (cf. ἃ καὶ

peal are plain enough: "God's way of bringing salvation to the world through the cross was hidden from all human understanding, but God had 'prepared' this plan from before the foundation of the world for those who love him."[135] Notice also that, once again, by applying "scripture," if that is how Paul regarded this citation, to the newly revealed christological mystery, scripture itself becomes newly and differently revelatory. Thus what scripture once concealed it now proclaims, and differently.[136]

Two additional questions now arise. First, if this mystery has been hidden and, more than that, if it previously transcended human comprehension, then how does it become knowable? And, second, if it has been necessary to conceal this mystery from the rulers of this age, then to whom is it made known? As 2:10 explains, the process of revelation involves, first, God, who is the source of revelation (ἀπεκάλυψεν), and, second, the Holy Spirit, who is the designated agent by which the revelation occurs.[137] As for who receives the revelation, it is given "to us" (ἡμῖν). The precise identity of the "us" is not here defined, and so the extent of the inclusivity remains ambiguous, but given the context the emphasis must be on the apostolic convoy (or the implied subjects of the plural λαλοῦμεν).

In 2:10b–16 Paul proceeds to explain, in syllogistic fashion, just how it is that "we" have come to know these revealed gifts of God through the agency of the Spirit. Following the plural ἅ in 2:9, he no longer speaks about a singular wisdom but instead about "the things being given to us by God" (τὰ ὑπὸ τοῦ θεοῦ χαρισθέντα ἡμῖν), "spiritual things" (πνευματικά), and "the things of the Spirit of God" (τὰ τοῦ πνεύματος τοῦ θεοῦ). He does, however, in 2:13 again contrast speaking "in the instructed words of human wisdom" (ἐν διδακτοῖς ἀνθρωπίνης σοφίας λόγοις) with speaking "in the instruction of the Spirit" (ἐν διδακτοῖς πνεύματος). He also further defines the latter as "interpreting spiritual

---

λαλοῦμεν in 2:13). As Lindemann, *Der Erste Korintherbrief*, contends, "ἀλλά markiert nicht den Gegensatz zu V. 8, sondern steht parallel zu ἀλλὰ λαλοῦμεν in V. 7" (65). Taken this way, the verse, while awkward, is not necessarily anacoluthic. Instead, as Robertson and Plummer, *First Epistle of St. Paul to the Corinthians*, read it, "The relative is co-ordinate with ἥν in v. 8, refers to σοφία, and therefore is *indirectly* governed by λαλοῦμεν in v. 7" (40). Cf. also Garland, *1 Corinthians*, 97; Schrage, *Der erste Brief*, 255–56.

135 Hays, *First Corinthians*, 45.
136 The neuter plural antecedent is thus significant. Whatever it originally referred to, it *did not* say exactly what Paul is using it to say. Paul thus creatively bends it to apply to new Christian circumstances.
137 Cf. the relationship of the Spirit to the utterance of mysteries in 14:2. Dan (Th) 4:9 is also relevant: "O Balthasar, ruler of the enchanters! I knew the Spirit of a Holy God was in you and that no mystery was too difficult for you." See also Wis 9:13–17.

things for spiritual people" (πνευματικοῖς πνευματικὰ συγκρίνοντες),[138] and, in turn, defines "spiritual people" as those who discern spiritual things (2:14), judge all things but are judged by no one (2:15), and possess "the mind of Christ" (νοῦν Χριστοῦ) (2:16). Amid all this elevated language about πνευματικοί who enjoy exceptional cognitive abilities by virtue of the Spirit of God and the mind of Christ, it is important to remember the fundamental message being revealed – that of an executed messiah. Therefore, far from indulging in elaborate esoterica, the spiritual person is being envisaged as a person privy to God's wisdom as revealed in Christ's saving death. Moreover, the chief effect of Paul's rhetoric is to redefine categories such as mystery, wisdom, spirit, and status in terms of divine revelation and the cross. It thus cunningly subverts aspirations of worldly prestige or human accomplishment and so, just as in 1:18–26, in 2:6–16 Paul continues his assault on human boasting by reshaping human and theological conceptions in conformity with the now determinative λόγος τοῦ σταυροῦ.

With 3:1 Paul begins a new section of his letter, but the relationship between 3:1–5 and 2:6–16 is important for appreciating the rhetorical design of Paul's argument. Thus far Paul has largely avoided specific descriptions of the identities of the apparently advantaged τέλειοι (2:6), the ἡμεῖς (2:7, 10, 12, 13, 16), and the πνευματικοί (2:13, 15; 3:1).[139] The Corinthian readers, many perhaps presuming themselves to be among these honorific groupings, are, however, in 3:1 warned otherwise: κἀγώ, ἀδελφοί, οὐκ ἠδυνήθην λαλῆσαι ὑμῖν ὡς πνευματικοῖς ἀλλ' ὡς σαρκίνοις, ὡς νηπίοις ἐν Χριστῷ ("and I, brothers, was not able to speak to you as spiritual people but as fleshly, as babes in Christ").[140] It is important to notice that although Paul claims that he could not speak to the Corinthians as πνευμα-

---

[138] For this translation of συγκρίνω, see Gen 40:8, 16, 22; 41:12, 13, 15; Dan 5:7, 12 (Th), 16. The expression could also be translated "combining/comparing spiritual things with spiritual things," thus reading πνευματικοῖς as neuter and understanding συγκρίνω as Paul uses it in 2 Cor 10:12. The chief problem with such a translation is that the πνευματικοί seem to be contrasted with the ψυχικός ἄνθρωπος in v. 14, and so should be masculine in gender.

[139] On this term see esp. John M.G. Barclay, "Πνευματικός in the Social Dialect of Pauline Christianity," in *Pauline Churches and Diaspora Jews* (WUNT 275; Tübingen: Mohr Siebeck, 2011), 205–15.

[140] Not often considered is the question of *when* Paul was unable to speak to them as spiritual people. Given the shift from the present to the aorist in 3:1 (οὐκ ἠδυνήθην λαλῆσαι ὑμῖν) and the use of κἀγώ, which appears to reiterate the κἀγώ in 2:1, Paul is clearly referring to some previous visit or correspondence. Contrary to the usual assumption, this does not have to be his founding visit and could instead refer to an intervening visit or even a previous letter (see 5:9). For the use of λαλέω in relation to written correspondence, see Rom 7:1; 1 Cor 9:8; 2 Cor 11:17, 23.

τικοί, he does not in any way portray them as unbelievers. In fact, he does not even deny that they are in fact πνευματικοί, instead stating that he could not speak to them *as though* they were such (ὡς πνευματικοῖς). In 3:1 he refers to them additionally as ἀδελφοί and "babes in Christ," even though they still appear to be "fleshly people" (ὡς σαρκίνοις).[141] He says he had to feed them milk as opposed to solid food because they were not ready, and even now they are not ready (3:2).[142] Morna Hooker, in attempting to avoid an apparent reference to "esoteric teaching" in this passage, posits that Paul's "meat does not differ from his milk" and thus that "the Corinthians' failure to understand the wisdom spoken in a mystery is not due to the fact that Paul is withholding it from them, but is the result of their own inability to digest what he is offering them."[143] But Paul does quite clearly say that he has had to withhold solid food from them and thus that "two quite different diets"[144] are indeed in view. More probable is that the milk/food contrast here is, as in Heb 5:12–14, 1 Peter 2:1–2,[145] and elsewhere,[146] not about esoteric teaching versus public teaching but instead is about rudimentary ethical exhortation (or censure) as opposed to mature theological instruction. Hence Paul is bemoaning the fact that, as at points in the past, so now he has to contend with the Corinthians on basic issues of conduct, particularly party strife. As he reminds them in 3:3–4, the principal issue encumbering their progress, and so the chief cause of their infancy, is the factional discord that persists among them (see 1:10–17).[147] In lamenting that the

---

141 The use of σάρκινος instead of ψυχικός (2:14) is perhaps significant. The ψυχικός ἄνθρωπος appears to be a non-Christian, or someone who rejects the Spirit, finding the things of the Spirit foolish (cf. the use of ψυχικός in Jas 3:15; Jude 1:19). The σάρκινος person, by contrast, here seems to represent a Christian, but one who is still being controlled by the desires of the flesh. Thus Lindemann, *Der Erste Korintherbrief*, contends that "σάρκινος meint anders als ψυχικός nicht *Feindschaft* gegenüber dem Geist (vgl. 2,14), sondern entspricht νήπιος ἐν Χριστῷ (vgl. Röm 7,14, wo die starker negative Wertung aus dem Hinweis auf die ἁμαρτία hervorgeht)" (77).
142 He has also already unequivocally described them as Christians 1:1–9.
143 M.D. Hooker, "Hard Sayings: 1 Corinthians 3:2," *Theology* 69 (1966): 19–22, 20–21.
144 Hooker, "Hard Sayings: 1 Corinthians 3:2," 21.
145 Admittedly, while there is not a milk/food contrast in this passage, "the rational, pure milk" (2:2) that Peter exhorts his readers to seek is still related to their need to put an end to interpersonal ethical transgressions (2:1). This passage is thus quite relevant to the problem of communal discord in 3:1–5.
146 The milk/food trope is also applied in an ethical manner in Philo, *Agr.* 9. The metaphor is similarly related to correct behavior in Epictetus, *Diatr.* 2.16.39–41.
147 The definitive study on this subject is Margaret M. Mitchell, *Paul and the Rhetoric of Reconciliation: An Exegetical Investigation of the Language and Composition of 1 Corinthians* (HUT; Tübingen: J.C.B Mohr [Paul Siebeck], 1992). Mitchell does not discuss at any length the rhetorical relationship of 3:1–5 and 1:18–2:16.

Corinthians cannot be addressed as πνευματικοί, Paul is lamenting that their spiritual lives are not reflecting their professed spiritual beliefs. Therefore, as in Gal 6:1, the designation πνευματικοί does not delimit who is Christian and who is not. It rather identifies the ethically consistent Christians in contrast to Christian transgressors—or, in the case of the Corinthian community, discordant partisans.[148] And so, in accord with his advice in Gal 6:1, Paul assumes the responsibility of the πνευματικός by attempting to rehabilitate Corinthian transgressors "in a spirit of gentleness."[149]

When 2:6–16 is reconsidered in light of 3:1–4, Paul's rhetoric in these two sections appears all the more biting. He is not just questioning the Corinthians' conduct. He is also questioning whether or not they have truly understood the wisdom of God as manifested in the mystery of the crucified Christ. By juxtaposing and integrating his discourse on the facts of divine revelation and conditions of Christian epistemology (2:6–16) with his indictment of the persisting strife and factionalism in Corinth (3:4), Paul is thereby demonstrating the inextricable union of Christian knowledge and Christian behavior.[150] For Paul, a deficiency in

---

[148] Cf. also 1 Cor 14:37, where πνευματικός appears to be a distinct category of Christians.
[149] For a similar reading, cf. Sigurd Grindheim, "Wisdom for the Perfect: Paul's Challenge to the Corinthian Church (1 Corinthians 2:6–16)," *JBL* 121 (2002): 689–709, esp. 707–9. As Grindheim notices, "There seems to be an intentional ambiguity on Paul's part. Paul is challenging the Corinthians to define themselves in relation to his gospel.... To be spiritual is thus at the same time a status bestowed upon every Christian and a goal for which every Christian must strive" (708).
[150] While I agree with Gerd Theissen, *Psychological Aspects of Pauline Theology* (trans. John Galvin; Philadelphia: Fortress, 1987 [1983]), that "[i]n the preaching of the cross [1:18–31] and in the wisdom teaching [2:6–16] the same symbol stands materially at the center – the cross"..., and that "2:6ff. is clearly a further development of the preaching of the cross," I believe Theissen is incorrect in limiting the wisdom discourse in 2:6–16 to "a higher stage of consciousness" in which "the perfect penetrate what happens to them and in them" and so "perfect wisdom consists in making conscious a previously unconscious content" (352). What I believe Theissen has failed to emphasize is the unannounced ethical dimension of 2:6–16, which comes to the fore when it is related to Paul's subsequent censure of the Corinthians in 3:1–4. Paul's point is indeed that "the perfect penetrate what happens to them and in them," but much more than just "a higher stage of consciousness," Paul insists that spiritual knowledge of God's wisdom as displayed in the mystery of the cross necessarily shows forth in spiritual behavior. For an excellent analysis of the subtle but sophisticated ways in which Paul has rhetorically integrated his theological statements with ethical indictments and exhortations throughout 1 Cor 1–4, see Peter Lampe, "Theological Wisdom and the 'Word About the Cross': The Rhetorical Scheme in 1 Corinthians 1–4," *Int* 44 (1990): 117–31. Applying a rhetorical principle from Quintilian, Lampe characterizes Paul's arguments in 1:18–2:16 as a "Trojan horse" (128) and as staging a "suspicion-causing 'silence'" (131) with respect to the issue of Corinthian factionalism. As Lampe concludes, "In 1:18–2:16 Paul nowhere refers to the party

one implies a deficiency in the other. To comprehend the mystery of the crucified Christ is not a matter of the intellect alone; to know the divine wisdom that has been manifested in the cross is to live according to it as well, as correct Christian knowledge occasions a new way of life.

2.3 Conclusion

In conclusion, it is important to highlight one distinctive aspect of the revelation schema in 1 Cor 2:6–16 that will become even more apparent in what follows. As we shall see in the analysis of μυστήριον in Ephesians, Colossians, the Pastoral Epistles, and the doxology of Rom 16:25–27, the hidden/revealed mystery schema is repeatedly arranged in an explicitly chronological manner, accenting the division of history into a *previous* era of hiddenness and the *present* era of revelation. In 1 Cor 2:6–16, however, the accent is less on a division in history and more on the ongoing interpersonal division among those who do and those who do not comprehend the mystery of God's wisdom as revealed in the cross. This is not to deny that there is a chronological dimension in 2:6–16, which is clearly expressed in 2:9. It is simply to point out that whereas in the deuteropauline texts the hidden/revealed binary is consistently organized, as Michael Wolter puts it, "als zeitliches *Nacheinander*," in 1 Cor 2:6–16 there is a strong accent on hiddenness and revelation "als zeitgleiches *Nebeneinander*."[151] Hence the mystery of God's wisdom in 1 Cor 2 is described as remaining concealed from "the rulers of *this* age" (2:8), as incomprehensible to the ψυχικὸς ἄνθρωπος (2:14), and as withheld from the σάρκινοι (3:1), but as specially revealed to the apostles (2:6–7, 10), who then make it known to the τέλειοι (2:6) and πνευματικοί (2:15).[152] As Gerd Theissen observes:

---

strife *directly*. Nevertheless, I have asserted that this whole section not only produces general theological statements but, on a second level, also targets in covert form the specific problem of party disorder" (128). Peter Stuhlmacher, "The Hermeneutical Significance of 1 Cor 2:6–16," in *Tradition and Interpretation in the New Testament: Essays in Honor of E. Earl Ellis* (ed. Gerald F. Hawthorne and Otto Betz; Grand Rapids: Eerdmans, 1987), 328–47, also correctly notes that "Paul returns to speak about divisive factions in 3:1–4. Thus from the standpoint of the structure of the text, 1:18–2:16 is inserted into the apostle's admonition about party divisions at Corinth, and therefore is to be understood as part of this exhortation" (333).

151 Michael Wolter, "Verborgene Weisheit," 298.

152 And these latter two groups are represented as possessing the Spirit (2:10–12) and having "the mind of Christ" (2:16).

> What is striking...is that nowhere except in 1 Corinthians 2 is the passing on of revelation restricted to a particular circle of Christians; on the contrary, passing on of revelation is identical with the mission of preaching. It is directed to 'every man' (Col. 1:28), encompasses Jews and Gentiles (Eph. 3:2–8; Rom. 16:26) and is public preaching, as the terms *kerygma* (Rom. 16:25) and *kerux* (2 Tim. 1:11) show. Paul, on the contrary, [in 1 Cor 2] restricts the passing on of revelation to the circle of the perfect. The perfect human is not the goal of the preaching (Col. 1:28) but its presupposition (1 Cor. 2:6; 3:1ff).[153]

The many similarities and important contrasts that exist between 1 Cor 2:6–16 and the mystery schema in the deuteropauline letters will become even clearer as we now turn our attention to those texts.

---

[153] Theissen, *Psychological Aspects*, 346–47.

3 Μυστήριον and the Deuteropauline Mystery Schema of Revelation.
Part 1: Ephesians and Colossians

3.1 Introduction

The objectives in this chapter and the next are twofold. The first is to continue to map the use of μυστήριον in the Pauline corpus, now in the so-called deuteropauline letters. Many basic features of μυστήριον remain consistent in these letters. Most notable among these is that μυστήριον, now exclusively in the singular, repeatedly signals the existence of some previously hidden but newly revealed reality. Therefore, rather than naming sources of incomprehension, μυστήριον continues to identify a recent divine disclosure that, while perhaps unforeseen and extraordinary, is nonetheless plainly stated and comprehensible to the Christian to whom it has been revealed.[1] There are some critical differences that emerge as well, differences that bind these texts to each other while at the same time setting them apart from the undisputed letters. Most notable among these is the consistent and emphatic historical configuring of the hidden/revealed binary and the attendant bifurcation of time into contrasting eras of concealment and disclosure. To continue the cartographical metaphor, if the map that emerged in the previous chapter could be described as something like a random grouping of assorted locales in a city, and so the samples are scattered and diverse but share commonalities and are by and large contiguous, the picture that emerges from these disputed letters is more like a single neighborhood in that city. Hence the new instances coalesce within the previously established margins but are so densely interconnected with each other that they are

---

[1] That it is plainly stated and rationally understood does not entail that it is exhaustively comprehended or appreciated. Even Paul, after disclosing the mystery regarding the Gentiles' and Israel's ultimate salvation in Rom 11:25, remains in wonder: "O the depth of the riches and wisdom and knowledge of God! How unsearchable are his judgments and inscrutable his ways!" (11:33). As Steven D. Boyer, "The Logic of Mystery," *RelS* 43 (2007): 89–102, notes, "A revelational mystery...can be known without forfeiting its status as a mystery. It may be 'known', but it is never 'solved'.... Instead, it is known precisely *as* a mystery. Prior to its being made known, it might not have been a mystery at all: it might not have risen even to the status of an 'unanswered question', might not have been the faintest blip on my epistemological radar screen. Yet when it is revealed, it is revealed *as* a mystery: the depths have been discovered, and they are simultaneously discovered to be too deep to penetrate" (92).

clearly distinguishable from the previous samples, joining together to form a distinct pattern.

The second objective of this chapter is to trace the contours and inner workings of this new pattern, which is to say, to trace the common terms and rule-governed variation that define this deuteropauline mystery discourse. As the key components of this pattern emerge, it will be important also to consider its rhetorical and theological effects, as well as the comprehensive reconception of history and God's eternal purposes that it entails. This new historical conception will prove critical for the investigation of μυστήριον in subsequent chapters and for appreciating many early Christian approaches to divine revelation.

3.2 Colossians

In deference to the critical consensus that Colossians was composed prior to Ephesians and perhaps even served as its literary model, I treat Colossians first, even though for current purposes I am uncommitted to Colossian's priority.[2] While agreements and disagreements with Ephesians will be noted, I postpone any detailed examination of the significance of the variances with Ephesians until we examine that letter.

3.2.1 Colossians 1:24 – 2:5

The word μυστήριον occurs three times in Col 1:24 – 2:5 and is integral to the principal statements of this portion of the letter. Structurally these verses can be grouped into two adjacent sections: 1:24 – 29 and 2:1 – 5. The first section begins in v. 24 with Paul's expression of joy in suffering on behalf of the church, a statement further supplemented by a series of relative clauses in vv. 25 – 29. In the second section Paul again refers to his apostolic ἀγών, but now by relating his missionary travails to the wellbeing and ongoing fidelity of the church.[3] Since the

---

[2] For more on the potential literary dependency of Colossians on the other Pauline letters see esp. Outi Leppä, *The Making of Colossians: A Study on the Formation and Purpose of a Deutero-Pauline Letter* (Publications of the Finnish Exegetical Society 86; Göttingen: Vandenhoeck & Ruprecht, 2003).

[3] For more detailed and specific proposals regarding the structural organization of these two sections, see Jean-Noël Aletti, *Saint Paul: Épitre aux Colossiens* (EBib 20; Paris: Gabalda, 1993), 130 – 31; John Paul Heil, *Colossians: Encouragement to Walk in All Wisdom as Holy Ones in Christ* (SBLECL 4; Atlanta: Society of Biblical Literature, 2010), 21 – 23, 83. The extend-

various assertions in this passage unfold in tightly connected clauses that mutually inform one another, a detailed analysis of the whole is needed.

Verse 24, which introduces the first section, has become one of the most controversial statements in the entire Pauline corpus:[4]

> νῦν χαίρω ἐν τοῖς παθήμασιν
> ὑπὲρ ὑμῶν
> καὶ ἀνταναπληρῶ τὰ ὑστερήματα τῶν θλίψεων τοῦ Χριστοῦ
> ἐν τῇ σαρκί μου
> ὑπὲρ τοῦ σώματος αὐτοῦ,
> ὅ ἐστιν ἡ ἐκκλησία.
>
> Now I rejoice in the sufferings on behalf of you and complete what is lacking from the afflictions of Christ in my flesh on behalf of his body, which is the church.

Read in isolation, Paul's claim that his own sufferings compensate for some deficiency in the afflictions of Christ could be taken as contradicting other clear statements in Colossians (and the rest of the Pauline corpus as well) regarding the exclusive sufficiency of Christ's passion and death (see esp. Col 1:13–22; 2:13–14).[5] Rightly suspicious of such a reading, modern scholars frequently import ideas foreign to Colossians or even the other Pauline letters in order to avoid it – such as a treasury of merit earned by saints and martyrs,[6] or an established

---

ed chiasm outlined by Heil is convincing, but it does not contribute significantly to the interpretation of these verses. Heil's organization does, however, exhibit the frequent resumption of language and themes through 1:24–2:5 and the importance of treating the passage as a whole.
4 On the reception history of this verse, see the excellent study by Jacob Kremer, *Was an den Leiden Christi noch mangelt: Eine interpretationsgeschichtliche und exegetische Untersuchung zu Kol. 1,24b* (BBB 12; Bonn: Peter Hanstein, 1956).
5 The confidence of Philipp Vielhauer, *Geschichte der urchristlichen Literatur: Einleitung in das Neue Testament, die Apokryphen und die Apostolischen Väter* (Berlin/New York: de Gruyter, 1975), on this matter is characteristic of many scholars, particularly those who question the integrity of Colossians: "Dieser Gedanke, die 'Trübsale Christi' – und dh nichts anderes als seine Heilstat – seien unvollständig und müssten durch den Apostel komplettiert werden, der Gedanke vom Apostel als dem Christus prolongatus, widerspricht der Kreuzestheologie des Paulus und kann nicht von ihm stammen" (199).
6 This proposition, though frequently voiced, is rarely seriously considered in recent scholarship. For the predictable but now rarely valid Protestant critique of this position, see John Calvin's commentary on this verse. For the debate on this issue among an earlier generation of Protestant and Catholic scholars, see the discussions in J.B. Lightfoot, *Saint Paul's Epistles to the Colossians and to Philemon* (London/New York: Macmillan, 1904), 164–65; T.K. Abbott, *The Epistles to the Ephesians and the Colossians* (ICC; Edinburgh: T&T Clark, 1897), 230–31.

ledger of messianic tribulations,[7] or a mystical union with Christ.[8] A simpler and more contextually sensitive solution (and one that has the support of the earliest ancient interpreters)[9] is to approach the relation of Christ's afflictions and Paul's vicarious sufferings in terms of Paul's apostolic self-understanding and missionary task. Read in this way the shortage in question is not related to the atoning work of Christ but rather to the apostolic imperative to extend to all humanity the riches accrued by Christ (1:27). The afflictions (θλίψες) then are not those of Christ *per se*, but rather, as the word order indicates, they are "the afflictions of Christ in my (that is, Paul's) flesh." The θλίψες then are the Christ-like sufferings (παθήματα) that Paul is destined to endure.[10] Paul's sufferings on behalf of the Colossians in 1:24a and "the afflictions of Christ in my flesh" on behalf of the church in 1:24b should therefore be equated.[11] The phrase τὰ ὑστερήματα τῶν θλίψεων τοῦ Χριστοῦ ἐν τῇ σαρκί μου thus refers to the fact that the redemptive accomplishment of Christ's afflictions is yet to be announced to "every human"

---

[7] This hypothesis, which nowhere else emerges in Paul's letters, is especially prominent in recent scholarship. Jerry L. Sumney, "'I Fill Up What Is Lacking in the Afflictions of Christ'," *CBQ* 68 (2006): 664–80, provides an inventory of the scholars who uphold this position (665 n. 5). See also his critique of it (668), as well as the criticism of Markus Barth and Helmut Blanke, *Colossians: A New Translation with Introduction and Commentary* (AB 34B; New York: Doubleday, 1994), 292–93. As Kremer, *Was an den Leiden*, 118–19, has shown, this view is relatively new, being first proposed by Johann Albrecth Bengel.

[8] The most influential statement of this view is Adolf Deissmann, *Paulus: Eine kultur- und religionsgeschichtliche Skizze* (Tübingen: Mohr Siebeck, 1911). Among other problems with it is the fact that, as Dunn, *Colossians*, points out, the "'mystical union with Christ'...leaves unexplained the 'lack in Christ's afflictions'" (115).

[9] See Kremer, *Was an den Leiden*, 5–56. Also helpful is John Reumann, "Colossians 1:24 ('What is Lacking in the Afflictions of Christ'): History of Exegesis and Ecumenical Advance," *CurTM* 17 (1990): 454–61. Other early advocates of this type of reading include Chrysostom, Theodoret, Severian, Augustine, and Ambrosiaster.

[10] Scholars frequently note that θλῖψις is nowhere else applied to Christ and is instead usually associated with Christians. As Andrew Perriman, "The Pattern of Christ's Sufferings: Colossians 1:24 and Philippians 3:10–11," *TynBul* 42 (1991): 62–79, points out, "this need only reflect the fact that the sufferings have been transferred from Christ to Paul" (67 n. 15). He points to 1 Thess 1:6 as similarly associating θλῖψις with Christ and extending that association to the experience of Christians.

[11] The full phrase τῶν θλίψεων τοῦ Χριστοῦ ἐν τῇ σαρκί μου, particularly the syntactical positioning of ἐν τῇ σαρκί μου, is critical for this understanding and often ignored by interpreters. As Aletti, *Épitre aux Colossiens*, recommends, "Il faut en effet scrupuleusement respecter l'ordre des lexèmes, et lire ensemble la séquence 'ce qui manqué aux tribulations du Christ en ma chair'" (135).

(1:28). To "complete" or "distribute"[12] what is lacking is to dispense to the world "the wealth of glory" and "the treasures of wisdom and knowledge" that have been credited to humanity in Christ (1:27; 2:2–3).[13] The deficit in these afflictions remains only because there is missionary work still to accomplish.[14] As for what such a proposition means in soteriological terms, Pokorný states the matter eloquently:

> Der Apostel kämpft und leidet, damit die Menschen "erkennen", dass ihr Heil in Jesus Christus schon vollendet ist, damit sie im Glauben an der schon vollendeten Versöhnung teilnehmen können.... Der abwesende Apostel kämpft und leidet für die Adressaten, damit sie erkennen, dass sie im Glauben schon die Auferstehung und das neue Leben haben.... Das, was noch "aussteht", ist die menschliche Aufnahme des schon vollendeten Heils.[15]

Theodore of Mopsuestia (ca. 350–428), who is among the earliest extant commentators on this verse, states roughly the same:

> What was it that was lacking (προσλεῖπον)? For you, by learning what things were achieved (κατορθωθέντα) for you by him, to receive the promise concerning them. It would not be possible in any way for this to come about without toils and afflictions. So for these things

---

12 Barth and Blanke, *Colossians*, translate ἀνταναπληρόω as "repay." Although I would endorse a translation that highlights the fiscal sense of this word, I do not think "repayment" is the correct idea. Rather than *re*-paying something, in filling up Christ's afflictions in his own apostolic ministry Paul is instead announcing the new credit that has been vouchsafed by Christ. He is, in other words, distributing a gift rather than returning something owed.
13 As Paul routinely points out in his letters, the work of bringing the gospel to all the nations necessarily entails participation in Christ-like suffering (see, i.a., 2 Cor 4:7–12). Thus Eduard Schweizer, *The Letter to the Colossians: A Commentary* (trans. Andrew Chester; Minneapolis: Augsburg Publishing House, 1982 [1976]), while noting that this interpretation is supported by the majority of ancient commentators, writes, "On the one hand there is the suffering of Jesus, which brings about reconciliation, that is, the cosmic event of the death of Jesus. On the other hand there is the suffering which is still lacking, that is, suffering which is connected with the proclamation, or in particular with the Gentile mission and the further growth of the community" (101–2).
14 So also R. McL. Wilson, *A Critical and Exegetical Commentary on Colossians and Philemon* (ICC; London/New York: T&T Clark, 2005), writes, "The reference then is to Paul's personal contribution (ἐν τῇ σαρκί μου), made for the sake of Christ's body, which is the church.... What is lacking, still to be completed, is then not the atoning sacrifice of Christ but Paul's own share in the sufferings that must be faced in the present age, before the dawn of the new era" (171).
15 Petr Pokorný, *Der Brief des Paulus an die Kolosser* (THKNT 10/1; Berlin: Evangelische Verlagsanstalt, 1987), 83.

Paul suffers, going about preaching to all what has been accomplished (τὰ κατορθωθέντα).[16]

In presenting this reading of 1:24 I have tried to use the language of economy and finance since Paul also, throughout 1:24–2:5, associates the mystery that is being presented to humanity with fiscal imagery: "the economy of God" (1:25), "the riches of the glory" (1:27), "all the riches of the assurance of understanding" (2:2), and "the treasures of wisdom and knowledge" (2:3).[17] Such imagery continues in v. 25 as Paul begins to articulate his apostolic self-understanding by discussing his appointment as "a manager according to the economy of God" (διάκονος[18] κατὰ τὴν οἰκονομίαν τοῦ θεοῦ).[19] He states that this responsibility was given to him for the sake of his readers and in order "to fulfill the word of God."

As was discussed in the previous chapter, John Goodrich has demonstrated that whatever the particular form of employment (and there could be many), the usual duties of οἰκονόμοι – and so the οἰκονομία entrusted to them – "primarily and consistently included the administration of public finances, particularly the payment of community expenses."[20] Paul's use of οἰκονομία is then probably always in some sense "economical," even if metaphorically so. In addition to Goodrich, Giorgio Agamben has also shown that although with Paul "the term *oikonomia* is transposed into a theological field," we should not "assume a theo-

---

[16] This slightly modified translation is from *Theodore of Mopsuestia: The Commentaries on the Minor Epistles of Paul* (trans. Rowan A. Greer; SBLWGRW 26; Atlanta: Society of Biblical Literature, 2010), 396–97.
[17] Integrating 1:24 with the whole of 1:25–2:5 is, I submit, crucial and yet all too often overlooked by interpreters. Thus Reumann, "Colossians 1:24," remarks, "It is surprising, in the long history of interpretation, how rarely 1:24 has been treated in conjunction with 1:29–2:1 and the *agōn* motif…. Paul's ministry (1:23, 25) in God's *oikonomia*…includes the apostle's struggles (1:29, 2:1) 'for you' (in Colossae and those in Laodicea and others, 1:24, 2:1)" 461.
[18] Cf. Col 1:23. On this term see esp. John N. Collins, "A Monocultural Usage: διακον- words in Classical, Hellenistic, and Patristic Sources," *VC* 66 (2012): 287–309; *Diakonia: Re-interpreting the Ancient Sources* (New York: Oxford University Press, 1990). Correcting longstanding assumptions, Collins shows that διακον- terminology among Christian writers is, as elsewhere, "formal language" that has "no basic meaning" such as "service at a table." Moreover, it does not necessarily indicate low status, although it does imply "the carrying out of a commission from a person or institution – with whatever level of authority or power this requires" ("A Monocultural Usage," 295–96). A διάκονος from God presumably obtains a degree of authority.
[19] I take the κατά as indicating reference or respect. Cf. the parallel expression in Eph 3:7.
[20] John K. Goodrich, *Paul as an Administrator of God in 1 Corinthians* (SNTSMS 152; Cambridge: Cambridge University Press, 2012), 69–70.

logical sense that is not necessitated by the text."²¹ Agamben contends that even in the case of Paul the denotation of the term still remains within the sphere of finances.²² He recommends translating οἰκονομία in Col 1:25 as "fiduciary duty,"²³ rightly insisting that any attempt to read something like a "divine plan of salvation" into Paul's use of the term, as many scholars do, anachronistically presses later theological developments upon Paul's usage.

Additional information about the οἰκονομία that has been assigned to Paul is provided in the next verse, which also contains the first occurrence of μυστήριον in the letter:

…τὸ μυστήριον
   τὸ ἀποκεκρυμμένον
      ἀπὸ τῶν αἰώνων καὶ ἀπὸ τῶν γενεῶν
   νῦν δὲ
   ἐφανερώθη τοῖς ἁγίοις αὐτοῦ…

…the mystery which has been hidden from the ages and from the generations but now is disclosed to his saints…

With this appositional clause Paul identifies "the word of God" as a previously hidden but recently manifested mystery. Since τὸν λόγον τοῦ θεοῦ is the principal responsibility of Paul's οἰκονομία, the μυστήριον is therefore also to be viewed as fundamental to the οἰκονομία allocated to Paul and so likewise a matter of "economy" (cf. 1 Cor 4:1). As in 1 Cor 2:7, ἀποκρύπτω appears in the form of

---

21 Giorgio Agamben, *The Kingdom and the Glory: For a Theological Genealogy of Economy and Government* (trans. Lorenzo Chiesa with Matteo Mandarini; Stanford: Stanford University Press, 2011), 20; see also 21–25.

22 Agamben, *The Kingdom and the Glory*, 22. In his use of the terms "sense" and "denotation," Agamben is presumably following Gottlob Frege's logical (and then linguistic) distinction between *Sinn* and *Bedeutung*. According to Frege, we should differentiate what a sign refers to (for example, the number 7) and how it refers to it (3 + 4 or 8 – 1). Frege labels the latter *Sinn* and the former *Bedeutung*. The key point is that different *Sinne* can refer to a single *Bedeutung* and so signs such as = or "is" may be preceded by different terms and still refer to identical *Bedeutungen*. In the case of οἰκονομία, Agamben is interested in tracing the "gradual analogical extension of its denotation (*Bedeutung*)" (20). He contends that "[i]n truth, there is no theological 'sense' of the term [οἰκονομία], but first of all a displacement of its denotation onto the theological field, which is progressively misunderstood and perceived as a new meaning" (21). In the case of Paul, Agamben argues that the *Sinn* and *Bedeutung* of οἰκονομία still reside within the context of economy, particularly fiduciary responsibility. In contemporary linguistics, it should be noted, the terms *Sinn* and *Bedeutung* are usually translated into English as "sense" and "reference."

23 Agamben, *The Kingdom and the Glory*, 22.

a perfect passive participle. In 1 Cor 2, however, the form is feminine because what "has been hidden" (ἀποκεκρυμμένην) is "the wisdom of God" (θεοῦ σοφίαν) being spoken "in a mystery." In Col 1:26 it is the mystery itself that is being described as previously hidden. Also like 1 Cor 2:7–8, this mystery is characterized as having been concealed from some αἰών. But there is a key difference. In 1 Cor 2:8 the concealment is applied to personal agents, whether human, or personified, or both: "the rulers of this age" (ἄρχοντες τοῦ αἰῶνος τούτου). In Col 1:26 concealment "from the ages" is not personal but rather temporal.[24] Thus in Col 1:26 it is not an entity associated with the current age but the ages themselves and the humans who lived in them (γενεαί) that have been prevented from knowing the mystery.[25] This is not to deny that there is a temporal dimension in 1 Cor 2:6–16; temporality is always in question when revelation is under discussion. It is simply to point out that whereas the accent in 1 Cor 2:6–8 is on the interpersonal arrangement of the hidden/revealed binary ("from the rulers of this age"), in Colossians 1:24–26 the stress is explicitly on the chronological dynamic ("from the ages and generations"). The emphasis on temporality continues with the description of the revelation: "but *now* it is disclosed to God's saints" (νῦν δὲ ἐφανερώθη τοῖς ἁγίοις αὐτοῦ).[26] This use of the eschatological νῦν (as it is sometimes called)[27] in an emphatic first position to describe the present timing of the revelation, along with the use of φανερόω to characterize it and the correlation of the revelation with the saints, are common features in many of the deuteropauline mystery schema passages, as well as in other more general statements of revelation (such as 2 Tim 1:9–10 and Titus 1:2–3).[28]

In the following verse Paul uses another relative clause to clarify God's reasons for making known the previously hidden mystery to the saints:

---

[24] Though strictly speaking indefinite, I take this expression as indicating that the mystery has been hidden by God from creation since the time of creation and, thus, as eternally hidden by God. Cf. John 9:32. See also 1 Cor 2:7; Eph 1:4; 2 Tim 1:9; Titus 1:2. The αἰῶνες and γενεαί are not, therefore, to be read as heavenly powers or hypostases.

[25] That concealment from humans is in view is made clear in the parallel passage in Eph 3:5 (ὃ ἑτέραις γενεαῖς οὐκ ἐγνωρίσθη **τοῖς υἱοῖς τῶν ἀνθρώπων**).

[26] I take the ἅγιοι to refer to all believers (1:2, 4, 12, 22; 3:12). For a discussion of alternative possibilities, see Markus N.A. Bockmuehl, *Revelation and Mystery in Ancient Judaism and Pauline Christianity* (WUNT 2/36; Tübingen: Mohr Siebeck, 1990), 183–84. Even if a restricted group of Christians is in view, the hiddenness is still being arranged primarily in chronological, as opposed to interpersonal, terms.

[27] Besides the passages discussed in this chapter, see also Rom 3:21 for this use of νῦν (νυνὶ δὲ χωρὶς νόμου δικαιοσύνη θεοῦ πεφανέρωται), which similarly brings together νῦν and φανερόω.

[28] Outside of Paul, see also 1 Peter 1:10–12.

> ...οἷς ἠθέλησεν ὁ θεὸς γνωρίσαι
> τί τὸ πλοῦτος τῆς δόξης **τοῦ μυστηρίου τούτου**
> ἐν τοῖς ἔθνεσιν,
> ὅ ἐστιν Χριστὸς
> ἐν ὑμῖν,
> ἡ ἐλπὶς τῆς δόξης...[29]

...to whom God wanted to make known what is the wealth of the glory of this mystery among the Gentiles, which is Christ in you, the hope of glory...

God's long hidden mystery is here defined as "the riches of glory" for the Gentiles.[30] In other mystery passages the Gentiles are repeatedly singled out as the primary recipients of God's newly manifested μυστήριον. As for the association of μυστήριον with τὸ πλοῦτος τῆς δόξης, in Ephesians the πλοῦτος of God is related to subjects such as redemption and forgiveness (1:7), inheritance (1:18), salvation (2:5–8), the gospel (3:7–8), and spiritual strengthening (3:16). In Col 1:27, however, "the wealth of the glory of this mystery"[31] is correlated with the λόγον τοῦ θεοῦ of v. 25 and then the presence of Christ among the Gentiles in v. 27b. To best appreciate the deployment of μυστήριον here it is important to attend to the full progression in vv. 25–27, which is compactly interconnected by the repetition of relative clauses. First, Paul describes his responsibility to distribute the λόγον τοῦ θεοῦ (1:25). Second, the λόγον τοῦ θεοῦ is described as a previously hidden but now manifested μυστήριον (1:26). Third, the μυστήριον and the λόγον τοῦ θεοῦ are then further characterized as τὸ πλοῦτος τῆς δόξης (1:27). Finally, this newly disclosed wealth is defined as Χριστὸς ἐν ὑμῖν and "the hope of glory."[32] These correlations all contribute to the definition of the μυστήριον. Rather than some abstract "plan," the previously hidden mystery is instead being envisioned both as a treasury of wealth that has been credited to the Gen-

---

29 Cf. the parallel in Eph 1:18.
30 Cf. 1:11–12 where "the strength of his glory" is associated with "inheritance" (κλῆρος). Cf. also Rom 9:23, where "the riches of his glory" is similarly associated with knowledge (ἵνα γνωρίσῃ τὸν πλοῦτον τῆς δόξης αὐτοῦ).
31 As for the relationship between πλοῦτος and μυστήριον, Abbott, *Ephesians and Colossians*, is correct that "the 'mystery' is not something distinct from the riches of the glory of it; those to whom the former is revealed are made acquainted with the latter" (235).
32 There is much debate about whether the phrase ἐν ὑμῖν should be taken in a participatory sense ("Christ in you") or a spatial sense ("Christ among you"). Reading ἐν ὑμῖν in parallel with ἐν τοῖς ἔθνεσιν, the spatial sense seems more likely. Either way, I agree with Bockmuehl, *Revelation and Mystery*: "Although one rendering tends to bear out a more mystical and the other a more objective slant, the question is perhaps less important than is sometimes assumed: each of the two emphases is consistent with Paul's thought and in light of the other can be said to obtain at least by implication" (185).

tiles through Christ and also a message that Paul has been commissioned to proclaim.³³ The equations in these verses all flow out of Paul's initial self-description in 1:25a as "an administrator according to the economy of God." The language of economy and wealth thus unite the whole progression, attracting the accompanying language into that thematic register.

In 1:28 Paul offers additional details regarding his missionary praxis. He describes Christ as the subject of his preaching (καταγγέλλω), teaching (διδάσκω), and admonition (νουθετέω) and then emphasizes the universal scope of his mission.³⁴ His message about the wealth of Christ accrued for the Gentiles is intended "for every person" (πάντα ἄνθρωπον), and the objective is "to present every person (πάντα ἄνθρωπον) as τέλειον ἐν Χριστῷ." The use of τέλειος in this context is reminiscent of the τέλειοι in 1 Cor 2:6, whom Paul singled out as the exclusive recipients of the hidden wisdom being spoken ἐν μυστηρίῳ. There is, however, another important but often overlooked discrepancy between 1 Cor 2:6–7 and Col 1:26–28. Whereas *being* τέλειος is the condition for being spoken to in the 1 Corinthians passage, *becoming* τέλειος is the goal of Paul's mystery proclamation in Colossians. Furthermore, instead of restricting the discussion of σοφία to those who are already τέλειος, as in 1 Cor 2:6–7, in Col 1:26–28 all humanity is to be instructed "in all wisdom" (ἐν πάσῃ σοφίᾳ) in order that they might all be presented as τέλειος. The precondition of Paul's mystery speech in 1 Cor 2 is thus now redefined as the purpose of that speech here in Col 1. This reversal of the status of the τέλειος person with respect to Paul's preaching, as well as the place of σοφία in that preaching, is quite conspicuous and made all the more evident by the threefold repetition of πάντα ἄνθρωπον.³⁵

---

33 Notice also the chiasm in 1:27: A ὁ πλοῦτος **τῆς δόξης** B τοῦ μυστηρίου τούτου **ἐν τοῖς ἔθνεσιν** B' ὅ ἐστιν Χριστὸς **ἐν ὑμῖν** A' ἡ ἐλπὶς **τῆς δόξης**. As the middle lines indicate, Christ is also equated with the mystery. This equation becomes explicit in 2:2 and 4:3. This, incidentally, is also the pinnacle of Heil's proposed extended chiasm. There are impressive parallels between this application of μυστήριον to Christ and the very similar correlation with Enoch's Son of Man. See Raymond E. Brown, *The Semitic Background of the Term 'Mystery' in the New Testament* (Philadelphia: Fortress Press, 1968), 55–56.

34 He now uses the plural, likely indicating that this should be the practice of any apostolic envoy, such as the one that first ministered in Colossae (1:7). As Eduard Lohse, *Colossians and Philemon* (trans. W. R. Poehlmann, and R. J. Karris; Hermeneia: Philadelphia: Fortress Press, 1971), observes, the verbs διδάσκω and νουθετέω are frequently paired. See the numerous examples he cites (77 n. 72).

35 Thus Lohse, *Colossians*, states, "Three times 'every man' (πάντα ἄνθρωπον) is referred to as the recipient of the apostolic admonition in order to stress the truly ecumenical character of the apostolic message which is proclaimed in all the world" (77). He then correctly notes, "This sharply contradicts any attempt to limit the teaching of wisdom to only a small circle of initiates" (77 n. 74). Is not 1 Cor 2:6–7 seemingly such an attempt?

There is also potentially a different nuance in the use of τέλειος in Col 1:28.[36] As many interpreters have noted, a concern for something akin to cultic mystery practices (or forms of popular pagan devotion) seems pronounced in this letter.[37] There are, for instance, good reasons for supposing that the "philosophy" being combatted in Col 2 was related to some variety of mystery practice and that some Colossian Christians "continued to embrace certain aspects of mystery cult belief and practice."[38] Given these circumstances, the reference to becoming τέλειος,[39] especially when placed alongside the three occurrences of μυστήριον in Col 1:26–2:2, perhaps deliberately invokes existing forms of cultic devotion. If this is the case, then Paul's stated desire to present every person as "an initiate in Christ" (τέλειον ἐν Χριστῷ)[40] would not be about pedagogical progress toward maturity (or "perfection"), as translations and interpretations usually suppose, but rather about the intiatory rite of baptism, particularly as it is described in 2:11–13. To present all humanity as τέλειος would thus be to present all humanity as having been fully inducted by ritual washing into Christ's resurrection (2:2).[41] It is important to point out that such a reworking of mystery initiation does not relegate Christ to just another foreign deity and the Christian assembly to just another cultic community. The consistent use of the singular μυστήριον is

---

[36] Cf. Col 4:12.
[37] See esp. Clinton E. Arnold, *The Colossian Syncretism: The Interface between Christianity and Folk Belief at Colossae* (WUNT 2/77; Tübingen: Mohr Siebeck, 1995), 103–57.
[38] Arnold, *The Colossian Syncretism*, 271.
[39] Recall that this is a technical term for an initiate in the Mysteries.
[40] BDAG recommends this sense for τέλειος in 1:28.
[41] There may be further parallels with mystery practices on this matter. As Marcel Simon, "The *religionsgeschichtliche Schule*, Fifty Years Later," *RelS* 11 (1975): 135–44, has pointed out, "The Christian Baptism as well as the Lord's Supper are rooted in Jewish ritual practice…. But once all due qualifications have been made regarding the views of the *religionsgeschichtliche Schule*, there subsists an element which Judaism is unable to account for: the idea of salvation mystically achieved through the baptismal rite by appropriation of, or identification with, the fate of a Saviour who died and rose again" (143). A similar idea does perhaps appear in the mysteries of Isis. See, for instance, the account of Lucius' initiation in Apuleius, *Metam.* 11.21–24. Perhaps a comparable species of this practice persisted in Colossae or was known by the author of this letter. It should be noted that Simon's remark regarding participation in a dying and rising savior is not as likely a feature in the Mysteries as was once supposed. See esp. Jonathan Z. Smith, "Dying and Rising Gods," *ER* 4:2535–40. It is still the case, however, that Lucius' initiation is described as being "performed in the manner of a voluntary death and the attainment of salvation" (*ad instar voluntariae mortis et precariae salutis celebrari*) (*Metam.* 11.21) and as an experience in which he approached "the boundary of death" (*confinium mortis*) and "came face to face with the gods below and the gods above" (*deos inferos et deos superos accessi coram*) (11.23).

significant in this regard: it names Christ as *the* mystery, not one among many.⁴²
The assertion that Christ is the mystery *par excellence* would also provide important preparation for Paul's subsequent condemnation in Col 2 of the shadowy philosophy and human traditions that were severing the Colossian Christians from Christ. Hence Paul's appropriation of popular cultic terminology would be part and parcel of his strategy to christianize available religious vocabulary and, in so doing, to submit all of creation to Christ, "the head of every rule and authority" (2:10).

The final occurrence of μυστήριον in this section is in 2:2. Having reaffirmed his fervent labor on behalf of the church (1:29 – 2:1), Paul reiterates in 2:2 – 3 the purpose of his many struggles: so that the Colossians, the Laodiceans, and all people who have not seen his face will be encouraged and united, realizing they have "all the wealth of the certainty of understanding, for knowledge of the mystery of God, which is Christ, in whom all the treasures of wisdom and knowledge are hidden." This statement, fitting as a conclusion to the section, condenses the major themes of the preceding verses. Paul again correlates μυστήριον with knowledge (cf. 1:27) and, albeit awkwardly, with Christ.⁴³ He also again describes his apostolic mission in financial terms, restating his hope that all people will come to know the πλοῦτος and θησαυροί that have been credited to them by Christ. It is difficult to say much about the cumbersome phrase πλοῦτος τῆς πληροφορίας τῆς συνέσεως, mostly because the word πληροφορία is rare. It is at least worth pointing out that the corresponding verb πληροφορέω is commonly used in fiscal contexts, such as when a creditor seeks to recover money "in full" or a debtor seeks to pay what is owed "in full."⁴⁴ The phrase "hidden treasures of wisdom and knowledge" conjoins conventional terminology from passages such as Isa 33:6, 45:3, and other Jewish wisdom traditions.⁴⁵ Somewhat ambiguous is the place or, more likely, the person in whom these treasures are hidden because it is not initially clear to whom or what ἐν ᾧ refers.⁴⁶ Since Christ has already been identified with the riches and the

---

42 Christ's preeminence was already emphasized in 1:15 – 20.
43 For a presentation of the complex textual problems here, see esp. Lohse, *Colossians*, 81 – 82. The array of textual variation related to the apparent appositional phrase τοῦ μυστηρίου τοῦ θεοῦ, Χριστοῦ would seem to indicate that many scribes also found it inelegant.
44 See LSJ I.3; MM 4135.
45 Prov 2:3 – 6; Sir 1:24 – 25; Wis 6:22; 7:13 – 14; Bar 3:15; 2 Bar 44:14; 54:13; *1 En.* 41:1 – 7; 46.3. Cf. also Rom 11:33.
46 The relative pronoun could, of course, be neuter and thus have μυστήριον as its antecedent. But, as Bockmuehl, *Revelation and Mystery*, notes, this correlation "would effect a malapropism: our earlier results suggest that the 'treasures' can hardly be hidden in a 'mystery', since the former are instances of the latter" (188).

newly manifest mystery, and since he is the nearest antecedent, Christ is almost certainly the person in whom these epistemological treasures are hidden. But notice that although he is a person of concealment, he is also the person in whom such treasures are made manifest. As Schweizer puts it, "The main point...is that these treasures of wisdom remain 'hidden' in the very act of their being disclosed; that is, they elude all human efforts to grasp them. It is God alone who can freely bestow them.... Thus Christ remains, as it were, the subject of all our knowing."⁴⁷

Finally, in the conclusion to this section (2:4–5), Paul's descriptions of Christ as God's newly disclosed mystery and the ultimate source of knowledge and understanding are presented as motivations for the Colossians to resist deceptive arguments (2:4) and to persist in fidelity to Christ (2:5). The repeated focus on mystery and knowledge and the application of these subjects to the Colossians' behavior is then not incidental. Paul's emphasis on these themes is designed to prepare the way for his subsequent attack in 2:8–23 on the so-called Colossian heresy, a movement that promoted epistemological notions Paul judged counterfeit (hence the focus on wisdom and knowledge) and may have involved customs associated with local cults (hence the focus on mystery and the true path to becoming τέλειος).⁴⁸

3.2.2 Colossians 4:3–4

The final use of μυστήριον in this letter comes in 4:3–4 and contributes little more to the preceding analysis than a further demonstration of the importance of the term for this author:⁴⁹

---

47 Schweizer, *Colossians*, 118.
48 So Joachim Gnilka, *Der Kolosserbrief* (HTKNT 10/1; Freiburg: Herder, 1980) explains, "Ist die alttestamentliche Weisheit als der Hintergrund...zu sehen, so muss als seine Besonderheit die antihäretische Spitze wahrgenommen werden" (111). Even Brown, *The Semitic Background*, who is ever eager to promote Jewish parallels, concedes, "Although what is said about the mystery of Christ to the Colossians is explicable against the background of the Semitic concept of mystery and has parallels in previous Pauline passages, it is not impossible that the mystery terminology of this letter is meant to counter the Colossian heretics who had reshaped Christianity in the image of a mystery cult" (55).
49 As James D.G. Dunn, *The Epistles to Colossians and to Philemon* (NIGTC; Grand Rapids: Eerdmans, 1996), puts it, mystery "was certainly a primary theme of the letter itself (1:26–27; 2:2), so the request at this point is a way of reinforcing the emphasis of the letter" (263).

...προσευχόμενοι ἅμα καὶ περὶ ἡμῶν, ἵνα ὁ θεὸς ἀνοίξῃ ἡμῖν θύραν τοῦ λόγου λαλῆσαι **τὸ μυστήριον τοῦ Χριστοῦ**, δι' ὃ καὶ δέδεμαι, ἵνα φανερώσω αὐτὸ ὡς δεῖ με λαλῆσαι.[50]

...praying also at the same time for us, that God may open for us a door for the word to speak the mystery of Christ, for which also I have been bound, in order that I should manifest it, as I am bound to speak.

Once again μυστήριον is linked to Paul's missionary endeavors and preaching, and again it is correlated with the verb φανερόω (cf. 1:26). Here, however, Paul identifies himself as the instrument of revelation, which is not explicitly stated in 1:26.[51] The idea that the mystery is manifested through proclamation, and often "speaking" (λαλέω), is frequently expressed in other Pauline mystery passages.[52] The full phrase "mystery of Christ"[53] evokes all the descriptions and identifications associated with μυστήριον in 1:24–2:5. Thus the mystery of Christ that Paul wishes to continue to make manifest denotes "the word of God" (1:25), "the riches of the glory among the Gentiles" (1:27), "the hope of glory" (1:27), and "the treasures of wisdom and knowledge" (2:3). Given the consistent conjoining of μυστήριον with Christ in the three previous mystery passages, the description "mystery of Christ" in 4:3 is an apt phrase.

The most difficult issue here is the relation of the expression δι' ὃ καὶ δέδεμαι to the rest of the statement. As printed, Paul's apparent imprisonment, which is what δέδεμαι is usually taken to indicate, is being characterized as a consequence of his mystery proclamation: he is bound because he has been speaking about the mystery of Christ. Paul is therefore asking the Colossian Christians to pray for his release so that he might continue to speak the mystery, which is what he is also "bound" (δεῖ) to do. Bockmuehl – preceded by critics such as Wettstein and Griesbach, and early readers such as Chrysostom and Photius – has noted that the phrase δι' ὃ καὶ δέδεμαι can also be printed as διὸ καὶ δέδεμαι.[54] Read this way, Paul would be not be asking the Colossians to pray for his release but instead to pray that even his imprisonment would manifest the μυστήριον τοῦ Χριστοῦ. Thus Bockmuehl offers the following paraphrase:

---

50 Cf. the parallel expression in Eph 6:19–20.
51 One might assume that the agent of revelation in 1:26 is God, especially given that in the very next verse Paul states that God "wanted to make known what are the riches of the glory of this mystery" (1:27). This may indeed be the case, but the fact remains that Paul has been chosen as God's designated administrator and so is a facilitator of this divine disclosure (1:24–25).
52 See 1 Cor 2:1, 7; 14:2; 15:51; Eph 6:19.
53 Cf. Eph 3:4.
54 Markus Bockmuehl, "A Note on the Text of Colossians 4:3," *JTS* 39 (1988): 489–94.

And pray that God may open for us an opportunity for proclamation, so that we may speak forth the mystery of Christ. For it is to this end that I have been imprisoned, in order that I might manifest it, as indeed I am obliged to do.⁵⁵

This alternative reading introduces a "conceptual connection between the apostle's physical bonds and his obligation to speak the word of Christ"; thus his chains may be seen as "illustrative, indeed as symbolic of his ministry: he is *bound* to speak."⁵⁶ The point then becomes "not simply that Paul is bound for the sake of the mystery of Christ; but that in fact his preaching and his very bonds constitute his manifestation of the mystery."⁵⁷ Bockmuehl also points to a possible chiasm involving the verbs λαλέω and δέω, which potentially reinforces the idea that the condition of imprisonment is itself a vehicle for apostolic proclamation:

λαλῆσαι τὸ μυστήριον τοῦ Χριστοῦ, διὸ καὶ **δέδεμαι,**
ἵνα φανερώσω αὐτὸ
ὡς **δεῖ** με **λαλῆσαι.**

A decision on the textual matter is difficult, but Bockmuehl's proposal certainly deserves a place in any critical apparatus. And as for viewing Paul's imprisonment as itself an instrument for demonstrating the mystery of Christ, even if it is not to be found in this passage, it is certainly in keeping with Paul's self-understanding (see my reading of 1 Cor 2:1–5 in the previous chapter).

3.2.3 Conclusion

Before turning to Ephesians, it will be helpful to summarize some of the key findings in this examination of μυστήριον in Colossians, particularly as they relate to the preceding chapter. In terms of continuity with the undisputed letters, the following features are noteworthy:
1) In agreement with most of the undisputed mystery passages, Colossians, like all the other deuteropauline letters, exclusively uses the singular form of the noun. Given the preference for the plural in Hellenistic and early Jewish sources, the prominence of the singular in Paul is a distinctive feature.

---

55 Bockmuehl, "A Note on the Text of Colossians 4:3," 492.
56 Bockmuehl, "A Note on the Text of Colossians 4:3," 491–92. We do find similar ideas elsewhere in Paul (see esp. Phil 1:12–14; 2 Tim 2:9).
57 Bockmuehl, "A Note on the Text of Colossians 4:3," 493.

2) As in the undisputed letters, the μυστήριον under Paul's stewardship in Col 1:24–2:5 and 4:3 (cf. 1:25; 1 Cor 4:1) is expressed especially in the apostle's missionary preaching. Thus the mystery is usually something proclaimed, spoken, or otherwise communicated and, hence, has definite and expressible content.

3) Like most of the undisputed passages, μυστήριον in Colossians in no way insinuates something like a cryptic teaching or impenetrable doctrine. Hence there is nothing deeply inscrutable about the basic content of the newly disclosed mystery. Although it is elaborated and nuanced in various ways in Col 1:24–2:5 and 4:3, the mystery essentially refers to the redemptive benefits secured by Christ specifically for the Gentiles.[58]

Alongside these mostly general parallels, however, there exist also a number of key developments, distinctive emphases, and even discontinuities:

1) While not exactly an unprecedented development, the repeated conjunction of μυστήριον with Christ in Colossians sets it apart from the assorted mysteries that are recounted in the undisputed letters. The union of μυστήριον and Christ is an important and shared characteristic of the deuteropauline letters.

2) Also characteristic of Colossians and the other deuteropauline letters is the recurrent association of μυστήριον with the benefits of Christ specifically for the Gentiles. While also not necessarily unprecedented (cf. Rom 11:25), it differentiates the deuteropauline texts from the undisputed letters and binds them together.

3) Another such characteristic is the prevalence of economic language in relation to μυστήριον. I have argued that financial motifs pervade 1:24–2:5 and that the mystery in this passage is deliberately presented as a form of symbolic capital entrusted to Paul. His apostolic οἰκονομία is thus the responsibility to distribute these already secured assets to their designated beneficiaries, the Gentiles. While this emphasis is perhaps anticipated, albeit in an undeveloped form, by 1 Cor 4:1, it is developed in some detail in the Colossians and Ephesians mystery passages.

---

58 Again, that the mystery is not inscrutable does not entail that it is exhaustively known or appreciated. On this feature of "revelational mysteries," see Boyer, "The Logic of Mystery," 90–94. As Boyer explains, "[W]hen thoughtful religious people talk about mystery, they seem to mean a dimensional depth of reality that calls for a rationality that is both logical and more than logical. Knowledge of this mystery is genuine rational knowledge, but it also involves a penetration into or a participation in a depth.... Clarity is important, but the goal is not merely to clarify or to organize" (100).

4) I have already identified some of the discontinuities between the use of μυστήριον in Col 1 and, specifically, 1 Cor 2:6–7. Principal among these is that whereas becoming τέλειος is the objective of mystery proclamation in Col 1, that status is presented as a prerequisite for such instruction in 1 Cor 2:6–7. Also in contrast to 1 Cor 2:6–7, "wisdom" instruction is not a subject that should be reserved exclusively for the τέλειοι. Instead, the Paul of Colossians instructs "all people" "in all wisdom" (ἐν πάσῃ σοφίᾳ) in the hopes that they might become τέλειοι (1:28).
5) Finally, and perhaps most significantly, in Col 1:26 we encounter the first clear systemization of the historically structured – or "once hidden, now revealed" – deuteropauline mystery schema of revelation. While there are certainly general instances in the undisputed letters of the "once hidden, now revealed" chronological arrangement, this historical schema is nowhere stated so plainly in those letters.

3.3 Ephesians

In Ephesians we find the most detailed uses of μυστήριον in the Pauline corpus. And though the uses of the term are diverse, it is still employed consistently throughout the letter in relation to the recent revelation of God's pretemporal plans for unity in the cosmos – whether that unity be the unity of the cosmos (1:9–10), the solidarity of Jews and Gentiles (3:2–12; 6:19–20), or the oneness of the church and Christ (5:31–32). Many of the main characteristics and emphases that accompanied the use of mystery in Colossians are similarly invoked in Ephesians. Especially noteworthy are: (1) the chronological arrangement of the hidden/revealed binary and the key terminology of the deuteropauline mystery schema; (2) the prominent correlation of the newly revealed mystery with the redemption of the Gentiles; and (3) the use of financial imagery for describing the "value" of the mystery for the Gentiles.

Before beginning I should say more about the relationship between Ephesians and Colossians. It is commonly acknowledged that much of the mystery material in Ephesians reiterates, often verbatim, language from Colossians. Much of the material also develops key terminology and motifs from Colossians in new ways, which makes the question of the relationship of Ephesians and Colossians all the more important. While some sort of literary dependency of Ephesians on Colossians is usually presumed,[59] there remain important challenges to this con-

---

[59] The evidence for this has been evaluated in multiple places. See esp. C. Leslie Mitton, *The*

sensus.⁶⁰ In dealing with this issue it is necessary to clarify what is meant by "dependence" in this instance. Does it mean meticulous extraction and reworking?, or conscious recollection without concern for exactitude?, or perhaps even subliminal influence? While I am persuaded that the author of Ephesians does know and, in some sense, "depends" on Colossians, I presume an unstructured and *ad hoc* form of reliance. Therefore, while I view Ephesians as often expanding or restating key themes from Colossians, and so routinely reworking or reapplying its language, I do not think this occurs in any systematic or especially scrupulous fashion.⁶¹

3.3.1 Ephesians 1:9

Ephesians 1:9 lies near the center of what is often described (and sometimes derided)⁶² as a complex yet intricately unified concatenation of doxological material running from vv. 3–14.⁶³ There have been varying approaches to the structure of this unit and numerous hypotheses regarding its generic classification,⁶⁴ but scholars now generally agree that the passage should be read as a whole, and most treat it as an extended eulogy of some sort (or, quite often, a Jewish *berakah*).⁶⁵ I am not interested in establishing a grand structure for this passage.

Epistle to the Ephesians: Its Authorship, Origin and Purpose (Oxford: Clarendon Press, 1951), 55–97; Michael Gese, *Das Vermächtnis des Apostels: Die Rezeption der paulinischen Theologie im Epheserbrief* (WUNT 2/99; Tübingen: Mohr Siebeck, 1997), 39–54.

60 Esp. E. Best, "Who Used Whom? The Relationship of Ephesians and Colossians," *NTS* 43 (1997): 72–96.

61 So also Mitton, *Ephesians*, similarly concludes, "The borrowing is exceedingly free. There is nothing mechanical about it. It is not at all the kind of borrowing that can be associated with a writer who has a document open in front of him as he writes and laboriously incorporates sections from it into his own work.... His acquaintance with Colossians is not dependent on what he reads in a document, but it is a familiarity which has become part of his own mental equipment" (57–58, 63).

62 Eduard Norden, *Agnostos Theos: Untersuchungen zur Formengeschichte religiöser Rede* (Leipzig/Berlin:Teubner, 1913), refers to it as "das monströseste Satzkonglomerat" (253).

63 For the large body of literature on this passage, see the bibliography provided by E. Best, *A Critical and Exegetical Commentary on Ephesians* (ICC; London/New York: T&T Clark, 1998), 103.

64 See esp. the inventory of approaches discussed by Andrew T. Lincoln, *Ephesians* (WBC 42; Dallas: Word Books, 1990), 10–19.

65 The most prominent stylistic features uniting this unit include the repetition of εἰς ἔπαινον δόξης (1:6, 12, 14), key aorist participles (esp. εὐλογήσας [v. 3], προορίσας [v. 5], and γνωρίσας [v. 9]), multiple relative pronouns, and ἐν phrases.

I am simply concerned with how the various parts of the discourse relate to and contribute to "the mystery of God's will" in 1:9. But since the announcement of the μυστήριον in v. 9 and the description of its content in v. 10 are often regarded as "the peak to which the eulogy has been building up"[66] and "the intellectual summit"[67] of the entire section, vv. 9–10 should be appreciated in relation to their larger context.

The section begins in v. 3a with Paul's opening eulogy: "blessed (εὐλογητός) is the God and father of our Lord Jesus Christ." This introductory avowal of God's blessedness is the fundamental proposition that each subsequent proposition in the discourse substantiates. The first corroborative proposition is presented in v. 3b where, immediately following Paul's blessing, God is acclaimed as "the one who blessed us (ὁ εὐλογήσας) in (ἐν) every spiritual blessing in (ἐν) the heavenly places in Christ (ἐν Χριστῷ)." Although the temporal relationship between Paul's blessing of God and God's blessing of "us" is not stated explicitly, it becomes clear from what follows that Paul is praising God's pretemporal election of humanity in Christ. It is therefore God's blessing of humanity (v. 3b) that precedes and provokes Paul's own acclamation of God (v. 3a). The primacy of divine action – that is, that God acts benevolently on behalf of humanity prior to any human response – is reiterated in the next two verses, as Paul further specifies the nature of God's blessing: God blessed us "insofar as he chose us (καθὼς ἐξελέξατο ἡμᾶς) before the foundation of the world to be holy and unblemished before him in love, predestining us for adoption (προορίσας ἡμᾶς εἰς υἱοθεσίαν)[68] through Jesus Christ for himself according to the pleasure of his will (κατὰ τὴν εὐδοκίαν τοῦ θελήματος αὐτοῦ)."[69] Paul explains in v. 6a God's purpose in electing humanity for adoption: "for the praise of his own glorious grace." He then in v. 6b explains the person in whom God's grace has been bestowed upon humanity: "in the Beloved One" (ἐν τῷ ἠγαπημένῳ).[70] As the preceding and subsequent ἐν constructions make plain,[71] the Beloved One who brings χάρις to humanity is Christ, the same Christ who has already been identified as the mediator of blessing, election, and predestination. In v. 7 Paul further identifies Christ (specifical-

---

66 Best, *Ephesians*, 139.
67 Best, *Ephesians*, 139 n. 52.
68 Paul will go on to connect this adoption (υἱοθεσία) with redemption (ἀπολύτρωσις) in v. 7. This association also occurs in Rom 8:23 (υἱοθεσία/ἀπολύτρωσις) and Gal 4:5 (υἱοθεσία/ἐξαγοράζω).
69 The προορίσας in this verse qualifies the ἐξελέξατο in 1:4.
70 D* F G et al. add υἱῷ αὐτοῦ to τῷ ἠγαπημένῳ, which is a good interpretation but dubious on text-critical terms.
71 I take these ἐν phrases as indicating location (and so participatory union), not instrumentality. The instrument of redemption in v. 7 is Christ's blood.

ly his blood) as the instrument of human redemption and the forgiveness of transgressions.[72] In vv. 7–8 Paul characterizes redemption additionally as the extension of divine χάρις, specifically describing this χάρις as "the wealth of his grace which he lavished on us in all wisdom and insight" (τὸ πλοῦτος τῆς χάριτος αὐτοῦ ἧς ἐπερίσσευσεν εἰς ἡμᾶς ἐν πάσῃ σοφίᾳ καὶ φρονήσει). Given some of the patterns we have already observed in 1 Cor 2 and Col 1, this mention of a provision of riches related to wisdom and cognition supplies an appropriate segue into the revealed μυστήριον in v. 9 and then the additional description of this μυστήριον as an οἰκονομία assigned to Christ in v. 10. It is worth pointing out that Paul returns to the images of wisdom, knowledge, revelation, and "the glorious wealth of inheritance" (ὁ πλοῦτος τῆς δόξης τῆς κληρονομίας) in vv. 17–18, which form the opening remarks in his prayer for the Ephesians.[73] The nexus of divine revelation and the endowment of riches is, therefore, as in Colossians 1, a matter of particular emphasis at the very outset of this letter.

To summarize the text thus far, in vv. 3–8 Paul has developed his initial ascription of blessing to God by variously illustrating the primacy of God's actions on behalf of humanity in Christ. Whether viewed within any of the assorted rubrics of election, predestination, adoption, redemption, the forgiveness of trespasses, or the generous endowment of wealth and wisdom, the consistent emphasis in these verses is on God's pretemporal determination to bless humanity in Christ.[74] Since the μυστήριον in v. 9 is woven into these various descriptions of humanity's predestined status by way of the aorist participle γνωρίσας, the mystery is clearly related to this pretemporal divine plan for humanity. But this plan is here widened to involve much more than the blessing of humanity alone:

...γνωρίσας ἡμῖν **τὸ μυστήριον τοῦ θελήματος αὐτοῦ**,
    κατὰ τὴν εὐδοκίαν αὐτοῦ
        ἣν προέθετο ἐν αὐτῷ

---

[72] Cf. Col 1:14. The "blood" here is a synecdoche for Christ's death. See esp. Eph 2:13 (ἐν τῷ αἵματι τοῦ Χριστοῦ) and Col 1:20 (διὰ τοῦ αἵματος τοῦ σταυροῦ αὐτοῦ). Cf. also Rom 3:25; 5:9; 1 Cor 10:16; 11:25–27.

[73] The language of πλοῦτος is prominent in this letter (see 1:7, 18; 2:7; 3:8, 16) and, as in Col 1:27 and 2:22, it is closely associated with God's newly revealed μυστήριον in both chs. 1 and 3. The term πλοῦτος is otherwise rare, only appearing 7x in the undisputed letters. Especially relevant for the usage in Ephesians and Colossians are Rom 9:23 (τὸν πλοῦτον τῆς δόξης αὐτοῦ); 11:12 (πλοῦτος κόσμου...πλοῦτος ἐθνῶν); and especially 11:33 (Ὦ βάθος πλούτου καὶ σοφίας καὶ γνώσεως θεοῦ).

[74] Notice that there is not any mention of just what the "problem" is – that is, the reason why humanity is in need of redemption and forgiveness.

> εἰς οἰκονομίαν τοῦ πληρώματος τῶν καιρῶν,
> ἀνακεφαλαιώσασθαι τὰ πάντα ἐν τῷ Χριστῷ,
> τὰ ἐπὶ τοῖς οὐρανοῖς
> καὶ τὰ ἐπὶ τῆς γῆς ἐν αὐτῷ.

...making known to us the mystery of his will, which he set forth in him [Christ] according to his good pleasure for the administration of the fullness of the times, to unify all things in Christ, the things in the heavens and the things on the earth in him.

Paul here supplies a third aorist participle (γνωρίσας)[75] to articulate in greater detail his opening claims in v. 3a.[76] As with the other verbs and participles in this section, God is the subject and, accordingly, the agent who has made the mystery known. The mystery itself is specifically qualified as "the mystery of his will" (τὸ μυστήριον τοῦ θελήματος αὐτοῦ).[77] Paul previously described the predestination of humanity as "according to the good pleasure of his will (τοῦ θελήματος αὐτοῦ)" (v. 5)[78] and, as there, the θέλημα in v. 9 concerns the pretemporal election of humanity. As Paul explains in vv. 9b-10, however, God's pretemporal design encompasses more than just humans. God also purposed a new arrangement for the fullness of the times by setting forth in Christ an οἰκονομία "to unify (or to concentrate or to condense or to summarize) all things in Christ" (ἀνακεφαλαιώσασθαι τὰ πάντα ἐν τῷ Χριστω).[79] Whatever the precise nuance of ἀνακεφαλαιόω,[80] the key point is that God's long established μυστήριον has been to incorporate all created reality in Christ, and this μυστήριον has now

---

[75] This verb (γνωρίζω) is commonly used in the deuteropauline mystery schema. Cf. Rom 16:25–26; Eph 3:3, 5, 10; Col 1:27.

[76] We can either read this participle as modifying ἐξελέξατο in v. 4, or we can take it in relation to the nearer verb, ἐπερίσσευσεν, in the previous verse. If read with ἐξελέξατο, the disclosure of the mystery is somehow epiphenomenal of God's election. The problem with such an association is that God's act of election is described, like the προορίσας in v. 5, as a singular and decisive act in the pretemporal past, whereas the disclosure of the mystery is presented as something that has recently occurred. If, however, the phrase is read with the immediately preceding ἐπερίσσευσεν, then the disclosed mystery becomes commensurate with "the riches of grace" that God has lavishly poured out on humanity. The association of a revealed μυστήριον with the provision of πλοῦτος is supported by Col 1:26–27, which similarly correlates the revealed mystery with the disclosure (γνωρίσαι) of "the wealth of the glory of this mystery."

[77] The genitive τοῦ θελήματος is perhaps best characterized as epexegetical ("the mystery which is his will").

[78] Cf. also κατὰ τὴν βουλὴν τοῦ θελήματος αὐτοῦ in v. 11.

[79] Cf., of course, the οἰκονομία in Col 1:25 and then Eph 3:2, 9.

[80] This verb is usually found in rhetorical contexts where it refers to the summing up or drawing together of the various points of an argument.

been made known by God to humanity.⁸¹ The previously established mystery of God's will is therefore every bit as much about the destiny of the cosmos as it is about the destiny of humans, and it is worth pointing out that while such a universal conception of Christ's preeminence is not necessarily unique in the Pauline corpus, the application of the term μυστήριον to the cosmic unification of creation is.⁸²

The next two verses (vv. 11–12) essentially reaffirm previous statements regarding God's predetermined plan (προορισθέντες)⁸³ and "the council of his will" (κατὰ τὴν βουλὴν τοῦ θελήματος αὐτοῦ).⁸⁴ In the final two verses (vv. 13–14) Paul pivots away from the status of humanity in Christ and turns to the role of the Holy Spirit. He again uses vocabulary of finance in relation to humanity's redemption, describing the Spirit as a pledge of inheritance (ἀρραβὼν τῆς κληρονομίας ἡμῶν)⁸⁵ given to Christians "for the redemption of the possession" (εἰς ἀπολύτρωσιν τῆς περιποιήσεως).⁸⁶ Thus with these concluding verses of his eulogy Paul reinforces the idea that humanity and Christ remain at the center of God's eternally planned but recently disclosed mystery to unify the cosmos in Christ.

3.3.2 Ephesians 3:2–13

Ephesians 3:2–13 represents the lengthiest and most detailed development of μυστήριον and the accompanying hidden/revealed schema in the Pauline corpus. This passage is usually characterized as a digression (although whether or not it is a proper *digressio* is disputed),⁸⁷ which ostensibly interrupts the first half of a prayer in 3:1 (τούτου χάριν…) and its resumption in v. 14 (τούτου χάριν…). The unit can be separated into two sections of six verses each: vv. 2–7 and vv. 8–13.⁸⁸ The first section is framed by verbal repetition:

---

81 Cf. Eph 1:20–23.
82 See Bockmuehl, *Revelation and Mystery*, 200.
83 Cf. 1:5.
84 Cf. 1:5, 9.
85 In support of the translation "pledge," by which I mean something along the lines of an offering of a security, see Yon-Gyong Kwon, "Ἀρραβών as Pledge in Second Corinthians," *NTS* 54 (2008): 525–41.
86 I take the περιποίησις to refer to humanity, who is thus God's rightful possession and adopted heir. Cf. the usage in 1 Peter 2:9.
87 See esp. Best, *Ephesians*, 293–94.
88 There are other, more detailed ways in which interpreters have structured these verses, and I am in no way doggedly committed to this particular arrangement, though I do find it heuristi-

v. 2: τὴν οἰκονομίαν τῆς χάριτος τοῦ θεοῦ τῆς δοθείσης μοι
v. 7: διάκονος κατὰ τὴν δωρεὰν τῆς χάριτος τοῦ θεοῦ τῆς δοθείσης μοι

The focus in this first section is on the earthly revelation of the mystery to human authorities: to Paul himself (vv. 2–4) and then to other "holy apostles and prophets" (v. 5). The second section is bracketed by expressions of Paul's lowly status (v. 8) and suffering (v. 13).[89] The focus in the second section also shifts. Rather than on the revelation of the mystery to Paul and other human emissaries, the focus is on Paul's own role as a witness to the mystery (vv. 8–9) and then on the role of the church in this regard (v. 10). The objective of both Paul and the church is to make "the administration of the mystery" (ἡ οἰκονομία τοῦ μυστηρίου) manifest to the entire created order, even to the rulers and authorities in the heavenly places (vv. 9–10). Thus whereas vv. 2–7 describe the individual revelation of the mystery to human leaders on earth, vv. 8–13 emphasize the cosmic disclosure of the mystery to every person and being in the universe. It is worth pointing out, however, that whether the disclosure occurs terrestrially to humans or celestially to cosmic powers, the revealed mystery in both halves of this discourse remains concentrated on the benefits of Christ for the Gentiles (vv. 6, 8).

Before turning to vv. 2–13, I should say a brief word about 3:1. Paul's characterization of his imprisonment as on behalf of the Gentiles might be perceived as an odd prelude to a discourse highlighting one's exceptional status as a privileged recipient and representative of a newly revealed divine mystery. At the conclusion to the mystery digression in v. 13, however, Paul again returns to his lowly status, but there he encourages his readers not to be dispirited by his sufferings on behalf of them, for these are in fact their glory. Hence Paul overtly juxtaposes suffering and glory in v. 13 in order to redefine the latter by the former. The same can be said of the juxtaposition of his imprisonment in 3:1 with the lengthy account of his commission to proclaim the mystery of Christ vv. 2–13. And so, when 3:1 is reconsidered in light of the subsequent discourse, it appears as though even the dishonor of incarceration cannot revoke Paul's exceptional status as a διάκονος of a divine οἰκονομία.[90] The focus on the Gentiles

---

cally useful. For an analysis of alternative approaches, see Chantal Reynier, *Évangile et Mystère: Les enjeux théologiques de l'épître aux Éphesiens* (LD 149; Paris: Cerf, 1992), 43–81.

[89] Verse 13 also recommences the thought of v. 1 and prepares the way for Paul's prayer in vv. 14–21.

[90] As Aaron Sherwood, "Paul's Imprisonment as the Glory of the *Ethnē*: A Discourse Analysis of Ephesians 3:1–13," *BBR* 22 (2012): 97–112, puts it, "Paul's concern for the digression is that his audience would wrongly understand his apostleship in terms of his imprisonment, and so he

in 3:1 is also significant. Just as Paul's imprisonment and sufferings are on behalf of the Gentiles and for their glory (v. 13), so also the mystery entrusted to Paul in vv. 2–13 specifically concerns the Gentiles. Once again we see the connection between Paul's self-understanding as an apostle to the Gentiles and his vocational charge as a herald of God's mystery.

Turning to the discourse itself, Paul opens the digression in vv. 2–4 by reminding his readers of the previous report they received regarding the μυστήριον that was made known to him via revelation.[91] It is not exactly clear what he is referring to (a previous letter? previous statements? some previous teaching?), and outside of his earlier remarks on the mystery in 1:9–10, the extent of their knowledge remains uncertain.[92] Paul first mentions an administration of divine grace that was given to him for his readers in v. 2 (τὴν οἰκονομίαν τῆς χάριτος τοῦ θεοῦ τῆς δοθείσης μοι εἰς ὑμᾶς), and then in v. 4 he specifically characterizes this administration assigned to him as his "insight in the mystery of Christ" (τὴν σύνεσίν μου ἐν τῷ μυστηρίῳ τοῦ Χριστου).[93] The association of οἰκονομία with μυστήριον was already seen in 1:9–10. We also observed the correlation of these terms is Col 1:25–26, which refers to a divine administration entrusted to Paul (τὴν οἰκονομίαν τοῦ θεοῦ τὴν δοθεῖσάν μοι). It is therefore no surprise to find Paul again using administrative (or, we might say, "economic") terminology to characterize his fiduciary responsibility over the mystery for the Gentiles. Also familiar is the direct correlation of μυστήριον with Christ, which is inferable from Col 1:27 and stated plainly in Col 2:2 and 4:3. As in those passages, the mystery under discussion can be equated with Christ because Christ has become the means of Gentile inclusion, his body the site in which Jew and Gentile become one (2:11–22). Notice, however, that the genitive expression "mystery of Christ" is not equivalent to "the mystery of God's will" in 1:9. Whereas "the mystery of God's will" names the source from which the mystery itself derives, the "mystery of Christ" names the person in whom that mystery is accomplished.

---

takes pains instead to interpret his imprisonment in terms of his apostleship. Otherwise, his role in God's eschatological plan could have been subverted and viewed as shameful" (108).

91 The εἴ γε formulation at the beginning of this verse is rare (cf. the usage in 4:21). It is, however, also used in Col 1:23, which is interesting in terms of the literary relationship between the Col 1 and Eph 3 discourses.

92 Decisions on this matter depend on a host of prior judgments about authorship, authenticity, date of composition, and so on.

93 Cf. the association of σύνεσις and μυστήριον in Col 2:2. There Paul wants his readers to have insight into the mystery of Christ. The term σύνεσις here, as in other contexts, appears to connote divinely enabled insight, such as was supplied to Daniel. See esp. Dan 1:17, 20; 2:21; Dan (Th) 5:11–14; 8:15; 9:22; 10:1.

In v. 3 Paul recounts how the mystery was made known to him via revelation: κατὰ ἀποκάλυψιν ἐγνωρίσθη μοι τὸ μυστήριον. The noun ἀποκάλυψις (cf. 1:17) is extremely rare prior to Paul, yet it appears some thirteen times in his corpus.[94] The most similar use of this noun is in Rom 16:25, where μυστήριον is again aligned with it (κατὰ ἀποκάλυψιν).[95] The verb γνωρίζω, which appears again in relation to μυστήριον in vv. 5 and 10 and then in 6:19, is similarly related to the disclosure of a μυστήριον in Rom 16:26, as it is in Col 1:27 and Eph 1:9. We should avoid trying to be too precise in describing just what sort of epistemological or phenomenological process is in view here, though it must be admitted that a communicative encounter with God would seem to be required.[96] As for the μυστήριον of Gentile inclusion, which is the focus of these verses, it seems to me most likely that in the case of the historical Paul such an exceptional disclosure was not comprehended in its totality during some singular moment of direct inspiration, such as a Damascus road epiphany, but rather that it was developed and articulated through sustained processes of reflection and missionary experience.[97] It is also possible, however, that a post-Pauline author of Ephe-

---

[94] On this terminology, see Morton Smith, "On the History of ΑΠΟΚΑΛΥΠΤΩ and ΑΠΟΚΑΛΥΨΙΣ," in *Apocalypticism in the Mediterranean World and the Near East: Proceedings of the International Colloquium on Apocalypticism, Uppsala, August 12–17, 1979* (ed. David Hellholm; Tübingen: Mohr Siebeck, 1983), 9–20. Most comparable to the Pauline usage here is Luke 2:32 (φῶς εἰς ἀποκάλυψιν ἐθνῶν). The noun is related to μυστήριον in Sir 22:22 (μυστηρίου ἀποκαλύψεως), but the reference there is simply to a friend's betrayal of personal secrets. The only place in the Greek Bible where the term is used in translation is 1 Sam 20:30, where it renders the Hebrew ערוה ("nakedness").

[95] Cf. also κατὰ ἀποκάλυψιν in Gal 2:2, which seems to indicate an instantaneous (or "charismatic") disclosure. See the discussion of this passage in Dieter Lührmann, *Das Offenbarungsverständnis bei Paulus und in paulinischen Gemeinden* (WMANT 16; Neukirchen-Vluyen: Neukirchener Verlag, 1965), 39–44. For an interesting comparison of Gal 2:2 and Eph 3:3, see Helmut Merklein, *Das kirchliche Amt nach dem Epheserbrief* (SANT 33; München: Kösel, 1973), 193–200.

[96] This matter is, of course, again all the more complicated by questions regarding the authorship and authenticity of this letter.

[97] Cf. the reflections of Best, *Ephesians*, 300–1. Also important is Best's "The Revelation to Evangelize the Gentiles," *JTS* 35 (1984): 1–30, esp. 24. I find the comments of William Wrede, *Paul* (trans. Edward Lummis; Eugene, OR: Wipf and Stock, 2001 [1904]), especially instructive on this matter: "If we go by [Paul's] account this consciousness of vocation was felt in its fullness from the beginning. The very moment of his conversion had shown him that he was ordained, not simply to apostolate, but to the apostolate of the Gentiles. But this looks like a slight self-deception. From a psychological point of view the perception, at such a moment, of so specific a vocation is hardly comprehensible. The perspective of memory is apt to foreshorten and bring together events which were originally separate, if only there is some intrinsic connection between them" (18). For a more detailed exegetical analysis of the evolutions in Paul's

sians presumed otherwise.[98] Whatever the actual circumstances may have been, the claim in v. 3 is clear in its emphasis: the mystery was revealed to Paul by divine initiative.

In the final three verses of this first section Paul submits two additional facts about the mystery that was revealed to him (vv. 5–6) and then reaffirms his divinely appointed status (v. 7). Paul first describes the mystery as having been concealed from humanity in previous ages but presently revealed to holy apostles and prophets by the Spirit. Paul's statement in v. 5 presents a nicely structured juxtaposition, indicating when (former generations), in what sense (cognitively), and from whom (humanity) the mystery was concealed (v. 5a) and then when (now), in what sense (by revelation), and to whom (holy apostles and prophets) it has been disclosed (v. 5b):

A which in other generations
    B was not made known
        C to the sons of humanity
A' as now
    B' it has been revealed by the Spirit
        C' to his holy apostles and prophets
	A ὃ ἑτέραις γενεαῖς
	    B οὐκ ἐγνωρίσθη
	        C τοῖς υἱοῖς τῶν ἀνθρώπων
	A' ὡς νῦν
	    B' ἀπεκαλύφθη...ἐν πνεύματι
	        C' τοῖς ἁγίοις ἀποστόλοις αὐτοῦ καὶ προφήταις

In Col 1:26 the mystery was described as hidden from both "the ages and the generations" (ἀπὸ τῶν αἰώνων καὶ ἀπὸ τῶν γενεῶν). In Eph 3 Paul instead refers first to the concealment from the "generations" in v. 5 and then later to the concealment from the "ages" (ἀπὸ τῶν αἰώνων) in v. 9. Thus in Eph 3 the "ages and generations" pair is uncoupled and its parts relocated to separate sections of the discourse. Given the distinct emphases of these two sections, this rearrangement is appropriate. In keeping with the focus of vv. 2–7, the attention in v. 5 is delib-

---

missionary practice and self-understanding, see Douglas A. Campbell, *The Deliverance of God: An Apocalyptic Rereading of Justification in Paul* (Grand Rapids: Eerdmans, 2009), 154–66. See also Campbell's "Galatians 5.11: Evidence of an Early Law-observant Mission by Paul?," *NTS* 57 (2011): 325–47.

98 I find the conclusions of Best, "The Revelation to Evangelize the Gentiles," judicious: "The anarthrous noun in κατὰ ἀποκάλυψιν may refer to *a* particular act of revelation, but more probably distinguishes how Paul believed or, more correctly, how the writer of Ephesians believed that Paul came to his view...; he was not told by others, the veil was not lifted from his eyes as he read the Old Testament, he did not deduce it by human reason from general principles.... These things, of course, may have influenced Paul without him realizing it. What is said is that he obtained knowledge by a direct and personal communication from God. We do not need to discuss how this took place. The aorist ἐγνωρίσθη suggests an event in the past but gives no indication as to its duration or date" (24).

erately on the previous eras of *human* history in which the mystery of Christ was unknowable. But why was it previously concealed from humanity? The text does not say, but it does not appear to have been due to any enduring shortcoming in those previous generations. The text simply states that it was not "made known" (ἐγνωρίσθη) because it had not "been revealed" (ἀπεκαλύφθη). As Eph 1:9 already made plain, it is God's prerogative to divulge the mystery of his will,[99] and so, apart from divine disclosure, the mystery remains veiled. But another question now arises: was it previously veiled in an absolute sense? This question is complicated by the ὡς νῦν formulation, which could be taken as indicating a relative or comparative difference between the previous age and the current age. That is, perhaps the mystery was not made known then "as now" in the sense that it was then known in part by humanity but now fully, or then known by just some among humanity but not by all.[100] Despite this possibility, it seems more likely that an absolute contrast is again being affirmed, as appears to be the case in the other Pauline mystery passages. This would be to take the ὡς νῦν as descriptive and hence as differentiating in unconditional terms the previous generations of concealment and the current era of revelation.[101] And so, in the case of the οὐκ ἐγνωρίσθη/ἀπεκαλύφθη juxtaposition, that which was not known in earlier generations was not in any way accessible to the human mind. It was, as v. 9 describes it, "hidden" without qualification.

Paul designates "the holy apostles and prophets" as the principal recipients of this revelation and the Spirit (ἐν πνεύματι) as the medium of disclosure.[102]

---

99 The necessity of divine disclosure is also plainly stated in Col 1:26–27.
100 Origen, for instance, argues that Israel's prophets, since they were wise men (quoting Prov 16:23), understood the mysteries they spoke, even though they concealed them. Thus the mystery was not known then "as now" in the sense that it was only known by the prophets, who then communicated it in concealed form. For Origen's reading of Eph 3:5, see Ronald E. Heine, "Recovering Origen's Commentary on Ephesians from Jerome," *JTS* 51 (2000): 478–514, 506–10. See also Origen's *Comm. Rom.* 8.6; 10.43.
101 The importance of contrasting eras is critical, as is the fact that the νῦν corresponds to the current era and not just a singular point in time. (A νυνί, as in Rom 3:21, might better capture this.) As Merklein, *Das kirchliche Amt*, comments, "Mit νῦν ἀπεκαλύφθη ist sicherlich nicht ein historisches Datum angesprochen. Doch ist damit nicht jeder historische Bezug ausgeschlossen. Insofern nämlich das νῦν den geschichtlichen Aspekt des Heilsbereiches Kirche meint, ist es auch historisch einzuordnen: im Kreuz Christi hat Kirche und νῦν den historisches Ausgangspunkt. Damit hat auch die Offenbarung an Apostel und Propheten ihren historischen Rahmen" (186).
102 There are multiple syntactical issues in these expressions that cannot be discussed here. I simply note that my decision to read τοῖς ἁγίοις ἀποστόλοις αὐτοῦ καὶ προφήταις as delimiting two groups (apostles and prophets) and ἐν πνεύματι in relation to verb ἀπεκαλύφθη are in line with the majority of commentators.

While Paul later describes himself as laboring to make the mystery known to every human (vv. 8–9), here, as Lincoln notes, "the narrowing of the recipients of revelation...to a particular group is striking" and likely reflects "the author's already expressed interest in the foundational role of the apostles and prophets in the Church (cf. 2:20)."[103] Such a narrowing of authority to apostles and prophets may indeed, from a certain perspective, be striking, but this passage also expands responsibility for the mystery beyond Paul in ways not specifically stated by any other mystery passage. Insofar as the mystery is defined in vv. 6–8 in terms of the Gentile mission, the claim that other apostles have likewise been confronted by God with the revelation of Gentile inclusion provides implicit apostolic corroboration for Paul's missionary endeavors among the nations – an observation that becomes all the more intriguing when read in light of a text like Gal 2.[104] Finally, the association of πνεῦμα with revelation appeared previously in 1:17 (πνεῦμα ἀποκαλύψεως), and the Spirit's role in disclosing mysteries is frequently described elsewhere.[105] Indeed, the association of a revealed mystery with pneumatic illumination is typical.

Although Paul freely refers to the μυστήριον made known to him in vv. 3–5, it is not until v. 6 that he describes its precise content:

> ...εἶναι τὰ ἔθνη συγκληρονόμα καὶ σύσσωμα καὶ συμμέτοχα τῆς ἐπαγγελίας ἐν Χριστῷ Ἰησοῦ διὰ τοῦ εὐαγγελίου...
>
> ...for the Gentiles to be co-heirs, co-members, and co-partakers of the promise in Christ Jesus through the Gospel...

The triad of adjectival συν- compounds exhibits the key components of the μυστήριον: "the Gentiles are co-heirs (συγκληρονόμα), co-members of the body (σύσσωμα), and co-partakers of the promise (συμμέτοχα)."[106] While the association of the newly revealed mystery with the Gentiles is a recurrent feature in

---

[103] Lincoln, *Ephesians*, 178.
[104] Once again, what one makes of these observations depends in large part on the question of the authenticity and authorship of this letter.
[105] See esp. Dan (Th) 4:8–9; 1 Cor 14:2. Cf. also the Spirit's role in Eph 2:22.
[106] As Sigurd Grindheim, "What the OT Prophets Did Not Know: The Mystery of the Church in Eph 3,2–13," *Bib* 84 (2003): 531–53, points out, "The fact the Gentiles are included in the divine promise is nothing new...and Paul elsewhere stresses how the salvation of the Gentiles is in accordance with the promises of God in the Old Testament"; the question that remains, therefore, is "what was previously unknown about the mystery in Eph 3:6?" (533). While I do not necessarily agree with some specifics in his answer to this question, I think Grindheim is correct that "the mystery [in Eph 3:6] can be referred to as previously unknown because of the unexpected manner in which the Gentiles are saved" (547).

the deuteropauline mystery schema, this passage is unique in its specific emphasis on the coequal status of the Gentiles alongside Israel.[107] The identity of Israel must, of course, be inferred here but, given the preceding context of 2:11–22, such an inference is uncomplicated. The first aspect of the mystery is that the Gentiles have become "co-heirs" (συγκληρονόμα)[108] and thus, in Christ, now stand as rightful beneficiaries of God's inheritance. Paul previously referred to the inheritance (κληρονομία) that awaits the saints in 1:14 and 18. Though it is not spelled out explicitly, this announcement of the Gentiles' status as heirs of a divine inheritance is seemingly why Paul refers to his missionary commissioning as an οἰκονομία in v. 2 and also as an assignment to preach to the Gentiles "the inexhaustible wealth of Christ" in v. 8. The second fact of the mystery is that the Gentiles are now joined in one body with Israel (σύσσωμα).[109] Images of unity and oneness were variously presented in 2:11–22, with somatic unity being especially prominent (vv. 13–16). And, as those verses make clear, the body in which Jew and Gentile are joined together is that of Christ. Finally, the mystery also includes the fact that the Gentiles are equal participants in the promise (συμμέτοχα τῆς ἐπαγγελίας). The content of the promise is not stated, but it likely refers to the "covenants of promise" mentioned in 2:12 and thus indicates that the Gentiles also enjoy all the advantages of God's ancient covenantal pledges.

In concluding this statement of the mystery's content, Paul adds two additional qualifications. First, the site of Jew and Gentile unity is "in Christ Jesus" (ἐν Χριστῷ Ἰησοῦ). And second, this unity is brought about "through the gospel" (διὰ τοῦ εὐαγγελίου). The ἐν Χριστῷ expression has become a familiar refrain in the letter. Here it marks the location in which the three συν- expressions occur and so the person in whom Jew and Gentile are united. The term εὐαγγέλιον only appears three other times in the letter. Especially important, however, are 1:13, where Paul explains that in Christ "the gospel of salvation" is heard, and 6:19, where he asks for prayers that he might have occasion and boldness "to make known the mystery of the gospel" (γνωρίσαι τὸ μυστήριον

---

[107] It is important to point out that this unity occurs in a new entity. As Lincoln, *Ephesians*, writes, "[Paul] is not celebrating the relationship of Gentiles with Israel or the Jewish people as such.... [T]he writer views the Church as a new entity which transcends old divisions and categories, and what for him is at the heart of God's disclosure is that the Gentiles are an essential constituent of this new entity" (180).
[108] This compounded form also appears in Rom 8:17, but in a different sense.
[109] This compound term is perhaps coined by Paul.

τοῦ εὐαγγελίου).¹¹⁰ It would seem then that the mystery of Gentile inclusion, which is synonymous with their salvation, occurs "through the gospel" insofar as the gospel itself proclaims that mystery. The mystery is synonymous with gospel, just as the gospel is synonymous Christ.

In the final verse of this opening section (v. 7), Paul returns to the subject of his divine commissioning. He refers to himself as a διάκονος of the mystery and, slightly altering his claim in v. 2, he notes that his divinely appointed status is "according to the gift of the grace of God" (κατὰ τὴν δωρεὰν τῆς χάριτος τοῦ θεοῦ). Such an expression again indicates the extent to which the apostle's affiliation with the mystery of Christ is being envisioned as a fiduciary obligation, a theme only amplified in the ensuing verses.

Economic vocabulary continues to gather alongside the mystery motif in the second part of the discourse (Eph 3:8–13). Paul states again in v. 8 that to him ("to the least of all the saints") a χάρις has been entrusted. This χάρις assigned to Paul is "to announce to the Gentiles the good news about the inexhaustible wealth of Christ" (τοῖς ἔθνεσιν εὐαγγελίσασθαι τὸ ἀνεξιχνίαστον πλοῦτος τοῦ Χριστοῦ).¹¹¹ I have thus far translated the χάρις given to Paul very generally as a "grace," but perhaps a more tangible (or monetary) image is in view. First, it is important to notice that the previous uses of χάρις in this passage are in immediate proximity to economic terminology, as Paul speaks of "the administration of grace" (τὴν οἰκονομίαν τῆς χάριτος) that was given to him in v. 2 and "the gift of grace" (τὴν δωρεὰν τῆς χάριτος) that was given to him in v. 7. The association of χάρις with material benefits is in fact one that recurs throughout the letter: "the wealth of his grace" (τὸ πλοῦτος τῆς χάριτος αὐτοῦ) (1:7); "the immeasurable wealth of his grace" (τὸ ὑπερβάλλον πλοῦτος τῆς χάριτος αὐτοῦ) (2:7); "the grace was given according the measure of Christ's gift" (ἐδόθη ἡ χάρις κατὰ τὸ μέτρον τῆς δωρεᾶς τοῦ Χριστου) (4:7). It is therefore unsurprising that the χάρις assigned to Paul in v. 8 is characterized as a calling to publicize the extraordinary riches that have been credited to the Gentiles by Christ. The correlation of χάρις with financial benefits is itself unsurprising since it is typical in the broader cultural contexts of benefaction and wealth management.¹¹² More-

---

110 The only other instance is 6:15, where Paul refers to feet secured with "the gospel of peace."
111 For a similar correlation of πλοῦτος and ἀνεξιχνίαστος (and in proximity to μυστήριον) see Rom 11:33.
112 See esp. James R. Harrison, *Paul's Language of Grace in its Graeco-Roman Context* (WUNT 2/172; Tübingen: Mohr Siebeck, 2003). As Harrison amply demonstrates, the idea that χάρις has some basic "theological sense" is patently false. The term is most frequently used in ordinary contexts of benefaction. Also helpful is Zeba A. Crook's *Reconceptualising Conversion: Patron-*

over, Paul himself uses the term in this way when referring to the Jerusalem collection in 1 Cor 16:3 and 2 Cor 8–9.[113] We also find it used in a monetary sense in other general discussions of οἰκονομία, such as in Philodemus' important treatise on this subject. In his characterization of the wise οἰκονόμος Philodemus writes, "The wealth (π[λοῦ]τος) that he has will not bring him trouble nor, to the extent that it does trouble him, will it do so more than it will render the benefits back (τὰς χάριτας [ἀ]ποδώσει)." (*On Property Management*, 19.34–46).[114] Other examples of χάρις connoting tangible beneficence could be easily multiplied,[115] but one especially suggestive instance comes from Ephesus itself, in an inscription discovered in 1958. The monument reads, "By means of [t]he [favou]r (χαριτ[ι]) of Caesar August[us] from the sacred reven[ues] (εκ των ιερων προσο[δων]) [w]hich he himself [gave] freely (εχαρι[σατο]) to the goddess a road was laid under the procons[ul] Sextos Appoleios."[116] As Harrison remarks, with his ascent to power Augustus began to style himself as "the iconic example of beneficence" and so this "inscription represents another instance of the Augustan 'age of grace'."[117] Given the similar correlation of χάρις with fiscal terminology throughout Ephesians, it would seem that the χάρις assigned to Paul to proclaim in Eph 3 should be viewed, at least in some sense, as an alternative form of redemptive capital that has been secured for the Gentiles by the God of Israel.[118] This then is precisely why Paul's missionary task is an οἰκονομία to publicize the fact of God's beneficence.[119]

---

age, Loyalty, and Conversion in the Religions of the Ancient Mediterranean (BZNW 130; Berlin/New York: de Gruyter, 2004), esp. 132–50.

113 See 2 Cor 8:1, 4, 6–7, 9, 19; 9:8, 14. See also the discussion on these passages in Harrison, *Paul's Language of Grace*, 294–303.

114 See the recent text, translation, and notes provided by Voula Tsouna, Philodemus, *On Property Management* (WGRW 33; Atlanta: Society of Biblical Literature, 2012).

115 As Crook, *Reconceptualising Conversion*, explains, "The term χάρις occurs in numerous settings…in which it clearly means benefaction or favour, and refers to the conferral or reception of something concrete" (140); furthermore, "the meaning of concrete benefaction is far more common a usage than χάρις as a generous disposition" (134).

116 See the text and discussion in J.R. Harrison, "The 'grace' of Augustus paves a Street at Ephesus," in *NewDocs* 10 (2012): 59–63.

117 Harrison, "The 'grace' of Augustus," 60.

118 For a similar reading of the χάρις in this passage as "soteriological wealth," see Harrison, *Paul's Language of Grace*, 242–47. Harrison contends that the language here would have had a polemical edge in the context of local mystery and cultic practices in Asia Minor, particularly as they are represented in magical papyri. Thus the use of χάρις in Ephesians is perhaps "directed against the influence that magic and the Artemis cult wielded in Ephesus and throughout the province of Asia" (243).

119 Recall that this agrees with my reading of Col 1:24–25.

In the next verse Paul defines himself in his vocation as a courier of Christ's χάρις also as a herald of "the administration of the mystery" (v. 9). Whereas the revelation from God in vv. 2–7 was limited to Paul and then the apostles and prophets, Paul's own work of revelation is "to enlighten all" (φωτίσαι πάντας), meaning not just apostles and prophets.[120] The verb φωτίζω occurs one other time in this letter where Paul prays that his readers will be enlightened (πεφωτισμένους) so as to recognize "the wealth of the glory of God's inheritance" (1:18). Insofar as the content of the revelation is "the administration of the mystery" (ἡ οἰκονομία τοῦ μυστηρίου), the enlightenment in question in 3:9 is correspondingly fiscal. While elsewhere the relationship between οἰκονομία and μυστήριον is only indirectly coordinated, there is no need to characterize the phrase ἡ οἰκονομία τοῦ μυστηρίου as "patently a contradiction"[121] of Paul's other formulations. In v. 2, as in Col 1:25, the divine οἰκονομία given to Paul refers to his commission as an administrator of God's μυστήριον. Here in v. 9, however, Paul further explains the content of this οἰκονομία. It is the οἰκονομία "of the mystery which has been hidden from the ages by the God who created all things" (ἡ οἰκονομία τοῦ μυστηρίου τοῦ ἀποκεκρυμμένου ἀπὸ τῶν αἰώνων ἐν τῷ θεῷ τῷ τὰ πάντα κτίσαντι). Thus the οἰκονομία *from* God is the οἰκονομία *of* the mystery.

While mystery is similarly coordinated with the perfect passive participle of ἀποκρύπτω in 1 Cor 2:7 (τὴν ἀποκεκρυμμένην), the formulation here in v. 9 is most similar to that of Col 1:26 (τὸ μυστήριον τὸ ἀποκεκρυμμένον ἀπὸ τῶν αἰώνων καὶ ἀπὸ τῶν γενεῶν). As mentioned above, Paul appears to have reserved the temporal portion of the Colossian concealment schema (ἀπὸ τῶν αἰώνων) for this point,[122] having already dealt with the generational half in v. 5. And again, its placement here is fitting since Paul shifts the addressees of revelation in this section beyond humans to the whole cosmos (v. 10), and then affirms that this all occurs according to God's eternal plan – a "plan of the ages" (πρόθεσιν τῶν αἰώνων) as he characterizes it in v. 11. But something has been added to the Colossian 1:26 expression as well. In Eph 3:9 Paul describes the mystery as having been hidden from the ages "by the God who created all things" (ἐν τῷ θεῷ

---

120 The πάντας here is textually uncertain but has early (P46) and widespread support. Cf. also the threefold repetition of πάντα ἄνθρωπον Col 1:28. A cosmic extension of the mystery is, of course, plainly stated in Eph 3:10, but it is unclear whether the πάντας here in 3:9 should be taken as indicating all people or, as in 1:10, all reality.

121 So Agamben, *The Kingdom and the Glory*, 23.

122 That the αἰῶνες here potentially refer to heavenly beings (as in gnostic aeons), while intriguing in light of the contrast with the rulers and authorities in v. 10, is unlikely. See the discussion in Hoehner, *Ephesians*, 456–57. Cf. the ostensibly temporal use of αἰών in Eph 1:21; 2:7; 3:11, 21.

τῷ τὰ πάντα κτίσαντι).[123] The intended effect of the additional appellative is presumably to underscore a point that Paul has already stressed and will again return to: the mystery, though long hidden, has always remained integral to the creator God's eternal purposes.

Whereas v. 9 relates how the mystery has been hidden, v. 10 explains God's rationale for keeping it hidden: in order that it would be made known *now*, the "now" referring to the era inaugurated by Christ, the era, as 1:10 puts it, of "the fullness of the times."[124] In explaining this Paul also specifies the addressees (ταῖς ἀρχαῖς καὶ ταῖς ἐξουσίαις), instrument (διὰ τῆς ἐκκλησίας), and precise content (ἡ πολυποίκιλος σοφία τοῦ θεοῦ) of the new disclosure:

> ...ἵνα γνωρισθῇ νῦν ταῖς ἀρχαῖς καὶ ταῖς ἐξουσίαις ἐν τοῖς ἐπουρανίοις διὰ τῆς ἐκκλησίας ἡ πολυποίκιλος σοφία τοῦ θεοῦ...
>
> ...in order that the manifold wisdom of God should be made known now through the church to the rulers and the authorities in the heavenly places...

Once again new revelation is conveyed with a form of γνωρίζω (cf. Rom 16:25–26; Eph 1:9; 3:3, 5; 6:19; Col 1:27), and the present timing of the revelation is indicated by the particle νῦν (cf. Rom 16:25–26; Col 1:26). There are, however, some interesting variations in this expression. Despite its syntactical proximity, it is not "the administration of the mystery" that is to be made known to the heavenly rulers but rather, despite its syntactical deferral, "the manifold wisdom

---

123 The expression ἐν τῷ θεῷ could, of course, just as easily be taken as locative ("in the God…"), but the contrast with God's agency in revelation (1:9; 3:3, 5) suggests God's instrumentality in concealment as well. Nevertheless, whether the emphasis is on God as the place where the mystery has been hidden or the agent who has hidden it, the implications seems identical.
124 There is, it must be admitted, much debate about how the ἵνα should be connected with what precedes it. Most recent interpreters read it with all that follows from the ἐδόθη in v. 8 or with one or both of the infinitive expressions in vv. 8 (εὐαγγελίσασθαι) and 9 (φωτίσαι). Read in either way the accent is on the evangelistic assignment given to Paul and then the church's witness to the powers: Paul was given this assignment in order that the church would witness to the powers. But, as Abbott, *Ephesians and Colossians*, observes, since "γνωρισθῇ is directly opposed to ἀποκεκρ., and νῦν to ἀπὸ τῶν αἰώνων, the most natural interpretation is that the secret or mystery was concealed in former times in order that now the wisdom of God might be manifested in its fulfilment" (88). Read in this way the accent is on the previous era of concealment and the current era of revelation: God previously concealed the administration of the mystery in order that now, in the current era of Christ, the wisdom of God should be made known. Or, as Theodore of Mopsuestia, writes, "For this was concealed from all in this way because it was destined to be dispensed through Christ, so that neither the rulers not the authorities…could have first known the things that were to come" (*Ad Ephesios*, 235 [trans. Greer]).

of God."¹²⁵ While the σοφία τοῦ θεοῦ in this instance is certainly interrelated with the mystery under discussion in the previous verses,¹²⁶ this shift to wisdom is significant. Rulers (ἄρχοντες) are also mentioned in relation to the wisdom of God spoken "in a mystery" in 1 Cor 2:7–8, but there the rulers are designated as subjects whose *ignorance* (οὐδεὶς τῶν ἀρχόντων...ἔγνωκεν) of God's wisdom is vital to its manifestation, a point crucial to the logic of those verses. In Eph 3:10, by contrast, the rulers are marked as subjects for whom *knowledge* (γνωρισθῇ...ταῖς ἀρχαῖς) of God's wisdom is intended. This is a striking revision of the rationale in 1 Cor 2.¹²⁷ This verse also differs from the other mystery passages in that the church is designated as a vehicle through which the heavenly authorities are instructed. The text gives no indication as to how the church makes God's wisdom known to the heavenly powers,¹²⁸ but insofar as the church's witness in this regard abets "the administration of the mystery," this represents an important democratization of mystery proclamation. That is, while vv. 2–9 seem to restrict responsibility for the mystery of Christ to Paul and other ecclesial authorities, v. 10 clearly invests the entire church with some role, even if simply that of a witness, in making the newly revealed mystery of Gentile inclusion known. It is also worth pointing out that since the content of the mystery – which is to say, the product of God's manifold wisdom – remains concentrated on the unified community of Jew and Gentile, the church's part in exhibiting this wisdom to the heavenly powers in some sense prefigures the comprehensive ends of God's mystery as described in 1:9–10. In other words, as it embodies unified diversity, the church anticipates the ultimate destiny of the cosmos, which is the unification of all things in Christ.

The final three verses bring the discourse to its close. As in the conclusion to the letter's opening eulogy, so in 3:11 Paul locates the new revelation in God's

---

125 I take it that "the inexhaustible wealth of Christ" (v. 8), "the administration of the mystery" (v. 9), and "the manifold wisdom of God" (v. 10) are all more or less synonymous.
126 As Chrys C. Caragounis, *The Ephesian* Mysterion: *Meaning and Content* (ConBNT 8; Lund: Gleerup, 1977), puts it, "The *mysterion* is shaped by God's wisdom, it is a product of it. At the same time God's wisdom is reflected and revealed in the *mysterion*" (108).
127 Cf. Ign. *Eph*. 19.1, which seems to adapt the 1 Cor 2:7–8 tradition.
128 It seems to me most likely that the church is being envisioned as a material witness to God's newly revealed and multifarious wisdom. As Peter T. O'Brien, *The Letter to the Ephesians* (Pillar; Grand Rapids: Eerdmans, 1999), writes, the phrase διὰ τῆς ἐκκλησίας "signifies that the very existence of the new multiracial community in which Jews and Gentiles have been brought together in unity in the one body is the manifestation of God's richly diverse wisdom. Its presence is the means by which God himself discloses to the powers his own richly diverse wisdom" (246).

"eternal purpose" (κατὰ πρόθεσιν τῶν αἰώνων)[129] and then designates Christ as the specific mediator of that plan.[130] Paul thus insists again that the recent revelation of God's wisdom is not a reaction to shifting circumstances. It is rather the long-planned manifestation of the pretemporal design to unify creation – and Jews and Gentiles in particular – in Christ.

3.3.3 Ephesians 5:32

This passage appears at the conclusion of the first main section of the *Haustafeln* (vv. 22–33), which concerns husbands and wives. The mystery statement in v. 32a immediately follows the quotation of Gen 2:24 (v. 31)[131] and immediately precedes its interpretive gloss (v. 32b):

> ἀντὶ τούτου καταλείψει ἄνθρωπος [τὸν] πατέρα καὶ [τὴν] μητέρα καὶ προσκολληθήσεται πρὸς τὴν γυναῖκα αὐτοῦ, καὶ ἔσονται οἱ δύο εἰς σάρκα μίαν. **τὸ μυστήριον τοῦτο μέγα ἐστίν**· ἐγὼ δὲ λέγω εἰς Χριστὸν καὶ εἰς τὴν ἐκκλησίαν.
>
> "For this reason a man will leave his father and mother and be joined to his wife, and the two will be one flesh." This mystery is great; and I am speaking about Christ and the church.

Although the citation of Gen 2:24 lacks an introductory formula, it is nonetheless an extended and easily identifiable quotation which flows appropriately from what precedes it.[132] The μυστήριον in v. 32 is linked to the citation by the neuter demonstrative pronoun τοῦτο, which refers "this mystery" back to the remark about a man and a woman becoming one flesh.[133] But "this mystery" is also explicated by the supplemental gloss in v. 32b, which is introduced by the emphatic

---

129 See 1:11 (κατὰ πρόθεσιν τοῦ τὰ πάντα ἐνεργοῦντος). Cf. also 2 Tim 1:9 (κατὰ ἰδίαν πρόθεσιν...τὴν δοθεῖσαν ἡμῖν ἐν Χριστῷ Ἰησοῦ πρὸ χρόνων αἰωνίων).
130 Notice how Paul again resumes the refrain of ἐν phrases: ἐν τῷ Χριστῷ Ἰησοῦ τῷ κυρίῳ ἡμῶν.
131 The only major departures from the Septuagintal traditions are the initial ἀντὶ τούτου, which is conventionally rendered ἕνεκεν τούτου, and the absence of the pronoun αὐτοῦ, which is found after both πατέρα and μητέρα.
132 In other words, in context it needs no introduction because the ἀντὶ τούτου appropriately links it with the preceding. Cf. the use of this text in 1 Cor 6:16 and the focus on the "one flesh" aspect of the quotation in Matt 19:5–6; Mark 10:7–8.
133 Admittedly, the τοῦτο could be read as pointing forward to v. 32b as it does, for instance, in 4:17, but we would then expect some sort of conjunction separating vv. 31 and 32. The contrastive (or explanatory) δέ dividing v. 32 would also be odd on such a reading.

ἐγὼ δὲ λέγω εἰς ("but I am referring to..."). [134] Therefore, by bridging the citation and its explanation, the μυστήριον is related to both, as they themselves are likewise being related to each other. The mystery is then neither *just* the one-flesh human relationship described in Gen 2:24 nor *just* the reference to Christ and the church in v. 32b, which on its own is undefined. The mystery is what emerges when the two are superimposed. Thus the mystery is that Christ and the church, like the man and woman of Gen 2, have also become a singular body.[135] Put in hermeneutical terms,[136] the mystery is what we might call the christo-ecclesial meaning that Paul is evoking with the words of Gen 2:24.[137] Whether allegorically playful or a serious demonstration of inspired spiritual exegesis (or something in between), what Paul is offering is nonetheless a new interpretation of those scriptural words.[138] But why does he label this interpretation a mystery? If μυστήριον is being used here as elsewhere in Paul, then it is not meant to signify that the unification of Christ and the church is some inscrutable or particularly mysterious proposition.[139] Rather it marks this unification as somehow previously hidden and yet now revealed. So where was it hidden and how is it revealed? The most likely answer in this context is that it was hidden in Gen 2:24, which now, when read in light of the Christ who loved and gave himself for the church

---

[134] Interestingly, the very same ἐγὼ δὲ λέγω expression is used verbatim by the Matthean Jesus in his famous antitheses (ἠκούσατε ὅτι ἐρρέθη...ἐγὼ δὲ λέγω). See Matt 5:22, 28, 32, 34, 39, 44. It appears nowhere else in the New Testament or LXX. For a similar use of λέγω εἰς, see Acts 2:25.

[135] As Heinrich Schlier, *Der Brief an die Epheser: Ein Kommentar* (Düsseldorf: Patmos, 1957), puts it, "Τὸ μυστήριον meint in V.32 nicht das Geheimnis der Schriftstelle als solcher, aber auch nicht das Geheimnis der Ehe als solcher, sondern den in der Schriftstelle angedeuteten Vorgang, der ja ein Typos auf Christus und die Ekklesia ist" (262).

[136] This is not to suggest that there is some sort of hermeneutical "method" at work here. As Best, *Ephesians*, remarks, "It is probably best not to fit what [the author of Ephesians] is saying into some given hermeneutical method or some predetermined dogmatic pattern, but simply to view him as providing a scriptural basis and theological justification for the drawing together of the husband-wife relation and the Christ-church relation.... He uses the word 'mystery' with its sense of a secret now revealed because he believes what he says is not something which he has thought up on his own but comes from God" (557).

[137] To be clear, the words of Gen 2:24 alone are not the mystery. It can be said that those words contain (or conceal) the mystery, but they can only be called a mystery insofar as they are interpreted in accordance with the Christ-church reality.

[138] As Lincoln, *Ephesians*, notes, "The emphatic ἐγώ and the particle δέ in v 32b make clear that the writer is stressing that this particular interpretation of Gen 2:24 as a reference to the profound mystery of the union between Christ and the church is his own" (382).

[139] Almost all interpreters acknowledge this. One recent exception is Frank Thielman, *Ephesians* (BECNT; Grand Rapids: Baker, 2010), who insists that the mystery here is "especially" and "unusually mysterious" (389–90).

so that she might be presented as holy to him (vv. 25–27), is newly perceived to disclose it. To be clear, this is not to suggest that an especially clever reader prior to Christ could get from Gen 2:24 the interpretation being attributed to it. It is to say that, for the author of Eph 5:32 at least, Gen 2:24 is now read as prefiguring Christ and the church because the new reality revealed by Christ has created this new hermeneutical possibility. Although this passage is generally acknowledged to be without parallel in the Pauline corpus, it is not necessarily an outright anomaly. We observed in the previous chapter how in passages like Rom 11:25–27 and 1 Cor 15:51–57 Jewish scripture can be creatively reapplied, and so reread, when appropriated in light of a newly revealed mystery. We shall also observe in Rom 16:25–26 the straightforward hermeneutical claim that the prophetic scriptures now newly disclose a previously concealed mystery.[140] As we shall discover in later chapters, this hermeneutical use of the hidden/revealed mystery schema becomes the most common use of mystery terminology in subsequent Christian authors.[141]

The specific application of μυστήριον here in Eph 5 to the unity of Christ and the church is in keeping with its earlier usage where unity, whether cosmic (as in 1:9) or interpersonal (as in 3:2–8), is the focus.[142] Thus once again in Ephesians the newly revealed mystery concerns reconciliation in Christ. As for the characterization of this mystery as "great," if the μυστήριον indeed marks something as previously hidden but now revealed, then the predicate adjective μέγα is not attributing any heightened obscurity to the mystery. It is instead emphasizing its immense importance or profundity.[143]

---

140 Cf. again 1QpHab 7:1–8, which is an excellent example of scripture concealing and then revealing important mysteries.
141 This was already noted by Brown, *The Semitic Background*, 65–66.
142 So Lincoln, *Ephesians*, observes, "Different aspects of this mystery can be highlighted according to the context..., and in chap. 3 it has a particular focus in the coming together in Christ of Jews and Gentiles in the one Church. It is most likely, then, that here in 5:32 the term has the same Christ-event in view, highlighting the aspect of it which has been central in this passage, namely the intimate union between Christ and his Church" (380).
143 Cf. the similar construction in 1 Tim 3:16 (μέγα ἐστὶν τὸ τῆς εὐσεβείας μυστήριον). As J. Armitage Robinson, *St Paul's Epistle to the Ephesians* (2d ed.; London/New York: Macmillan, 1904), explains, "The Apostle does not mean that the complete union of husband and wife as 'one flesh'...is a very mysterious thing, hard to be understood. In English we can speak of 'a great mystery' in this sense, using the epithet 'great' simply to emphasise or heighten the word to which it is attached; as in the familiar phrases 'a great inconvenience', 'a great pity'. But the corresponding word in Greek is not so used: it retains its proper meaning of magnitude or importance" (126).

3.3.4 Ephesians 6:19

The final occurrence of μυστήριον in this letter comes at its conclusion, as Paul asks for prayers that he would have boldness "to make known the mystery of the gospel" (γνωρίσαι τὸ μυστήριον τοῦ εὐαγγελίου).[144] This verse and the next are noticeably similar to Col 4:3–4, where Paul asks for prayers that God would "open a door for the word to speak the mystery of Christ." Here in Eph 6:19, however, Paul asks that a λόγος be given to him "in the opening of my mouth" (ἵνα μοι δοθῇ λόγος ἐν ἀνοίξει τοῦ στόματός μου).[145] In both passages Paul refers to his imprisonment on behalf of the mystery (ὑπὲρ οὗ πρεσβεύω ἐν ἁλύσει [Eph 6:20]; δι᾽ ὃ καὶ δέδεμαι [Col 4:3]) and to his obligation to speak about the mystery (ὡς δεῖ με λαλῆσαι [Eph 6:20; Col 4:4]). Perhaps the most notable distinctive in Eph 6:19–20 is Paul's stated desire to make known the mystery "with boldness" or "with openness" (ἐν παρρησίᾳ).[146] It should be noted that the very suggestion that the mystery of the gospel be announced with such openness – or "publicity," as παρρησία could also be translated – is a surprising proposition since in the ancient world divine μυστήρια were almost by definition supposed to be shrouded by initiates bound by an oath of silence.

The function of the genitive in the phrase τὸ μυστήριον τοῦ εὐαγγελίου is difficult to define with precision: is it subjective ("the gospel that announces the mystery"), or objective ("the mystery about the gospel"), or partitive ("the mystery which is part of the gospel"), or epexegetical ("the mystery that is the gospel")? In 3:6 the content of the mystery, which is the unity that characterizes Jews and Gentiles, is described as being realized διὰ τοῦ εὐαγγελίου. Thus, whatever their precise relationship, the terms μυστήριον and εὐαγγέλιον are intimately related, as is μυστήριον and Χριστός (cf. 3:4), and they are both appropriately applied to Paul's proclamation of the new unity of Israel and the Gentiles in the body of Christ.[147] As for this proclamation, apparently it has become the cause of

---

[144] The qualifier τοῦ εὐαγγελίου is omitted in B F G b m* et al.

[145] As Schlier, *Der Brief an die Epheser*, emphasizes, the "opened mouth" is a common biblical expression, especially for prophetic inspiration. Thus he contends, "Bei ἐν ἀνοίξει τοῦ στόματός μου denkt der Apostel also wahrscheinlich im Sinn dieser alttestamentlichen Wendungen daran, dass Gott ihm den Mund öffnen mögen zum Verkündigen des pneumatischen Wortes Gottes, und zwar so, dass er ihm dieses sein Wort geben möge" (303).

[146] Cf. the ἐν αὐτῷ παρρησιάσωμαι in v. 20. The verb παρρησιάζομαι, which is otherwise rare, is frequently applied to Paul's preaching in Acts (see 9:27, 28; 13:46; 14:3; 19:8; 26:26; cf. also 1 Thess 2:2).

[147] As Brown, *The Semitic Background*, notes, "The two phrases 'of Christ' and 'of the gospel' are only different aspects of the same basic reality, because the gospel announces the mystery, which is salvation for all in Christ" (64). Similarly, Werner Bieder, "Das Geheimnis des Christus

Paul's imprisonment. In v. 20 he describes himself, in something of an oxymoron, as "an ambassador in chains" (πρεσβεύω ἐν ἁλύσει)[148] on behalf of the mystery. The mystery discourse in 3:2–13 was also preceded by a reminder of Paul's incarceration in 3:1 and then concluded with a reference to his vicarious suffering in v. 13. The necessity of Paul's sufferings and his responsibility for mystery proclamation is similarly indicated in Col 1:24–26. Exactly why this mystery so frequently lands him in bondage and distress is never stated, but the correlation is a consistent and prominent theme in Ephesians and Colossians. Insofar as the heart of the Pauline gospel is the convicted and crucified messiah, then presumably the living witness of the apostle in chains is an opportune complement to the gospel itself.

3.4 Conclusion

Although μυστήριον is applied in Ephesians to matters as comprehensive as the destiny of the universe and to matters as specific as the benefits that the Gentiles now share with Jews, the term still orbits in every instance around the theme of unification in Christ. This newly revealed mystery of unification in Christ is presented in the letter as a previously hidden divine plan that has been recently disclosed to world, although to and through Paul in particular. Paul himself therefore now serves as a specially chosen administrator of this mystery, having been commissioned by God with the task of proclaiming the surpassing wealth of this mystery to the world, and to the Gentiles in particular. The similarities with Colossians are thus quite apparent.

While incongruities between Ephesians and Colossians are for the most part rare, the distinctive emphases in Ephesians are once again worth pointing out in summary form. To begin with, the comprehensive mystery that comes at the outset of Ephesians in 1:9–10 is probably the most obvious development in the letter. There is certainly no other mystery in the Pauline corpus that is so universal in scope. But such a development could be viewed as an elaboration of what is already implied in Col 1:15–20. As for the lengthy Eph 3 discourse, the most notable variations with Colossians are (1) the expansion of special revelation be-

---

nach dem Epheserbrief," *Theologische Zeitschrift* 11 (1955): 329–43, suggests that all three genitive constructions with μυστήριον – "of God's will" (1:9), "of Christ" (3:4), and "of the gospel" (6:19) – when read together, present a helpful summary of the content of the mystery: "Es geht bei diesem Geheimnis, allgemein gesagt, um den göttlichen Willen, der auf Christus bezogen ist und im Evangelium verkündigt wird" (330).

148 Cf. the use of πρεσβεύω in 2 Cor 5:20.

yond Paul to other apostles and prophets (v. 5); (2) the precise details of the mystery described in v. 6 and, in particular, the stress on unity between Jews and Gentiles (as opposed to Gentile inclusion alone, which is what is presented in Colossians);[149] (3) the addition of the church as an agent involved in making the mystery known (v. 10); and (4) the imperative to make the mystery known not only to humans but also to "the rulers and authorities in the heavenly places" (v. 10). As for elsewhere in the letter, while the usage in 5:31–32 is unique insofar as it specifically correlates μυστήριον with the interpretation of scripture, it is not without some precedent in the Pauline corpus, and the usage in 6:19–20 appears to be very similar to the statement in Col 4:3–4.

Especially noteworthy are the ways in which Ephesians, like Colossians, presents an account of the newly revealed mystery that differs from what is found in the undisputed Paulines, particularly 1 Cor 2. Most significant is the way in which the mystery schema in Ephesians, as in Colossians, takes up the language of hiddenness from 1 Cor 2:7 (again using the perfect passive participle of ἀποκρύτω) but arranges the hidden/revealed binary in an explicitly temporal fashion. Thus in Eph 3:5 the mystery is described as unknown "in other generations" but revealed "now." Then in 3:9 "the administration of the mystery" is described as "having been hidden from the ages" but made known "now" so that through it the rulers and authorities in the heavenly places might come to comprehend "the manifold wisdom of God." Knowledge of the mystery in Ephesians is, as in Colossians, thoroughly democratized. Paul's objective is to make the mystery known to "all people," even to the rulers and authorities in heavenly places. Therefore, whereas in 1 Cor 2 the wisdom of God spoken "in a mystery" is reserved for specific groups of people (τέλειοι) and, in addition, is purposefully concealed from "the rulers of *this age*," in Eph 3 Paul's desire is to announce the mystery to all people (v. 9) and to make the wisdom of God associated with it known *especially* to "the rulers and authorities in the heavenly places" (v. 10). In other words, whereas in 1 Cor 2 God's mystery is *restricted to some people* and God's wisdom is *hidden from ἄρχοντες*, in Eph 3 God's mystery is *envisioned*

---

149 Bockmuehl, *Revelation and Mystery*, emphasizes this point: "Here in Eph 3:6 the central mystery of Christ is now the fact 'that the Gentiles are fellow heirs, and fellow members of the body, and fellow partakers of the promise in Christ Jesus through the gospel'. This of course is by no means to deny that the salvation of both Gentiles and Jews was a central feature of Paul's gospel from the beginning; but simply to point out that it seems here to have become a fully acceptable *definition* of the 'mystery of Christ'. Nevertheless, it would not be correct to consider that this notion of the incorporation of the Gentiles is an innovation.... We are merely dealing with a change in emphasis, seconded by a concomitant shift...in the presentation of the gospel, viz. from a christological (Gal 1:12, 15) to an ecclesiological focus" (202).

for all people and God's wisdom is *intended for ἄρχοντες*. While these seeming discrepancies need not necessarily be flattened to outright contradictions, they are nonetheless intriguing modifications and, I maintain, further evidence of the distinct deuteropauline codification of a Pauline mystery discourse.

As for the implications of this discourse, we shall continue to chart its effects in the next chapter. It is perhaps most important now simply to emphasize again the particular historical consciousness that undergirds it. Just as the mystery schema entails a specific understanding of the workings and designs of revelation, it entails equally a specific understanding of the workings and designs of history. By dividing history into adjacent eras – the previous era of hiddenness and the current era of disclosure – the deuteropauline mystery schema situates the advent of Christ as the determinative event upon which these two eras hinge and as the determinative revelation that reconfigures how reality in both eras is perceived (and re-perceived). As this chapter has demonstrated, the consequences of this new historical consciousness are varied and profound, ranging from the theological (Col 1:25–27) through to the eschatological (Eph 1:9–10), the ecclesial (Eph 3:5–10), and the hermeneutical (Eph 5:31–32). Ensuing appropriations and adaptations of this apocalyptic historical consciousness will be the subject of the remainder of this study.

4 Μυστήριον and the Deuteropauline Mystery Schema of Revelation.
Part 2: The Pastoral Epistles and the Romans 16:25–27 Doxology

4.1 Introduction

If Ephesians and Colossians represent the original codification of the historically structured Pauline mystery discourse, then the Pastoral Epistles and the Rom 16:25–27 doxology demonstrate the early success of this apocalyptic perception of history within Pauline circles (presuming their later, non-Pauline status, that is).¹ This is not to suggest these documents mechanically reproduce what is found in Ephesians and Colossians. There are in fact significant modifications in these texts, both semantic and thematic, but these variances likely reflect the absorption of the discourse by different authors in different circumstances, and so in no way do they depart from the fundamental discursive pattern established in the previous chapter: the apocalyptic schema in which the previously hidden or unknown mystery is now, in the person and proclamation of Christ, disclosed to the world, and particularly to the Gentiles. Much more than just a patterned discourse or mode of reasoning, however, we shall continue to observe how the deuteropauline mystery discourse gives expression to a particular and totalizing historical understanding, and one that engenders some of the most basic propositions in subsequent Christian theology – the inclusion of the Gentiles in the eternal designs of God merely the first among them.

4.2 Romans 16:25–27

I treat this passage first because it can be viewed as something of a "middle term" between the mystery schemas in Ephesians and Colossians and then the abbreviated versions in the Pastorals.² While the Rom 16 doxology adheres to

---

1 Along with the majority of scholars, I consider the Pastorals to be post-Pauline compositions and, as I shall discuss in more detail below, I also consider the Rom 16 concluding doxology to be a later addendum to early forms of the letter.
2 Scholarly judgments about the authenticity of the doxology are frequently predetermined by prior decisions regarding the authenticity of the disputed letters. Thus the doxology is often guilty or innocent by association. This is why one finds, on the one hand, C.K. Barrett, *A Commentary*

the usual pattern in its combination of μυστήριον with a description of previous concealment, the passive form of φανερόω, and the temporal marker νῦν, other terminology in these verses also reappears in the Pastorals, and only there in the Pauline corpus. As J.K. Elliot, in his meticulous word-by-word analysis of the doxology, concludes, "Much of the doxology occurs elsewhere in the Pastoral Epistles...and may well have originated at a similar date to those books, possibly at a time when Paul's preaching was having a revival and his extant writings were being gathered together and imitated."[3] Before considering such matters in more detail, the first issue to discuss is the integrity and provenance of these verses.[4]

The textual history of this so-called "wandering doxology" is notoriously tortuous, and the majority of critics now view it as a later addition.[5] It sometimes appears after 14:23 (L Ψ and sometimes in Origen et al.), once after 15:33 (P46), sometimes after both 14:23 and 16:23 (A P et al.), sometimes after 16:23 alone (P61 ℵ B C D et al.; in vg and Old Latin it comes after 16:24), and sometimes nowhere at all (F G exemplar for D et al.).[6] The circuitous syntax and stylistic similarities with the supposed deuteropauline letters – the Pastorals in particular – is perhaps indicative of a later date of composition, if not also a common author.[7] Tied to the textual integrity of 16:25–27 is that of ch. 16 as a whole and, indeed, the entire letter, which is extant in some fourteen text forms.[8] The most plausible genealogical reconstruction of these versions is that of Peter Lampe, who contends that 16:25–27 was appended as a new ending

---

on the Epistle to the Romans (HNTC; New York: Harper & Brothers, 1957), claiming that the doxology is a "not very convincing imitation of Paul's style" and in content "not distinctively Pauline" (286), and then, on the other hand, Walter Schmithals, Der Römerbrief: Ein Kommentar (Gütersloh: Gütersloher Verlagshaus Gerd Mohn, 1988), plainly declaring, "Mit Sicherheit unpaulinisch ist kaum etwas in der Doxologie" (568).
3 J.K. Elliott, "The Language and Style of the Concluding Doxology of the Epistle to the Romans," ZNW 72 (1981): 124–30, 129.
4 Literature on the textual history of these verses and, in fact, the whole of Rom 16 is massive. A detailed inventory need not be reproduced here. Perhaps the best place to begin, however, is Robert Jewett, Romans (Hermeneia; Minneapolis: Fortress Press, 2007), 4–9, 997–1005.
5 Raymond F. Collins, "The Case of a Wandering Doxology: Rom 16,25–27," in New Testament Textual Criticism and Exegesis: Festschrift J. Delobel (ed. A Denaux; BETL 161 Leuven: Leuven University Press, 2002), 293–303.
6 It is also absent in early Latin versions. Thus Tertullian does not appear to know it, and it is absent in Priscillian of Avila's Canons on the Letters of Paul (mid-fourth century) as well.
7 It is the lengthiest doxology in the New Testament and most similar to Jude 24–25.
8 Immensely valuable for these matters is Harry Gamble, The Textual History of the Letter to the Romans: A Study in Textual and Literary Criticism (SD 42; Grand Rapids: Eerdmans, 1977).

to Romans after Marcion's supposed deletion of 15:1–16:24,[9] which belonged to the *Urtext*.[10] If correct, this suggests that the doxology was added to Romans sometime in the second century, though it could have been composed earlier, perhaps independently of Romans, or even evolved through stages of redaction.[11] It should be noted that critics who defend its originality often appeal to its fittingness as a conclusion to Romans. As Brevard Childs notices, "Romans closes with a doxology which has been patterned after the praescript and which serves to encompass the entire book within the same consistently christological context."[12] Such an observation, while likely correct, hardly amounts to an argument in text-critical terms. There is no reason why a subsequent redactor should be precluded from fabricating a conclusion that could appear every bit as fitting as an original author. In the end, therefore, while it is possible the doxology is original and unrecoverable accidents of history have accounted for its erratic textual positioning, this seems unlikely. More probable is that it is a later addition and – whether it was composed independently of Romans, specifically for Romans, or redacted in multiple stages – that it was treated by subsequent editors of Romans as an apt conclusion for numerous forms of the letter. It also seems reasonable to assume that its marked similarities with the disputed letters, particularly the Pastorals, suggest that it stems from similar circles, if not the same

---

9 The actual effects of Marcion's editorial activity at this juncture are not as certain as is sometimes supposed. According to Origen's *Commentary on Romans*, it does not appear that Marcion deleted the final two chapters of Romans in their entirety but rather that he omitted the Rom 16 doxology in whole (*penitus abstulit*) and then heavily redacted (*desecuit*) the material from 14:23 to the end of the letter (see *Comm. Rom.* 10.43.2). It should be noted that Origen would actually have no way of knowing whether Marcion himself deleted the doxology or whether his *Vorlage* simply lacked it.

10 Peter Lampe, "Zur Textgeschichte des Römerbriefes," *NovT* 27 (1985): 273–77. On this point Lampe is in agreement with the earlier reconstruction of Kurt Aland, "Der Schluss und die ursprüngliche Gestalt des Römerbriefes," in *Neutestamentliche Entwürfe* (TB 63; Munich: Kaiser, 1979), 284–301, esp. 287–90. Cf. also David Trobisch, *Die Entstehung der Paulusbriefsammlung: Studien zu den Anfängen christlicher Publizistik* (NTOA 10; Göttingen: Vandenhoeck & Ruprecht, 1989), 75–79. One major advantage of this proposal is that it accounts for the varying locations of the doxology, particularly those that have it after 14:23.

11 There have been several hypotheses about the possible redactional development of the doxology, all of which are prompted by its awkward style and syntax. Jewett, *Romans*, 1002–05, has most recently proposed a three stage editorial process, wherein scribes gradually revised a Hellenistic Jewish doxology into a suitable, post-Marcionite Christian ending for the letter. Jewett's reconstruction is tidy in theory but, in my view, unduly speculative.

12 Brevard Childs, *The New Testament as Canon: An Introduction* (Philadelphia: Fortress Press, 1984), 254.

author or communal context.¹³ These issues aside, what matters is that the doxology exists and that its importance in Paul's literary legacy is highlighted by its inclusion in most extant versions of Romans.

Sorting out the dynamic of revelation in this passage first involves sorting out the convoluted syntax, especially the syntactical arrangement of the three passive participles: σεσιγημένου, φανερωθέντος, and γνωρισθέντος. The most economical ordering of these verbals (and the one most commentators and translations adopt) regards the τε in v. 26 as separating διά γραφῶν προφητικῶν from the adjacent φανερωθέντος and so coordinating "through the prophetic scriptures" with the concluding γνωρισθέντος:

> ...κατὰ ἀποκάλυψιν μυστηρίου
> **χρόνοις αἰωνίοις σεσιγημένου**
> **φανερωθέντος δὲ νῦν**
> **διά τε γραφῶν προφητικῶν**
> κατ' ἐπιταγὴν τοῦ αἰωνίου θεοῦ
> εἰς ὑπακοὴν πίστεως
> εἰς πάντα τὰ ἔθνη
> **γνωρισθέντος.**
>
> ...according to the revelation of the mystery that has been kept silent for eternal ages but now has been disclosed, and through the prophetic writings made known, according to the command of the eternal God for the obedience of faith for all the Gentiles.

Read this way, the current manifestation of the mystery is being contrasted with the previous epochs of silence, and the "being made known through the prophetic scriptures" then further specifies exactly how (or where) the mystery is now disclosed.

The doxology opens by acclaiming God's power "to strengthen"¹⁴ believers in accordance with Paul's gospel (κατὰ τὸ εὐαγγέλιόν μου) and "the proclamation of Jesus Christ" (τὸ κήρυγμα Ἰησοῦ Χριστου).¹⁵ This gospel and its proclamation are then further defined as being "according to the revelation of the mystery." This second κατά phrase is perhaps modeled on Eph 3:3 (κατὰ ἀποκάλυψιν ἐγνωρίσθη μοι τὸ μυστήριον), where the revelation is specific to

---

13 Cf. also the conclusions of Collins, "Wandering Doxology," 302–03.
14 Cf. 1:11.
15 Most commentators read the genitive here as objective: "the proclamation *about* Jesus Christ." As Ulrich Wilckens, *Der Brief an die Römer (Röm 12–16)* (EKK VI/3; Zürich/Neukirchen-Vluyn: Benziger/Neukirchener, 1989), 148, notes, the καί connecting these phrases can also be read as an *explicativum* ("according to my gospel *which is* the proclamation of Jesus Christ").

Paul. In 16:25 there is no such limitation,[16] and the ἀποκάλυψις appears instead to be generally accessible to all readers of the prophetic scriptures. Any additional information about this ἀποκάλυψις remains unclear: does it occur with or without pneumatic aid? privately or communally? in a singular moment or through a process of scriptural exposition – perhaps the exposition of a uniquely inspired exegete?[17] These questions remain unanswerable, but more can be said about the μυστήριον itself given its coordination with the kerygma of Christ and Paul's gospel. The association of the revealed mystery with τὸ εὐαγγέλιον is present in Eph 3:6 and especially 6:19 (cf. 2 Tim 1:10), and the association of new revelation with κήρυγμα is found in Titus 1:3. The explicit association of the mystery with Christ is, of course, common in the Ephesians and Colossians. Therefore, in terms of its general content, the mystery in Rom 16:25 is squarely in line with the larger deuteropauline tradition.

The passage next describes the former concealment of the mystery: "having been kept silent for eternal ages." The use of σεσιγημενός for concealment, as opposed to ἀποκεκρυμμένος,[18] is unique in the Pauline corpus. As we shall see in the next chapter, similar images of inaudibility recur in Ign. *Eph.* 19.1 with the noun ἡσυχία ("three mysteries of a cry which were accomplished ἐν ἡσυχίᾳ θεοῦ") and then again in Ign. *Magn.* 8.2, where Christ is lauded as "a word proceeding from silence" (λόγος ἀπὸ σιγῆς προελθών). The passive σεσιγημένου presumably indicates that God is responsible for this concealment.[19] While it is not stated from whom the mystery has been concealed, or exactly why, there is nothing to indicate that anything less than absolute concealment is in view, which would entail that no human at any time prior to its divine man-

---

[16] It should be noted, however, that κατὰ ἀποκάλυψιν μυστηρίου is paralleled with κατὰ τὸ εὐαγγέλιόν μου, and so the gospel proclamation specific to Paul.

[17] Cf. the Teacher of Righteousness in 1QpHab 7:1–8. Perhaps also a passage like Luke 24:44–48 provides a comparative model.

[18] I see no reason to presume any significant shift in meaning in this variance. Thus C.E.B. Cranfield, *A Critical and Exegetical Commentary on the Epistle to the Romans* (ICC; Edinburgh: T&T Clark, 1979), concludes, "It is pedantic to try to make a significant distinction between a secret which is ἀποκεκρυμένον and one that is σεσιγημένον.... σιγᾶν in this connexion is surely no more than an equivalent of a negative of γνωρίζειν, λαλεῖν, λέγειν, or καταγγέλειν...and the distinction between ἀποκεκρυμένον and σεσιγημένον is really only a matter of whether the mystery is thought of in terms of seeing or in terms of hearing" (2:810 n. 3).

[19] As Wilkens, *Der Brief an die Römer*, discerns, "σεσιγημένου is passivum divinum wie entsprechend φανερωθέντος" (149). Interesting, as Jewett, *Romans*, notes, "Apart from this verse, the perfect participle σεσιγημέν- is unattested before the second century C.E., but Irenaeus *Adv. haer.* 1.1.1.43 refers to the twelve aeons that are οἱ σεσιγημένοι καὶ μὴ γινωσκόμενοι ('kept secret and unknown')" (1007 n. 75).

ifestation could have perceived this mystery.[20] As for the timing of the concealment (χρόνοις αἰωνίοις),[21] the explicitly diachronic delineation is, as we have seen time and again, typical of the deuteropauline schema, and the similar πρὸ χρόνων αἰωνίων formulation in 2 Tim 1:9 and Titus 1:2 is another correspondence drawing the Romans doxology and the Pastorals together.

In contrastive juxtaposition with the statement of prior concealment is the statement of present revelation: φανερωθέντος δὲ νῦν. We have already examined the nearly identical expressions in Col 1:26 (νῦν δὲ ἐφανερώθη) and the other instances of νῦν in relation to μυστήριον and verbs for disclosure (Eph 3:5, 10).[22] The phrase φανερωθεῖσαν δὲ νῦν in 2 Tim 1:10 is obviously relevant as well. What is clear is that this is all formulaic language of the deuteropauline schema. Moreover, once again the historical hinge upon which the hidden/revealed dynamic pivots must be the advent of Christ and the ongoing proclamation of this event. Unlike Col 1 and Eph 3, however, there is no indication as to whom the manifestation occurs, but since it is oriented toward the obedience of Gentiles, they are presumably again the primary audience.

The doxology next clarifies the means by which the manifestation of the mystery occurs: διά τε γραφῶν προφητικῶν…γνωρισθέντος. While the verb γνωρίζω is familiar from other mystery passages (Eph 1:9; 3:3, 5, 10; 6:19; Col 1:27), there is no other text in the Pauline corpus where the revelation of a divine mystery is so explicitly characterized as a hermeneutical event. The interpretive gloss in Eph 5:32 comes close, but Rom 16:26 is unique in that the texts of scripture themselves explicitly function as the medium of revelation. The question thus becomes: how do Israel's scriptures, as documents produced during the era of silence, now make known the new mystery of Christ? Stated differently: how is it that Israel's scriptures appear to have concealed the very thing they now reveal? There have been occassional attempts by modern scholars to evade this question by submiting that since this doxology is probably a post-Pauline fabrication the "prophetic scriptures" here must be Christian scriptures, Paul's own letters perhaps principal among them (cf. 2 Peter 3:16). Among the numerous problems with this proposal is the fact that it is almost impossible in the context of Romans. When read as the conclusion to the letter, the prophets in question must be the same prophets routinely cited throughout it. Comparison with the prescript of the letter (1:1–2) strengthens this claim since there Paul explicitly

---

[20] The only potential exception would be the prophets, whose scriptures now make the mystery known.
[21] The temporal dative here addresses the question of "how long?" (or duration of time) as opposed to the question "when?" (or point in time). Cf. BDF §201.
[22] Cf. also Rom 3:21 (νυνὶ δὲ χωρὶς νόμου δικαιοσύνη θεοῦ πεφανέρωται).

equates "the gospel of God" with what was "promised beforehand through God's prophets in holy scriptures (διὰ τῶν προφητῶν αὐτοῦ ἐν γραφαῖς ἁγίαις)." Therefore, even if the doxology, or portions of it, originated elsewhere and at some point in its editorial odyssey referred to prophetic Christian writings, for the redactors who affixed it to Romans, as for the readers of Romans, διὰ γραφῶν προφητικῶν must, like διὰ τῶν προφητῶν in 1:2, be Israel's scriptures. Thus the question still stands: how do Israel's scriptures now make known the mystery they previously concealed?

In answering this question it is important to point out first that the mystery is not made known *exclusively* through the prophetic scriptures. It is also apparently made manifest in Paul's gospel and the proclamation of Christ. Hence the scriptures are simply here being highlighted as an additional locus of disclosure. Furthermore, since the mystery is not the scriptures themselves but rather the gospel proclamation of Christ, it is probably the case that, as in other Pauline mystery passages (most notably Rom 11:25–26), the new manifestation of Christ activates latent christological meanings in the antecedent revelation of the prophetic scriptures. Thus, through a hermeneutical transformation, scripture *becomes* newly and retrospectively prophetic, witnessing openly to the gospel it formerly concealed.[23] The affirmation that Israel's scriptures make known the gospel of Christ is therefore contingent on the prior revelation of Christ himself.[24] This does not diminish the revelatory function of the scriptures; it simply means that the Christ event is what is hermeneutically determinative, restructuring the perception of reality on either side of its occurrence and so enabling the reader to discern Christian realities that previously were not even thinkable.[25] As we shall see in the subsequent chapters, the use of mystery to designate newly revealed christological meanings in scripture becomes the most widespread use of mystery terminology in the early church. Whether a primary source for such developments or a reflection of them, the importance of Rom 16:26 for early Christian hermeneutics has not been sufficiently appreciated.

As for the remainder of the doxology, the only matter in need of comment is the reference to the Gentiles's faith. The full expression εἰς ὑπακοὴν πίστεως εἰς πάντα τὰ ἔθνη is nearly identical to Rom 1:5 (εἰς ὑπακοὴν πίστεως ἐν πᾶσιν τοῖς

---

23 Again, the idea that scripture can conceal and then reveal particular meanings is not without precedent. See esp. 1QpHab 7:1–8.

24 Perhaps something similar is being expressed in Rom 3:21.

25 Cf. Simon Légasse, *L'Épître de Paul aux Romains* (LD 10; Paris: Cerf, 2002), who also notes that what we observe here is "le thème d'une révélation accordée grâce à une lecture correcte (et inspirée) de l'Écriture. Un theme apocalyptique est ainsi repris d'après lequel la revelation eschatologique donne la clé des prophéties" (977).

ἔθνεσιν), which lends additional support to the possibility that the doxology was composed specifically as an ending for Romans.²⁶ The most significant aspect of this mention of the Gentiles is simply their inclusion in the mystery schema. The prominent role of the Gentiles in relation to God's previously concealed but presently revealed mystery is one of the most important features that binds the deuteropauline mystery passages together and, at the same time, sets them apart from the data in the undisputed letters. If the disputed letters are indeed not products of Paul and instead are the work of some later tradent of the Pauline legacy, then it would appear that the "once hidden/now revealed" mystery schema became something of a codified discourse with which later Paulinists justified Paul's legacy as God's apostle to the Gentiles while further legitimizing non-Torah observant Gentiles' special status as God's eternally elect people. The extent to which Paul's legacy and Gentile inclusion were at stake for the Christians among which the disputed letters originated and first circulated can only be a matter of speculation. The implication of the mystery discourse is, however, clear: to question Paul's career as the apostle to the Gentiles and the Gentiles *qua* Gentiles as blessed by God is to question divine revelation.

4.3 The Pastoral Epistles

As Nils Dahl noted some time ago, aspects of what he calls the Pauline *Revelations-Schema* are present in the Pastorals but in noticeably different and truncated forms.²⁷ While Dahl only treated 2 Tim 1:9–11 and Titus 1:2–3, where μυστήριον does not in fact appear, the mystery texts in 1 Tim 3:9 and 3:16 should be considered as well.

---

26 On the "recapitulating function" of Pauline letter closings, see Jeffery A.D. Weima's *Neglected Endings: The Significance of the Pauline Letter Closings* (JSNTSup 101; Sheffield: JSOT Press, 1994).
27 Nils Alstrup Dahl, "Formgeschichtliche Beobachtungen zur Christusverkündigung in der Gemeindepredigt," in *Neutestamentliche Studien für Rudolf Bultmann* (Berlin: Alfred Töpelmann, 1957): 3–9. Dahl actually classified these as a second category in which "[d]as Schema wird frei variiert" (5).

4.3.1 1 Timothy

The word μυστήριον occurs only twice in the Pastorals, both of which are in 1 Timothy (3:9, 16).[28] These two instances are in close proximity to one another and are generally regarded as more or less synonymous noun phrases. In 3:9 Paul adds to the qualifications of deacons that they "hold to the mystery of the faith" (ἔχοντας τὸ μυστήριον τῆς πίστεως) with a pure conscience.[29] The "faith" in this instance is usually taken to refer to basic confessions of Christian doctrine or, more generally, to a whole way of life (cf. 1:2; 4:1, 6; 5:8; 6:10, 21), which is to be contrasted with the various theological and ethical betrayals of "the faith" detailed at length in this letter. Comparison with 3:16 suggests that something like "creedal orthodoxy" (to speak anachronistically) is likely in view. But "the mystery of the faith" – like "the mystery of devotion" – is probably referring more specifically to the historical facts of Christ's manifestation in the world, as outlined in 3:16b. Therefore, the requirement that deacons not waver from "the mystery of the faith" is a requirement that they continue to confess the church's foundational story, namely, the story of Christ's incarnation, earthly sojourn, and ascension.[30] Presumably such articles of the faith are termed a mystery because they, along with Christ himself, are realities newly revealed to the world.

Although the exact expression τὸ μυστήριον τῆς πίστεως is unique in the Pauline corpus, it is perhaps anticipated by a text like Eph 6:19 (τὸ μυστήριον τοῦ εὐαγγελίου) or even 1 Cor 2:1, 7, where μυστήριον appears to be a shorthand expression for the saving power of the cross and so the historical fact of Christ's existence. Also relevant is 1 Cor 4:1–2, where Paul refers to himself and Apollos as "administrators of the mysteries of God" and then mentions the importance of an administrator's enduring fidelity, much like the need for a deacons' enduring fidelity.[31] The use of the singular μυστήριον in 1 Timothy becomes all the more interesting in light of the plural in 1 Cor 4 and likely reflects the strict use of the singular in the deuteropauline tradition. It may also reflect the tendency in the Pastoral Epistles to articulate Christian dogma as a singular body of tradition – ἡ παραθήκη as it is termed in 6:20 – from which others have departed.

---

[28] Again, these two passages were not considered by Dahl, "Formgeschichtliche Beobachtungen," but 3:16 in particular has much to contribute to his proposed *Revelations-Schema*.
[29] Cf. 1:19 (ἔχων πίστιν καὶ ἀγαθὴν συνείδησιν).
[30] The genitive τῆς πίστεως should probably be read as appositional; hence the whole phrase could be glossed along the lines of "the mystery that is expressed in the faith."
[31] It is also worth pointing out that Paul defines himself as a διάκονος when referring to the μυστήριον revealed to him in Eph 3:3–9 and Col 1:23–26.

More can be said about the expression μέγα ἐστὶν τὸ τῆς εὐσεβείας μυστήριον in 3:16 (much of which can also be applied to 3:9)[32] because of the following hymnic formulation that further defines it.[33] I treat this formulation as a composition in six lines:[34]

1. ὃς ἐφανερώθη ἐν σαρκί,
2. ἐδικαιώθη ἐν πνεύματι,
3. ὤφθη ἀγγέλοις,
4. ἐκηρύχθη ἐν ἔθνεσιν,
5. ἐπιστεύθη ἐν κόσμῳ,
6. ἀνελήμφθη ἐν δόξῃ.

1. Who was manifested in the flesh,
2. was vindicated by the Spirit,
3. was seen by angels,
4. was preached among the Gentiles
5. was believed in the world,
6. was taken up in glory.

Secondary literature on this verse is sizable—partly because of the preoccupation in New Testament scholarship with identifying preformulated hymnic material, and partly because it is often considered to be "the rhetorical and christological highpoint of the letter"[35] – but not every subject of scholarly interest needs to be addressed here.

The initial mystery exclamation is reminiscent of Eph 5:32, and here, as there, the predicate adjective μέγα does not signal great *mysteriousness* but the great *significance* of the mystery itself. The mystery is qualified as "the mystery τῆς εὐσεβείας." The word εὐσεβεία is rare in Jewish literature – though it appears several dozen times in 4 Maccabees – and also in the New Testament. Eight of the fifteen New Testament occurrences are, however, in 1 Timothy, and so it constitutes a major theme of the letter. The virtue of εὐσεβεία (and

---

[32] As I. Howard Marshall, *A Critical and Exegetical Commentary on the Pastoral Epistles* (ICC; Edinburgh: T&T Clark, 1999), notes, "The language [of 3:16] picks up the thought adumbrated in v. 9, where church leaders are to be people who hold the mystery of the faith with a clear conscience. In effect, the nature of this mystery is now delineated, and the shift from τῆς πίστεως to τῆς εὐσεβείας need not imply that a different mystery with a different content is in mind" (523).
[33] Cf. *Diogn.* 4.6 (τὸ δὲ τῆς ἰδίας αὐτῶν θεοσεβείας μυστήριον).
[34] Cf. *Diogn.* 11.2–3, which is almost certainly dependent on this passage.
[35] So Philip H. Towner, *The Letters to Timothy and Titus* (NICNT; Grand Rapids: Eerdmans, 2006), 276.

of *pietas*, the Latin equivalent) was highly esteemed in Hellenistic culture.[36] The translation "devotion" – which I view as the least worst option – hardly captures its comprehensive nature. A life of εὐσεβεία envisions a total way of being – a "Lebensführung"[37] as Angela Standhartinger puts it – and hence it "is characterized by both devotion to the deity and by familial and imperial duty."[38] That Paul wishes those under Timothy's care to embody a form of life (ἀναστρέφεσθαι)[39] that corresponds with the truth (ἡ ἀλήθεια) and is thus fitting for the "household of God" (ἐν οἴκῳ θεοῦ) is clearly indicated in 3:14–15. Hence the "mystery of devotion" outlined in 3:16b is, we must presume, what is to be regarded as the founding story of the new Christian way of life. As for parallel expressions, besides the near synonym in 3:9, a rarely considered but suggestive analogue is "the mystery of lawlessness" (τὸ μυστήριον τῆς ἀνομίας) in 2 Thess 2:7. In both of these passages μυστήριον is modified by an abstract quality (ἀνομία or εὐσεβεία); in both passages the mystery is associated with a person of eschatological note (the man of lawlessness or Christ); and in both passages the mystery is linked to that person's revelation to the world (ἀποκαλυφθήσεται or ἐφανερώθη). One could, therefore, read the full account of "the mystery of devotion" in 1 Tim 3:16 as the christological obverse of the "mystery of lawlessness" in 2 Thess 2:3–12.

As for the use of mystery here, L. Ann Jervis has presented an intriguing case for understanding μυστήριον in this verse in comparison with ἱεροὶ λόγοι traditions from mystery cults.[40] She explains:

> In the ancient Mediterranean world the word μυστήριον had several meanings, one of which was to refer to the divine drama forming the basis of Hellenistic mystery religions. The ceremonies of the mystery religions included recitations and reminders of the foundational mystic drama. 'Mystery,' then, may refer to the story which forms the basis for a cer-

---

36 See esp. Angela Standhartinger, "*Eusebeia* in den Pastoralbriefen: Ein Beitrag zum Einfluss römischen Denkens auf das entstehende Christentum," *NovT* 48 (2006): 51–82; Mary R. D'Angelo, "Εὐσέβεια: Roman Imperial Family Values and the Sexual Politics of 4 Maccabees and the Pastorals," *BibInt* 11 (2003): 139–65.
37 Standhartinger, "*Eusebeia* in den Pastoralbriefen," 52.
38 D'Angleo, "Εὐσέβεια: Roman Imperial Family Values and the Sexual Politics," 162.
39 Cf. 2 Cor 1:12; Eph 2:3. As Luke Timothy Johnson, *The First and Second Letters to Timothy: A New Translation with Introduction and Commentary* (AB 35 A; New York: Doubleday, 2001), emphasizes, the verb ἀναστρέφω "is used in moral discourse not simply for 'behavior' in the narrow sense, but for 'manner of life' in accord with certain guiding principles" (231).
40 For more on these traditions, see Albert Henrichs, "*HIEROI LOGOI* and *HIERAI BIBLOI*: The (Un)Written Margins of the Sacred in Ancient Greece," *HSCP* 101 (2003): 207–66. See also Walter Burkert, *Ancient Mystery Cults* (Cambridge: Harvard University Press, 1987), 69–78. Cf. the ἱερὰ γράμματα in 2 Tim 3:15, which is almost certainly a reference to Jewish scripture.

tain worldview and religious understanding. It is this sense which is most likely conveyed by the word 'mystery' in 1 Tim 3:16. As the *Homeric Hymn to Demeter* was fundamental to the Eleusinian cult, so the readers of 1 Timothy have a foundational story, a mystery. This is the story of Jesus Christ which the author outlines in 3:16.[41]

As provocative as this proposal is – and while evocations of mystery associations are always possible when a term like μυστήριον is in use – we should exercise care in making too much of this possibility in the context of 1 Tim 3. One major problem is the fact that mystery cults did not by and large produce individuals or communities that were characterized by a new or distinctive εὐσεβεία, which is clearly what is being expected in 3:14–16. As Helmut Koester explains:

> Mysteries also possess sacred stories (ἱεροὶ λόγοι) that tell the fate of the deity, often the god's suffering and death. This sort of story establishes a new relationship with the deity and intimacy with the fate of the gods, thus taking the initiate into personal experiences of the realm beyond the tangible reality of mortal life and its social context.... What mysteries normally do not accomplish, however, is the creation of a new community that is committed to alternative moral, social, and political values.[42]

The "normally" in the above quotation is significant because there are important exceptions. One such exception that is illuminating for 1 Tim 3:16 is reported by Diodorus Siculus (c.a. 60–30 B.C.E.) and concerns the mysteries of the Kabeiroi on the island of Samothrace (cf. Acts 16:11):

> The fame has travelled wide of how these gods appear (ἡ τούτων τῶν θεῶν ἐπιφάνεια) to humans and bring unexpected aid to those initiates of theirs who call upon them in the midst of perils. The claim is also made those who have taken part in the mysteries (τοὺς τῶν μυστηρίων κοινωνήσαντας) become more pious (εὐσεβεστέρους) and more just (δικαιοτέρους) and better in every respect than they were before.[43]

---

41 L. Ann Jervis, "Paul the Poet in First Timothy 1:11–17; 2:3b–7; 3:14–16," *CBQ* 61 (1999): 695–712, 707. As far as I am aware, Jervis is the first scholar to suggest this.
42 Helmut Koester, *History, Culture, and Religion of the Hellenistic Age* (2d ed.; New York/Berlin: de Gruyter, 1995), 170. Similarly, Jervis refers to Burkert, *Ancient Mystery Cults*, who explains that "despite a vocabulary often applied to ancient mysteries without much circumspection, the existence of mystery communities, *Mysteriengemeinden*, cannot be taken for granted. There are important differences among the various mysteries in regard to social organization and coherence, but none of them approaches the Christian model of a church, *ekklesia*" (30–31).
43 Diodorus Siculus, *The Library of History*, 5.49.6. My translation adapts that of C.H. Oldfather, LCL.

While Diodorus appears to present the piety instigated by these mysteries as an atypical case, the correspondence of divine epiphany (ἐπιφάνεια),⁴⁴ mysteries (μυστήρια), and improved devotion (εὐσεβέστερος) make for a fascinating comparison with τὸ τῆς εὐσεβείας μυστήριον in 3:16 and certainly renders Jervis' proposal all the more suggestive.⁴⁵

Paul opens his statement in 3:16 with the adverb ὁμολογουμένως,⁴⁶ which evokes mutual agreement – as in, "most certainly we all confess this." The "mystery of devotion" is then defined in the metrical account of Christ's appearance on earth (ἐφανερώθη) and final return to heaven (ἀνελήμφθη). There have been numerous proposals concerning the structure of these lines and nearly as many hypotheses concerning their classification (a hymn, a poem, a creed, a spontaneous construction?).⁴⁷ While decisions on organization and genre certainly affect how they are eventually interpreted, particularly in the case of lines two and three, I am mostly concerned with lines one, four, and six, which are relatively uncontroversial.

Line one provides the first detail about the mystery: ὃς ἐφανερώθη ἐν σαρκί. The initial ὅς is peculiar since one expects the neuter ὅ given the neuter antecedent μυστήριον. This peculiarity is reflected in the textual tradition, where in later manuscripts one finds both ὅ (D* lat) and even θεός (אᶜ Aᶜ C² D² Ψ et al.) as ostensible correctives. There is little debate that ὅς should be viewed as the original reading and that, in its original context (if there was one prior to this verse), the ὅς had Christ as its antecedent. But notice that even if the ὅς is residual from a prior context (that is, from the hymn or creed to which it previously belonged), the fact that it appears in 3:16 to have μυστήριον as its antecedent exhibits, whether awkwardly or evocatively, the intimate association between

---

44 This term is important in the Pastorals. See 1 Tim 6:14; 2 Tim 1:10; 4:1, 8; Titus 2:3. It otherwise only occurs in the New Testament in 2 Thess 2:8. For more on the word and its significance in the Pastorals, see Andrew Y. Lau, *Manifest in Flesh: The Epiphany Christology of the Pastoral Epistles* (WUNT 2/86; Tübingen: Mohr Siebeck, 1996), 179–259.

45 For analysis of the potential relevance of the Cabirus cult on a Pauline community, see Karl P. Donfried, "The Cults of Thessalonica and the Thessalonian Correspondence," *NTS* 31 (1985): 336–56.

46 Cf. *Diogn.* 5.4 (καὶ ὁμολογουμένως παράδοξον ἐνδείκνυνται τὴν κατάστασιν τῆς ἑαυτῶν πολιτείας).

47 Besides the major commentaries, see esp. Mark M. Yarbrough, *Paul's Utilization of Preformed Traditions in 1 Timothy: An Evaluation of the Apostle's Literary, Rhetorical, and Theological Tactics* (LNTS 417; New York/London: T&T Clark, 2009), esp. 95–102.

μυστήριον and Christ.⁴⁸ Thus the apparent anacoluthon is interpretively suggestive, bending grammar in order to bind the μυστήριον and Christ. As for the full statement, the use of φανερόω in relation to μυστήριον is standard (see Rom 16:25–26; Col 1:26; 4:3–4), and while there is no verb for hiddenness here, as there is in Rom 16:25–26 and Col 1:26, the "once hidden/now revealed" structure would seem to be implied.⁴⁹ Also, as in Rom 16:25–26 and Col 1:26, the passive form of φανερόω likely indicates that God is the cause of Christ's manifestation ἐν σαρκί. The key point is that at the head of this mystery is the fact of Christ's historical appearance in human form.⁵⁰

Lines two (ἐδικαιώθη ἐν πνεύματι) and three (ὤφθη ἀγγέλοις) have been interpreted in varying ways, and exegetical decisions here largely depend on how one understands the structure of the hymn and, along with it, the historical moments to which these lines presumably correspond. The key element for our purposes is Christ's appearance before the angels in line three. If this is a reference to heavenly beings,⁵¹ or perhaps even to something like the imprisoned ἄγγελοι in Jude 6, it is interesting in light of Eph 3:10, where Paul explains that the mystery is to be made known "to the rulers and authorities in the heavenly places," and then 1 Cor 2:8, where "the rulers of this age" are apparently prevented from knowing such a mystery.⁵² More important is line four: ἐκηρύχθη ἐν ἔθνεσιν.⁵³

---

48 As Marshall, *Pastoral Epistles*, concludes, "It is not, therefore, necessary to assume that he has created a grammatical tension here by making a citation. Rather, the mystery is at one and the same time the message about Christ and the Christ-event" (523).

49 So also Marshall, *Pastoral Epistles*, notes, "The 'once hidden/now revealed' pattern of thought found elsewhere in the [Pastoral Epistles] is probably echoed here also" (524). The subject of preexistence is, it must be admitted, a major issue here, and scholars are divided on the matter. See esp. the discussion in Lau, *Manifest in Flesh*, 92–99. If previous hiddenness is implied in the association of μυστήριον and φανερόω, then the preexistence of Christ is implied along with it since μυστήριον and Christ are so tightly correlated in this verse.

50 The manifestation here should perhaps not be limited to a singular event like Christ's birth, and instead it should be applied to the whole of his human existence. Thus Wolfgang Metzger, *Der Christushymnus 1. Timotheus 3,16: Fragment einer Homologie der paulinischen Gemeinden* (AzTh 62; Stuttgart: Calwer, 1979), concludes that "der Eintritt in die Sphäre des Fleisches in einer menschlichen Geburt und dann der Verlassen dieser Sphäre in Tod am Kreuz sind die Fakta, welche für den Glauben der Gemeinde das Verweilen des Offenbarers im Fleische charakterisieren" (76).

51 Almost all interpreters take it this way. One notable exception is R.W. Micou, "On ὤφθη ἀγγέλοις, I Tim. iii. 16," *JBL* 11 (1892): 201–5, who argues for human messengers.

52 For a reading of lines two and three in relation to Christ's descent into Hades, see Robert H. Gundry, "The Form, Meaning and Background of the Hymn Quoted in Timothy 3:16," in *Apostolic History and the Gospel: Biblical and Historical Essays presented to F.F. Bruce on his 60th Birthday* (ed. W. Ward Gasque and Ralph P. Martin; Grand Rapids: Eerdmans, 1970), 203–22.

The correlation of God's newly revealed μυστήριον with the Gentile mission is, of course, a characteristic motif of the deuteropauline schema.[54] It is thus fitting to find a specific mention of Christ's (and, by association, the mystery's) proclamation among the Gentiles.[55] The choice of ἐν ἔθνεσιν perhaps stands out since an alternative such as ἐν ἀνθρώποις could have been used and would have provided a more corresponding and mellifluous juxtaposition with the ἀγγέλοις of the previous line. As for the final two lines, the fifth affirms the effect of the proclamation of Christ among the Gentiles – "he was trusted in the world" – and the sixth likely refers the historical fact of the ascension – "he was taken up in glory." Both, therefore, likewise correspond to events of Christ's human history.

In conclusion, the historical events recounted in this hymn, taken as a whole, provide the founding narrative for the church's "mystery of devotion" and, therefore, are to be understood as central to the way of life embodied by Christians.[56] To return to the earlier suggestion that the use of μυστήριον here should be viewed as analogous to pagan mystery practices, and to ἱεροὶ λόγοι traditions in particular, perhaps the chief problem with this possibility is our fractional and indirect understanding of the mysteries themselves and their ἱεροὶ λόγοι in particular. These traditions were, by design, intended to remain secret and so, by custom, were not committed to any material record. They have vanished with the people who possessed them.[57] If, however, we are on firm footing in assuming these λόγοι were often etiological myths related to the founding of a particular cult, as we have in the account of Kore and Demeter in the *Homeric Hymn to Demeter*, then the "mystery of devotion," so briefly sketched in hymnic form in 1 Tim 3:16, is certainly something of a parallel species insofar as it outlines the story of Christ, the deity of Christian worship, and the beginnings of the church he founded among the Gentiles. But there are incongruities as well. The Christian ἐκκλησία was an ethically peculiar community in a manner that is not conventionally expected of the mysteries,[58] and clearly in 1 Tim 3

Gundry takes line two as referring to Christ's "vindication through descent into hades" and then line three as "the sight of the vivified Christ in spirit-form by the 'spirits in prison'" (215).
53 Cf. *Diogn.* 11.3 (διὰ ἀποστόλων κηρυχθείς ὑπὸ ἐθνῶν ἐπιστεύθη).
54 See esp. the ἐν τοῖς ἔθνεσιν in Col 1:27.
55 Cf. 1 Tim 2:7, which also emphasizes Paul's labor among the Gentiles.
56 For a similar reading of the "contextual function" of the hymn, see Lau, *Manifest in Flesh*, 107–14.
57 See esp. the discussion in Henrichs, "HIEROI LOGOI and HIERAI BIBLOI," 207–10, 239–50.
58 Koester, *History, Culture, and Religion*, points to the mysteries of Bacchus and, in particular, to "the missionary strength and revolutionary potential" (175) of that cult as a possible exception to the claim that the mysteries did not produce alternative moral communities. (He is refer-

"the mystery of faith" and "the mystery of devotion" are bound to a particular manner of conduct or εὐσεβεία in the household of God and the world at large.[59] In the words of 1 Tim 6:3, those who devote themselves to the λόγοι of the Lord Jesus Christ will discover the teaching that accords with εὐσεβεία.[60] Thus the mystery of εὐσεβεία and the λόγοι of Christ that define it are presented in 3:16 not simply as an etiology of origins or a simple narrative of the dealings of the divine on earth, like most pagan μῦθοι and λόγοι. The mystery of Christian εὐσεβεία, as demonstrated in the story of Christ's earthly manifestation, also entails a morally converted way of life.[61] The Samothracian mysteries were thus not the only form of worship to connect honor of the gods with "a more devout" (εὐσεβεστέρους) form of life.

4.3.2 2 Timothy and Titus

Although the word μυστήριον never appears in 2 Timothy or Titus, both letters do have passages that were originally classified by Nils Dahl in his *Revelation-Schema* and so require consideration since they replicate some key features of the diachronic mystery schema. The first text to consider is 2 Tim 1:9–10:

...τοῦ σώσαντος ἡμᾶς
 καὶ καλέσαντος κλήσει ἁγίᾳ,
  οὐ κατὰ τὰ ἔργα ἡμῶν
  ἀλλὰ κατὰ ἰδίαν πρόθεσιν καὶ χάριν,
   τὴν δοθεῖσαν ἡμῖν ἐν Χριστῷ Ἰησοῦ
   πρὸ χρόνων αἰωνίων,
   φανερωθεῖσαν
    δὲ νῦν διὰ τῆς ἐπιφανείας τοῦ σωτῆρος ἡμῶν Χριστοῦ Ἰησοῦ,
     καταργήσαντος μὲν τὸν θάνατον

---

ring to the famous *senatus consultum de Bacchanalibus* of 186 B.C.E.) If we take the case of the Bacchic *thiasoi* as such evidence, it still renders those mysteries an interesting moral inverse to the virtues extolled in the Pastorals. This, incidentally, appears to be how Clement of Alexandria treated them (see *Protr.* 12.119–120).
59 Cf. again Diodorus Siculus, *The Library of History*, 5.49.6.
60 This verse actually characterizes a "heterodox" person (τις ἑτεροδιδασκα) as someone who μὴ προσέρχεται ὑγιαίνουσιν λόγοις τοῖς τοῦ κυρίου ἡμῶν Ἰησοῦ Χριστοῦ καὶ τῇ κατ' εὐσέβειαν διδασκαλίᾳ. There is much debate about how the λόγοι here should be understood, but I am persuaded that the expression is best read as I have insinuated above, i.e., as referring to the "accounts of our Lord Jesus Christ." Cf. also 1 Tim 1:15 (πιστὸς ὁ λόγος...ὅτι Χριστὸς Ἰησοῦς ἦλθεν εἰς τὸν κόσμον ἁμαρτωλοὺς σῶσαι).
61 Cf. the contrast in 4:6–7 between being trained τοῖς λόγοις τῆς πίστεως as opposed to "profane and absurd myths" (τοὺς βεβήλους καὶ γραώδεις μύθους).

> φωτίσαντος δὲ ζωὴν καὶ ἀφθαρσίαν
> διὰ τοῦ εὐαγγελίου...

> ...who saved us and called us to a holy calling, not by virtue of our works, but according to his own design and grace, which was given to us in Christ Jesus before eternal ages, and being disclosed now through the appearing of our savior Jesus Christ, who abolished death and brought to light life and immortality through the gospel...

Although this passage lacks μυστήριον and any specific mention of concealment, there is still much that is familiar.[62] Terms like πρόθεσις (Eph 1:11; 3:11), χάρις (Eph 1:6, 7; 3:2, 7, 8), the passive form of φανερόω (Rom 16:26; Col 1:26; cf. also 1 Tim 3:16), νῦν (Rom 16:26; Eph 3:5, 10; Col 1:26), and φωτίζω (Eph 3:9) are all featured in other deuteropauline mystery passages, and expressions like τὴν δοθεῖσαν ἡμῖν (cf. Eph 3:2, 7, 8; Col 1:25), ἐν Χριστῷ (Eph 1:10; 3:6, 11; Col 1:28), πρὸ χρόνων αἰωνίων (cf. Rom 16:25; 1 Cor 2:7; Eph 1:4; 3:5, 9; Col 1:26), and διὰ τοῦ εὐαγγελίου (Eph 3:6; cf. 6:19) are found there as well. Taken together, therefore, these two verses present a dense assemblage of vocabulary and phrases commonly associated with μυστήριον in the Pauline letters, but especially the deuteropauline letters. Also, there is a reference in v. 8 to Paul's imprisonment (ἐμὲ τὸν δέσμιον αὐτου) and suffering (συγκακοπάθησον), which are correlated with mystery passages in both Ephesians (3:1, 13; 6:19–20) and Colossians (1:24; 4:3). In v. 11 there is the association with Paul's proclamation (cf. τὸ κήρυγμα in Rom 16:25), apostleship (cf. Eph 3:5), and teaching ministry (cf. Col 1:28), which are likewise themes in other mystery texts in the deuteropauline Pauline letters. Especially noteworthy in v. 11 is the fact that Paul distinguishes himself as having received a specific appointment (εἰς ὃ ἐτέθην ἐγώ) to be a representative of this gospel of the newly disclosed grace of God, which is reminiscent of Col 1:25 and Eph 3:2, 7–8.

The most redolent aspect of the deuteropauline mystery schema, however, is the description of the pretemporal divine plan (πρὸ χρόνων αἰωνίων) that has become presently manifest (φανερωθεῖσαν δὲ νῦν) in Christ's earthly epiphany (ἐπιφάνεια):[63]

> κατὰ ἰδίαν πρόθεσιν καὶ χάριν,
> τὴν δοθεῖσαν ἡμῖν ἐν Χριστῷ Ἰησοῦ
> πρὸ χρόνων αἰωνίων,
> φανερωθεῖσαν δὲ
> νῦν διὰ τῆς ἐπιφανείας τοῦ σωτῆρος ἡμῶν Χριστοῦ Ἰησοῦ

---

[62] Notice that even the style, with the concatenation of aorist participles, is similar to the Ephesians and Colossians mystery passages.

[63] Again, for the importance of this term in the Pastorals, see Lau, *Manifest in Flesh*, 179–259.

4.3 The Pastoral Epistles — 127

Although hiddenness is not explicitly mentioned, it would seem to be implied in the "previously planned but presently revealed" structure, and although μυστήριον is likewise absent, it could have been incorporated via an additional subordinate clause at almost any point. Also important is that this eternal plan for salvation is formed by God's "design and grace given to us in Christ Jesus." Thus the pretemporal plan and its temporal manifestation are both enacted "in Christ," which agrees with the christological emphases in the other deuteropauline mystery texts.[64] In sum, although mystery is missing, other important characteristic features of the historically structured schema are present, the most important being the chronological arrangement of the "eternally planned but now revealed" binary.

Much of the same is true of Titus 1:2–3:

...ἐπ' ἐλπίδι ζωῆς αἰωνίου,
  ἣν ἐπηγγείλατο ὁ ἀψευδὴς θεὸς
    πρὸ χρόνων αἰωνίων,
  ἐφανέρωσεν δὲ
    καιροῖς ἰδίοις
      τὸν λόγον αὐτοῦ ἐν κηρύγματι,
        ὃ ἐπιστεύθην ἐγὼ
          κατ' ἐπιταγὴν τοῦ σωτῆρος ἡμῶν θεοῦ...

...in the hope of eternal life, which the God who never lies promised before eternal ages and at the proper time disclosed it in his word through proclamation, of which I have been entrusted according to the command of God our savior...

Here eternal life is what God promised before eternal ages, and the proclamation of this life is what God, according to his prearranged timetable, has recently made manifest through apostolic proclamation. The expression πρὸ χρόνων αἰωνίων is identical to 2 Tim 1:9, and the use of aorist active ἐφανέρωσεν, as opposed to a passive form, unambiguously identifies God as the agent of this revelation. In place of νῦν this passage has καιροῖς ἰδίοις,[65] but the sense is probably identical. The same καιροῖς ἰδίοις formulation also occurs in 1 Tim 2:6 and 6:15 and there, as here, it indicates a predetermined moment in which God discloses something through the doings of Christ, such as his death (1 Tim 2:6) or his still future epiphany (1 Tim 6:15). Therefore, even though there

---

[64] This passage is unique in aligning the newly revealed benefit with "salvation" (τοῦ σώσαντος ἡμᾶς... τοῦ σωτῆρος ἡμῶν Χριστοῦ Ἰησοῦ), but this is a prominent theme in the Pastorals. See Martin Dibelius and Hans Conzelmann, *The Pastoral Epistles* (trans. Philip Buttolph and Adela Yarbro. Hermeneia; Philadelphia: Fortress Press, 1972 [1955]), 100–03.
[65] Cf. Gal 6:9 (καιρῷ ἰδίῳ).

is no specific mention of hiddenness, since the promise was enacted by God prior to creation and only disclosed by God in the Christian kerygma, we can infer that it was not knowable to humanity prior to the recent manifestation and so, in that sense, hidden. Admittedly, while there is nothing overtly christological in Titus 1:2–3 itself, the phrase τὸν λόγον αὐτοῦ ἐν κηρύγματι,[66] which is the object of the verb ἐφανέρωσεν,[67] is to be understood as the kerygma about Christ entrusted to Paul as Christ's apostle (v. 1), which itself must be a kerygma about eternal life (v. 2). The salvation secured by Christ and the hope of eternal life are, in fact, again explicitly correlated in 3:6–7. Thus the contrast in these verses is between the eternal life promised by God *prior to creation* and then the divinely ordained *present* disclosure of that promise in apostolic preaching.[68] Once again, therefore, as with 2 Tim 1:9–10, the basic structure of the deuteropauline mystery schema is in place despite the absence of μυστήριον and any specific mention of hiddenness.

4.4 Conclusion

To conclude, I would like to return to the Rom 16 doxology because it offers a fitting segue as we move from the larger discussion of the deuteropauline mystery schema to the appropriation of that particular apocalyptic schema in second-century Christian theology. On the one hand, as I have noted, the Rom 16 doxology conjoins linguistic features of the Ephesians and Colossians schemas, and then the versions found in the Pastorals as well. It is, therefore, something of an epitome of the various iterations of the diachronic mystery schemas. On the other hand, however, insofar as the Rom 16 schema restates the apocalyptic division of history, which is the most basic feature of the deuteropauline schema, but then accents the prophetic scriptures as a special site for the mystery's new hermeneutical disclosure, the passage anticipates the two dominant trajectories

---

[66] Cf. Rom 16:25 (τὸ κήρυγμα Ἰησοῦ Χριστου).

[67] The construction is odd because one expects the object of this verb to remain the same, and so perhaps for it to be preceded by an additional ἥν. The phrase τὸν λόγον αὐτοῦ ἐν κηρύγματι is a new object. Towner, *The Letters to Timothy and Titus*, correctly observes that "in choosing a new object ('his word in proclamation') for the verb 'manifested,' Paul has not moved on to a new subject; he has instead chosen a way of referring to the promise in its fulfillment, that is, the preaching of the gospel" (672).

[68] Notice also, and once again, the concurrence of the human and the divine in this disclosure: that which is made manifest is God's word, but that manifestation occurs in the kerygma entrusted to Paul, which itself is "according to the command (κατ' ἐπιταγὴν) of our savior God." The phrase κατ' ἐπιταγὴν also appears verbatim in Rom 16:26.

of the mystery discourse in later Christian authors. Whether it be to divide time along the axis of Christ's advent and, in so doing, to bind the newness of Christianity to God's eternal plans (Ignatius and the *Epistle to Diognetus*), or to identify the once latent but now newly revealed christological meanings of prophetic scripture (Justin, Melito), and so to identify Christ with the God of Israel, as well (Tertullian), the logic of the "once hidden, now revealed" mystery discourse supplies subsequent Christian thinkers with the essential conceptual apparatus for dealing with these pressing issues.

5 Mystery and History in the Letters of Ignatius and the *Epistle to Diognetus*

5.1 Introduction

Within a cultural world in which proof of antiquity was usually synonymous with legitimacy, the Christian pronouncement of God's recent and definitive revelation in the person of Jesus Christ was for many a precarious proposition. As the pagan inquirer Diognetus asks of his Christian counterpart, if Christianity is indeed true, then "why did this new race or practice enter the world now and not earlier?" (*Diogn.* 1.1). It was of course the case that certain traditional facts about Christian origins tied the new movement to Israel's more suitable history (or at least for most this was the case), and this union with Israel was at times useful for defending Christianity's acceptable pedigree. To charges of novelty the Christian could point to Israel's ancient ancestry and thus maintain that the church was not a foundationless novelty within the Roman religious economy but rather the continuation, even fulfillment, of long-esteemed traditions. Nevertheless, as the earliest Christian assemblies became unattached to synagogues, various Christian leaders often threatened to undo any purported ties with Israel, her scriptures, and her God. In Marcion (ca. 85–160) the prospect of severing the creator God of Israel from the recently revealed Christ fully materializes. For the majority of other early Christians, however, there remains an impulse to hold together both the new and the old and to work out what is required in order to maintain this – a new and totalizing social and historical comprehension.

Ignatius of Antioch and the author of the *Epistle to Diognetus* are two such figures who attempt to hold together the new and the old by reconceiving history according to a temporally ordered hidden/revealed framework. Within this framework time is divided into contrasting eras of concealment and disclosure with Christ acting as the fulcrum between these two ages. These authors thereby integrate the new and the old by creatively reapplying the totalizing historical trope that is the deuteropauline mystery schema of revelation. "Creatively reapplying" is a key qualification since these authors do not merely reproduce Pauline (or deuteropauline) texts or arguments. They instead utilize the hidden/revealed historical schema for sometimes quite different theological ends, and in the case of how the schema is mobilized with respect to historical Israel and ongoing Jews, these ends are such that it is hard to imagine Paul himself (or those who propagated his epistolary legacy) would have recognized them.

5.2 Ignatius of Antioch

Little can be said about the letters of Ignatius or the man himself with much certitude. A collection of letters ascribed to the "bishop of Antioch"[1] are preserved in three recensions conventionally referred to as the short, the middle, and the long. Almost all modern scholars now accept that the seven letters of the middle recension represent the earliest recoverable stratum of their textual history, but not all are convinced that these seven letters are authentic missives from an historical Ignatius. Nor is there universal agreement about when the letters purported to be from this Ignatius were composed.[2] In what follows I simply assume the critical consensus and treat the middle recension form of the seven letters as our best textual witness.[3]

According to Eusebius (*Hist. eccl.* 3.36.2–4) Ignatius was martyred in Rome during the tenth year of Trajan's reign (107 C.E.), but scholars have long doubted the accuracy of these claims.[4] As Andreas Lindemann judiciously measured the situation in 2005, "[T]he traditional dating of the letters…very early in the second century in the time of the emperor Trajan is probably no longer acceptable. On the other hand, there are no convincing reasons to date the letters in the late second century."[5] Timothy Barnes has recently presented what he alleges is sufficient evidence for finally jettisoning the Eusebian tradition in favor of a date some decades later. Barnes contends that Ignatius makes reference to the Valen-

---

[1] This is the title traditionally assigned to him, but Ignatius himself never claims the designation. He instead refers to himself as "the bishop of Syria" (ὁ ἐπίσκοπος Συρίας) (*Rom.* 2.2).
[2] The most recent introduction to these and other issues is Hermut Löhr, "The Epistles of Ignatius of Antioch," in *The Apostolic Fathers: An Introduction* (ed. Wilhelm Pratscher; Waco: Baylor University Press, 2010), 91–115.
[3] This consensus reaches back to Theodor Zahn, *Ignatius von Antiochien* (Gotha: Perthes, 1873).
[4] The general uncertainty regarding the date of the letters is demonstrated by the series of articles and responses in the *Zeitschrift für Antikes Christentum*. See Reinhard M. Hübner, "Thesen zur Echtheit und Datierung der sieben Briefe des Ignatius von Antiochien," *ZAC* 1 (1997): 44–72; Andreas Lindemann, "Antwort auf die 'Thesen zur Echtheit und Datierung der sieben Briefe des Ignatius von Antiochien'," *ZAC* 1 (1997): 185–94; Georg Schöllgen, "Die Ignatianen als pseudepigraphisches Briefcorpus: Anmerkung zu den Thesen von Reinhard M. Hübner," *ZAC* 2 (1998): 16–25; M.J. Edwards, "Ignatius and the Second Century: An Answer to R. Hübner," *ZAC* 2 (1998): 214–26. For a presentation of 20th century scholarship on the date of Ignatius, see William R. Schoedel, "Polycarp of Smyrna and Ignatius of Antioch," *ANRW* 27.1 (1992): 272–358. The most recent introduction to all issues related to dating the letters is Timothy D. Barnes, "The Date of Ignatius," *ExpTim* 120 (2008): 119–130.
[5] Andreas Lindemann, "Paul's Influence on 'Clement' and Ignatius," in *Trajectories through the New Testament and the Apostolic Fathers* (ed. Andrew F. Gregory and Christopher M. Tuckett; Oxford/New York: Oxford University Press, 2005), 9–24, 17.

tinian disciple Ptolemy in *Pol.* 3.2 and that this, along with other data, likely places Ignatius' martyrdom in the 140s, during the reign of Antoninus Pius.[6] A decision on this question does not necessarily affect my analysis, but my overall findings confirm that the theological profile of the letters fits best within first half of the second century, which is still in line with Barnes' claims. Specifically, in his use of μυστήριον Ignatius does not, like later second-century authors, employ the term in any sort of hermeneutical sense. Instead he applies it in a general historical sense, dividing time into a previous era in which the mystery of Christ was kept silent and the current era in which this mystery has become revealed. This usage also agrees with the *Epistle to Diognetus*, which is also customarily dated to the first half of the second century and thus may provide an additional anchor for dating Ignatius' letters.

5.2.1 Ignatius and Paul

Literature on the relationship between Ignatius and Paul is vast.[7] Potential citations and allusions to the Pauline letters have been frequently catalogued, and

---

[6] Barnes, "The Date of Ignatius." Although Barnes identifies *Pol.* 3.2 as an almost certain allusion to a description of the teachings of Ptolemy reported by Irenaeus in *Haer.* 1.1.1, it is not entirely clear to me why the direction of influence, if it indeed exists, cannot be reversed. For further critique of Barnes' argument, see Sebastian Moll, *The Arch-Heretic Marcion* (WUNT 250; Tübingen: Mohr Siebeck, 2010), 136 n. 2. It is worth noting that Barnes' proposed date agrees with the conclusions of the early Adolf Harnack, *Die Zeit des Ignatius* (Leipzig: J.C. Hinrischs'sche Buchhandlung, 1878) and more recently Allen Brent, *Ignatius of Antioch and the Second Sophistic Movement: A Study of an Early Christian Transformation of Pagan Culture* (STAC 36; Tübingen: Mohr Siebeck, 2006). Barnes additionally notes that on the basis of this dating "it is chronologically possible that some passages in his letters, especially in the *Letter to the Smyrneans* (2–3), reflect a repudiation of the teachings of Marcion" (126). Markus Vinzent also develops this possibility in "'Ich bin kein körperloses Geistwesen': Zum Verhältnis von κήρυγμα Πέτρου, 'Doctrina Petri', διδασκαλία Πέτρου und IgnSm3," in *Der Paradox Eine: Antignostischer Monarchianismus im zweiten Jahrhundert* (ed. Reinhard M. Hübner; Leiden/Boston: Brill, 1999), 241–86, esp. 265–73, 286. I am not persuaded by Vinzent's arguments or his conclusion that the letters belong to the second-half of the second century. And even if Barnes is correct that the letters were composed in the 140s and Ignatius was somehow familiar with Marcion's work, I still find no sufficient evidence in the letters to conclude that Ignatius considered Marcion a threat or that he was influenced by his ideas in any meaningful way. I therefore concur with the assessment of Moll, *The Arch-Heretic Marcion:* "In the end, one may certainly date Ignatius' letters much later than 110, even as late as 140, but the appearance of such men as Ptolemy and Marcion remains the *terminus ante* not *post quem*" (136 n. 2).
[7] See esp. Heinrich Rathke, *Ignatius von Antiochien und die Paulusbriefe* (TU 99; Berlin: Akademie, 1967). For a comprehensive analysis of the literary relationship between Paul and Ignatius,

the importance of Paul for Ignatius' theology and self-presentation is beyond dispute.[8] As for the question of whether or not Ignatius derives his use of μυστήριον from Paul, it is of course *prima facie* likely that Paul's use of the term had some influence on Ignatius since Paul is the principal Christian source for the word and the only Christian author prior to Ignatius to connect μυστήριον explicitly with Christ, which Ignatius does explicitly as well. Also intriguing for the connection between mystery and the Pauline letters is *Eph.* 12.2, where Ignatius describes his readers in Ephesus as συμμύσται, or "co-initiates," with Paul.[9] This depiction of the Christians in Ephesus as μύσται with the Apostle suggests that Ignatius associates Paul with mystery practices and terminology.[10] There are, therefore, good reasons for suspecting even at the outset that Ignatius' use of μυστήριον is deeply informed by Pauline precedent.

---

see Albert E. Barnett, *Paul Becomes a Literary Influence* (Chicago: The University of Chicago Press, 1941), 152–70. For recent general introductions to the topic, see the studies by Andreas Lindemann, which include *Paulus im ältesten Christentum: Das Bild des Apostels und die Rezeption der paulinischen Theologie in der frühchristlichen Literatur bis Marcion* (BHT 58; Tübingen: J.C.B. Mohr [Paul Siebeck], 1979), 82–87; "Paul in the Writings of the Apostolic Fathers," in *Paul and the Legacies of Paul* (ed. William S. Babcock; Dallas: Southern Methodist University Press, 1990), 25–45; and "Paul's Influence on 'Clement' and Ignatius." Also helpful are Ernst Dassmann, *Der Stachel im Fleisch: Paulus in der frühchristlichen Literatur bis Irenäus* (Münster: Aschendorff, 1979), 126–49; David K. Rensberger, "As the Apostle Teaches: The Development of the Use of Paul's Letters in Second-Century Christianity" (Ph.D. diss., Yale University, 1981), 65–67; and Carl B. Smith, "Ministry, Martyrdom, and Other Mysteries: Pauline Influence on Ignatius of Antioch," in *Paul and the Second Century* (ed. Michael F. Bird and Joseph R. Dodson; LNTS 412; London/New York: T&T Clark, 2011), 37–56.

8 See, for instance, David M. Reis, "Following in Paul's Footsteps: *Mimēsis* and Power in Ignatius of Antioch," in *Trajectories through the New Testament and the Apostolic Fathers* (ed. Andrew Gregory and Christopher Tuckett; Oxford/New York: Oxford University Press, 2005), 287–305. Ignatius does not routinely cite Paul verbatim, but given the difficulties of his imprisonment (see his remarks on this in *Rom.* 5.1), we would not expect him to have the luxury of his own personal library. Thus Lindemann, "Paul in the Writings of the Apostolic Fathers," characterizes Ignatius' relationship with Paul as follows, "Ignatius, we might say, was making an entirely unforced use of Paul, implicit rather than explicit, without rather than with any special thought or attention. If this view is correct, however, the allusions to Paul are all the more remarkable; they demonstrate just how far-reaching the Pauline influence on Ignatius apparently was" (40).

9 For a reading of Ignatius as a self-styled θεοφόρος of the mystery cult that is the church, see Allen Brent, "Ignatius and Polycarp: The Transformation of New Testament Traditions in the Context of Mystery Cults," in *Trajectories through the New Testament and the Apostolic Fathers* (ed. Andrew Gregory and Christopher Tuckett; Oxford/New York: Oxford University Press, 2005), 325–49, and also Brent's *Ignatius of Antioch and the Second Sophistic*, esp. 121–230.

10 Given the prominence of μυστήριον in Ephesians (the term appears six times), it is perhaps unsurprising that Ignatius would associate that Pauline community with mystery initiation.

5.2.2 Μυστήριον in the Ignatian Letters

Ignatius is perhaps our earliest witness to the use of μυστήριον in second-century Christianity, but his witness is limited to just three occurences (*Trall.* 2.3; *Magn.* 9.1; *Eph.* 19.1).[11] Since *Trall.* 2.3 is the least specific of the mystery passages and in several ways unlike the other two, I treat it first:

> And it is necessary for the deacons, being of the mysteries of Jesus Christ (ὄντας μυστηρίων Ἰησοῦ Χριστοῦ), to be pleasing in every way to all people, for they are not deacons of foods and drinks but helpers of the church of God. Therefore, they must keep themselves from accusations as from fire.

This passage is most often read in light of 1 Cor 4:1, where Paul describes himself and those laboring alongside him as "servants of Christ and administrators of the mysteries of God" (οἰκονόμους μυστηρίων θεοῦ).[12] Worthy of mention as well is 1 Tim 3:9, where Paul similarly addresses deacons, emphasizing that they must "hold the mystery of faith in a clean conscience." This guardianship of the mystery is presented as a key qualification for serving as a deacon. In nearly identical fashion Ignatius here describes the deacons as "being of the mysteries" in order to underscore that they bear responsibility as servants of the church of God. They are not merely ministers of food and drink but helpers of the church, and so they must guard their reputations "as from fire." If the content of μυστήριον is as elsewhere in Ignatius, then the expression refers to something like the deacons's responsibility for preserving essential Christian beliefs, such as belief in Christ's incarnation and death, and perhaps tutoring others in these revealed truths.[13] It is important to note that the association of "mysteries"

---

[11] Setting aside the Synoptic Gospels and Revelation, which almost all scholars would date prior to Ignatius, the only other non-Pauline Christian use of μυστήριον also likely prior to Ignatius is *Did.* 11.11. This passage warns that no approved and true prophet "working for the earthly mystery of the church" (ποιῶν εἰς μυστήριον κοσμικὸν ἐκκλησίας) should be condemed. There have been numerous proposals for what this so-called "earthly mystery of church" is but, as Kurt Niederwimmer, *The Didache* (trans. Linda M. Maloney; Hermeneia; Minneapolis: Fortress Press, 1998), explains, "Its formulation is probably cryptic by design, although the original audience certainly understood what it was about" (180).

[12] Among those who emphasize a literary connection between these passages, see J.B. Lightfoot, *Apostolic Fathers Part II, Ignatius and Polycarp: Volume 2* (London/New York: Macmillan, 1889), 156; Henning Paulsen, *Die Briefe des Ignatius von Antiochia und der Briefe des Polykarp von Smyrna: zweite, neubearbeitete Auflage der Auslegung von Walter Bauer* (HNT 18; Tübingen: Mohr Siebeck, 1985), 59; William R. Schoedel, *Ignatius of Antioch* (Hermeneia; Philadelphia: Fortress Press, 1985), 141.

[13] In *Phld.* 11.1 the deacon Philo is descibed as serving Ignatius in the word of God.

with sacraments is a much later development, and so there is no basis for assuming a connection here, though it is perhaps not impossible.[14]

More interesting is *Magn.* 9.1–2. This passage occurs in the context of a series of warnings about the false teachings of those who live κατὰ Ἰουδαϊσμόν (chs. 8–11). As Schoedel notes, this entire section forms "the heart of the letter,"[15] and so to appreciate the use of μυστήριον here it will be necessary to consider this larger context, especially the immediate context of 8.1–9.2. But we should first take a look at the primary text in question:

> 9.1 Therefore, if those who lived in the old ways came to a newness of hope (καινότητα ἐλπίδος), no longer keeping Sabbath (μηκέτι σαββατίζοντες), but rather living according to the Lord's day (κατὰ κυριακὴν ζῶντες), upon which also our life sprung up through him and his death, which some deny, through which mystery we have obtained faith (δι᾽ οὗ μυστηρίου ἐλάβομεν τὸ πιστεύειν) and through this we endure so that we might be found disciples of Jesus Christ, our only teacher. 9.2 [If this is the case] how will we be able to live without him under whom even the prophets were disciples in the spirit (ὄντες τῷ πνεύματι), anticipating him as a teacher and, therefore, rightly expecting him who, when he came, raised them from the dead?

Ignatius is here contrasting two fundamentally irreconcilable ways of life:[16] the life characterized by "keeping Sabbath" (σαββατίζοντες)[17] and life ordered around "the Lord's day" (κυριακὴν).[18] The latter is purportedly based on decep-

---

14 Schoedel, *Ignatius*, suggests that Ignatius "may have had the eucharist in mind" (141) since deacons are associated with the distribution of the eucharistic bread and wine as early as Justin (*Apol.* 1.65.7; 1.67.5). Lightfoot, *The Apostolic Fathers*, however, observes that "[i]n a later writer διακόνους μυστηρίων would probably refer to their attendance on the priest when officiating at the eucharist. But such a restriction of μυστηρίων would be an anachronism in Ignatius. He apparently uses the word in the same wide sense in which it is used by S. Paul, 'revealed truths'" (2.2.156).
15 Schoedel, *Ignatius*, 118. Cf. the similar line of argument in *Phld.* 5–9.
16 Schoedel, *Ignatius*, similarly writes that "the expressions 'keeping Sabbath' and 'living in accordance with the Lord's day' serve primarily to characterize two whole ways of life" (123). See also Karl-Wilhelm Niebuhr, "'Judentum' und 'Christentum' bei Paulus und Ignatius von Antiochien," *ZNW* 85 (1994): 218–33. Niebuhr similarly remarks, "'Judentum' und 'Christentum' bei Ignatius bezeichnen nicht Religionsgemeinschaften oder Glaubenssysteme, sondern Lebensweisen. Beide Stichworte haben in ihrem jeweiligen Kontext rhetorische Funktion" (232). For Ignatius' own thoughts on the incompatibility of these two competing "life systems," see esp. *Magn.* 10.1–3.
17 Cf. Col. 2:16.
18 For κυριακός in relation to Sunday worship see Rev 1:10 and *Did.* 14.1. In these two texts, however, the term is coordinated with ἡμέρα, which is not the case here. Though there have been attempts to read the expression in relation to things other than Sunday worship (particularly by Seventh Day Adventists!), these are quite strained given the common use of κυριακός in relation

tive ancient customs (8.1) that have become an "evil leaven" (10.2).[19] The former, by contrast, is a new way of being in the world that originates in the person and death of Christ, the mystery that grants faith and generates obedience.[20] Those who have benefited from this mystery of Christ's life and death are disciples who have a "newness of hope."[21] They observe Sunday worship, as opposed to Sabbath, and learn from Christ alone, the source of their life. Even though this mystery of Christ and the attendant Christian way of life, which is here typified by worship ordered around the Lord's day, are indeed new, they were not, according to Ignatius, entirely unforeseen. As 9.2 explains, even the prophets of old were disciples of Jesus in the spirit (τῷ πνεύματι)[22] and awaited (προσδοκάω) Christ as their teacher.[23] Therefore, long prior to the life-creating mystery of Christ's life and death, the prophets of Israel had already become his proleptic disciples, having learned from him despite the fact that he had not yet appeared.[24] But how could this be, and what does it mean for the designation of Christ himself and his death as a mystery? To better understand the underlying framework of revelation being presupposed in this correlation of the mystery of Christ with prior prophetic expectation, it is necessary to examine the immediately preceding passage.

---

to Sunday and the clear contrast with Sabbath in this passage. For further discussion see Schoedel, *Ignatius*, 123–24 and Judith M. Lieu, *Image & Reality: The Jews in the World of the Christians in the Second Century* (Edinburgh: T&T Clark, 1996), 33–34.

19 Barnett, *Paul Becomes a Literary Influence*, identifies the whole of 10.2 as a "free quotation" of 1 Cor 5:7 and suggests that Ignatius "carries the metaphor through more logically in that he makes Christ the 'new yeast,' whereas Paul makes him the new Passover" (158).

20 Thus Lightfoot, *The Apostolic Fathers*, writes, "This 'living after the Lord's day' signifies not merely the observance of it, but the appropriation of all those ideas and associations which are involved in its observance" (129).

21 Cf. Rom 6:4; 7:6. Paul is the only New Testament author to use the word καινότης.

22 Schoeldel, *Ignatius*, writes, "The fact that the prophets were disciples 'in the spirit' reminds us that they did not have the advantage of looking back to Christ's fleshly presence" (124). See also Paulsen, *Die Briefe des Ignatius*, 53. Cf. the connection Paul makes between "the prophets" and ἐν πνεύματι in Eph 3:5.

23 Cf. the similar description of the prophets in 1 Pet 1:11–12.

24 As Schoedel, *Ignatius*, notes, "For Ignatius the main thing is that the prophets lived 'according to Jesus Christ' and not (it may be inferred) 'according to Judaism'. Their way of life presupposes...anticipation of the coming of Christ, but at this point the emphasis must be on their refusal to observe Jewish customs.... This is not an anachronistic summary of the prophetic message...but a statement about the faith elicited by that message after the coming of Christ. The view is that for all except a few everything falls into place only after the fulfillment of the prophecies.... Consequently, appeals to scripture are indecisive apart from that fulfillment..., and we see why the refusal to abandon Jewish ways 'until now' – after the grace of Christ has become generally accessible – is what is so incomprehensible to Ignatius" (119–20).

As previously mentioned, 8.1–2 introduces the new section on the dangers and errors of Judaism. Ignatius begins by warning the Magnesians of "heterodoxies" (ἑτεροδοξίαι)[25] and "old fables"[26] that are profitless and deceive. As the next sentence makes clear, he has contemporary Jews (or perhaps some variety of Judaizing Christians) in mind:

> For if until now we should live according to Judaism (κατὰ Ἰουδαϊσμόν) we admit that grace has not been received.

It is important to notice that the contrast here is not between grace and some Jewish particularity such as Torah (a more Pauline sounding opposition) but rather between grace and Judaism as such.[27] This more generalized contrast sets up "Judaism" and "Christianism" as two conflicting life systems that epitomize fundamentally incompatible modes of existence, the former of which is profitless and misleading.[28] To amplify the incongruity of these two ways of life Ignatius enlists the Jews' own prophets in 8.2 as evidence in contradiction of Judaism:

> For the most divine prophets lived according to Christ Jesus. For this reason they were also persecuted, being inspired by his grace so that the disbelieving would be convinced that God is one, this God who revealed himself (ὁ φανερώσας ἑαυτὸν) through Jesus Christ his son, who is his word proceeding out of silence (ὅς ἐστιν αὐτοῦ λόγος ἀπὸ σιγῆς προελθών), who in all ways pleased the one who sent him.

By claiming that even the prophets lived κατὰ Χριστόν (and not, by implication, κατὰ Ἰουδαϊσμόν), Ignatius conscripts the Jews' own scriptural progenitors as proto-Christians who, like Ignatius, were persecuted, preached truth, and hoped to be resurrected. The insinuation is that since the prophets of Israel rejected the deceptive practices of "Judaism" and lived Christianly, any in the Magnesian church who persist in Judaism should instead conform their lives to the

---

25 Cf. 1 Tim 1:3; 6:3.
26 Cf. 1 Tim 1:4; 4:7; Titus 1:14.
27 Cf. 10.1–3.
28 The text is unclear about just what the objectionable parts of Judaism are. "Strange doctrines" and "old fables" are derided in 8.1 and Sabbath in 9.1, but no other precise doctrines or practices are mentioned. Circumcision is almost certainly implied, and in fact the longer version of *Magn.* 8.1 adds circumcision to what it means to live "according to Judaism." Cf. also the contrast in *Phld.* 6.1. For more on the question of circumcision in Ignatius, see Shaye J. D. Cohen, "Judaism without Circumcision and 'Judaism' without 'Circumcision' in Ignatius." *HTR* 95 (2002): 395–415.

Christian pattern, which is in fact also exemplified by the "most divine" prophets of ancient Israel.

What is most important in this passage for understanding the larger construal of revelation in 8.1–9.2, and the sense in which Christ is a mystery in particular, is the statement that the one God proclaimed by the prophets is now revealed in Christ, who is the "word of God proceeding from silence (ἀπὸ σιγῆς προελθών)."[29] This expression is in several ways similar to the mystery passage in *Eph.* 19.1, which will be discussed below, but there are other helpful parallels for understanding this idea of the "word proceeding from silence." Wis 18:14–15 is the passage most commonly associated with *Magn.* 8.2:

> For when all things were surrounded in quiet silence (ἡσύχου γὰρ σιγῆς περιεχούσης τὰ πάντα) and the night was in the middle of her own quick course, then your almighty word leaped from heaven (ὁ παντοδύναμός σου λόγος ἀπ' οὐρανῶν), from the royal throne (ἐκ θρόνων βασιλείων).

In this passage God's λόγος from heaven is the divine agent who slaughters Egypt's firstborn. This is, then, not exactly a positive example of divine revelation, but the arrival of this "stern warrior" does cause the Egyptians to recognize Israel as God's child (Wis 18:13). More similar to the image of the Word proceeding out of silence in *Magn.* 8.2 is Rom 16:25–26, which describes the revelation of the mystery of Christ's advent as having been kept silent (σεσιγημένου) for eternal ages but now revealed (φανερωθέντος) and made known through the prophetic writings. Like Rom 16:25–26, Ignatius also brings together the prophets, new revelation, a previous era of silence, and the mystery of Christ. Also like Rom 16:25–26, Ignatius organizes this cluster of terms and ideas in order to express an understanding of history in which the Christ event is a previously concealed (or silent) reality that has become newly manifested (or spoken) to the

---

29 Cf. *Magn.* 7.2, where Christ is described as "proceeding from the one Father" (ἀφ' ἑνὸς πατρὸς προελθόντα). There is no need to seek some sort of Gnostic conception of Christ as the revealer of the unknown Father. Even if Ignatius is consciously borrowing from a specific precursor tradition, he is still sufficiently reworking it in relation to his own concerns, and therefore it is imperative to attend to his particular theological formulation. See the critique of Gnostic hypotheses in Schoedel, *Ignatius*, 120–21. Schoedel also notes that silence and mystery were commonly associated with one another in antiquity. See e.g. Plutarch, *Garr.* 504A; 505F. Paulsen, *Die Briefe des Ignatius*, also correctly notes that "die Identifizierung von Gott und σιγή in der antiken Religiosität weit verbreitet war, läßt sich kaum übersehen" (52). See also Paulsen's *Studien zur Theologie des Ignatius von Antiochien* (Göttingen: Vandenhoeck & Ruprecht, 1978), 110–121, which is the most thorough treatment of the themes of silence and revelation in Ignatius.

world. Christ himself is God's λόγος[30] who interrupts and brings to a close the previous era of silence by speaking forth a new reality. As Ignatius elsewhere puts it, "Jesus Christ will reveal these things to you because I say truly he is the mouth without lie in whom the Father truly spoke" (*Rom.* 8.2). Thus Schoedel is correct in remarking that in *Magn.* 8.2 "Christ is thought of as emerging from a sphere of silence only in the sense that his appearance brings the hidden purpose of God to light."[31] But again, although this reality has only recently been inaugurated, it is not without prior authoritative witnesses. One finds confirmation of Christianity when one retrospectively examines the pattern of piety exhibited by the prophets. When viewed in light of Christ, the prophets thus come to yield new significance for the Christian, and so it can be said, as Clement of Alexandria will later put it, that as God's newly revealed λόγος Christ "breaks the mystic silence (τὴν μυστικὴν...σιωπήν) of the prophetic enigmas" (*Protr.* 1.10.1). Since we now observe that the prophets too lived κατὰ Χριστὸν Ἰησοῦν (or so Ignatius insists), those who still persist in Judaism should abandon their misleading myths and wicked practices and embrace the grace offered by the mystery of Christ.

This assertion of the prophetic witness to Christianity entails an important question, and one we considered in relation to Rom 16:25–26 in the previous chapter. If Christ truly "proceeds from silence," and if this means that a new revelation has occurred, then how can Christ also have been anticipated by the prophets who lived during that era of silence? As 9.2 makes clear, the prophets were not unwitting or accidental witnesses to Christ. They were rather his disciples "in the Spirit," somehow anticipating his arrival. But does this entail that the particularities of Christ's advent and death – which is to say "the mystery" – were somehow generally knowable (or even predictable) prior to his appearance? If this were the case then one could not say in an absolute sense that Christ was God's word "proceeding from silence." Though Ignatius never explicitly spells it out, it is most likely that he understands the prophets to be somehow proleptic or latent representatives of God's mystery and so, as in Rom 16:25–26, they only testify to the mystery after the fact of its occurrence. Perhaps Ignatius would even go so far as to say the prophets were an exception in the previous era of concealment, and so they were somehow specially granted knowledge of life "according to Christ" so that they would later become *ex post facto* demonstrations of Christianity to indict those who "until now" practice Judaism.[32] Ei-

---

[30] Cf. the manifestation of God's λόγος in Titus 1:2–3.
[31] Schoedel, *Ignatius*, 122.
[32] As Schoedel, *Ignatius*, writes, "The prophets are recalled for the purpose of putting the Judaizers to shame" (124).

ther way the reasoning here corresponds to Rom 16:25–26, where the prophetic writings, when viewed through the fact of the revealed mystery, become channels of Christian revelation. Even though both passages replicate the same schema of revelation from silence, however, the main point in *Magn.* 8.1–9.2 is quite different. Whereas the prophets in Rom 16:26 function positively in order to make known the mystery "to all Gentiles for the obedience of faith," for Ignatius the prophets are enlisted primarily for the negative purpose of increasing the blameworthiness of all who live according to Judaism. With their esteemed ancestors allegedly substantiating the new Christian way of life, those practicing Judaism become even more culpable for failing to live in accordance with the new Christian manner.

When considered in the larger context of 8.1–9.2, then, Ignatius' use of μυστήριον in 9.1 participates in a larger discourse that embodies many key features of the deuteropauline mystery schema, and of the Rom 16:25–26 instantiation of it in particular. As coordinated by Ignatius in this passage, history is divided into a previous age of silence and a current age in which the mystery is revealed. But even though the mystery of Christ's life and death is a "word proceeding from silence" that is now being made known, it is also retrospectively corroborated by the antecedent witness of Israel's prophets – "for the most divine prophets lived according to Jesus Christ." And so, since even the prophets were disciples of Christ (or so the assertion goes), Jews likewise should abandon whatever belongs to "Judaism" and convert to the newly revealed Christian way of life as well. Much like Rom 16:25–26, therefore, Ignatius claims Israel's prophets as confirming Christian realities,[33] but unlike Rom 16:25–26, Ignatius stylizes Israel's prophets in a way that undermines Judaism.[34] True Israel according to Ignatius is, it seems, Christianity.

---

[33] It is important to emphasize again that this appeal to the prophets is nothing like a prospective prophecy-fulfillment schema in which they serve a predictive function prior to the Christ event. For Ignatius they only become witnesses from the retrospective vantage point of Christ's revelation. Prior to this the mystery was kept silent.

[34] It is not even clear if Ignatius believed in a preparatory function for Israel. See Lieu, *Image & Reality*, 35–37, who correctly notes that as Ignatius construes them, the prophets "have no true significance except in the light of Jesus Christ" (37). Though he never explicitly states it, his arguments seem to imply that the prophets not only thought correct thoughts about Jesus but also fully embodied the Christian way of life and thus, perhaps, were not law observant (or at least did not practice Sabbath). For the idea that the prophets did not practice Sabbath, see the argument in *Barn.* 15.8 with reference to Isa 1:13.

We turn now to the final mystery passage, *Eph.* 19.1.³⁵ Here μυστήριον again appears in a schema of revelation that is, for the most part, structurally identical to the arrangement found in *Magn.* 8.1–9.2. This passage occurs near the end of the letter and at the conclusion to the major section on eschatological warnings that begins at 11.1:

> And the virginity of Mary eluded (ἔλαθεν) the Ruler of this age (τὸν ἄρχοντα τοῦ αἰῶνος τούτου), and her giving birth as well, and the death of the Lord: three mysteries of a cry that were accomplished in the quietness of God (τρία μυστήρια κραυγῆς ἅτινα ἐν ἡσυχίᾳ θεοῦ ἐπράχθη).

The content of the three mysteries is here stated plainly: the virginity of Mary and the birth and death of Jesus.³⁶ As the immediately preceding verses indicate (18.1–2),³⁷ these three mysteries are believed to be sources of salvation brought about in accordance with the οἰκονομία of God. There are, however, three more complicated questions that require greater attention: (1) Why and how did these mysteries elude the ruler of this age? (2) What is the meaning of the expression "mysteries of a cry" and the statement that these "mysteries of a cry" were accomplished ἐν ἡσυχίᾳ θεοῦ? And (3) if these proclaimed mysteries disrupted a time of divine quietness (if not total inaudibility), ending that era, and yet still remained unknown to the ruler of this age, then how were they also announced and made known to the world?

First to consider is the significance of the statement that these mysteries "eluded" (ἔλαθεν)³⁸ the ruler of this age.³⁹ A form of λανθάνω occurs two

---

35 This passage is the most commented on from Ignatius' corpus. So Paulsen, *Die Briefe des Ignatius*, writes, "Kaum ein Text der ign Briefe hat in einem solchen Ausmass die Aufmerksamkeit auf sich gezogen wie Eph 19" (43). Lightfoot, *The Apostolic Fathers*, 2.2.76–77, offers a helpful summary of the Patristic reception of this passage.
36 The angel Gabriel's promises that Mary "will conceive by means of this word" and give birth to Jesus (*Prot. Jas.* 11:5–8) are also described by the narrator as μυστήρια in *Prot. Jas.* 12:6–9 (following the versification of Ronald F. Hock, *The Infancy Gospels of James and Thomas* [The Scholars Bible 2; Santa Rosa, CA: Polebridge Press, 1995]). Particularly interesting is the fact that whereas in Ignatius the mysteries are said to have "eluded" the ruler (using an aorist form of λανθάνω) in *Protoevangelium James* the mysteries are said to have been "forgotten" by Mary (using a cognate aorist form in the compound ἐπιλανθάνομαι) (12:6).
37 The association of μυστήριον with Christ is of course in keeping with the Pauline precedent, though no Pauline text makes the exact correspondences that Ignatius does.
38 The verb is singular and, therefore, its precise subject is not clear. Though it is possible that it agrees only with the nearest subject and not the entire collective, it is more likely that the neuter plural τρία μυστήρια should be read as the subject. The sense does not significantly change either way.

other times in this letter (14.1; 15.3), and in both instances some sort of active concealment is described along with the reason for why something has remained unknown to someone else. As will become clear below, the sense here is likely also that knowledge of the mysteries escaped the ruler because God deliberately concealed them from him.[40] The association of "the ruler of this age" with ignorance of a Christian mystery is almost certainly dependent on 1 Cor 2:7–8. In that passage Paul states that the plural "rulers of this age" did not know the hidden mystery of God's wisdom because if they had then they would not have crucified the Lord of glory. By doing so they instead abetted God's plan for redeeming humanity and so contributed to their own undoing. The same rationale can be inferred here. The mysteries of salvation eluded the ruler of this age because if the ruler had been aware of their true significance then he would not have permitted their occurrence.[41] The visible and very public mysteries of Christ's advent and death thus remained riddles to the ruler in the sense that he remained unaware of what they truly were even while helping to bring them about. As Lightfoot puts it, "It is not…the fact of the death, but the significance and effects of the death, to which Ignatius refers. The prince of this world instigated the death of Christ, not knowing that it was ordained to be the life of mankind. Thus the deceiver was himself deceived."[42]

The next critical issue is the meaning of the final phrase: "three mysteries of a cry which were accomplished ἐν ἡσυχίᾳ θεοῦ." This expression corresponds to *Magn.* 8.2, where the revelation of God in Christ is described as the "word of God proceeding from silence (ἀπὸ σιγῆς)," which is Ignatius' way of stating that Christ's advent brings to an end a previous era of concealment. Here the

---

[39] Cf. also *Ascen. Isa.* 11.16, where Christ's birth is described as being hidden "from the heavens, all princes, and every god of this world."
[40] This is why translators such as Kirsopp Lake (LCL) render the verb passively: "were hidden."
[41] See *Eph.* 17.1 for the deceptive intent of the ruler.
[42] Lightfoot, *The Apostolic Fathers*, 2.2.77. I should note that the alignment of this text with 1 Cor 2 is also supported by the allusions to 1 Cor 1:19, 20, and 23 in 18.1. Therefore, mirroring the structure of Paul's argument in 1 Cor 1–2, Ignatius raises the subject of the scandal (σκάνδαλον) of the cross in 18.1 (cf. 1 Cor 1:23) – even referring nearly verbatim to the rhetorical questions posed by Paul in 1 Cor 1:20. Then in 18.1–19.3 he turns to the revelation of Christ's mysteries and the reasons for their concealment. So also Lightfoot, *The Apostolic Fathers*, observes, "As Ignatius has quoted the context of this passage of S. Paul just before, we must suppose that he had the Apostle's words in his mind here" (2.2.78). Paulsen, *Die Briefe des Ignatius*, also emphasizes the importance of 1 Cor 2 for understanding this passage while at the same time attending to Ignatius' independent use of the traditional material: "Ign setzt dies überlieferte Material im Kontext eigener Theologie ein" (44).

"three mysteries of a cry"[43] include the totality of Christ's earthly sojourn – his conception, birth, and death – and "in the quietness of God" designates the point in time in which the "cry" of these events occurred – during the era of concealment.[44] Read in this way, κραυγή corresponds to ἡσυχία[45] in the same way that disclosure corresponds to concealment: the latter countermands the former. The mysteries of Christ's incarnation and death are, therefore, mysteries "of a cry" because, for those who properly comprehend them, they newly announce what was previously kept hushed. And so once again in *Eph.* 19.1 Ignatius synchronizes mystery, Christ's advent, and a previous era of concealment in a manner quite similar to Rom 16:25–26, but in this instance he also integrates the "previously hidden, presently revealed" schema with the depiction of the unknowing ruler drawn from 1 Cor 2:8.

The third question is raised by Ignatius himself at the outset of 19.2. If the revelation of Christ's mysteries conclude the previous era of concealment but yet still remained concealed from the ruler of this age, "then how was [Christ] revealed (ἐφανερώθη) to the world (τοῖς αἰῶσιν)?"[46] Ignatius answers this question in the so-called "star hymn" in 19.2–3:[47]

> A star shined in heaven above all the other stars, and its light was unspeakable (ἀνεκλάλητος), and its newness (καινότης) caused astonishment, and all the other stars, together with the sun and the moon, formed a chorus with this star, but its light was surpassing all the others. And there was perplexity as to this new thing (καινότης), so unlike the others. From

---

43 There is no reason, like David Daube, "Τρία μυστήρια κραυγῆς: Ignatius, *Ephesians*, XIX. I," *JTS* 16 (1965): 128–29, to connect the cry with something as specific as the cry of Elizabeth in Luke 1:42 and the cry of Jesus on the cross.
44 In commenting on this passage Guy Stroumsa, *Hidden Wisdom: Esoteric Wisdom and the Roots of Christian Mysticism* (Leiden/New York: Brill, 1996), perceptively notes, "'Mystery' is here used in a highly idiosyncratic way: the term refers to events which are not kept secret. On the contrary, they represent the apex of God's new revelation to mankind. These events, hence, are highly visible although, through a cunning of some sorts, they remain hidden from Satan.... Hence, what is hidden is also what is revealed, but can be understood only through faith, not through wisdom" (162–63).
45 The term ἡσυχία also denotes silence in *Eph.* 15.2.
46 Ignatius' other uses of αἰών confirm the translation "world" here. In 8.1 the Ephesian church is described as "renowned throughout the world (τοῖς αἰῶσιν)," and in 1.1 they are described as predestined "before the world" (πρὸ αἰώνων). There is then little basis for finding a reference to Valentinian aeons here.
47 Theories on the source and background of the "star hymn" in 19.2–3 abound (see Schoedel, *Ignatius*, 87–89). The Gnostic hypothesis has recently been rehabilitated by Thomas Lechner, *Ignatius adversus Valentinianos? Chronologische und theologiegeschichtliche Studien zu den Briefen des Ignatius von Antiochen* (Leiden: Brill, 1999). Allen Brent, *Ignatius of Antioch and the Second Sophistic*, 240–42, provides a convincing rebuttal of Lechner's thesis.

it all magic was being destroyed and every bond of wickedness was being obliterated, ignorance was being deposed, and the old kingdom was being destroyed. God was being manifested as a man (θεοῦ ἀνθρωπίνως φανερουμένου) for the newness of eternal life (εἰς καινότητα ἀϊδίου ζωῆς), and this was the beginning of what had been prepared by God. Hence all things were in commotion on account of the plot to destroy death.

Here Ignatius describes the appearance of a star in heaven – a new thing exceeding all other celestial bodies and receiving their worship – as the herald and sign of Christ's manifestation.[48] From the moment of the star's appearance, which corresponds to the moment in which God was revealed as a human, the collapse of the old kingdom began (which included magic, wickedness, and ignorance)[49] and at the same time the manifestation of God's pre-established plan for the abolition of death and the "newness" (καινότητα)[50] of eternal life occurred. This cosmic presentation of Christ's manifestation in 19.2–3 confirms that the "three mysteries" were not absolutely hidden from the ruler. They were enacted publically – even cosmically – and visible to the entire cosmos. But, as in 1 Cor 2:8, the ruler did not comprehend the true significance of the events which he even facilitated. Therefore, Christ's incarnation and death are designated mysteries because, as Schoedel explains, these "unheralded events of salvation cry out their meaning to those who are able to grasp their significance."[51] The ruler failed to grasp this meaning, and so for him the signifier is disclosed but the signified remains unknown.

It is important to note in conclusion that this description of revelation emphasizes both the historical (or *Nacheinander*) as well as the interpersonal (or *Nebeneinander*) orientation of the hidden/revealed dynamic. On the one hand, the manifestation of Christ's mysteries divides history into contrasting eras of concealment and universal disclosure. On the other hand, however, *Eph.* 19.1 also maintains the persistence of the hidden/revealed dynamic with respect to the ruler of this age. And so even though the mysteries of Christ's birth and death have been cosmically unveiled, those mysteries are only truly known when they are correctly perceived as inaugurating the deliverance of humanity.

---

48 Cf. Matt 2:1–12 and the remarkably similar language in Clement of Alexandria, *Exc.* 69–75 and *Prot. Jas.* 19.2.
49 The imperfect verbs used for the undoing of the old kingdom in 19.3 likely have an inceptive sense. Thus the collapse has begun but is not yet complete.
50 This noun appears only one other time in Ignatius, in *Magn.* 9.1, where it is applied to the newness of Christian hope. Thus the idea of the "newness" of the Christian mystery is emphasized in both places. Cf. the observations of Barnett, *Paul Becomes a Literary Influence*, 157.
51 Schoedel, *Ignatius*, 91.

5.2.3 Revelation in Ignatius

Before concluding this section on mystery in Ignatius, I should offer a few comments on revelation more generally in the letters. The only other detailed statement about revelation is Ignatius' personal claim to special esoteric knowledge in *Trall.* 5.1–2:

> Surely I am not unable to write to you heavenly things, but I fear lest, being infants, I harm you. Pardon me, lest you be choked by what you cannot handle. For I myself, even though I am bound and able to know heavenly things and the angelic places and the archonic compositions – things visible and invisible – besides all this I am a disciple even now.

This passage weaves together Pauline intertexts as Ignatius depicts himself, like Paul, as possessing privileged access to heavenly visions (cf. 2 Cor 12:1–4) – ὁρατά τε καὶ ἀόρατα (cf. Col 1:16). But he does not share this information with the Trallians because they are not yet mature (cf. 1 Cor 2:6; 3:1–2).[52] This does not mean that Ignatius is in principle opposed to Christians pursuing knowledge of the heavenly realms, for he exhorts Polycarp to pray "that invisible things might be revealed" to him so that he should lack nothing and abound in every gift (*Pol.* 2.2). The pursuit of revealed esoterica is indeed an edifying Christian ambition, but only for those who have attained a certain degree of maturity.

The place of Israel's scriptures as sources of revelation for Ignatius is notoriously difficult to gauge.[53] Though possible biblical allusions can be variously multiplied or curtailed, he quotes scripture explicitly in only three places (*Eph.* 5.3 [Prov 3:34];[54] *Magn.* 12 [Prov 18:17]; *Trall.* 8.2 [Isa 52:5]),[55] but these are rather vague, proverbial expressions (two are from Proverbs!). He does refer to the prophets on six occasions and always positively (*Magn.* 8.2; 9.2; *Phld.* 5.2; 9.1; 9.2; *Smyrn.* 7.2).[56] But, as already discussed, these ostensible Israel-

---

[52] The best recounting of potential allusions in this passage is Lightfoot, *The Apostolic Fathers*, 163–65.
[53] On this question see Matthew W. Mitchell, "In the Footsteps of Paul: Scriptural and Apostolic Authority in Ignatius of Antioch," *JECS* 14 (2006): 27–45.
[54] Cf. the citation of this passage in Jas 4:6; 1 Pet 5:5; and *1 Clem.* 30.2.
[55] Only *Eph.* 5.3 and *Magn.* 12 mark the citation with an introductory formula involving γέγραπται.
[56] There is, curiously, little mention and no citation of Torah in the letters (see, however, the passing reference to the νόμος Μωύσεως in *Smyrn.* 5.1). But Ignatius clearly opposes those who practice aspects of it. For more on how Ignatius' historical understanding relates to the ongoing question of Jewish law, see Peter Meinhold, "Die geschichtstheologischen Konzeptionen des Ignatius von Antiochien," in *Studien zu Ignatius von Antiochien* (Wiesbaden: Franz Steiner, 1979), 37–47.

ite voices have been mostly divested of any Jewish particularity, being converted into pre-Christian prototypes of the Christian way of life. As Ignatius himself writes, "And let us also love the prophets because of the fact that they also proclaimed the gospel and hoped in [Jesus] and waited for him, and believing in him were saved" (*Phld.* 5.2).

The most discussed passage for evaluating Ignatius' view of scripture is the dispute he reports concerning the "archives" in *Phld.* 8.2.[57] The critical questions in this passage concern the meaning of τὰ ἀρχεῖα and then their relationship to τὸ εὐαγγέλιον. If, as most scholars conclude, the "archives" refer to Israel's sacred scriptures, then this passage is a clear statement of Ignatius' subordination of "Old Testament" to gospel tradition. Interestingly, Ignatius does not actually question his opponents' slogan: "If I do not find it in the archives, I do not believe in the gospel." Seemingly confident in the gospel's scriptural foundation, Ignatius avers that "it" – presumably some doctrine or fact related to the gospel – has been written (γέγραπται). But when his opponents remain unconvinced that "it" has been written ("that is the question" they reply) Ignatius changes course and asserts the superior authority of Christ's revelation: "the archives (ἀρχεῖα) are Jesus Christ, the inviolable archives (τὰ ἄθικτα ἀρχεῖα) are his cross and death and the faith which is through him – in these I want to be justified through your prayers." And so what initially appeared to be an acknowledgement that the gospel is rooted in the "archives" of Israel's scriptures turns into a statement of Christ's superior authority.[58]

In the end Ignatius' attitude toward scripture appears to be one of ambivalence (no better demonstrated than in *Phld.* 8.2). Though he does not seem to be averse to it,[59] when he recovers scriptural voices and figures such as the prophets they are stripped of anything that might smack of "Judaism" and instead are restyled as proto-disciples of Christ. He certainly does not appear to have felt obliged to interact with Israel's "archives" in any extended way.[60] A similarly un-

---

[57] There has been extensive comment on this passage. See Mitchell, "In the Footsteps of Paul," 36–40 and the bibliography and analysis provided in William R. Schoedel, "Ignatius and the Archives," *HTR* 71 (1978): 97–106.

[58] As for his view on Torah, again, one can only speculate since he does not cite or comment on it. Its absence is likely another indicator of the deep rift between Christianity and Israel in Ignatius' thought.

[59] As he says himself, the Christian should "attend to the prophets, but above all to the gospel" (*Smyrn.* 7.2).

[60] I agree with Mitchell, "In the Footsteps of Paul," who concludes that Ignatius' "infrequent reliance on the Jewish scriptures derives from a desire to subordinate the Old Testament to other sources of authority. The letters of Ignatius thus reflect a transitional state in early Chris-

certain posture toward Jewish scripture is to be found in the *Epistle to Diognetus* as well, and it is to this that we now turn.

5.3 Epistle to Diognetus

"No text and no context. These circumstances confront the investigator of the document known as the *Epistle to Diognetus*" – so Paul Foster candidly states the uncertainty surrounding this document.[61] The only medieval copy of the manuscript of *Diognetus* was destroyed by fire in 1870, and so our knowledge of the text depends entirely on the transcriptions that have been preserved.[62] Further magnifying the obscurity surrounding this text is the fact that prior to its discovery in Constantinople around 1436, it was evidently unknown to ancient and medieval Christian authors. There are no extant citations of it and, to the best of our knowledge, it is never otherwise referred to. In spite of this document's insignificance prior to the 15th century, however, modern scholars have not been dissuaded from regarding it as an important and likely very early work of Christian apologetics.

The text as we have it is anonymous. Since the other writings in the codex in which it was originally found (*Argentoratensis*) are ascribed to Justin Martyr, early critics assumed Justin to be the author. The differences between *Diognetus* and the writings of Justin are now recognized to be so great that this is no longer a tenable position, but no other options have garnered widespread agreement. As Meecham described the situation some decades ago, "The door of speculation thus stands open, and many have not hesitated to enter boldly in."[63] Such spec-

---

tianity wherein the phrasing of Paul's writings serves as a normative exemplar, although there is not yet any reference to exclusively Christian written authorities" (27; from the abstract).

61 Paul Foster, "The *Epistle to Diognetus*," in *The Writings of the Apostolic Fathers* (ed. Paul Foster; London/New York: T&T Clark, 2007), 147–56, 147. The most comprehensive and recent Englsh language introduction to *Diognetus* is Clayton N. Jefford, *The Epistle to Diognetus (with the Fragment of Quadratus): Introduction, Text, and Commentary* (Oxford: Oxford University Press, 2013). See also Horacio E. Lona, *An Diognet: Übersetzt und erklärt* (KFA 8; Freiburg: Herder, 2001).

62 For the history of the manuscript, see most recently Jefford, *The Epistle to Diognetus*, 5–8. See also Foster, "The *Epistle to Diognetus*," 147–48; Horacio E. Lona, "Diognetus," in *The Apostolic Fathers: An Introduction* (ed. Wilhelm Pratscher; Waco: Baylor University Press, 2010), 197–213, 197.

63 Henry G. Meecham, *The Epistle to Diognetus: The Greek Text with Introduction, Translation and Notes* (Manchester: Manchester University Press, 1949), 16. As evidence of the wide-ranging speculation, see the list of some fifteen scholarly proposals provided by Henri Irénée Marrou, *A*

ulation continues today,⁶⁴ but I regard the author simply as an erudite yet unnamed Christian apologist.

More pressing is the question of date. Scholarly opinions run the gamut, but I find the evidence to favor a date of composition sometime in the middle or early part of the second century. This judgment is based primarily on appraisal of the key similarities and differences that exist between *Diognetus* and other later second-century apologies.⁶⁵ As Bart Ehrman writes, "The book embodies concerns and emphases comparable to other apologists of the second century, although it shows no familiarity with (or, at least, regard for) arguments based on 'proof from prophecy' or with the 'logos doctrine' that proved so popular among them."⁶⁶ Also absent is any trace of a Marcionite conflict, or any anxiety about any other Christian "heresy" for that matter.⁶⁷ There are thus plausible reasons for regarding *Diognetus* as one of the earliest instances of a formal Christian apology.⁶⁸ This perhaps also accounts for why the document was unknown or unimportant to subsequent authors: it was simply overshadowed by the more

---

Diognète: Introduction, édition critique, traduction et commentaire (SC 33; Paris: Cerf, 1951), 242–43.

64 Among the more recent explorations of this question is Charles E. Hill, *From the Lost Teaching of Polycarp: Identifying Irenaeus' Apostolic Presbyter and the Author of* Ad Diognetum (WUNT 186; Tübingen: Mohr Siebeck, 2006).

65 *Diognetus* is most similar to the *Apology* of Aristides, especially in the shared absence of the "proof from prophecy" argumentation that is characteristic of the later apologists and also the lack of any specific mention of heresy. Klaus Wengst, *Schriften des Urchristentums 2: Didache (Apostellehre), Barnabasbrief, Zweiter Clemensbrief, Schrift an Diognet* (Darmstadt: Wissenschaftliche Buchgesellschaft, 1984), 308–9, argues that *Diognetus'* relationship with the apologetic genre suggests a date of composition in the latter part of the second century but, again, such a judgment does not take into account some of the major differences between the style of argumentation in *Diognetus* and the more developed and standardized apologies.

66 Bart D. Ehrman, *Apostolic Fathers* (vol. 2; LCL; Cambridge: Harvard University Press, 2003), 127. Ehrman tentatively suggests that "this should be regarded as one of the earlier apologies, written during the second half of the second century, possibly closer to the beginning than the end of that period." Meecham, *Diognetus*, 19, provides similar but more detailed reasons for an early date.

67 For dating *Diognetus* prior to Marcion, see Charles M. Nielsen, "The Epistle to Diognetus: Its Date and Relationship to Marcion," *AThR* 52 (1970): 77–91.

68 For instance, Ehrman, *Apostolic Fathers*, further notes that *Diognetus* "makes almost no use of the writings that later came to be canonized as the Christian Scriptures; and its striking theological assertions (esp. chs. 7–8) are not characterized by the nuance and refinement found among equally educated Christian authors at later times" (127). Cf. also the list of arguments for an early date supplied by Meecham, *The Epistle to Diognetus*, 19.

mature works of the great mid to late second- and third-century apologists.[69] I should add that the use of μυστήριον in the text lends further support to an earlier date. On the one hand, the prevalence of the term in the document accords with other mid to late second-century authors such as Justin, Melito, and Tertullian.[70] But on the other hand, the use of the term in relation to the division of history into adjoining ages of concealment and revelation – and not in relation to hermeneutical claims about scriptural meaning – belongs to a time period closer to Ignatius and the various Pauline letters than to those authors situated in the second-half of the second century.

5.3.1 Literary Structure and Content

Among the more difficult issues that interpreters of *Diognetus* face is the fragmentary nature of the text as we now have it. Two problems with this manuscript are major: the first is a lacuna of unknown length at 7.6, and the second is the abrupt break and literary shift in the final two chapters (11–12). The textual break between 10 and 11 is especially critical, and scholars have long suspected that chs. 1–10 and 11–12 are separate works,[71] possibly even from separate authors, that were inadvertently fused together.[72] The foremost reason for this conclusion is that whereas chs. 1–10 constitute an apology addressed to a pagan inquirer named Diognetus, 11–12 appear to be something like a homily addressed to a plural audience who is already Christian ("those becoming disciples in the truth" [11.1]). While sensitive to all possibilites in my analysis, I am persuaded, following L.W. Barnard, that though these two sections of text belong to separate works, they do not belong to separate authors.[73] The consistent use of μυστήριον in 1–10 and 11–12 supports the judgment of a single author.[74]

---

69 Nielsen, "The Epistle to Diognetus," makes a similar point, contending that *Diognetus* 1–10 was neglected by later authors because these chapters were composed "before Marcion came on the scene and were therefore relevant neither to him nor his enemies." Moreover, these chapters "had so many dangerous points of contact with Marcionism, the Catholics could not be expected to preserve them" (82).
70 Bornkamm, "μυστήριον, μυέω," also notices that "[f]rom the time of the early apologetic the term acquires increasing importance" (*TDNT* 4:825).
71 The conclusion that these chapters belong to a separate works goes back to the first editor of the document, Henricus Stephanus, in 1592.
72 For more on these matters see Ehrman, *Apostolic Fathers*, 124.
73 For more on this see L.W. Barnard, "The Epistle Ad Diognetum: Two Units from One Author," *ZNW* 56 (1965): 130–37.

As for literary structure, the document is organized as follows:

1	Prologue
2.1–10	The Errors of Paganism
3.1–4.6	The Errors of Judaism
5.1–6.10	The Distinctive Character of the Christian Religion
7.1–9	The Divine Origin of Christian Revelation
8.1–8.11	God's Eternal Plan and the Revelation of God's Son
9.1–9.6	The Revelation of God's Plan and the Contrast of the Two Ages
10.1–8	Becoming an Imitator of God

Appended Homily

11.1–8	The Newness of the Word
12.1–9	An allegory on Genesis 3

The prologue opens with an address to an otherwise unidentified Diognetus who is described as zealous to learn more about "the religion (τὴν θεοσέβειαν) of Christians."[75] This Diognetus has apparently posed a series of questions about Christians: (1) Who is their God? (2) How do they worship? (3) Why do they disregard the world and not fear death? (4) Why do they acknowledge neither the gods of the Greeks nor the religion/superstition (δεισιδαιμονία)[76] of the Jews? (5) What is the nature of the love they have for one another? And finally (6) "why did this new race or practice (γένος ἢ ἐπιτήδευμα) enter the world now and not formerly?"[77] The remainder of 1–10 addresses these questions and can be divided into two, unequal parts. The first (2–4) presents a negative account of pagan and Jewish worship, focusing especially on what the author regards as their absurdities – ritual sacrifice being foremost. The second and lengthier section (5–10) offers a positive account of Christianity, describing its unique position in the world (5–6), its origins in God's recent self-revelation in the Son's advent (7–8), the reasons God deferred this revelation until only recently (9), and the benefits of embracing Christian truth (10). The appended

---

74 Hill, *From the Lost Teaching of Polycarp*, likewise notices that the "common development of the idea of God's μυστήριον...also connects the two portions of text" (125).
75 There is no way to determine who this figure is. The tutor of Marcus Aurelius is the most common suggestion (*Meditations* 1.6).
76 Given the use of this term in 4.1, the sense here is likely derogatory. The denigration of Judaism is in fact something that the Christian author and his pagan addressee can agree upon.
77 For an excellent treatment of race and ethnicity, see Denise Kimber Buell, *Why this New Race: Ethnic Reasoning in Early Christianity* (New York: Columbia University Press, 2005). Though Buell takes the title of her book from the prologue of *Diognetus*, the idea of Christianity as a new γένος does not elsewhere appear in the letter, and so *Diognetus* is only briefly treated by Buell.

homily also treats the theme of Christianity as newly revealed in the Word's advent (11). It then provides a creative rereading of the two trees planted in Eden (12), the goal of which is to recover the place of knowledge within the life of faith.

Also important to the structure of the text is the strategic placement of μυστήριον across the whole of the document. It appears in this relatively short work seven times, two times in the singular (4.6; 8.10) and five in the plural (7.1, 2; 10.7; 11.2, 5). The first three occurrences at 4.6 and 7.1, 2 are in literary seams that serve as bridges between major sections, concluding what precedes and introducing the principal topic that ensues. The use of the term in 8.10 also occurs within the concluding statement of that section. Though the two occurrences of μυστήριον in 11.2, 5 are not necessarily significant for the structure of that chapter, the term is integral to its central subject, which concerns the eternal existence of the Son/Word and his recent manifestation to the world. Therefore, both the prevalence of the term as well as its structural locations confirm Meecham's observation that μυστήριον is "a favourite word of the author."[78] It is an especially important one for the theology of the author as well.

5.3.2 Diognetus and Paul

Unlike in Ignatius' letters, the name of "Paul" is never explicitly invoked in *Diognetus*, but this is typical of an apologetic work.[79] There is, however, a reference to "the Apostle" in 12.5 with an accompanying quotation of 1 Cor 8:1, but the significance of this citation depends on one's assessment of the integrity and authorship of chs. 11–12. Despite the absence of overt references to Paul in 1–10, distinctly Pauline terms and expressions do frequently appear – the repeated use of μυστήριον being one example.[80] Meecham has identified some eighteen

---

78 Meecham, *Diognetus*, 107.
79 Thus Rensberger, "As the Apostle Teaches," writes, "As we have come to expect in apologetic works, no mention is made of Paul or of his letters. But the influence of Paul is stronger in this short 'epistle' than in any other apology of our period" (288).
80 For research on the relationship between the Pauline letters and *Diognetus*, see Einar Molland, "Die literatur- und dogmengeschichtliche Stellung des Diognetbriefes," *ZNW* 33 (1934): 308–10; Rudolf Brändle, *Die Ethik der "Schrift an Diognet": Eine Wiederaufnahme paulinischer und johanneischer Theologie am Ausgang des zweiten Jahrhunderts* (ATANT 64; Zürich: Theologischer Verlag Zürich, 1975), esp. 202–16; Dassmann, *Der Stachel im Fleisch*, 254–59; Andreas Lindemann, "Paulinische Theologie im Brief an Diognet," in *Kerygma und Logos: Beiträge zu den geistesgeschichtlichen Beziehungen zwischen Antike und Christentum* (Göttingen: Vandenhoeck & Ruprecht, 1979), 337–50 and Lindemann's *Paulus im ältesten Christentum*, 343–50; K. Wengst, "'Paulinismus' und 'Gnosis' in der Schrift an Diognet," *ZKG* 90 (1979): 41–62; Re-

potential allusions and near citations of Paul's letters,[81] with 5.8–16 being a particularly dense site of characteristic Pauline terms and expressions.[82] I concur with the judgment of Andreas Lindemann, "Dieser 'Brief' enthält zwar keine Erwähnung des Heidenapostels, aber es finden sich in relativ großem Umfang Gedanken und Formulierungen, die als Anspielungen auf die paulinischen Briefe... anzusehen sind."[83] And so, "Richtig ist aber, dass sich seine Paulus-Rezeption auf einem Niveau bewegt, das vor ihm kein anderer uns bekannter christlicher Autor – die Vf. von Kol und Eph vielleicht ausgenommen – erreicht hat und daß insofern Dg in der ältesten Theologiegeschichtliche ohne Vorbild ist."[84] In what follows I shall make the case that, like Ignatius, this author's use of μυστήριον very likely originates in Paul's own usage, and in the deuteropauline mystery schema in particular.[85] And so, like Ignatius, this author adopts the deuteropauline discourse of the newly revealed Christian mystery to divide history into temporally adjacent eras of hiddenness and revelation with the arrival of the Son as the decisive event effecting the division.

5.3.3 Mystery and Revelation in Diognetus

The presentation of Christianity as newly revealed, and so unknowable apart from God's prior initiative, is the most prevalent theological emphasis in *Diogne-*

---

nsberger, "As the Apostle Teaches," 286–93; Michael F. Bird, "The Reception of Paul in the *Epistle to Diognetus*," in *Paul and the Second Century* (ed. Michael F. Bird and Joseph R. Dodson; LNTS 412; London/New York: T&T Clark, 2011), 70–90.
81 Meecham, *Diogneus*, 54–58.
82 In 5.8 Christians are described as appearing ἐν σαρκί but not living κατὰ σάρκα (cf. Rom 8:12, 13; 2 Cor 10:3). Thus they pass their time on earth but have their citizenship in heaven (ἐν οὐρανῷ πολιτεύονται) (5.9) (cf. Phil 3:20). But all does not necessarily go well for them. They are also a persecuted people (5.10–11). In a near quotation of 2 Cor 6:9–10, they are described as "unknown (ἀγνοοῦνται)...put to death and gaining life; they are poor and make many rich" (5.12–13). Freely quoting 1 Cor 4:12, the author further describes the Christians as "being abused but also blessing (λοιδοροῦνται καὶ εὐλογοῦσιν)" (5.15), for they understand that when injured they can rejoice in receiving life (5.16).
83 Andreas Lindemann, "Paulinische Theologie im Brief an Diognet," 337–38.
84 Lindemann, "Paulinische Theologie im Brief an Diognet," 350.
85 In his analysis of μυστήριον in *Diognetus*, Brändle, *Die Ethik der "Schrift an Diognet"*, also finds that "Der Vf des 'Ad Diognetum' schliesst sich an den Mysterienbegriff des Paulus, vor allem aber des Eph und Kol an" (10).

tus, and so the description of Christianity as a recently revealed μυστήριον is unsurprisingly integral to this theme.⁸⁶

The first appearance of μυστήριον in 4.6 comes at the conclusion of the first two sections on the errors of pagan and Jewish worship. Having recounted the alleged absurdities of pagan worship (2.2–20) and the reasons why Christians do not worship "in the same ways" as the Jews (3.1–4.5), the author resumes his direct address to Diognetus in 4.6, warning him that even though he now knows the reasons for the Christian rejection of the above religious traditions, he should not now presume to be able to learn from any human "the mystery of the Christian's own religion" (τὸ...τῆς ἰδίας αὐτῶν θεοσεβείας μυστήριον). The point here is one that recurs throughout the rest of the letter. The Christian mystery is not discernible by any earthly *a priori* because it is only knowable when and where God chooses to disclose it. As is the case throughout the text, the precise content of the μυστήριον is undefined, but since "the mystery of the Christian religion" is contrasted with the all-encompassing religious routines of paganism and Judaism, it most likely refers to the entire array of Christian beliefs and practices, or the total Christian way of life.⁸⁷ Such a broadening of μυστήριον is comparable to the expressions in 1 Tim 3:9 and 3:16, which refer to "the mystery of faith" and "the mystery of devotion" as shorthand phrases for fundamental aspects of Christian doctrine.

Emphasis on the divine and revelatory origins of the Christian way of life – and thus its exceeding value and incontrovertible truth – is repeated again in 5.3, which states that no aspect of Christian knowledge (μάθημα) "has ever been discovered by the intellect (ἐπινοία) or meditation (φροντίς) of meddlesome people." The notion that Christian teaching is not found by human reason is fundamental for the author, and so, as Meecham puts it, since "no argumentative skill or subtlety can avail to win Diognetus to the Faith... [the author] points him now to the *life* of the Christians – the unanswerable proof."⁸⁸ The primary purpose of chs. 5–6 is indeed to demonstrate that because the Christian religion is not of human origin, so also the Christian way of life is not of this world (5.1–17).

---

86 Cf. Walther Eltester, "Das Mysterium des Christentums: Anmerkungen zum Diognetbrief," *ZNW* 61 (1970): 278–93, who similarly describes the relationship between μυστήριον and revelation in *Diognetus*: "Das Christentum ist eben keine menschliche Erfindung, sondern beruht auf Offenbarung. Nichts anderes als die absolute Transzendenz des Ursprungs der christlichen Lehre, ihr supranaturaler Character, wird durch den wiederholten Gebrauch des Wortes Geheimnis (μυστήριον) bezeichnet" (283).
87 Similarly Brändle, *Die Ethik der "Schrift an Diognet"*, writes, "Auf die Bemerkung in 4,6 folgen nicht etwa Ausführungen über Religion und Kultus der Christen, sondern eine Schilderung ihres Lebens" (117).
88 Meecham, *Diognetus*, 107.

The author further develops this point in ch. 6 with an image of Christians as the soul of the world. Just as a soul dwells in a body and spreads throughout it, so Christians reside in the world as inhabitants but not members (6.1–10).

The subject of divine revelation does not reappear again until 7.1, but this passage serves as an introduction to the extended treatment of the topic in chs. 7–9, which form the document's central theological section:

> For it is not, as I said, an earthly discovery (ἐπίγειον...εὕρημα) that was given to them, nor is it some mortal system of thought (θνητὴν ἐπίνοιαν) which they regard themselves worthy to guard diligently, nor is it an economy of human mysteries (ἀνθρωπίνων οἰκονομίαν μυστηρίων) to which they have been entrusted (πεπίστευνται).

Although 7.1 introduces the next major section on revelation, the "as I said" links it with the previous claims about Christianity's divine origins made in 4.6 and 5.3, resuming the emphases of those passages. Once again, therefore, the author insists on the transcendent nature of Christian knowledge by opposing the earthly with the heavenly and the human with the divine.[89] Christians have not been granted a mere οἰκονομία of human mysteries but rather – or so it is implied – they have been entrusted with the οἰκονομία of divine mysteries. The phrase οἰκονομίαν μυστηρίων almost certainly depends on Paul, who uses similar language in several places and, prior to *Diognetus*, is the only extant author to bring these two words together.[90] The most relevant Pauline passages are 1 Cor 4:1,[91] where Paul describes himself and his coworkers as οἰκονόμοι μυστηρίων, and Eph 3:9, where Paul speaks of his commission to enlighten all people about ἡ οἰκονομία τοῦ μυστηρίου which has been hidden from the ages.[92] Directly following Paul, the author of *Diognetus* presents Christians as specially chosen custodians who have gained possession of an assemblage of newly revealed divine μυστήρια that require their stewardship. Additional detail on how these heavenly μυστήρια were entrusted to Christians is supplied in 7.2:

---

[89] These "human mysteries" could conceivably be a reference to cultic rites, although Eltester, "Das Mysterium des Christentums," insists, "Mit dem Ursprung des Begriffs im antiken Mysterienkult hat seine Verwendung in Kapitel 1–10 nichts mehr zu tun" (284).
[90] They also appear together in *Acts of John* 106; *Acts of Andrew* 16; and Justin *Dial.* 134.2; 141.4.
[91] Brändle, *Die Ethik der "Schrift an Diognet"*, 111–12, also identifies a connection with 1 Cor 4:1.
[92] Cf. also Eph 1:10; 3:2; Col 1:25. Paul also associates the term οἰκονομία with the perfect passive of πιστεύω in 1 Cor 9:17.

> But truly God himself – the all-powerful, all-creating, unseen God – founded and established from heaven the truth and the holy word – which is incomprehensible to humans – in their hearts. He did not do this, as one might suppose, by sending some servant or angel or ruler or someone who manages earthly things or someone entrusted with the administration in heaven. Rather he sent the designer and maker of all things himself, through whom he created the heavens…whose mysteries all the elements of creation guard faithfully (οὗ τὰ μυστήρια πιστῶς πάντα φυλάσσει τὰ στοιχεῖα).

The author again emphasizes here that what God has revealed is "incomprehensible" (ἀπερινόητος) to the unaided human mind. This revelation – previously unknown, even unthinkable – arrives from heaven, from the unseen God (ἀόρατος θεός).[93] Lona is correct in noting that the very image of an unseen God would seem to entail "the undeniable need for a revelation to achieve knowledge of God."[94] If God has been unseen, then he can only become seen (or known) through an act of self-revelation, which is exactly how the author characterizes the Son's incarnation. It is the Creator himself who comes to the world, being sent by God and even appearing "as God" (7.3).[95] The revelation of the Son to the world is therefore at the same time God's self-revelation, the event by which the unseen God and all divine mysteries are unveiled. There is then no longer any need for heavenly στοιχεῖα[96] to guard God's mysteries, for these secret designs have now been manifested in the sending of his Son.

The account of this act of divine disclosure is elaborated in the following chapter, which begins with the question: "Who among all humans understood (ἠπίστατο) at any time what God is?" (8.1). The answer to be inferred is that no human understood anything about God prior to the advent of God's Son because knowledge of this God is beyond human discovery. Any claim to the contrary made by human teachers is "fraudulent and the deception of tricksters" (8.4). The author develops this point about deception in 8.2–4, but in 8.5–11 he returns to the topic of the Son as the definitive revelation of the Father. He begins by reiterating that though God was previously unseen, he has now become visible: "For no human saw or made him known, but rather he showed

---
[93] Cf. Col 1:15; 1 Tim 1:17.
[94] Lona, "Diognetus," 204. This idea of the previously undetected God is repeated in 8.5: "No human saw him or made him known, but he revealed himself."
[95] For more on the Christology of *Diognetus*, see Joseph T. Lienhard, "The Christology of the Epistle to Diognetus," *VC* 24 (1970): 280–89. The relationship between Father and Son in this text is closely drawn, but the relationship between the two is also not precisely defined. Various aspects of the Son are simply unselfconsciously stated but never extrapolated and certainly not circumscribed by later strictures of christological dogma.
[96] As the remainder of 7.2 makes clear, the στοιχεῖα who guard the mysteries are the elements of creation: the sun, moon, stars, etc. Cf. Wis 7:17; 19:18; Gal 4:3, 9; Col 2:8, 20; 2 Pet 3:10, 12.

himself" (αὐτὸς δὲ ἑαυτὸν ἐπέδειξεν). In 8.7–8 the author addresses the character of this God, describing him as kind to humans, longsuffering, and not wrathful. Then in 8.9–11 the author situates God's self-revelation historically, explaining how this recent revelation is in fact the consummation of a design determined long ago. He makes this point by utilizing the discursive structure and key vocabulary of the deuteropauline mystery schema:

> And thinking a great and inexpressible thought, he communicated it to the child alone. Therefore, insofar as he concealed it in a mystery (κατεῖχεν ἐν μυστηρίῳ) and preserved his wise counsel (τὴν σοφὴν αὐτοῦ βουλήν), he seemed to neglect and have no concern for us. But then he revealed (ἐπεὶ δὲ ἀπεκάλυψε) it through his beloved child, and manifested (ἐφανέρωσε) the things prepared from the beginning. He gave all things to us at the same time, and to participate in his good deeds and to see and understand (ἰδεῖν καὶ νοῆσαι). Who of us at any time expected this?

As Meecham notes, "The essential point in these sections (the divine design for long kept secret – the possible charge against God of neglect of man – the consequent blessings contrary to all man's expectations) are drawn from Paul's teaching."[97] More specifically, in this passage all the essential ingredients of the deuteropauline mystery schema are present: the eternal plan for salvation concealed ἐν μυστηρίῳ; the previous era of hiddenness; the revelation of the mystery through the Son's agency; the connection with wisdom; and the mention of the ensuing benefits of Christian cognition. The idea of God's eternal plan for salvation as being concealed ἐν μυστηρίῳ coincides with the language of 1 Cor 2:6–8, where Paul speaks of God's wisdom being spoken in a mystery and unknown to the rulers of this age (the interpersonal or *Nebeneinander* emphasis), but the larger schema agrees with the chronological partitioning of history into two temporally successive epochs of concealment and disclosure with the apocalypse of the Son as the revelatory agent who performs the division (the diachronic or *Nacheinander* emphasis).

In ch. 9 the nature of these two eras is further defined in relation to Diognetus' question in the prologue concerning Christianity's belated appearance in the world. The author begins by terming the two historical epochs "the former time of unrighteousness" (τῷ τότε τῆς ἀδικίας καιρῷ) and "the present time of righteousness" (τὸν νῦν τῆς δικαιοσύνης).[98] Within this chapter the author then repeatedly contrasts these two eras in similar terms:[99]

---

97 Meecham, *Diognetus*, 126.
98 Paul is often cited as possible background for *Diognetus*' contrast of ages. See esp. Rom 3:21–26; Eph 2:1–9; Titus 3:3–7.

1) "as long as the former time (τοῦ πρόσθεν χρόνου) endured" (9.1) // "and then our unrighteousness was fulfilled" (9.2).
2) "not in the former time of unrigheousness (τῷ τότε τῆς ἀδικίας καιρῷ)" (9.1) // "but the present time of righteousness (τὸν νῦν τῆς δικαιοσύνης)" (9.1).
3) "in the former time" (ἐν τῷ τότε χρόνῳ) (9.1) // "now" (νῦν) (9.1).
4) "in the prior time" (ἐν μὲν τῷ πρόσθεν χρόνῳ) (9.6) // "but now" (νῦν δέ) (9.6).

Having planned everything long ago with the Child, the Father permitted humans to indulge their perverse desires during the former age. This forbearance of human iniquity in the former time, however, was not an endorsement of that behavior (9.1). Rather the purpose of the former age was, first, to make it plain to humanity that entering the kingdom of God is only possible by the power of God (9.1) and, second, to allow humans to appreciate more fully the incomparable kindness of God (9.1, 6). When the ledger of human iniquity was finally full – and thus humans were properly prepared to appreciate God's goodness – the time came for God to manifest his kindness by sending his righteous Son as a ransom (λύτρον) – "the innocent for the guilty" (9.2). The remainder of this chapter (9.2–6), in a quintessentially Pauline register, eulogizes this event in which the righteousness of the one man makes the many lawless ones righteous as well (9.5; cf. Rom 5:15–21).[100]

In ch. 10, the final extant chapter of the main document, the author offers a few reflections on the benefits of Christian knowledge and of becoming an imitator of God.[101] Again addressing Diognetus directly, the author explains that if he achieves full knowledge of God's love, then he in turn will be inspired to extend such love to his neighbors. In so doing he becomes an imitator of God, and to those who receive him he even "becomes a god" (θεὸς γίνεται) (10.6). Though he remains on earth, he will be permitted to see that God lives in heaven and he will begin to speak the μυστήρια θεοῦ to others (10.7).[102] The idea here is that

---

99 Cf. Lienhard, "The Christology of the Epistle to Diognetus," who remarks on these temporal juxtapositions: "Time, for the author, is clearly divided into two parts; and the event which separates them is the coming of the Son.... [H]is absolute division of time into two ages demands an absolute event that marks the division—precisely what modern authors mean by 'the Christ event', a decisive, historical occurrence that radically and permanently alters the course of cosmic history" (285).
100 Commenting on these passages, Meecham, *Diognetus*, writes, "Our author's thought is deeply Pauline" (130).
101 On the μιμητὴς θεοῦ theme in Diognetus, see Michael Heintz, "Μιμητὴς θεοῦ in the *Epistle to Diognetus*," *JECS* 12 (2004): 107–19.
102 Cf. 1 Cor 14:2.

just as the Son manifested the Father's love and revealed the mysteries of God to humans, so too the Christian, in perhaps something even akin to a moment of theosis, can participate in the divine task of revealing the mysteries of Christianity to other humans.[103]

The text breaks off at 10.8 and what is most likely a separate document commences at 11.1.[104] Although ch. 11 probably belongs to a separate work, the use of μυστήριον as denoting unspecific aspects of Christian identity and belief agrees with what is found in chs. 1–10. Chapter 11 begins with a self-description of the author. He claims to be a "disciple of the apostles" and a "teacher of Gentiles"[105] who desires to be a worthy servant of what has been handed down to him for "those who are becoming disciples of truth." After this introduction, the author then states the reasons for his commitment to apostolic authority (11.2–3):

> 11.2 For who, being rightly taught and becoming pleasing to the Word, does not seek to learn exactly the things made known plainly through the Word to the disciples? The Word appeared and revealed (ἐφανέρωσεν ὁ λόγος φανείς) to them these things, speaking openly to them (though he was not understood by unbelievers). He related fully these things to the disciples who, when they were reckoned faithful by him, came to know the mysteries of the father (ἔγνωσαν πατρὸς μυστήρια). 11.3 And for this reason he sent the Word in order that he should be manifest (φανῇ) to the world – this one who was dishonored by the people (ὑπὸ λαοῦ), was proclaimed (κηρυχθείς) through the apostles, was believed by the Gentiles (ὑπὸ ἐθνῶν ἐπιστεύθη).

The author claims to submit to the tradition of the disciples of the Word because of the fact that they were the original human trustees of the Father's mysteries.[106] The content of the "mysteries of the Father" is not defined, but since they are related to traditions given to the disciples (11.1–2), they likely refer to something like the gospel and perhaps also subsequent liturgical and theological teaching. What is unmistakable here is the emphasis on the Word as God's special envoy of revelation. There is no explicit mention of a previous era of concealment, but the description of the Word who has appeared and revealed mysteries entails the division of time into an era in which the Word did not reveal mysteries and the current era in which he has revealed mysteries.[107] Another characteristic feature

---

[103] Once again the content of these mysteries is undefined, and so once again they should probably be read as referring generally to the Christian way of life.
[104] The manuscript has a marginal note identifying that the text has broken off at this point.
[105] Cf. 1 Tim 2:7; 2 Tim 1:11. The focus on the Gentiles reappears in 11.3.
[106] Cf. the entrusting of the οἰκονομίαν μυστηρίων in 7.1–2.
[107] There is also an interpersonal dimension to the hidden/revealed discourse in that the Word, though he is revealed and speaks openly to the disciples, is not understood by unbelievers.

of the deuteropauline mystery schema present in this passage is the identification of the Gentiles as those who trusted the Word. The entire expression concerning the proclaimation (κηρυχθείς) of the Word's manifestation through the apostles and it being believed by the Gentiles (ὑπὸ ἐθνῶν ἐπιστεύθη) is a near citation of 1 Tim 3:16, which, in similar creedal style, equates "the mystery of Christian devotion"[108] with "what was proclaimed to Gentiles, believed in the world" (ἐκηρύχθη ἐν ἔθνεσιν, ἐπιστεύθη ἐν κόσμῳ).[109] Thus in typical Pauline fashion, the Gentiles in *Diognetus* are singled out and contrasted with the people of Israel (ὁ λαός)[110] who dishonored the Word and his revelation. The connection with Paul on this matter is further strengthened by the author's earlier self-description as a "teacher of Gentiles."

In 11.4–5 additional details are given about the Word's manifestation:

> 11.4 This is the one who was from the beginning, who appeared new and was found old, who is always being born new in the hearts of saints. 11.5 This one is the eternal one, who today is reckoned the Son, through whom the church is enriched and grace is unfolded and multiplied to the saints. This grace offers understanding (χάρις...παρέχουσα νοῦν), manifests mysteries (φανεροῦσα μυστήρια), announces times, rejoices in the faithful, and is given to those who seek, among whom the pledges of faith (ὅρκια πίστεως)[111] are not broken, nor the boundaries of the Fathers (ὅρια πατέρων) transgressed.

Here the author again underscores that the Word (who is also the Son) is in fact eternal even though he appears new from the vantage point of the world ("he appeared new and was found old"). Emphasis is also again placed on the Word's revelation as an act of grace that opens up new cognitive possibilities for humanity ("this grace offers understanding") and makes knowable previously unknown mysteries. Also once again the author restricts this grace and those mysteries to the faithful, who neither break "the pledges of the faith" nor transgress "the boundaries of the Fathers."[112] As is the author's consistent pattern, the contents of these μυστήρια are nowhere elucidated, and so they probably again refer generally to the Christian mode of existence.

---

108 Cf. again *Diogn.* 4.6.
109 The Gentiles are never discussed in chs. 1–10 and so are not incorporated into the revelation schema there, but this is almost certainly due to the subject and audience of those chapters and the fact that the inclusion of the Gentiles into the promises of Israel's God was not among Diognetus' stated concerns in the prologue.
110 This is a common designation for Israel. The contrasts between ὁ λαός for Israel and τὸ ἔθνος for other nations in the Greek Bible are numerous.
111 The phrase ὅρκια πίστεως is Lachmann's conjecture for the manuscript reading ὅρια πίστεως. Almost all editors have followed Lachmann's emendation, and I have as well.
112 Cf. 8.6; 10.1; 11.5.

This concludes the occurrences of μυστήριον in *Diognetus*. The author's use of this word, as well as his more comprehensive theology of revelation, is in important ways consonant with the Pauline precursors – and the deuteropauline mystery schema in particular – and is most likely dependent on them. Both Paul and the author of *Diognetus* associate the revelation of God's mystery with Christ's advent, and both view this happening as a punctiliar moment that in turn peroidizes history into eras of concealment and disclosure. Furthermore, both characterize God's mystery as belonging to an οἰκονομία newly entrusted to humanity, and yet they also describe this mystery as having been determined pretemporally by God but previously concealed. There are of course differences between the deuteropauline versions of the mystery schema and what is found in *Diognetus*. Perhaps most significant is the lack of emphasis in *Diognetus* on the revealed mystery as specifically relevant for the Gentiles. Although there is a special focus on the Gentiles in ch. 11, the accent throughout 1–10 is on the mysteries of God as generally accessible to all believers with no exceptional status apportioned to any particular social grouping, but this fact is easily explained by the genre of those chapters. The generality reflected in these chapters is also characteristic of the author's unspecific use of μυστήριον.[113] Whereas the deuteropauline letters correlate the revealed mystery specifically with the profit of Christ for the Gentiles, in *Diognetus* the term occurs without any such specific correlation and instead appears to refer unspecifically to the new Christian way of life. This generalization of both the term and the discourse is, however, unsurprising given that the subject of the inclusion of Gentiles within the God of Israel's salvific plans is never raised. Although this problem surfaces in and sometimes dominates various Pauline letters, the argumentative necessities in *Diognetus* differ from those of Paul, and most plainly in the fact that the document addresses a pagan inquirer and not a Jew or some individual Christian community. The chief concern in *Diognetus* is to account for the existence of Christianity, particularly its recent appearance in the world. The generalization of the mystery discourse in *Diognetus*, therefore, represents a creative reapplication of the deuteropauline mystery schema in relation to a different social situation and a different circumstance of polemical pressure.

---

113 Markus N.A. Bockmuehl, *Revelation and Mystery in Ancient Judaism and Pauline Christianity* (WUNT 2/36; Tübingen: Mohr Siebeck, 1990), 219–20, also notes the tendency toward generalization.

5.3.4 Conclusion: Christian Revelation and the Question of Judaism

A key question that remains is one we encountered with Ignatius as well. What does the newness of Christian revelation mean for the status of historical Israel and the ongoing relationship of Christianity and Judaism? Many interpreters have concluded that when the author of *Diognetus* maintains that there is no knowledge of God prior to the Son's advent, he means this to be true of ancient Israel as well. According to Meecham, "No place is given to Judaism as a *praeparatio evangelica*.... The pre-Christian world, pagan and Jewish alike, stands under condemnation."[114] Meecham goes on to describe the author's "temper" as "Marcionite in ignoring the historical link between Judaism and Christianity."[115] Lona's appraisal is equally stark: "The distance of Christians from Judaism is so great that they are too estranged for a relationship to have ever existed."[116] Lona additionally claims that the presentation of Christianity in this letter as something of a "third race" entails that both Judaism and paganism "lie equally far from Christianity."[117]

Admittedly, the generalization of the mystery schema in this text and the description of God's revelation as exclusively located in the incarnation would seem, if viewed in isolation, to support these views. In contrast to the deuteropauline letters, which define the revealed mystery specifically as the extension of the God of Israel's promises to the Gentiles, the argument of *Diognetus* appears to broaden the recently revealed mystery to include all knowledge of the divine, even God's existence. The implication of this would seem to be that rather than some aspect of God's plan being hidden from Israel, God's own identity would have been hidden at all times from Israel as well. Just like the pagans, therefore, Israel and ongoing Jewish adherents would have no claim to privileged status or even awareness of this God. The God to which *Diognetus* refers would be the God of Christians alone, a view that would, it seems, indeed accord with Marcion's total bifurcation of the creator God and Christ.

There are, however, problems with this supposedly definite divide between Christianity and Judaism (or Israel) in *Diognetus*. First, for such a position to remain tenable, it requires that one treat 11–12 as either from a different author or from an author who has undergone a major theological transformation on this issue. There is still a critique of Israel (or ὁ λαός) for dishonoring the Word who appeared and revealed mysteries in 11.3, but there is also the unequivocal ap-

---

114 Meecham, *Diognetus*, 29.
115 Meecham, *Diognetus*, 38.
116 Lona, "Diognetus," 204.
117 Lona, "Diognetus," 204.

preciation for Jewish scripture in 11.6, which equates "fear of the Law" (φόβος νόμου) and "the grace of the prophets" (προφητῶν χάρις) with "the faith of the Gospels" and "the tradition of the apostles." Furthermore, the entirety of ch. 12 is an extended interpretation of the fall narrative in Genesis. Therefore, it cannot be said that the author of 11–12 had Marcionite inclinations or viewed Jews as equally distant from Christianity as pagans. Second, there is evidence even within 1–10 that the author recognizes some special status for Israel, as well as a necessary relationship between Christianity and Judaism. In 3.1, the point where the text makes a transition from the critique of paganism to Judaism, the author writes: "And next I suppose that you are especially desiring to hear why the Christians do not worship in the same ways (κατὰ τὰ αὐτά) as the Jews." Throughout the critique of Judaism, the issue is never the identity of the God that the Jews worship but rather how they worship this God. This differs from the description of pagan religion, which derides both the ways in which pagans worship as well as the gods of pagan worship. The author's approval of the God whom the Jews worship is explicitly stated in 3.2, where he explains that insofar as the Jews avoid worshiping their God in the same ways as the pagans, they can claim "truly to worship the one God of the universe (καλῶς θεὸν ἕνα τῶν πάντων σέβειν) and regard him as master." Such a statement affirms that at least some Jews have indeed known the God now revealed in the advent of his Son. It is therefore not accurate to characterize *Diognetus* as Marcionite or to equate the author's characterization of Judaism as equal to his characterization of paganism.

What remains uncertain is how the Jews could ever have worshiped – and therefore known – this God when understanding of "what he is" (8.1) has only become possible after his self-revelation in the sending of the Son. The author does not ever clarify this, and this is likely the reason why some interpreters of *Diognetus* 1–10 have mistakenly characterized the document as Marcionite. There is no denying that the author's critique of Judaism is severe, but this does not require it to be unconditional. Perhaps like Ignatius (also an author of harsh Jewish criticism) the author would have restricted this authentic pre-Christian knowledge of God to a special class of figures within Israel, like the prophets, who both truly knew God and also refrained from improperly worshipping him. Or perhaps he would have distinguished between awareness of this God's existence (*that* he is) and more exact knowledge of his identity (*what* he is). Either way, the author did not compose a treatise on the problem of Jewish-Christian relations and so it was not his task to clarify such subtleties. What is certain is that even if mostly muted, the author of this apology still recognizes indissoluble continuity between the God worshipped by Jews and the God worshipped by Christians even if, much like Ignatius, the Judaism he presupposes is severely truncated and recast exclusively in Christian terms.

6 Mystery, Scriptural Meaning, and the "Grace to Understand" in Justin Martyr's *Dialogue with Trypho*

6.1 Introduction

Whereas Ignatius' letters are written to fellow Christians, and the *Epistle to Diognetus* addresses a pagan inquirer, the bulk of Justin's *Dialogue* rehearses a dramatic conversation between a Christian convert and an otherwise unknown Jew named Trypho and his small band of companions.[1] The principal subject of the *Dialogue* is the meaning of Israel's scriptures and the alleged correlation of those scriptures with the advent of Christ and consequent Christian realities. The drama unfolds therefore in many respects as an in-house contest played out on the shared field of sacred scripture—a textual field that both participants honor as authoritative and claim as their own.[2] To prove his case that Christians are now the people truly on the side of scripture—and, therefore, the God of Israel as well—Justin performs a totalizing rereading of those scriptures, frequently reproducing protracted biblical quotations with protracted commentary on them in order to systematize his central conviction that all scripture attests to the story of Jesus Christ and the church that worships him.[3] In his revisionary interpretations of these lengthy biblical passages, Justin's exegetical project begins at every point with the premise that Christ and consequent Christian realities provide the essential interpretive framework for perceiving what scripture is truly saying. And so, as Francis Watson puts it, Justin's objective is "the transformation of Jewish scripture into the Christian Old Testament, not by converting these texts into a mere quarry for an *ad hoc* polemic or apologetic, but by reimagining

---

1 By "dramatic" I mean that it is composed according to the Platonic template, even though it most often reads more like a monologue than a dialogue.
2 As Francis Watson, *Text and Truth: Redefining Biblical Theology* (Grand Rapids: Eerdmans, 1997), explains, "This Jewish-Christian dialogue takes place on the premise of the Jewishness of Christianity…. Among the foundations of the Christian faith represented by Justin are a Jewish view of God as the creator and revealer, and the Jewish prophets who point forward to the day when the divine Word himself will be manifested in the form of a Jewish humanity, born of a Jewish mother…. The dispute between Justin and Trypho is indicative not of the insensitivity of the Gentile outsider to a supposed essence of Judaism but to a profound rupture within Judaism or Jewishness itself" (313).
3 On the nature and sources of Justin's scriptural citations, indispensable is Oskar Skarsaune, *The Proof from Prophecy: A Study in Justin Martyr's Proof-Text Tradition Text-Type, Provenance, Theological Profile* (NovTSup 56; Leiden: Brill, 1987).

the whole in the light of the Christ-event and its enduring aftermath."[4] At the end of this project Justin emerges as Christianity's first comprehensive biblical exegete, yet Trypho and his Jewish companions, not surprisingly even to Justin, remain unconvinced by his exegesis. Converted by the mystery of Christ, Justin newly perceives the mystery of scripture, which is to perceive it as christological prophecy. But Trypho and his Jewish companions, unconverted by the mystery of Christ, read scripture as it had always otherwise been read.

The word μυστήριον appears thirty-seven times in the *Dialogue*, a number greatly exceeding any other Jewish or Christian document prior to it,[5] but besides sheer numerical prominence, the "once hidden, now revealed" discursive formula plays a critical role in the argumentative aims and tactics of the text.[6] Given the dramatic setting of the *Dialogue* and the social circumstances it reflects, we should expect to find Justin's employment of the mystery discourse doing very different theological work than in previous authors.[7] And we do. Justin's primary aim is to demonstrate that the historical fact of Christ and the words of prophetic scripture reciprocally illuminate each other, and that in this hermeneutical helix Christ is the catalyst who supplies the generative pressure driving the exegetical circularity.[8] Justin appropriates the chronologically ordered mystery schema to achieve this specific end.

6.2 Justin Martyr

Owing to his impressive literary output and to biographical details from the likes of Eusebius,[9] quite a bit is known about the life of Justin, or at least can be reasonably deduced, but such details will only be introduced in what follows when

---

[4] Francis Watson, *Text and Truth*, 310.
[5] The rate of occurrence in the *Dialogue* (.069%) is actually lower than in the *Epistle to Diognetus* (.26%), but it is still slightly higher than in the 13 letter Pauline collection (.061%).
[6] Markus Bockmuehl, *Revelation and Mystery in Ancient Judaism and Pauline Christianity* (WUNT 2/36; Tübingen: Mohr Siebeck, 1990), writes, "With [Justin] we encounter an author whose knowledge and use of the motif of 'mysteries' would again merit an independent study – if only for the frequency with which the term μυστήριον occurs" (218). This chapter offers just such a study.
[7] Perhaps the most pressing historical circumstance within the drama of the *Dialogue* is Hadrian's banishment of the Jews from Jerusalem (*Dial.* 16.2).
[8] Although not all of his interpretations of scripture are explicitly about the person of Christ, most of them are, and even when some Christian reality other than the person of Christ is in view, the fact of Christ remains the original event that makes the Christian reading possible.
[9] Eusebius lists the works attributed to Justin in *Hist. eccl.* 4.18.2–6. Of these, only the *Apologies* and the *Dialogue* are extant and generally considered authentic.

and where they assist the main analysis. As for the date of his extant writings, the *Apologies* are usually placed between 150–155 C.E. The *Dialogue*, since it makes reference to the *First Apology*,[10] was likely composed between 155–160 C.E in Rome, where Justin spent the latter years of his life. Since Justin's distinctly Christian use of μυστήριον appears almost exclusively in the *Dialogue*, it is the focus of this chapter.[11]

Although composed near the end of Justin's life, the literary setting of the *Dialogue* appears to be some two decades earlier, when the failed Bar Kochba revolt (132–135 C.E.) remained a topic of fresh conversation (see *Dial.* 9.3).[12] Unfortunately, no more exact details about the setting of this debate are provided by the text, although Eusebius (*Hist. eccl.* 4.18.6) claims that it took place in Ephesus. Among the most debated questions in scholarship on the *Dialogue* are those related to the audience and purposes of the work. Everything from the conversion of Jews,[13] to the encouragement of Christians and preparation for evangelism,[14] to competition for Gentile adherents,[15] to the production of a distinct Christian self-identity vis-à-vis the theological Jewish "other"[16] has been put forward as a chief aim.[17] Ultimately, it is unnecessary to maintain an either/or approach to these issues, and so I concur with the judgment of Judith Lieu:

> [I]t is dangerous to posit too exclusive alternatives. Internal Christian concerns have shaped Justin's sources as well as his present argument; a tradition of missionary concern which

---

10 *Dial.* 120.6.
11 The text of the *Dialogue* is preserved in a single 14th century manuscript (*Parisinus gr* 450). My citations are based on a comparison of Goodspeed's collation of that manuscript with the recent critical editions produced by Miroslav Marcovich, *Iustini Martyris: Dialogus cum Tryphone* (PTS 47; Berlin/New York: Walter de Gruyter, 1997) and Philippe Bobichon, *Justin Martyr: Dialogue avec Tryphon* (Paradosis 47/1–2; Fribourg: Academic Press Fribourg, 2003).
12 Throughout this chapter all unmarked citations are to the *Dialogue*.
13 Theodore Stylianopoulos, *Justin Martyr and the Mosaic Law* (SBLDS 20; Missoula, MT: Society of Biblical Literature and Scholars Press, 1975).
14 Stephen Wilson, *Related Strangers: Jews and Christians 70–170 C.E.* (Minneapolis: Fortress Press, 1995).
15 Claudia J. Setzer, *Jewish Responses to Early Christians: History and Polemics, 30–150 C.E.* (Minneapolis: Fortress Press, 1994); David Rokéah, *Justin Martyr and the Jews* (Leiden/Boston/Köln: Brill, 2002).
16 Daniel Boyarin, *Border Lines: The Partition of Judaeo-Christianity* (Philadelphia: University of Pennsylvania Press, 2004); Denise Kimber Buell, *Why this New Race: Ethic Reasoning in Early Christiantiy* (New York: Columbia University Press, 2005); Nina E. Livesey, "Theological Identity Making: Justin's Use of Circumcision to Create Jews and Christians," *JECS* 18 (2010): 51–79.
17 For a more detailed rehearsal of the most recent scholarship on this question see Livesey, "Theological Identity Making," 51–57.

included those who might equally be attracted by Judaism can also not be excluded; sympathetic pagans might be swayed by some of the arguments. However, the *Dialogue* is what it purports to be, a contribution to debate with Jews.[18]

While acknowledging the error of exclusive alternatives, I nonetheless agree with the growing number of recent scholars who appreciate the importance of the *Dialogue* for an internal Christian audience and the process of self-definition in early Christianity. Daniel Boyarin and others have argued that, as an emerging religious minority, to carve out its identity Christianity "needed religious difference, needed Judaism to be its other – the religion that is false."[19] Though I am not persuaded that Justin thought he needed religious difference,[20] much less that he thought that he was "constructing" it, the *Dialogue* does offer a depiction of Christianity which exploits a fundamental contrast with Judaism. In what follows I shall show how the mystery discourse played an essential role in reifying and advancing this Jewish/Christian divide.[21]

6.3 Justin and Paul

The question of Justin's relationship with Paul is one of longstanding controversy.[22] According to the once widespread story of Paul in the second century, Jus-

---

[18] Judith Lieu, *Image & Reality: The Jews in the World of Christians in the Second Century* (Edinburgh: T&T Clark, 1996), 108.
[19] Daniel Boyarin, *Border Lines*, 11. See also Buell, *Why this New Race*; Livesey, "Theological Identity Making."
[20] The fact that Justin believes a Jew who professes Christ can still observe the commandments of the Mosaic Law and be saved (*Dial.* 47) shows that his goal is not just one of difference making. That he proves flexible on this matter shows that his aim is not simply to "construct" difference when and where possible.
[21] On the subject of "otherness" and the rhetorics that create it, see esp. Jonathan Z. Smith, "What A Difference A Difference Makes," in *"To See Ourselves as Others See us": Christians, Jews, "Others" in Late Antiquity* (eds. Jacob Neusner and Ernest S. Frerichs; Chico, CA: Scholars Press, 1985), 3–48. As Smith explains, "'Otherness'…is a matter of relative rather than absolute difference. Difference is not a matter of comparison between entities judged to be equivalent; rather difference most frequently entails a hierarchy of prestige and ranking. Such distinctions are found to be drawn most sharply between 'near neighbors,' with respect to what has been termed the 'proximate other.' This is the case because 'otherness' is a relativistic category inasmuch as it is, necessarily, a term of interaction. A 'theory of otherness' is, from this perspective, essentially political" (15).
[22] The literature on this topic is vast and regularly multiplying. Perhaps the best place to start for an account of the history of scholarship is still David K. Rensberger, "As the Apostle Teaches: The Development of the Use of Paul's Letters in Second-Century Christianity" (Ph.D. diss., Yale

tin's writings provided the principal proof that as the apostle became increasingly identified with "heretical" groups and thinkers like the Gnostics and Marcion, he was increasingly abandoned by "orthodox" theologians like Justin. This "proof" was based primarily on the observation that whereas Paul supposedly plays a predominant role in the writings of various "heretical" authors of the second century, he is nowhere named or cited in the works of Justin. This is all the more odd because, no matter how he viewed him, Justin certainly would have known Paul and recognized his importance. Living in Rome during the middle part of the second century, Justin was writing at the same time and in the same city as "heterodox" Paulinists such as Marcion and those associated with the school of Valentinus.[23] It was often assumed, therefore, that the absence of Paul in Justin must be due to hostility to the Paul who had been taken over by Justin's opponents.

In recent years this speculative construal of Paul in the second century has come under heavy and finally devastating criticism.[24] Scholars now increasingly recognize that there are good reasons for the apparent absence of Paul in Justin's extant writings. The argumentative aims of both the *Dialogue* and the *Apologies* would not have been served by citations of someone the encoded audiences (whether a Jew or pagan emperor) would not consider an authority.[25] Therefore,

---

University, 1981), 1–61, 162–92. Also excellent is the recent study by Judith M. Lieu, "The Battle for Paul in the Second Century," *ITQ* 75 (2010): 3–14.

23 He mentions them specifically in 35.6.

24 The most important challengers to the old position are Andreas Lindemann, *Paulus im ältesten Christentum: Das Bild des Apostels und die Rezeption der paulinischen Theologie in der frühchristlichen Literatur bis Marcion* (BHT 58; Tübingen: J.C.B. Mohr [Paul Siebeck], 1979), and Rensberger, "As the Apostle Teaches." See also Lieu, "The Battle for Paul," who writes, "While Marcion and Justin Martyr represent very different styles of...remembering, the changing fortunes of the remembered Paul should not be explained by his supposed status as 'apostle of the heretics' or by simplistic reconstructions of a binary division within the early church; rather Paul serves as a 'hero from the past' through whom different patterns of practice, of communal structure, of confrontation with contemporary society and ideas, of authority, could be explored and negotiated" (3; from the abstract).

25 At the beginning of the *Dialogue*, when Justin first cites Christian traditions about Jesus in order to demonstrate that they have been prefigured by the prophets (17.3–4), he explains that he has done this only because he knows that Trypho has also read these traditions (18.1). This passage demonstrates Justin's sensitivity to the inappropriateness of citing texts that are not known by or authoritative for both parties. Furthermore, when Justin later refers to the "memoirs" (ἀπομνημονεύματα) of the apostles, he does this in an isolated section, and again he does not cite them as though they were equivalent to Israel's scriptures. Rather he merely refers to them for the historical details they provide about Christ's life which, when approached in light of scripture, are seen to have been prophetically prefigured (or so Justin contends).

no Christian authorities are ever mentioned by Justin, and though he occasionally refers to the "memoirs of the apostles" and other Jesus traditions, he does not cite these as equal to prophetic scripture.[26] Second, and closely related to the first, the apparent absence of direct citations from Paul need not necessarily indicate disregard, opposition, or even a lack of extensive influence. One should rather consider some of the more complex ways in which Justin might relate to Pauline traditions. Third, it is unlikely that if Justin was widely understood as an anti-Paulinist he would have been so eagerly embraced by slightly later figures such as Irenaeus[27] and Tertullian,[28] who did highly regard Paul's authority and felt no anxiety about revering both Paul and Justin. And finally, though Paul is never named by Justin, there are still numerous places where distinctly Pauline language, ideas, emphases, and patterns of exegesis and biblical citation appear. Though scholars fall scattered onto a minimalist or maximalist continuum when it comes to assessing potential instances of Pauline influence, the majority agree that "[t]here is no reason to doubt that Justin made extensive use of Paul's letters,"[29] and that there are many reasons to doubt that "Justin's 'neglect' of Paul had anything to do with his antagonism toward Marcion."[30]

The primary purpose of this chapter is not necessarily to make a novel contribution to this debate about Justin and Paul, but I do contend that Justin's distinctive employment of the mystery discourse represents a creative (and positive) appropriation of Pauline material. But I should note that in making this judgment I am presuming more elastic understandings of notions such as "tradition," "influence," and "use" than are often found in recent literature. One of the greatest inadequacies in previous studies is that they have operated with naïve understandings of the manifold ways in which a later thinker might be described as relating to the language and ideas of a previous thinker. However we might speak about or imagine "traditions," they are not compartments of data with definite and impermeable borders. Outside of those who coin neologisms perhaps, there are no sole proprietors of words and ideas. Whenever someone takes up language and ideas from someone else, mixture and transformation is bound to occur. To speak something again is necessarily also to speak it differ-

---

26 The degree to which they were somehow authoritative for Justin is another question. On this matter, see esp. Craig D. Allert, *Revelation, Truth, Canon and Interpretation: Studies in Justin Martyr's Dialogue with Trypho* (VCS 64; Leiden/Boston: Brill, 2002), 187–220.
27 *Haer.* 4.6.2; 5.26.2.
28 *Val.* 5.1.
29 Oskar Skarsaune, "Justin and His Bible," in *Justin Martyr and His Worlds* (ed. Sara Parvis and Paul Foster; Minneapolis: Fortress Press, 2007), 53–76, 73.
30 Rensberger, "As the Apostle Teaches," 192.

ently. And so the historical task is more about articulating differences and continuities than affirming or denying pristine replication. Furthermore, too often scholars have presumed that "influence" – or the interaction with "traditions" – is only present (or demonstrable) when language or ideas are repeated (or "received") with the least degree of variation. But to define influence as a matter of uncreative dependence and repetition is an impoverished notion of how this process actually works.[31] A more nuanced approach considers the assorted ways in which identifiably Pauline ideas and terms might be creatively reused by subsequent authors. Therefore, instead of judging the "influence" of Paul on a later author exclusively in terms of repetition, a more fruitful endeavor is to offer comparative descriptions of the many possible ways in which Pauline traditions have been reused, transformed, or subverted (perhaps even unconsciously or unintentionally) by later authors.

A helpful model for assessing the potential influence of Pauline traditions on Justin has been provided by Rodney Werline.[32] Werline begins by demonstrating that the question of whether Justin knew Paul is beyond dispute.[33] Therefore, the task in evaluating influence is first to identify potential instances of similarity and then to consider the ways in which Justin may follow, modify, or even possibly oppose the precursor Pauline tradition. What Werline shows is that time and again Justin takes up distinctly Pauline themes, and especially instances of scriptural exegesis, but he reapplies them in relation to different theological dilemmas and with different polemical ambitions. As Werline explains, "While Justin clearly borrows ideas and exegetical arguments from Paul, albeit without citing him, he consistently recasts the apostle's arguments for his own purposes and in response to the changing relationship between Jews and Christians in the mid- and late second century CE."[34] Such differences are not symptoms of antagonism, nor are they failures of understanding, but rather they are the result of changed historical circumstances and the resourceful appropriation of the language and ideas of an earlier and fecund theological mind.

As for the specific question of Justin's use of μυστήριον and the probability that Paul's prior use of the term had some impact on Justin's own usage, there is

---

[31] I remind the reader of Harold Bloom's theory regarding literary influence as an oedipal agon waged between poets and their precursors (see esp. Bloom's *The Anxiety of Influence: A Theory of Poetry*, [New York: Oxford University Press, 1973]). Bloom's work exemplifies how relations of influence can be variously and complexly imagined.
[32] Rodney Werline, "The Transformation of Pauline Arguments in Justin Martyr's Dialogue with Trypho," *HTR* 92 (1999): 79–93.
[33] Werline, "The Transformation of Pauline Arguments," 79–80.
[34] Werline, "The Transformation of Pauline Arguments," 92.

strong evidence suggesting that this is indeed the case. To begin with, there is the simple fact that Paul is the original Christian author to use this language. The Pauline letters are also the only Christian documents prior to Ignatius to associate the term explicitly with Christ, which is how Justin uses the term as well. The term is also quite rare in the Jewish literature that Justin might have been aware of (including, of course, the Greek scriptural traditions). Even Philo, one of the major Jewish employers of the term, only uses it some eighteen times, a rate which, given his massive corpus, pales in comparison to the twenty-one occurrences in the comparatively tiny Pauline letter collection.[35] Also suggestive is Justin's preference for the singular form of the noun. This agrees with the convention in the Pauline letters (especially the deuteropaulines) and departs from the trend in Jewish[36] and Greco-Roman literature, where the singular is extremely uncommon.[37] Justin's recurrent use of the ἐν μυστηρίῳ formula is also, I shall contend, very likely an instance in which he has adapted a Pauline expression (see 1 Cor 2:7). Therefore, even prior to any detailed examination, there are compelling reasons to suppose that Justin's use of the term extends from Pauline exemplars, even as he bends them.

6.4 Μυστήριον in Justin

The word μυστήριον appears forty-five times in the extant writings of Justin. Of the eight incidences of the term outside of the *Dialogue*, all but one are in reference to the pagan mystery cults and so do not in any way represent a uniquely Christian use of the terminology. In such passages Justin introduces several of the well-known pagan mysteries either to show the alleged superiority of Christian temperance or to demonstrate the derivative nature of all non-Christian

---

35 Erwin R. Goodenough, *The Theology of Justin Martyr* (Jena: Frommannsche Buchhandlung, 1923), 113–22, has argued for Justin's dependence on Philo and that Justin was "unmistakably a follower of Alexandrine tradition" (116). Willis A. Shotwell, *The Biblical Exegesis of Justin Martyr* (London: SPCK, 1965), however, disputes this hypothesis, demonstrating that there is no reason to posit such a historical connection (see esp. 93–111). For a more detailed history of scholarship on this question, see Rokéah, *Justin Martyr and the Jews*, 22–28.
36 Returning to Philo again for comparative purposes, he only uses the plural.
37 With the exception of Paul and the four appearances of the term in Revelation, no such preference for the singular exists in any of the Christian texts prior to Justin. In the Synoptic pericope, Matthew and Luke use the plural and Mark the singular. The singular also appears once in *Did.* 11.11. Ignatius twice uses the plural (*Eph.* 19.1; *Trall.* 2.3) and only once the singular (*Magn.* 9.1). The *Epistle to Diognetus* only twice uses the singular (4.6; 8.10) and 5x the plural (7.1, 2; 10.7; 11.2; 11.5).

forms of worship.³⁸ The only place in the *Apologies* where a Christian use of the term appears is in *1 Apol.* 13.4 where, in defending the worship of Christ as the son of the true God, Justin states:

> For it is there they declare our madness to be manifest, saying we give the second place after the unchangeable and eternal God and begetter of all to a crucified man (ἀνθρώπῳ σταυρωθέντι), as they do not know the mystery in this (ἀγνοοῦντες τὸ ἐν τούτῳ μυστήριον), to which we urge you to give your attention, as we expound it.³⁹

As the remainder of the *Apology* makes clear, the μυστήριον of the crucified man is the total economy of salvation that God has enacted for humanity through Christ's death. To those who understand this mystery, salvation is realized and Christ is properly worshipped. To those who do not comprehend this mystery, worship of the crucified Christ appears to be nothing short of lunacy. The characterization of Christ's crucifixion as a mystery is common in the *Dialogue*, but prior to Justin this specific connection is only otherwise explicit in Ign. *Eph.* 19.1,⁴⁰ though it is certainly inferable from the wider context of 1 Cor 2:7.

As in the *Apologies*, on three occasions in the *Dialogue* Justin refers to specific pagan μυστήρια – once of Dionysius (69.2) and twice of Mithras (70.1; 78.6) – but Justin's normal practice is to describe (1) some aspect of Christ himself as a mystery (as in *1 Apol.* 13.4); (2) the christological meaning of some scriptural *object* or *event* as a mystery; or (3) the christological meaning of some scriptural *statement* as having been uttered "in a mystery."

(1) The first class of mystery texts differs from the other two in that it is not something in scripture that is designated a mystery but rather some fact about Christ. Although Justin once speaks of "the mystery of Christ's birth" (43.3) and another time more simply of "the mystery of Christ" (44.2),⁴¹ he otherwise always associates μυστήριον with the salvation achieved through Christ's suffering and death. In 74.3, for instance, Justin explains that the charge in Psalm 96

---

38 Justin refers to the sexual frenzy associated with the mysteries of Adonis (*1 Apol.* 25.1); the emasculations associated with the mysteries of "the mother of the gods" (Cybele) (*1 Apol.* 27.4); the perversion of involving licentious sex with a mystery rite (*1 Apol.* 29.2); the mysteries of wine in the cult of Dionysius, which Justin argues derive from the prophetic words of Moses (*1 Apol.* 54.5 – 6); the mysteries of Mithras, which Justin argues are demonically inspired imitations of Christian eucharist (*1 Apol.* 66.4); and finally the mysteries of Kronos (*2 Apol.* 12.5).
39 Trans. by Denis Minns and Paul Parvis, *Justin, Philosopher and Martyr: Apologies* (Oxford Early Christian Texts; Oxford/New York: Oxford University Press, 2009). All translations of the *Dialogue* are my own.
40 The "death of the Lord" is the third of Ignatius' "three mysteries of a cry" in *Eph.* 19.1.
41 Cf. the identical expression in Col 4:3.

(95 LXX) to sing to the Lord a new song is now a command to all Christians to sing out to the world the salvific mystery (τὸ σωτήριον τοῦτο μυστήριον) of Christ's suffering and crucifixion. The mystery of salvation is equated with the suffering of Christ in this passage because while Christians perceive this event for what it truly is – the securing of salvation – the unconverted understand it simply for what it appears to be – a criminal execution. A similar equation is made in 97.3–4, where Justin pronounces Trypho and his companions blind if they cannot admit that Psalm 22 (21 LXX) refers to Christ's suffering and death "in a mystical parable" (ἐν παραβολῇ μυστηριώδει).[42] According to Justin the "parable" of Psalm 22 rehearses beforehand the story of Christ "who died through this mystery (διὰ τούτου τοῦ μυστηρίου), which is the crucifixion." The crucifixion is a mystery because just as one must have the hermeneutical disposition to receive Psalm 22 as a prefigurative recitation of Christ's death, so to comprehend the cross as a saving event one must understand its hidden meaning, which is to say one must understand it not as the mere putting to death of a man but as the mystery of salvation. In each place where Justin speaks of "the mystery of the crucified one" (106.1), or of "the despised and shameful mystery of cross" (131.2), or simply of "the mystery of the cross" (134.5; 138.2), the emphasis is on Christ's death as the onset of salvation for all humanity. To understand this event as a mystery is to understand it in terms of its latent salvific sense.

Though the specific association of μυστήριον with Christ's death is most similar to 1 Cor 2:6–8, where the hidden wisdom of God spoken by Paul "in a mystery" corresponds to the foolishness of the cross described in 1 Cor 1:17–31, this first class of mystery texts is also in many ways similar to the deuteropauline tradition, which likewise coordinates μυστήριον with Christ and Christian salvation.[43] Incidentally, Justin (44.2) and Paul (Eph 3:4; Col 2:2; 4:3) are also the first two authors to refer explicitly to "the mystery of Christ." Furthermore, in several places where Justin speaks of the mystery of Christ's death, he uses it as an occasion to stress that the salvation achieved through this event is extended beyond Israel to include "every race" (πᾶν γένος) (106.1), for it occurred "on behalf of all diverse races and varied peoples" (ὑπὲρ τῶν ἐκ παντὸς γένους

---

[42] See Naomi Koltun-Fromm, "Psalm 22's Christological Interpretive Tradition in Light of Christian Anti-Jewish Polemic," *JECS* 6 (1998): 37–58. Koltun-Fromm shows how Justin's (and others') christological exegesis of this Psalm "is intrinsically linked to early Jewish-Christian polemic and Christian self-identification.... It is an outcome of real, or perceived, early Jewish-Christian debates and most likely originates with Justin Martyr" (38).

[43] The major difference here is that Justin most often combines the mystery idea with Christ's suffering and death, which is never so precisely linked in the deuteropauline schema.

ποικίλων καὶ πολυειδῶν ἀνθρώπων) (134.5).⁴⁴ In 138.2, Justin speaks in the language of Col 1:15 of Christ as the "first born of every creature" (πρωτότοκος πάσης κτίσεως)⁴⁵ and as having established "another race" (ἄλλου γένους) through the mystery of his cross. This emphasis on the work of Christ as on behalf of all humanity closely resembles the deuteropauline schema's concentration on the Gentiles. The Pauline emphasis on the extension of God's promises to the Gentiles is, in fact, one that recurs throughout the *Dialogue*. In *Dial*. 11, 23, and 119 Justin even follows Paul in appealing to the Abraham narrative to make this point.⁴⁶ Just like Paul in Rom 4, Justin brings together Gen 12:3, 15:6, and 17:24 in order to underscore the point that Abraham was justified by faith before his circumcision.⁴⁷ This theme of the inclusion of the Gentiles is also specifically coordinated with the mystery of Christ in 131.2. In the context of a lengthy discussion on how through Christ the "Gentiles rejoice with his people, which is to say Abraham, Isaac, Jacob, the prophets, and all those from that people" (130.2), Justin pressures Trypho to admit that the Gentiles have indeed been called by God through the mystery of the cross. Therefore, in agreement with the characteristic emphasis of the deuteropauline mystery schema, Justin also links the mystery of Christ with the inclusion of Gentiles within the promises of God.⁴⁸ It must be admitted, however, that Justin is not in full agreement with Paul on this matter insofar as Justin aligns the inclusion of the Gentiles with the

---

44 For more on the importance of "ethnic reasoning" in Justin, see Denise Kimber Buell, *Why This New Race*, esp. 95–115. On the issue of Christians as a new "race," Buell contends that "Justin vacillates among three views: (1) Christians are *the* Israelite *genos* or *ethnos* (thereby effacing the right of any other group to this identity) or the people promised to Abraham; (2) Christians are a second, superior, Israelite people; and (3) Christians are a distinct people formed out of individuals from all human races, including Jews" (99).
45 The term πρωτότοκος appears 10x in Justin and exclusively in the *Dialogue*: 84.1 (2x); 84.2; 85.2; 91.1; 100.2; 116.3; 125.3; 138.2. Paul uses the term in Rom 8:29; Col 1:15; 1:18. Cf. also Luke 2:7; Heb 1:6; 11:28; 12:23; Rev 1:5.
46 See Werline, "The Transformation of Pauline Arguments," 83–86. As Werline notes, although much of Justin's argumentation in these passages follows Paul's precedent, Justin nonetheless "has transformed it by coupling it with his ideas of the new covenant, new people, and understanding of the Hebrew prophets as witnesses to Jewish unfaithfulness and rejection" (86).
47 See esp. *Dial*. 11 and 23. In 119.5 Justin, like Paul in Gal 3:7, refers to Christians as having become "children of Abraham" by their faith. For more on Justin's "Pauline" argumentation in these chapters, see Werline, "The Transformation of Pauline Arguments," 82–86.
48 In 140.1 Justin even uses the word συγκληρονόμα to describe the status of the Gentiles with respect to Christ. This rare word is ascociated with μυστήριον in Eph 3:6. It only otherwise appears in the New Testament in Rom 8:17; Heb 11:9; 1 Pet 3:7. It also appears 6x in the works of Philo, but it never appears prior to Paul.

wholesale exclusion of Judaism.⁴⁹ Therefore, even though Justin reiterates a characteristic Pauline emphasis, he also significantly modifies its implications vis-à-vis Israel.

(2) In the second class of texts, μυστήριον is used to signal a new Christian understanding of some *object* or *event* described in scripture. By designating an object or an event a mystery, Justin identifies it as prefiguring an ensuing Christian reality. Importantly, the claim that some scriptural object or event is a mystery, and therefore functions prefiguratively, does not erase any earlier (or "literal") sense or deny it of its original historical meaning and function. Rather it alleges that an additional meaning has newly become knowable after (and in light of) the historical occurrence of Christ. The following table organizes the various biblical artifacts and events that Justin coordinates with Christian realities:

Text	Expression	Antecedent Sign	Signified Reality
24.1	μυστήριον	The eighth day	Not declared⁵⁰
40.1	μυστήριον	Passover lamb	Christ and his blood
86.6	μέγα μυστήριον⁵¹	Birth of twins	Not declared⁵²
111.2	μυστήρια	Actions of prophets⁵³	Two comings of Christ
112.3	μυστηρίου γέγονε	Moses' brazen serpent	Crucifixion of Christ
120.5	μυστήριον	Sawing of Isaiah⁵⁴	Division of Israel
125.3	διὰ τοῦ μυστηρίου	Jacob's wrestling	Final victory of Christ

---

49 As Werline, "The Transformation of Pauline Arguments," concludes, "In [his] new social and historical context, Justin shifts Pauline arguments for inclusion of Jew and Gentile to exclude Jews from the promises and God's mercy. Essentially, Justin ignores the original contexts of Paul's letters and reads them through his own sociohistorical setting and theological agenda.... Reading Paul through these lenses, Justin makes Abraham the father of the Gentiles only, and as a result, Gentile Christians are the true, spiritual Israel" (93). See also Matthew W. Bates, "Justin Martyr's Logocentric Hermeneutical Transformation of Isaiah's Vision of the Nations," *JTS* 60 (2009): 538–55.
50 Justin notes that he could explain the mystery of the eighth day, which has been made known to Christians, but he will not, lest Trypho accuse him of digressing from the subject under discussion (circumcision). See, however, his remarks on the eighth day in 138.1, where he connects it with the appearance of the resurrected Jesus.
51 Cf. the "great mystery" in Eph 5:32.
52 This passage occurs in the context of a catalogue of instances of wood in scripture. Justin brings up the birth of twins from Tamar in relation to the rod of Judah. It is unclear just what the mystery is.
53 In the immediate context Justin is discussing the actions of Moses (making the form of the cross) and Joshua (leading the battle) in Exod 17 in relation to the two comings of Christ – the first in suffering, the second in victory.
54 This is a widespread early Christian tradition. See Bobichon, *Justin Martyr*, 2.875–76 n. 16.

Text	Expression	Antecedent Sign	Signified Reality
131.4	μυστήρια	Various scriptural events[55]	Crucifixion of Christ
134.2	μεγάλων μυστηρίων	Patriarch's multiple wives	Inclusion of Gentiles in Christ
139.1	ἄλλο μυστήριον	Blessing of Noah's sons	Inclusion of Gentiles in Christ
141.4	μυστήρια	Patriarchs' multiple wives	Inclusion of Gentiles in Christ

Again, in each of these instances a prior historical phenomenon is termed a mystery in order to indicate that some subsequent christological (and also historical) reality is signified by it. The anterior historical reality comes to correspond to the posterior historical reality only when viewed through the fact of the historically posterior event. For instance, in 40.1 Justin explains, "The mystery (τὸ μυστήριον) of the lamb, then, which God ordered you to sacrifice as a Passover was truly a type of Christ (τύπος ἦν τοῦ Χριστοῦ), with whose blood the believers, in proportion to the strength of their faith, anoint their homes, that is, themselves." The Passover lamb now represents a type of Christ because details of that event are perceived by Justin to align with, and therefore prefigure, details of Christ and Christian experience: instead of covering their homes with the blood of a lamb, Christians anoint themselves with Christ's saving blood. Similarly construed typological correspondences are applied to objects such as the brazen serpent (a type of Christ's cross) and events like the wrestling of Jacob (a type of Christ's ultimate victory). In two closely related passages, Justin links a precursor scriptural event with a subsequent Christian reality, but instead of labeling the event itself the mystery, he defines that which the event signifies the mystery. Thus the first class of mystery texts and the second class merge together. In 138.1, during a discussion of Noah and the flood, Justin explains how "the mystery of saved humanity (τὸ μυστήριον τῶν σωζομένων ἀνθρώπων) has appeared (γέγονεν) in the deluge." And once more in 138.2 Justin coordinates "the mystery of the cross" with the wood of the ark that saved Noah and his family. The only difference in these two passages is that it is the Christian occurrence that is the mystery and not its antecedent type. It is therefore proper for both historical analogues to be termed mysteries since both conceal and reveal nonliteral significations.

Justin's use of mystery in this second class of texts has no exact equivalent in the Pauline data, but there are some important parallels. That scripture can be shown to make known to Christians previously hidden mysteries is of course anticipated by Rom 16:25–26 (assuming this ostensible interpolation was indeed composed prior to Justin). Paul also designates an event described in scripture

---

[55] In the immediate context the brazen serpent and the outstretched arms of Moses are discussed, both of which are routinely connected to Christ's crucifixion.

as a "great mystery" prefiguring a Christian reality in Eph 5:31–32. Other instances of Pauline exegesis are also quite similar to Justin's own interpretive offerings and likely served as models, even though they lack the exegetical designation "mystery." For instance, Paul draws typological correspondences (and uses the language of τύπος) in Rom 5:14 with Adam and Christ and in 1 Cor 10:6 with the events of the exodus and Christian morality. Other exegetical moments in Paul also resemble some of the exegetical moves that Justin makes. The exegesis of 1 Cor 9:9–10, the whole exegesis in 1 Cor 10:1–11, Moses' veil in 2 Cor 3:7–18, and the Sarah/Hagar allegory in Gal 4:22–31 are most notable.[56] Therefore, though this particular use of μυστήριον is in several respects distinct, it may very well depend on the Pauline precedent.

(3) The final class of mystery passages differs from the previous one only in that it is not an event or object in scripture that is designated a mystery but scripture itself, or some scriptural personage, that is said to speak "in a mystery" (ἐν μυστηρίῳ). In 68.6, for instance, Justin explains how what was spoken by God ἐν μυστηρίῳ to David was later "interpreted" (ἐξηγήθη) by Isaiah to refer to Christ.[57] Justin then states the general hermeneutical proposition (which Typho agrees with in 68.7) that "many of the sayings which were expressed in mysteries (μυστηρίοις)…were later interpreted by the prophets who lived after those who had uttered or done them." The point here is that scripture speaks "in mysteries" when it is shown to possess latent meanings which require later elucidation. Similarly, in 75.1, Justin explains that through Moses "it was proclaimed in a mystery" (ἐν μυστηρίῳ … ἐξηγγέλθη) in the book of Exodus that "the name of God was also Jesus" – a fact not revealed (δεδηλῶσθαι) to Abraham or Jacob. The identical "in a mystery" phraseology appears in 76.2, where Justin explains how Daniel made various veiled allusions (αἰνίσσεται) "in a mystery" (ἐν μυστηρίῳ) to Jesus and aspects of his identity. In 78.9 the description of Damascus in Isa 8:4 is applied to the story of the Magi from Jesus' birth narrative and, accordingly, scripture is shown to signify "in a mystery" (ἐν μυστηρίῳ ἐσήμαινεν) the destruction of the wicked demon that dwelt in Damascus.[58] In 81.3 the words of Genesis are said to reveal (μηνύει) "in a mystery" (ἐν μυστηρίῳ) truths about the

---

[56] For the use of these and other Pauline passages within the history of the Christian tradition of allegorical exegesis, see the excellent study by Ronald E. Heine, "Gregory of Nyssa's Apology for Allegory," VC 38 (1984): 360–70. As Heine shows, it was the Pauline interpretive model on display in these passages that provided Gregory his primary ammunition against attacks from the so-called Antiochene school.

[57] The passage in question is Isa 7:14.

[58] The association here of Christ's birth, the magi story, and the defeat of demonic powers is quite similar to Ign. Eph. 19.2–3.

reality of an end time millennial period. And finally, in 100.1, Justin characterizes the blessings of Joseph and Judah in Genesis as having announced (κεκηρύχθαι) "in a mystery" (ἐν μυστηρίῳ) things about Jesus. This recurrent claim that scripture communicates various things about Christ "in a mystery" is a statement about the nature of scripture and the way in which it is to be interpreted. To affirm that something was uttered "in a mystery" is to affirm the presence of some previously hidden but now revealed christological meaning. It is therefore to affirm the need for a christological hermeneutic, which is to say, a hermeneutic that is ordered around the revealed mystery of the crucified Christ. Listened to through the story of this newly revealed mystery, scripture itself is newly perceived to speak "in a mystery" about the mystery that is Christ himself.

To conclude: although there are three distinguishable ways in which Justin uses the term μυστήριον, these really fall into just two more general categories: (1) the mystery of Christ and (2) the mystery of scripture. When Justin speaks of the mystery of Christ, he is usually referring to the event of the crucifixion. This event is termed a mystery because for the Christian it is no mere death; it is an act of salvation. Similarly, when Justin equates mystery and scripture, he is avowing that some scriptural event, object, or speech act possesses both an original (or literal) meaning and also a concealed christological (or more generally Christian) meaning. This concealed christological meaning is only perceived when approached from the perspective of the mystery of Christ. Therefore, the mystery of Christ reveals the mystery of scripture and, in turn, the mystery of scripture reveals the mystery of Christ. Notice that in this circularity both the interpersonal and the chronological configurations of the mystery schema are present. The mystery of Christ necessarily produces a synchronic division between those who do and who do not recognize Christ as a source of salvation. And the mystery of scripture, since it is only discernable in light of the mystery of Christ, depends on the temporal division of history with the story of Christ as the critical pivot.

As a mode of reading, this mystery hermeneutic is decidedly retrospective. Since the story of Christ functions as scripture's transfiguring prism, prior to and when lacking a commitment to the Christian narrative (as in the case of Trypho and his companions), the mystery of scripture remains unperceived. Therefore, despite the fact that Justin and Trypho are equal in their estimation of scripture's divine and prophetic character, their approaches to scripture remain unpersuasive to one another. For Trypho scripture simply appears as it has always appeared from within his own interpretive prism of Jewish tradition and law observance, and not necessarily any less comprehensible. For Justin, however, with the hermeneutical framework of the Christian story, a comprehensive interpretive transformation has taken place, providing him with an alternative and correspondingly comprehensive account of Israel's bible – or so he contends.

6.5 Μυστήριον and Justin's Hermeneutical Vocabulary

In order to better understand the nuances and inner workings of Justin's repeated approach to Israel's scriptures as expressing mysteries that prefigure Christian realities, it is necessary to situate his use of μυστήριον in relation to his larger hermeneutical vocabulary.[59] The following table displays Justin's most frequently used exegetical terms in the *Dialogue*:[60]

μυστήριον[61]	σημεῖον[62]	σύμβολον	τύπος	παραβολή
24.1; 40.1; 43.3; 44.2 (2x); 68.6 (2x); 74.3; 75.1; 76.1; 78.9; 81.3; 85.7; 86.6; 91.1; 91.3; 94.2; 94.4; 97.4; 100.1; 106.1; 111.2; 112.3; 115.1; 120.5; 125.3; 131.2; 131.4; 134.2; 134.5; 138.1; 138.2; 139.1; 141.4	84.1; 84.2; 90.3; 90.5; 91.4; 93.5; 94.1 (2x); 94.2; 94.3; 94.5; 107.1 (4x); 108.1; 111.4; 112.1; 112.2; 131.4; 137.1	14.2; 40.3; 42.1; 42.4; 53.4; 68.6; 78.6; 86.1; 88.8; 90.5; 111.1; 111.4 (2x); 112.2; 120.2; 131.5; 138.1; 138.2; 138.3	22.3; 40.1; 41.1; 41.4; 42.4; 90.2; 91.2; 91.3; 91.4; 111.1; 111.2 (2x); 114.1; 131.4; 134.3; 140.1	36.2; 52.1; 63.2; 68.6; 77.4; 78.10; 90.2; 97.3; 113.6; 114.2; 115.1; 123.8

Immediately obvious from the above data is the prominence of μυστήριον. Besides sheer numerical distinction, however, closer inspection reveals that it is

---

[59] Cf. R.M. Grant, *The Letter and the Spirit* (London: SPCK, 1957), 75–78; Willis A. Shotwell, *The Biblical Exegesis of Justin Martyr*, 14–23; Daniel Bourgeois, *La sagesse des anciens dans le mystère du verbe: évangile et philosophie chez saint Justin, philosophe et martyr* (Paris: Téqui, 1981), 53–60; Giorgio Otranto, "La terminologia esegetica in Giustino," *VetChr* 24 (1987): 23–41.

[60] Other less used terms include προδήλωσις (foretelling), καταγγελία (announcement), and προαγγελία (foretelling).

[61] In 69.2, 70.1, and 78.6 the term appears, but in reference to pagan mysteries, and so these have been omitted in this table.

[62] In the early parts of the *Dialogue* this term appears in biblical citations, which do not represent Justin's own use of the term, as well as in places where Justin refers to circumcision or Sabbath as having been given to Jews as a sign to mark them off from other nations (this was so that they might suffer afflictions they justly deserve). Such usages do not count as properly exegetical or as Justin's own, and so I have excluded them in this table.

the catchall word in his interpretive idiolect as well.⁶³ The terms σημεῖον, σύμβολον, and τύπος, like μυστήριον, are used synonymously to mark a precursor physical object or event as having a corresponding Christian analogue. And the term παραβολή, like the ἐν μυστηρίῳ expression, always occurs in the dative and is used just like ἐν μυστηρίῳ to indicate that some scriptural speech act has a newly revealed Christian signification. Thus Bourgeois is correct in stating that for Justin "la réalité du μυστήριον" is what "les tient toutes ensemble."⁶⁴ To better demonstrate this point, it will be helpful to consider each term individually.

Since σημεῖον, σύμβολον, and τύπος are used synonymously to signal that some physical (or historical) event or object in scripture corresponds to and prefigures some later revealed Christian reality, these terms function as hermeneutical pronouncements signaling that, as Erich Auerbach would put it, "something real and historical…announces something else that is also real and historical. The relation between the two events is revealed by an accord or similarity."⁶⁵ For τύπος,⁶⁶ the mystery of the Passover lamb in Exodus is termed a type because Justin is able to demonstrate various ways in which it parallels and therefore prefigures aspects of Christ's story (40.1). Similarly, the offering of flour for the cleansing of leprosy (Lev 14:10) was a type of the eucharist, which Christ himself instituted for all who have been cleansed from sin (41.1). Other types include the actions of the prophets (90.2), the horns of the μονοκέρωτος (rhinoceros? unicorn?) (91.2), the brazen serpent (91.4; 131.4), the name of Joshua/Jesus (111.2; 131.4), and the marriages of Jacob (134.3; 140.1). Each of these is a type because in retrospect they appear to resemble and therefore to prefigure some Christian actuality. This new way of appreciating the type is only possible following the event of Christ – the newly disclosed fact that establishes the typological correspondence.

Exactly like the language of types, Justin also uses the term symbol (σύμβολον)⁶⁷ to identify earlier actions or artifacts as corresponding to subsequently revealed Christian facts (some more corresponding than others). The command to

---

63 So Shotwell, *The Biblical Exegesis of Justin Martyr*, concludes, "Thus, it may be seen that the term 'mystery' includes parable, sign, and type. Justin seems to have used the word 'mystery' as a general term for any portion of the hidden predictive element in Scripture" (14).
64 Bourgeois, *La sagesse des anciens dans le mystère du verbe*, 59–60. See also Ortanto, "La Terminologia Esegetica," 30–33.
65 Erich Auerbach, "Figura," in *Scenes from the Drama of European Literature* (Theory and History of Literature 9; Minneapolis: University of Minnesota Press, 1984), 11–76, 29.
66 This term is also widespread and used in nearly identical fashion in the *Epistle of Barnabas*: 6.11; 7.3, 7, 10, 11; 8.1, 2; 12.2, 5, 6, 9; 13.5; 19.7.
67 This word is extremely rare in biblical literature and never appears in the New Testament, but it occurs over 200x in the works of Philo.

roast the lamb whole in Exod 12:9, for instance, is now read as a symbol (σύμ-βολον) of Christ's passion (40.3) because while being roasted the lamb appeared in the form of the cross, and so its shape is now newly appreciated when viewed through the crucifixion story. Likewise, the twelve bells on the high priest's robe become a symbol of the twelve apostles (43.1) who relied upon Christ as their eternal priest.[68] Other such objects and activities which are read by Justin as symbolic prefigurations of Christian realities are the paschal unleavened bread (14.2), the Mosaic precepts (42.4), the ass in Zech 9:9 (53.4), various unspecified actions described in scripture (68.6), the cave of Christ's birth which was predicted by Isaiah (78.6), the tree of life and the rod of Moses (86.1), the carpentry work of Jesus (88.8), the stone on which Moses sat (90.5), the sacrificial goats (111.1), the blood on the doorposts at Passover (111.4), Rahab's red rope (111.4), the brazen serpent (112.2), the division of Jacob's offspring (120.2), the events in the battle against Amalek (131.5), the eight people saved in the ark with Noah (138.1), the wood of the ark (138.2), and other events of the flood (138.3). Justin identifies each of these antecedent historical realities as symbols because he reads them as signifying some Christian reality such as the cross, salvation, the inclusion of the Gentiles, or, in the case of Christ's carpentry vocation, the importance of a just and active life.

Justin also frequently applies the term sign (σημεῖον) as a hermeneutical marker, identifying objects or occurrences as having corresponding Christian referents. In the first half of the *Dialogue* Justin designates the practices of circumcision (16.2; 23.4; 23.5; 28.4) and Sabbath (21.1) as signs imposed upon Israel in order to set them apart from other nations because of their sins.[69] In the second half of the *Dialogue*, however, where scriptural demonstration becomes the focus, Justin uses the language of sign repeatedly to designate prior historical objects or occurrences as having supplementary Christian significations. The most common use of this term is in relation to the brazen serpent (91.4; 94.1–5; 112.1; 131.4) and the outstretched arms of Moses (90.3–5; 93.5; 112.2; 131.4), both of which are reimagined as prefigurative pictures of Christ's crucifixion. Other scriptural signs include the renaming of Joshua/Jesus (131.4), the blood placed on the doors of the Israelites during the Exodus narrative (111.4), and the "sign of Jonah" (107.1; 108.1). Justin interprets each of these as revealing something about Christ but, again, this hermeneutical revelation only happens

---

68 Exod 28:33–34, so far as extant manuscripts show, does not actually mention the number of bells on the priest's robe. Cf., however, the twelve stones in the high priest's breastplate in Exod 28:17–21.
69 See 16.2.

when read through the lens of Christ's own revelation. Apart from this revelation these meanings remained undetectable.

Despite obvious similarities, the final exegetical term, παραβολή,[70] cannot be said to be synonymous with the previous terms in exactly the same way that they are with each other. Unlike type, symbol, and sign, the expression "in a parable" – like the expression "in a mystery" – is reserved for scriptural *speech acts* that are newly understood to have christological meanings.[71] These are no less real or historical than the things designated types, symbols, and signs, but they are nonetheless a distinguishable class. Like the ἐν μυστηρίῳ expression described above, each occurrence of παραβολή is in the dative, and in eleven of the twelve occurrences the ἐν + dative formula is used. As with the "in a mystery" expression, something in scripture is said to have been conveyed "in a parable" because its christological sense was originally concealed.[72] Now, however, after the event of Christ, the christological sense is discernable, and so the previous utterance is newly comprehended as predictive prophecy.

The distinction between scriptural words, which are spoken either "in mystery" or "in parable," and then scriptural events or objects, which may be described as types or symbols or signs, is evident in 90.2, where Justin reminds his interlocutors of a point they have already agreed upon: "As much as the prophets said and did (εἶπον καὶ ἐποίησαν) they revealed (ἀπεκάλυψαν) these things in parables and types (παραβολαῖς καὶ τύποις), hiding the truth in them (κρύπτοντες τὴν ἐν αὐτοῖς ἀλήθειαν)." True to the pattern throughout the *Dialogue*, what the prophets "said" is correlated with "parables" and what they "did" with "types."[73] Though this passage attributes the production of parables to the prophets, it is usually the Holy Spirit who is responsible for speaking "in a parable." As 77.4 plainly states, it is an agreed upon fact that the Holy Spirit has spoken frequently "in parables (ἐν παραβολαῖς) and many similitudes." Justin demonstrates this claim in his exegesis of the prophecies of Jeremiah, who he

---

[70] This word is also quiet common in Jewish and early Christian literature, and it often appears in ways quite similar to Justin's use of it. It is also a preferred term of the Shepherd of Hermas, occuring numerous times in his writings. Cf. also *Barn.* 6.10; 17.2.

[71] Bobichon, *Justin Martyr*, correctly observes that παραβολή "est toujours... mis en relation avec des *paroles* de l'Esprit Saint: καλεῖν, λαλεῖν, λέγειν, μυστηριώδειν, κηρύσσειν" (2.680 – 1 n. 8).

[72] On the correspondence between these expressions, Otranto, "La Terminologia Esegetica," writes, "Nel *Dialogo* ricorre sei volte l'espressione ἐν μυστηρίῳ, con cui l'esegeta mette in rilievo il significato riposte di alcune profezie. In questi casi l'espressione equivale a ἐν παραβολῇ o ad alter simili" (30).

[73] So Bobichon, *Justin Martyr*, correctly notes, "Chez Justin, le mot παραβολή...se rapporte toujours à des paroles de Dieu ou de l'Esprit Saint, et τύπος...à des réalités vétérotestamentaires" (2.813).

contends spoke in various ways about Jesus "by the Holy Spirit in a parable" (ἐν παραβολῇ ὑπὸ τοῦ ἁγίου πνεύματος) (36.2). The Holy Spirit is similarly described as speaking "in a parable" through other prophetic figures such as Isaiah (114.2).[74] So also in 52.1 Justin explains that in the words of Gen 49 "the Holy Spirit has spoken these things ἐν παραβολῇ and in a concealed manner (παρακεκαλυμμένως)." Even when the Spirit is not specifically singled out as the inspiring source for some utterance, his agency is to be inferred.[75] And so in 63.2, although it is not the Holy Spirit but simply Moses who is described as speaking ἐν παραβολῇ, the reader can infer that the Holy Spirit has also enabled Moses to speak in this way.

It is important to emphasize that in every place where Justin maintains that words of scripture have been composed ἐν παραβολῇ, what is concealed in the parable is a christological reality. Thus what Zechariah "demonstrates in a parable (ἐν παραβολῇ), proclaiming it in a concealed manner (ἀποκεκρυμμένως κηρύσσοντι)" is "the mystery of Christ" (τὸ μυστήριον τοῦ Χριστοῦ) (115.1). And in Psalm 22 (21 LXX) David is said to speak "in a mystical parable" (ἐν παραβολῇ μυστηριώδει) because his words are now understood to reveal facts about the events that occurred at Christ's crucifixion (97.3). Indeed, throughout the scriptures "many sayings have been spoken in a concealed manner and in parables (ἐπικεκαλυμμένως καὶ ἐν παραβολαῖς)" (68.6), and now that the mystery of Christ has been revealed, what these parables previously concealed can now be made known.

In conclusion, whereas μυστήριον functions synonymously with σημεῖον, σύμβολον, and τύπος to designate some phenomenon in scripture as possessing a latent Christian analogue, and the ἐν μυστηρίῳ expression is used synonymously with the ἐν παραβολῇ expression to designate some scriptural speech act as possessing a supplementary christological sense, only μυστήριον is used to refer to the incarnate Christ and the salvation accomplished by his death. Thus the crucified Christ is neither type, nor sign, nor symbol, nor parable. He is a mystery – or rather *the* mystery of Christian salvation. And it is the mystery he embodies that creates the hermeneutical catalyst for Justin's interpretive approach, transforming the various antecedent types, signs, symbols, and parables into prophetic mysteries of the crucified Christ.

---

74 Cf. 78.8–10.
75 Cf. 7.1, where the old man explains that the authors of scripture only repeated what they heard and saw when inspired by the Holy Spirit. Interestingly, in 123.8 it is God, and not the Sprit, who is said to speak "in a parable" about Christ through Isaiah.

6.6 Prophecy and "the Grace to Understand"

Justin's insistence that scripture contains and speaks in mysteries – and that the various objects, events, and utterances in scripture represent signs, types, symbols, and parables – depends on epistemological assumptions that warrant more systematic consideration. Most critical is the question of how Justin holds together the ideas that prophetic scripture predicted the mystery of Christ and, at the same time, concealed it until the historical moment of Christ. Put more plainly: how can scripture simultaneously foretell Christ and veil Christ?[76]

Justin repeatedly refers to the mysteries in scripture as instances of prophetic foretelling (he frequently uses the πρόφημι/προφήτης word groups), and he insists that the biblical prophets, inspired by a prophetic spirit, predicted and performed the various mysteries long before their occurrence in Christ. Given the ordinary nature of foretelling, it would seem that since Christian realities have been told beforehand by the prophets, they must then also have been generally knowable beforehand. Prophetic foretelling, at least conventionally understood, is a form of communication that says or performs something guaranteed to later occur. As Francis Watson puts it, "If foretelling occurs, it must enable its hearers to imagine certain definite events that are to be actualized in the future, and believing it would entail a confident expectation of this actualization."[77] The words of the old man at the very outset of the *Dialogue* would seem to summarize this aspect of prophecy:

> A long time before those so-called philosophers, there lived ancient men who were blessed and just and loved by God who spoke through the Holy Spirit and predicted (θεσπίσαντες)[78] things that would occur in the future (τὰ μέλλοντα), which are happening now. They call these men prophets. They alone saw the truth and communicated it to humanity, whom they neither feared nor revered. Not cowering to glory, they only spoke what they heard and what they saw when full of the Holy Spirit (ἃ ἤκουσαν καὶ ἃ εἶδον ἁγίῳ πληρωθέντες πνεύματι).[79]

Just as much as Justin ensures that Christian realities were previously predicted by the biblical prophets, both in their words and their deeds, he also maintains that these prophetic mysteries were originally enacted in a concealed manner, or

---

[76] Recall the consideration of this question in relation to Rom 16:25–26.
[77] Francis Watson, *Text and Truth*, 319.
[78] This is a technical term associated with oracular foretelling. See Bobichon, *Justin Martyr*, 2.596 n. 6.
[79] 7.1. Cf. *Barn*. 5.6.

in such a way that they could not have been perceived until after the human event of Christ. As he explains in 76.6:

> For if it has been proclaimed in a concealed manner (παρακεκαλυμμένως κεκήρυκτο) through the prophets that Christ would suffer first and after these things be Lord of all, it was then not possible to be understood by anyone (ὑπ' οὐδενὸς νοεῖσθαι ἐδύνατο) until he convinced the apostles that these things were explicitly proclaimed (κεκηρύχθαι διαρρήδην) in the scriptures.

The mystery of Christ was therefore indeed announced beforehand by the prophets, but it was announced in such a way that it could not be known until after the event of Christ and his personal exegetical demonstration. In the language of Luke 24:45–46, it was in his own explanation that for the first time "he opened their minds to understand the scriptures, and he said to them, 'Thus it has been written that the Christ is to suffer and on the third day rise from the dead'." That Jews of any time did not and still have not understood that the facts of Christ were foretold by their own scriptures is not, then, so much a function of their own incapacity as it is a function of scripture itself and the Spirit which inspired it, concealing Christian prophecies in mysteries and parables.

With this description of prophecy Justin has considerably revised the usual sense of prophetic foretelling as communication imparting certain knowledge to its addressees. Rather than straightforward prediction, which persuades an audience of a future happening, the biblical prophecies and prefigurations of Christ were instead formulated in such a way that they could only be comprehended after the event. They thus only foretell in hindsight.[80] Scriptural foretelling of Christ did not then occur in the form of prospective preannouncements, but rather that "foretelling" is the result of a retrospective recognition. Interestingly, this view of scripture as a repository of veiled meanings is something Justin's interlocutors concede:

> "You have known," I said, "that as much as the prophets said and did—as was admitted by you – they revealed these things in parables and types, so as not to be understood (νοηθῆναι) easily by all, by hiding the truth in them (κρύπτοντες τὴν ἐν αὐτοῖς ἀλήθειαν)."[81]

The reason for hiding the mysteries of Christ in the prophetic scriptures was so that they would become comprehensible after the historical event of Christ and

---

[80] Justin speaks of two prophets, Daniel (31.7) and Zechariah (115.3), as having prophesied in a state of ecstasy. One may assume then that Justin thought that all the prophets, when inspired by the Spirit, underwent some form of ecstatic transformation. Cf. Grant, *The Letter and the Spirit*, 75.
[81] 90.2.

would then authenticate that event in hindsight. In 84.2, for instance, Justin states that the true sign of the virgin womb and its irrefutable proof "was enacted beforehand (προλαβών) by the prophetic Spirit in various ways, as I recorded for you. He announced it beforehand (προεκήρυξεν) in order that when it took place it would be understood (γνωσθῇ) as occurring by the power and will of the creator of all things." The purpose of prophetic foretelling, and thus all scripture's mysteries, was not, as is usually the case, to supply an earlier witness that anticipates an event before its occurrence. Rather it was to introduce concealed meanings that would lie latent until a subsequent revelation – a revelation that is itself a mystery. But how exactly does this revelation happen, and why does it happen for some, like Justin, and not for others, like Trypho?

It is important to appreciate first the emphasis in the *Dialogue* on God's initiative in self-revelation and the inability of the natural (or unaided) human mind to perceive the divine. The old man introduces this theme at the conclusion of his speech on the prior revelation of Christ in the prophets when he exhorts Justin to pray for enlightenment so that he also will be able to perceive these realities: "And pray above all for the doors of light to be opened (φωτὸς ἀνοιχθῆναι πύλας) for you. For nothing is intelligible (συνοπτά) or understandable (συννοητά) unless it is understood (συνιέναι) through God and his Christ" (7.3).[82] The old man already made the case in chs. 3–4 that it is absurd for philosophers to claim to speak truly about a God whom they have never seen nor heard (3.7). Knowledge of God requires divine illumination, and so God can only be known (or, better, is only made known) when and where God chooses – "Will the human mind (νοῦς) ever see God without having been equipped (or ordered) (κεκοσμημένος) by the Holy Spirit?" (4.1).[83] Therefore, while it is true that the prophets predicted Christ (7.1), comprehending this prediction only occurs through the epistemological gift of divine illumination.[84]

---

[82] On the doors of light in this passage, see A. Cacciarai, "In margine a Giustino, *dial.* vii, 3, le porte della luce," in *In Verbis verum amare* (ed. P. Serra Zanetti; Florence: La Nuova Italia, 1980), 101–34. Cacciarai examines this image and other similar formulations in ancient literature, noting that it is consistently employed to express a mystical experience of enlightenment or a mystagogical spiritual journey.

[83] Here Justin modifies a philosophical position stretching back to Plato (Socrates), and ultimately Anaxagoras, that "mind" is the principle that "orders" and causes all things. Socrates considers this doctrine as offering a possible basis for a type of "natural theology" (*Phaedo* 97C–98B) but then realizes its ultimate defectiveness (*Phaedo* 98C–99D). Cf. also *Philebus* 30C. As Justin's old man in 4.1 implies, it is the Holy Spirit who reorders the human mind and thereby enables knowledge of God.

[84] Cf. *Barn.* 1.7.

Justin most often refers to this spiritually enabled epistemology as a "grace" or, perhaps better, a "gift" (χάρις).⁸⁵ He also refers more specifically to the "grace to understand" (χάριν τοῦ νοῆσαι)⁸⁶ or the "grace to know" (χάριν τοῦ γνῶναι).⁸⁷ When one enjoys the new mental architecture generated by this "grace to understand," then scripture is no longer read as it previously had been—"carnally" (σαρκικῶς)⁸⁸ or "humbly" (ταπεινῶς)⁸⁹ or "unspiritually" (χαμερπῶς)⁹⁰ or "simply" (ψιλῶς)⁹¹ – and instead it is read according to its "design" (νόος)⁹² and its "power" (δύναμις)⁹³. As Justin explains:

> I intend to quote scriptures to you, but I do not strive after the merely artful organization of words, for such is not my strength (δύναμις). Rather a grace alone from God (χάρις παρὰ θεοῦ μόνη) was given to me in order to understand (εἰς τὸ συνιέναι) his scriptures, of which grace I invite all to share freely and abundantly.⁹⁴

> He revealed (ἀπεκάλυψεν) to us all things, which is as much as we have understood (νενοήκαμεν) from the scriptures through his grace (διὰ τῆς χάριτος αὐτοῦ).⁹⁵

> It was also given to us to hear and to understand (ἡμῖν οὖν ἐδόθη καὶ ἀκοῦσαι καὶ συνεῖναι) and to be saved through this Christ as well as to know (γνῶναι) all the things of the Father.⁹⁶

Since it is now the Christians who have been given this extraordinary exegetical χάρις, Justin exhorts the Jews to turn from their old traditions in order to perceive the new mystery of Christ that has been foretold in the mysteries of Jewish scripture:

> So it would be better for you, O men, what you have not understood (ἃ μὴ νενοήκατε), to learn from those who received the grace from our God (παρὰ τῶν λαβόντων χάριν ἀπὸ τοῦ

---

85 The term appears 29x in the *Dialogue*. Though I preserve the standard translation "grace," one should keep in mind that this χάρις is always something granted (or "gifted") by God to the Christian and thus carries a sense of divine beneficence.
86 119.1.
87 30.1. Justin also uses the language of "enlightenment" (φωτίζω): 39.2; 109.2; 122.1, 2, 3, 4, 5 (2x). Cf. also *Barn.* 1.2.
88 See 14.2.
89 112.1, 4; 114.4.
90 112.4; 114.4.
91 112.1.
92 29.2.
93 112.1.
94 58.1.
95 100.2.
96 123.4.

θεοῦ ἡμῶν), namely the Christians, and therefore not to struggle to defend your own teachings, which dishonor the things of God.⁹⁷

As long as Trypho and his fellow Jews lack this great grace to understand, they will continue to misapprehend scripture and altogether fail to see the mystery of Christ that the Spirit has revealed therein:

> If, therefore, someone were not bestowed (λάβοι) with the great grace from God (μετὰ μεγάλης χάριτος τῆς παρὰ θεοῦ) to understand (νοῆσαι) the sayings and the deeds of the prophets, it will not benefit him to communicate their words or actions when he is unable to give an account of them. Will they not seem despicable to the many since they are spoken by those not understanding them (ὑπὸ τῶν μὴ νοούντων αὐτά)?⁹⁸

The problem with Trypho from Justin's perspective is that because he lacks the "grace to understand" and remains bound to the tradition of his teachers he is fundamentally incapable of perceiving the truth in Justin's exposition of scripture's christological mysteries. Justin states this candidly in 38.2:

> I know that, as the word of God says, the great wisdom of the almighty God who created all things has been hidden from you (κέκρυπται ἀφ' ὑμῶν). Therefore with pity for you, I struggle to work harder, so that you might understand our paradoxes (τὰ παράδοξα),⁹⁹ but if not, I shall be innocent on the day of judgment, for even then you will hear other teachings seeming even more paradoxical (παραδοξοτέρους). But do not be disturbed; rather become more eager listeners and stay as investigators, disregarding the traditions of your teachers since, being unable to understand (νοεῖν), they are convicted by the prophetic Spirit of God, for they prefer to commit themselves to their own teachings.

Justin acknowledges that there is little chance that Trypho will actually come to understand what Justin claims is the true meaning of scripture.¹⁰⁰ The Christian and the Jewish interpretive approaches represent totally different hermeneutical frameworks, and so long as Trypho remains yoked to Jewish tradition, the mystery of scripture will remain hidden from him. To Trypho the Jew, of course, Justin's totalizing retelling of scripture as Christian prophecy is arbitrary and foolish

---

97 78.10. In 82.1 Justin again declares that the "prophetic charisms" (προφητικὰ χαρίσματα) were transferred (μετετέθη) to Christians.
98 92.1. Cf. 30.1.
99 Justin refers to the "paradoxes" of the Christian rereading of scripture on seven occasions: 38.2 (2x); 48.1 (2x); 48.2; 49.6; 133.1. In these passages Justin freely admits that his treatment of scripture must seem preposterous to Jews.
100 In 93.5 Justin states that though the Jews have "opportunities" (ἀφορμάς) to understand the christological signification of scripture, they refuse to.

(μωρόν).¹⁰¹ But to Justin the Christian, Trypho's incredulity represents a misguided allegiance to now outdated traditions and so is proportionally absurd.¹⁰²

Justin's repeated claim that Trypho's failure to perceive the mystery of Christ and scripture is because he remains bound to old traditions is an important one. Thus far I have emphasized the primacy of divine enabling for the Christian's special ability to perceive the mystery of Christ and scripture. It is crucial, however, to underscore in addition that just as much as Justin characterizes the Christian's ability to comprehend scripture's mysteries as some sort of exceptional cognitive competence, the Christian rereading of scripture is also, and irreducibly, a matter embracing a new tradition. In other words, just as much as the Christian exegetical framework is revealed, it is received by and through apostolic tradition as well.

For Justin, the origin of the Christian exegetical tradition is Jesus himself. As he explains in 76.6 (discussed above), the prophetic announcement of Christ's suffering and exaltation could not have been understood before the events themselves, for Christ had to convince (ἔπεισε) the apostles that these things were indeed predicted by the prophets.¹⁰³ Justin makes the same point in 53.5:

> For after he was crucified, his disciples who were with him were scattered until he rose from the dead and had convinced (πέπεικεν) them that it had been predicted (προεπεφή-τευτο) that he would suffer. And thus being convinced (πεισθέντες), they went out into the entire world and taught these things.¹⁰⁴

---

101 48.1.
102 Bruce Chilton, "Justin and Israelite Prophecy," in *Justin Martyr and his Worlds* (ed. Sara Parvis and Paul Foster; Minneapolis: Fortress Press, 2007), 77–87, astutely describes this impasse in the *Dialogue:* "So what is presented by Justin as a meeting of minds is in the event a missing of minds. Both Judaism and Christianity made the immediate reference to scripture ancillary to its systemic significance. But because Christianity was committed to the *Logos* as its systemic center, and Judaism to the Torah as its systemic center, the two could not understand one another. Any objection from one side to the other seems silly: it misses the point. In the absence of a language to discuss systemic relationship, the two sides fell to disputing which made better sense of the immediate reference (the 'literal meaning,' as would be said today) of the texts concerned. What is billed as a dialogue is really a shadow play: learned leaders reinforcing their own positions by arguing over what neither side believes really matters" (87).
103 Justin seems to be indebted to the traditions described in Luke 24. For the relationship of Justin to Lukan traditions, see esp. Susan Wendel, *Scriptural Interpretation and Community Self-Definition in Luke-Acts and the Writings of Justin Martyr* (NovTSup 139; Leiden/Boston: Brill, 2011).
104 Cf. *1 Apol.* 49.5; 50.12.

Justin understands Christ to be not only the subject of the Christian (and apostolic) exegetical tradition but also its sole founder. The Christian way of reading is then not the clever invention of later minds but a mode of interpretation that was initiated and bequeathed by Jesus himself.[105] So when Justin unravels the christological mystery of scripture for Trypho, he is following the tradition of reading learned from the apostles, who themselves learned it from the resurrected Christ when their minds had been opened to comprehend it. Described in this way, the "grace to understand" scripture's mysteries can be characterized as both a supernatural epistemological conversion as well as a matter of participating in a new pedagogical tradition and way of life.[106] The comprehensive christological hermeneutic that is born in the spiritually reordered Christian mind is consequently not arbitrary. Rather it reiterates the inherited tradition of apostolic

---

[105] As Oskar Skarsaune, *The Proof from Prophecy*, notes, Justin repeatedly emphasizes that his interpretations are not his own inventions but based on received tradition. This tradition is mediated through the apostles but has its origins in Christ's own exposition of scripture following his resurrection (see esp. 11–13).

[106] The phrase "grace to understand" and the relation of this grace to the larger question of epistemology in Justin have been widely contested. According to Nestor Pycke, "Connaissance rationnelle et connaissance de grace chez saint Justin," *ETL* 37 (1961): 52–85, Justin attributes his capacity to understand scripture's mysteries to the Spirit's enabling gift of a new cognitive capacity. Similarly, David E. Aune, "Justin Martyr's Use of the Old Testament," *BETS* 9 (1966): 179–97, 182, 186–87, argues that for Justin the Christian is, just like the Old Testament prophets, a privileged recipient of "charismatic illumination." Robert Joly, *Christianisme et Philosophie: Études sur Justin et les Apologistes grecs du deuxième siècle* (Bruxelles: l'Université de Bruxelles, 1973), 104–13, has challenged this view, contending that Justin's idea of a "grace to understand" merely indicates his confidence that his comprehensive rereading of scripture is entirely rational and simply a matter of scriptural proof. Skarsaune, *Proof from Prophecy*, follows the judgment of Joly but more precisely correlates the "grace to understand" with the received tradition of apostolic exegesis (12–13). The problem with Joly and Skarsaune is that they fail to recognize that supernatural illumination and the rational proof of apostolic exegesis are not an either/or choice. Joly and Scarsaune and others are correct in noticing the importance of apostolic tradition in Justin, but they are incorrect in dismissing the Spirit's role in illumination. One cannot ignore the passages that describe, albeit imprecisely, something like a new and divinely gifted interpretative capability. There is no way around the fact that Justin believes that the human mind cannot know God without the Spirit's aid – "Or will a human mind ever see God if it has not been arranged by the Holy Spirit?" (4.1). It also makes sense to suppose that if the prophets spoke while "filled with the Spirit" (and even in an ecstatic state), then interpreting their hidden christological messages would also require some corresponding spiritual endowment. It is also the case, however, that for Justin the new Christian mode of reading has been transmitted by tradition from Christ through his apostles. Therefore, I concur with the recent conclusion of Susan Wendel, *Scriptural Interpretation and Community Self-Definition*, that receiving the "grace to understand" "includes divine agency as well as the transmission of the apostle's teaching" (101 n. 46). Inspiration and tradition need not be incompatible.

exegesis that was inaugurated by Jesus. The "grace to understand" is thus what renders this tradition of christological rereading compelling. The rational and the spiritual coincide.

6.7 Conclusion: The Mystery of Christ, Scripture, and the Question of Judaism

As many other studies on the *Dialogue* have shown, the Christianity that emerges from the discursive world of this work is one that, on the one hand, insists on its continuity with the God of Israel and the history of that God and those people. Or, as Justin puts it in 11.5, "We are the true Israelites (Ἰσραηλιτικὸν...τὸ ἀληθινόν), the spiritual (πνευματικόν),[107] and a people of Judah and Jacob and Isaac and Abraham who, though uncircumcised, was approved and blessed by God because of his faith and was called the father of many nations."[108] On the other hand, however, and as is evident from the previous quotation, Justin insists on the critical difference between contemporary Jews and Christians, the latter group having been amputated from their own history.[109] To a Jew like Trypho such a notion is of course preposterous: it is the Christians who have no reasonable claim to participate in Israel's heritage. As a bewildered Trypho puts it to Justin, "You keep neither the feasts nor the Sabbath nor circumcision.... Have you not read that the one who is not circumcised on the eighth day will be cast out from his people?... But you, disregarding this covenant, scorn it, and then you try to persuade us you know God—you the one not doing what people who fear God do" (10.3). Trypho's reasoning is, of course, plain and consistent (I suspect Justin would even admit as much), but it fails to persuade Justin because for him a new revelation has occurred. A new mystery has been unveiled that provokes a complete revision of history and scripture. Justin's great task as a Christian exegete is to hold together and, indeed, to integrate the new revelation of Christ and the antecedent revelation of scripture. The consequence of this integration, however, is that as Justin claims Trypho's scriptures and history as his own,[110] he at the same time disavows Trypho's form of Judaism – or at least in part.[111]

---

[107] A characteristic Pauline term, appearing 19x in his letters. It never appears in the LXX, and it occurs only two times in the New Testament outside of the Pauline corpus (1 Peter 2:5 [2x]).
[108] Cf., of course, the very similar Rom 4:9–10.
[109] For the various ways in which Justin argues this point, see esp. *Dial.* 11–22.
[110] Justin's takeover of scripture is nowhere more overt than the oft-cited 29.2: "Aren't you aware of [the words of the biblical authors], Trypho? For they are preserved in your scriptures.

6.7 Conclusion: The Mystery of Christ, Scripture, and the Question of Judaism

As this chapter has shown, the hidden/revealed mystery schema supplied Justin with the necessary conceptual and rhetorical resources for this twofold project of appropriation (scripture and Israel) and contrast (Christianity vs. Judaism). Conceptually, Justin's argument asserts a diachronic continuity with Israel's history and a synchronic discontinuity with ongoing Judaism. The mystery discourse is adapted by Justin to achieve both this continuity and this discontinuity. Justin's reading of scripture as revealing new mysteries concerning Christ and the Christian way of life establishes the diachronic link between Christianity and Israel's bible and history. By telling the story of the mystery of Christ as one foretold in the mystery of scripture, but previously hidden and only knowable from scripture after the historical fact of Christ, history is accordingly divided into two concurrent ages with the revelation of Christ as the fulcrum of this chronological division. By situating history within this hidden/revealed framework, Justin is thereby able to hold together the unity of Israel's God and the apocalypse of that God in Christ. Justin also, however, asserts a social division by separating Christians from Jews, even claiming that Christians are the true descendants of Israel and those upon whom God's χάρις now rests. Therefore, by dividing Christians and Jews with the mystery of Christ and by substantiating the mystery of Christ by way of his totalizing rereading of scripture, Justin affixes Christianity to Israel's history but, in the same stroke, excludes Judaism from that heritage—not Judaism *in toto*, but Judaism insofar as it does not profess Christ.[112] Therefore, although structurally identical to the temporally and interpersonally ordered schemas in Paul, Justin's particular deployment of the mystery discourse nonetheless produces very different consequences.

Or rather, not yours but ours; we trust them but you read them and do not understand the sense in them."

[111] Recall again that Justin does allow for law observant Jewish Christians, even though he also thinks that the Mosaic precepts were instituted because of the Jews' hardness of heart (*Dial.* 47). This concession indicates that Justin's theology is not simply about the construction of difference.

[112] Recall again *Dial.* 47, where law observant Christians are admitted as a possibility.

7 Mystery, Scriptural Meaning, and Ritual Performance in Melito's *Peri Pascha*

7.1 Introduction

In the previous chapter we observed how Justin situates the hidden/revealed mystery discourse within the context of dispute with Jews over the identity of Jesus and the meaning of Jewish scripture and thus represents an important expansion of the Christian use of the mystery schema. It is fitting that this chapter follows the preceding one since Melito also describes the saving death of Christ as a newly revealed mystery that is retrospectively foretold in Jewish scriptures – scriptures that are themselves full of latent mysteries. Thus in his exegetical disclosure of the previously hidden mystery of Christ in various scriptural texts, Melito exhibits an exegetical technique that is in most respects identical to Justin's. But Melito's use of μυστήριον offers further advancements as well. By applying this language to the ritual setting of Israel's Pascha and within the context of Christian worship, Melito is perhaps the first extant Christian author to amplify the conventional cultic connotations of the terminology. By reframing the Pascha as an initiatory rite that prefigures Christ and Christian ritual practices, Melito recasts himself as a hierophant of the Christian mystery and his congregants as co-initiates in the exegetical and then ritual performance of the paschal celebration. If the Melito of this homily is indeed the Melito of Sardis described by Eusebius,[1] then the Christianity on display very much reflects the Hellenistic and Jewish milieu of that city, presenting a picture of a community resourcefully acculturating and accommodating both Jewish and pagan patterns of devotional life.[2] From Judaism, Melito inherits scripture and the paschal rite. And from the ambient Greco-Roman culture, Melito exploits common cultic vocabulary so as to portray the paschal celebration as a sacred mystery rite. As he and his gathered co-initiates are exegetically transported into the first cultic performance of Pascha, that Pascha is redrawn to prefigure key aspects of Christian iden-

---

[1] This is the position of most scholars, though there are important dissenting voices. More on this below.

[2] "Acculturation" and "accommodation" need not mean unqualified endorsement or cultural capitulation. These can also become creative, even subversive, forms of cultural resistance. Furthermore, when Alistair Stewart-Sykes, *The Lamb's High Feast: Melito,* Peri Pascha *and the Quartodeciman Paschal Liturgy at Sardis* (Supplements to Vigiliae Christianae 42; Leiden/Boston: Brill, 1998), notes a "growing interest in native religion at the time of Melito," it does not necessarily follow that "Melito's Judaism would to an extent exclude him from this interest" (10).

tity, the crucified Christ and new Christian sacramental rites being most prominent. By memorializing the Pascha as prefigurative of Christ's death and Christian sacramental customs,[3] Melito and his church again unveil the salvific slaughter of their Lord, the true paschal lamb, by rehearsing that event in their liturgy. In that moment exegetical demonstration and liturgical performance coalesce.[4]

Besides the cultic evocations in his use of μυστήριον, Melito also represents an alternative to previous authors in his hermeneutical approach to Israel. Up to now we have observed early Christians employing the mystery discourse mostly in order to deny Israel any independent worth apart from Christ. Justin goes so far as to denigrate practices such as circumcision, which he maintains was given to Israel solely on account of her sins. Melito offers a very different evaluation of Israel's history. His exegetical approach is more of a fusion of the hermeneutical mystery discourse with a model/reality schema such as is developed in Hebrews. Fundamental to this latter schema is the rhetorical technique known as *synkrisis*,[5] which is a common trope in ancient literature. It is described by Aristotle (*Rhet.* 1368A; *Rhet. Alex.* 1441A) and Quintillian (*Inst.* 2.4.21) and is routinely included in the *progymnasmata* of the ancient rhetoricians.[6] The figure of *synkrisis* is essentially a rhetorically organized appraisal of two entities (such as people or ideas), and it is usually employed in one of two ways. The first is for the purpose of praising both entities, and so the similarity of the *comparanda* is emphasized in order to augment their equivalent and exceptional worth; since both are supremely esteemed, the comparison amplifies the encomium. The second way is for the purpose of deprecating one and elevating the other. Thus the similarity

---

[3] I use the term "sacramental" in the most general sense and do not mean to imply some well worked out or fixed "sacramentology."

[4] The best analysis of this important feature of *Peri Pascha* is Dragoș-Andrei Giulea, "Seeing Christ through the Scriptures at the Paschal Celebration: Exegesis as Mystery Performance in the Paschal Writings of Melito, Pseudo-Hippolytus, and Origen," *Orientalia Christiana Periodica* 74 (2008): 27–47.

[5] For the basic uses of this trope along with numerous ancient examples see Friedrich Focke, "Synkrisis," *Hermes* 58 (1923): 327–68. On the use of this technique in early Christianity, see the excellent study by Daniel Sheerin, "Rhetorical and Hermeneutic *Synkrisis* in Patristic Typology," in *Nova et Vetera: Patristic Studies in Honor of Thomas Patrick Halton* (ed. John Petruccione; Washington, D.C.: Catholic University of America Press, 1998), 22–39.

[6] It is, for instance, discussed in all five progymnasmata anthologized by George A. Kennedy in *Progymnasmata: Greek Textbooks of Prose Composition and Rhetoric* (SBLWGRW 10; Atlanta: Society of Biblical Literature, 2003). It was also employed in biographies, most methodically in those of Plutarch. See Hartmut Erbse, "Die Bedeutung der Synkrisis in den Parallelbiographien Plutarchs," *Hermes* 84 (1956): 398–424; Hans Beck, "Interne *Synkrisis* bei Plutarch," *Hermes* 130 (2002): 467–89.

of the *comparanda* is ultimately in service of difference with the value or virtue of one of the entities being extolled as exceedingly superior when compared with that of the other. Although Melito's *synkrisis* would probably appear to non-Christians, and especially Jews, to be of this latter, negative type, it is actually something of a merger of the two approaches—or at least Melito appears to view it this way. While there is no disputing that Melito characterizes the old model of Israel (including her law and temple) as a once treasured but now defunct blueprint of the supreme reality of Christ, his *synkrisis* does not end here. By reincorporating the once valuable model into the now comprehensive reality of Christ, the old model is reinvested with new value – the value of prophetic foretelling. Again, this is not to deny that for outsiders, and especially Jews, Melito's *synkrisis* would probably be perceived as encomium via denunciation. It is, however, important to respect Melito's own insistence that the *comparanda* are still in fact both exceedingly valuable, although only insofar as the temporally prior Israel is reincorporated into the new totalizing fact of Christ. This is precisely why the old Pascha is not abandoned by Melito but reread and celebrated in his paschal homily and the church's liturgy, albeit in a newly transformed sense.

7.2 Melito and his Peri Pascha[7]

Prior to a series of fortuitous literary findings during the middle part of the twentieth century (1932–1960), what was known about Melito was based primarily on a few surviving fragments of his works and remarks from Eusebius (*Hist. eccl.* 4.26; 5.24), who, among other things, describes Melito as the former bishop of Sardis and a prominent Quartodeciman (someone celebrates Passover according to Jewish practice on the fourteenth of Nisan).[8] However, in 1932 Frederick G. Kenyon identified a previously unknown homily found in a fourth- or fifth-century codex.[9] The *editio princeps* was then published in 1940 by Campbell Bonner, who concluded that the ascription ΜΕΛΕΙΤΩΝ at the heading of the homily meant that it was written by the same Melito described by Eusebius as the erst-

---

[7] For discussion of the most recent research on this text and new text-critical observations, see Stuart G. Hall, "Melito *Peri Pascha*: Corrections and Revisions," *JTS* 64 (2013): 105–10.
[8] Eusebius also provides a list of the works attributed to Melito and reports that he was a eunuch (i.e., probably celibate), that he was buried in Sardis, that his whole career was "in the Holy Spirit," that he made a journey to Palestine and there learned the proper listing of the Old Testament books, that he wrote an apology to Marcus Aurelius, and that he wrote *PP* while Servillius Paulus was proconsul of Asia.
[9] Frederick G. Kenyon, "The Chester Beatty Biblical Papyri," *Gnomon* 8 (1932): 46–49.

while bishop of Sardis.[10] In the following years other Greek, Coptic, Syriac, and Latin portions of the homily were discovered, but the most significant moment in the homily's history came when another, nearly complete Greek copy was discovered in the Bodmer codex. This manuscript was published by Michel Testuz in 1960 and supplied an official title for the work: Περὶ Πάσχα.[11]

Should we be so certain that the "Melito" of *Peri Pascha* (hereafter *PP*) is in fact the same Melito who Eusebius claims was the Quartodeciman bishop of Sardis? The majority of scholars have concluded this is the case, but there are dissenters.[12] Most notable is Lynn Cohick who marshals the following observations and arguments against the traditional attribution of the work: (1) Eusebius is a notoriously unreliable historian, and so anything he reports should be critically scrutinized;[13] (2) the "Melito" of *PP* could very well be someone other than the one Eusebius identified as bishop of Sardis;[14] (3) later copyists, desiring an esteemed author for the homily, could have misattributed the work to Melito;[15] (4) when Eusebius cites *PP* in *Hist. eccl.* 4.26, those words are nowhere in *PP* as we have it, a fact suggesting that Eusebius' *PP* and our *PP* are not the same work and, therefore, may not be by the same author;[16] (5) there is nothing in *PP* that is unambiguously Quartodeciman;[17] and (6) nothing in *PP* indicates or requires the provenance of Sardis.[18] Although attributing *PP* to the second-century Melito described by Eusebius is intriguing, and having a provenance in Sardis for this text potentially illuminating, Cohick has established just how tenuous such a judgment is.

---

[10] Campbell Bonner, *The Homily on the Passion by Melito Bishop of Sardis with some Fragments of the Apocryphal Ezekiel* (SD 12; Philadelphia: University of Philadelphia Press, 1940).
[11] M. Testuz, *Papyrus Bodmer XIII, Méliton de Sardes Homélie sur la Pâque* (Geneva: Bodner, 1960). In this chapter I follow the critical text of Stuart G. Hall, *Melito of Sardis On Puscha and Fragments* (Oxford: Clarendon Press, 1979). Though all translations are my own, I try to stay as close to Hall as possible, only adjusting his rendering where I deem it necessary.
[12] See esp. P. Nautin, "L'homélie de 'Méliton' sur la passion," *Revue d'histoire ecclésiastique* 44 (1949): 429–38; and more recently Lynn Cohick, *The* Peri Pascha *Attributed to Melito of Sardis: Setting, Purpose, and Sources* (Brown Judaic Studies 327; Providence: Brown Judaic Studies, 2000), esp. 4–51.
[13] Cohick, *The* Peri Pascha *Attributed to Melito of Sardis*, 12.
[14] Cohick, *The* Peri Pascha *Attributed to Melito of Sardis*, submits that three other "Melitos" are known to have existed in the first and second centuries, and so she concludes that "the name 'Melito' itself was not extremely rare" (11).
[15] Cohick, *The* Peri Pascha *Attributed to Melito of Sardis*, 12–13, 21.
[16] Cohick, *The* Peri Pascha *Attributed to Melito of Sardis*, 16–19.
[17] Cohick, *The* Peri Pascha *Attributed to Melito of Sardis*, 13–15, 22–31.
[18] Cohick, *The* Peri Pascha *Attributed to Melito of Sardis*, 31–37.

As for dating Melito and his homily, the only specific evidence (or potentially specific) comes from Eusebius but, again, the value and relevance of such evidence is questionable. Eusebius reports that in his "two books on the Pascha" Melito supplies a date for the work: "While Servillius Paulus was proconsul of Asia, at which time Sagaris suffered martyrdom, there was much discussion in Laodicea, respecting the Passover, which occurred at that time in its proper season, and in which, also, these works were written."[19] No Servillius Paulus is known to have existed in the second century. According to Rufinus' Latin translation of Eusebius this Asian proconsul was Sergius Paulus, and there does appear to have been a Sergius Paulus who was proconsul in the 150s and again in 166–67. But Rufinus could have confused the proconsul mentioned by Eusebius with the proconsul of Cyprus mentioned in Acts 13:7 who is a namesake. In the end, therefore, the evidence for a precise date is uncertain. Internal features of the homily do, however, support a date in the 160s – or in the mid- to late-second century.[20] The exegetical style, and the use of μυστήριον as a hermeneutical term in particular, matches that of Justin, as does the absence of New Testament citations, which becomes quite common in later authors such as Irenaeus, Tertullian, and Clement of Alexandria. Furthermore, if Eusebius is correct that Clement knew *PP* and composed his own similar treatise because of it (*Hist. eccl.* 4.26.4), then Melito must be placed prior to the late-second or early-third century (assuming again the correspondence of Eusebius' Melito and the author of *PP*).

One of the major preoccupations of recent study of *PP* is whether or not it is something like a Christian Haggadah (a liturgical text utilized in formal paschal celebrations) or if it depends on haggadic traditions. This thesis was first put forward by F. L. Cross, who noted intriguing similarities between the Passover Haggadah in Mishnah *Pesahim* 10.5 and several specific themes in *PP*, as well as in the wording of *PP* 68.[21] This theory has been taken up and refined by, among others, Stuart Hall[22] and Alistair Stewart-Sykes.[23] As interesting as this possibility is, I am hesitant to make much of it. As Cohick has pointed out, the parallels are not as significant when one recognizes that much of the common language is simply

---

19 *Hist. eccl.* 4.26.3 (trans. C.F. Cruse). These are the words that never appear in our extant editions of *PP*. It is, however, not hard to image how and why they might at some point have been appended to Eusebius' version, whether by Melito himself or a later copyist.
20 As Cohick, *The Peri Pascha Attributed to Melito of Sardis*, demonstrates, on the basis of manuscript evidence, "[t]he latest possible date for the homily is sometime in the third century, perhaps early enough in that century to allow for three possible recensions and a Coptic translation" (6–7).
21 F.L. Cross, *The Early Christian Fathers* (London: Gerald Duckworth and Co., 1960), 104–9.
22 Stuart G. Hall, "Melito in the Light of the Passover Haggadah," *JTS* 22 (1971): 29–46.
23 Stewart-Sykes, *The Lamb's High Feast*, 60–66.

biblical and that many of the supposed shared themes are likewise present in other non-haggadic Jewish and Christian texts.[24] But whether formally haggadic or not, the homily explicitly invokes a liturgical context at its outset—and probably one related to the Christian celebration of Pascha – and it indeed focuses on the exposition of a liturgical event – Israel's first Pascha. These facts alone justify attending to the liturgical resonances in the work.[25]

The text is arranged in four sections, each of which ends with a doxological statement and a closing Amen:[26]
1) *Prologue:* Introduction to the mystery of the Pascha (*PP* 1–10)
2) Typological exposition of the mystery of the Pascha (*PP* 11–45)
3) The mystery of the Lord and the mystery of Scripture (*PP* 46–65)
4) The death of the Lord and the failure of Israel (*PP* 66–105)

There has been much debate about whether or not these four extant sections somehow comprise the "two books *On the Pascha*" mentioned by Eusebius. Many scholars have assumed this to be the case and usually divide the two "books" into *PP* 1–45 and *PP* 46–105. The decision to divide the document here is based primarily on the explicit division of the homily here in the Georgian version. This version, however, is in many ways unreliable and, curiously, attributes *PP* 1–45 to Melitius and *PP* 46–105 to John Chrysostom.[27] Whether or not *PP* as we now have it is for the most part what Eusebius had in his "two books" is not the concern of this study. I do contend, however, that too strong a division between *PP* 1–45 and *PP* 46–65 undermines what is actually a unified and logically ordered progression in these sections.[28] In *PP* 1–10, after concluding the liturgical reading of Exod 12, Melito introduces his exposition (διηγήσομαι) of this text. In *PP* 11–45 he then performs his rereading of Exod 12 as a christological mystery, and in *PP* 46–65 he demonstrates how the mystery of the Pascha,

---

24 Cohick, *The* Peri Pascha *Attributed to Melito of Sardis*, 27–29.
25 For more on the genre of *PP*, see the extensive analysis of Stewart-Sykes, *The Lamb's High Feast*, 55–113. Following the usual convention, I refer to the document as a homily. And although I agree with Stewart-Sykes that "the term 'homily' is largely undefined," I do not, like Stewart-Sykes, view this as a "problem" (56). I refer to it as a homily because it is a formal, exegetical address to a gathered community. Just because "it is not an exegetical synagogue homily along rabbinic lines" (60) does render such a designation inappropriate.
26 The term μυστήριον only appears in the first three sections.
27 See J.N. Birdsall, "Melito of Sardis, Περὶ τοῦ Πάσχα in a Georgian version," *Le Muséon* 80 (1967): 121–38; and M. Van Esbroeck, "Le traité sur la Pâque de Méliton de Sardes en georgien," *Le Muséon* 84 (1971): 373–94.
28 See also the additional arguments for unity offered by Cohick, *The* Peri Pascha *Attributed to Melito of Sardis*, 19–21.

which is Christ's saving death, is typologically prefigured in the rest of scripture as well. Therefore, *PP* 1–65 read quite naturally as a unified text, and it is only in *PP* 66–105 that the subject shifts as Melito moves from his exegetical demonstration of the mystery of Pascha to his vilification of "ungrateful Israel." The term μυστήριον, so central to the first three sections, also disappears entirely in the fourth. Thus whether or not there are "two books" somewhere in our *PP*, I read the homily as we now have it in our two early Greek codices—that is, as a unified text divided into four sections by doxologies.

7.3 Melito and Paul

Little can be said about Melito's use or estimation of Pauline traditions since Melito never mentions any Christian authorities, nor does he cite any Christian author. There are, however, a few notable instances in *PP* of literary overlap with Pauline phrasing.[29] The most noticeable is the juxtaposition in *PP* 45 of "the Jerusalem below" (ἡ κάτω Ἰερουσαλήμ) and the "Jerusalem above" (τὴν ἄνω Ἰερουσαλήμ), which closely resembles Paul's allegory in Gal 4:25–26 involving "the present Jerusalem" (τῇ νῦν Ἰερουσαλήμ) and "the Jerusalem above" (ἡ ἄνω Ἰερουσαλήμ). Also similar are *PP* 103 (ἐγὼ γάρ εἰμι ὑμῶν ἡ ἄφεσις...ἐγὼ τὸ λύτρον ὑμῶν) and Eph 1:7 (ἐν ᾧ ἔχομεν τὴν ἀπολύτρωσιν...τὴν ἄφεσιν τῶν παραπτωμάτων) and Col 1:14 (ἐν ᾧ ἔχομεν τὴν ἀπολύτρωσιν, τὴν ἄφεσιν τῶν ἁμαρτιῶν). Another potential Pauline intertext in *PP* 103 is the statement "I am the Pascha of salvation" (ἐγὼ τὸ πάσχα τῆς σωτηρίας), which may be based on 1 Cor 5:7 (τὸ πάσχα ἡμῶν ἐτύθη Χριστός).[30] Paul's alignment of Christ and Pascha in 1 Cor 5:7–8 may even have stimulated Melito's entire exegetical approach in the homily.[31] Melito's reference to ὁ πρωτότοκος τοῦ θεοῦ (*PP* 82) also has Pauline analogues in Rom 8:29 and Col 1:15, 18.[32] Finally, Melito's use of μυστήριον also appears to be a quite prominent instance in which he has creatively appropriated Pauline material. His extensive use of the term agrees with its relative prominence in the Pauline corpus. Melito also exclusively uses the singular form of the noun, which accords with the Pauline preference. Moreover, since Paul is the earliest author (and the only New Testament author) to link μυστή-

---

[29] For more on these potential literary links see Bonner, *The Homily on the Passion*, 40.
[30] For an analysis of Paul's innovative exegesis of Exod 12 and its impact in early Christianity, see Karl Gerlach, *The Antenicene Pascha: A Rhetorical History* (Liturgia condenda; Leuven: Peeters, 1998), 32–42.
[31] Justin, *Dial.* 40, anticipates Melito as well.
[32] See also Heb 1:6, which Melito might have taken as Pauline.

ριον with the person of Christ, it is likely that Melito is directly dependent upon Paul in frequently making this correlation as well. Melito also repeatedly associates "the mystery of the Lord" (by which he means Christ) with the crucifixion, which likewise agrees with the implied association in 1 Cor 2:7. Therefore, although there are no incontrovertible instances where Melito overtly reiterates Pauline traditions, there are nonetheless suggestive occasions where his theological idiom appears to have been shaped by Pauline exemplars – the use of μυστήριον being the most conspicuous and theologically significant.

7.4 Μυστήριον in Peri Pascha 1–65

The word μυστήριον appears seventeen times in *PP*,[33] and exclusively in the first three sections (*PP* 1–65). In terms of the rate of occurrence, this is higher than any preceding Christian text.[34] Similar to Justin, Melito applies the term in a strict twofold manner, referring either to the "mystery of the Lord" (which he identifies as Christ's crucifixion)[35] or to the mystery of scripture (and most frequently to the "mystery of Pascha"). To designate something a mystery is, for Melito, to invest it with a previously concealed or newly revealed meaning. In the case of Pascha, its mystery is revealed when that event is viewed through the subsequent occurrence of Christ's crucifixion. It is thus the newly revealed mystery of the Lord's death that reveals the anterior mystery latent in the Exodus account of Pascha. But the hermeneutical movement does not end here as Melito also shows how the old mystery of Pascha itself illuminates the new mystery of Christ. There is thus, for Melito, an ongoing loop of revelation: the new mystery enlightens the

---

[33] The term also appears in some of the fragments attributed to Melito. In fragment 9 Melito describes the binding of Isaac as a "new mystery" (μυστήριον καινόν). According to the context, this event is a mystery because Isaac's suffering has become a type of Christ's suffering. This use of the term is consistent with what is found throughout *PP*, and the expression "new mystery" occurs in *PP* 31 and 34. Fragment 13 (from a Syriac florilegium) also has the expression "new mystery," but this time the mystery is the crucifixion. This also is consistent with Melito's usage in *PP*.

[34] Perhaps a near contemporary of Justin, Melito's extensive employment of μυστήριον appears to be part of the rapidly spreading interest in this terminology from the middle decades of the second century and onwards. In later authors such as Clement of Alexandria, Origen, and Tertullian the association of the term with Paul becomes explicit.

[35] This phrase occurs 5x and always in reference to the crucifixion.

old mystery, and the old then becomes an illuminating prefiguration of the new as it, in fact, becomes new.[36]

7.4.1 Μυστήριον in Peri Pascha 1–10

The term first appears at the outset of the homily in an opening that introduces most of the primary themes that the rest of the address develops:

> 1 The scripture of the Hebrew Exodus has been read,
> and the words of the mystery have been plainly stated:
> how the sheep is sacrificed,
> and how the people is saved,
> and how Pharaoh is scourged through the mystery.
>
> 2 Understand, therefore, beloved: thus it is
> new and old,
> eternal and temporary,
> perishable and imperishable,
> mortal and immortal,
> the mystery of the Pascha.

> 1 ἡ μὲν γραφὴ τῆς Ἑβραϊκῆς ἐξόδου ἀνέγνωσται,
> καὶ τὰ ῥήματα τοῦ μυστηρίου διασεσάφηται
> πῶς τὸ πρόβατον θύεται,
> καὶ πῶς ὁ λαὸς σῴζεται,
> [καὶ πῶς ὁ Φαραὼ διὰ τοῦ μυστηρίου μαστίζεται].[37]
>
> 2 τοίνυν ξύνετε, ὦ ἀγαπητοί· οὕτως ἐστὶν
> καινὸν καὶ παλαιόν,
> ἀΐδιον καὶ πρόσκαιρον,
> φθαρτὸν καὶ ἄφθαρτον,
> θνητὸν καὶ ἀθάνατον,
> τὸ τοῦ πάσχα μυστήριον.

---

[36] For specific studies on Melito's hermeneutical approach, see Andrew Michael Manis, "Melito of Sardis: Hermeneutic and Context," *Greek Orthodox Theological Review* 32 (1987): 387–401; Henry Knapp, "Melito's Use of Scripture in *Peri Pascha*: Second Century Typology," *VC* 54 (2000): 343–74; and John Hainsworth, "The Force of the Mystery: Anamnesis and Exegesis in Melito's *Peri Pascha*," *St. Vladimir's Theological Quarterly* 46 (2002): 107–46.

[37] This line is present in the Latin epitome and the Georgian version but is absent in the Chester Beatty and Michigan papyrus.

The first words of the prologue signal the liturgical setting of the homily, which is likely a paschal celebration.[38] Some portion of Exod 12 has been publically read for the congregants,[39] and now Melito, designating it a mystery, will further expound it. The literal content of the scripture is plain enough – the sheep is sacrificed, the people are saved, Pharaoh is scourged – but, as Melito soon explains, the mystery of this event is not its historical or "literal" meaning. Rather than just an account of the first Paschal celebration, Exod 12 is also a prefigurative foretelling of Christ's own sacrificial slaughter and related Christian rites, principally baptism and post-baptismal unction.[40] Therefore, to treat the Pascha in Exod 12 as a mystery is to read it as prefiguring Christ's saving death and Christian sacramental customs.[41]

It is worth noting here at the outset that although thus far the cultic connotations of μυστήριον have been ignored, or perhaps deliberately suppressed, by Christian authors, Melito has no reservations about speaking of the mystery of Pascha and the mystery of the Lord in ways that evoke the cultic framework of pagan practices.[42] The very designation of a ritual practice as a μυστήριον provokes such associations. Moreoever, in *PP* 15–17, where Melito begins to recount Moses' performance of the Pascha rite, he explicitly labels this ritual celebration a μυστήριον and then clusters around this designation important sacramental language along with technical cultic terminology for "initiation" (διατελέω; τελέω; ἀμύητος). In so doing, Moses becomes the hierophant of the paschal

---

38 I say "likely" because although most scholars simply assume this to be the case, there is no direct evidence for it within the homily itself.
39 G. Zuntz, "On the Opening Sentence of Melito's Paschal Homily," *HTR* 36 (1943): 298–315, proposes that ἡ γραφὴ τῆς Ἑβραϊκῆς ἐξόδου ἀνέγνωσται refers to a reading of the Hebrew text of Exod 12. This thesis, however, has been sufficiently refuted. See esp. Cohick, *The Peri Pascha Attributed to Melito of Sardis*, 35–37; Stewart-Sykes, *The Lamb's High Feast*, 92–100, 172–6. Following Stuart Hall, "Melito *Peri Pascha* 1 and 2. Text and Interpretation," in *Kyriakon: Festschrift Johannes Quasten* (ed. Patrick Granfield and Josef A. Jungmann; Münster: Aschendorff, 1970), 236–48, I read the first two lines in parallel, and so as describing the single activity of reading. For the possibility that separate activities are in view, see Bonner, *The Homily on the Passion by Melito*, 30–36.
40 On the practice of post-baptismal unction see Tertullian, *Bapt.* 7.
41 Cf. Justin, *Dial.* 40.
42 For more on this aspect of Melito's usage see esp. Josef Blank, *Vom Passa: Die älteste christliche Osterpredigt* (Freiburg: Lambertus, 1963), 45–55. As Blank correctly emphasizes, "Das Wort 'Mysterium' hat in der Sprache Melitons einen vollen Klang mit zahlreichen Ober- und Untertönen" (46). Giulea, "Seeing Christ through the Scriptures," also rightly points out that "although the term μυστήριον appears in the Pauline corpus, a development of exegesis as mystery performance or cult does not seem to materialize in Christian context before Melito" (32).

mystery rite and the people of Israel co-initiates in that ritual celebration.⁴³ By evoking these cultic images within the context of the church's own liturgical celebration, Melito's paschal homily ties together exegetical demonstration and ritual performance by transforming Exod 12 into christological prophecy and the rites of Pascha into ceremonial prefigurations of Christian sacramental practice.⁴⁴ If the setting of the homily is indeed Sardis, then this ritual evocation becomes all the more intriguing since that city had a long and diverse history of mystery cults.⁴⁵ But even if not, Melito's homily nonetheless represents an important stage in what will soon become a common way of imagining ecclesial identity vis-à-vis pagan mysteries and of referring to Christian sacraments as "the mysteries."⁴⁶ One passage in which Clement of Alexandria appropriates cultic pagan images for constructive purposes should suffice to show the development of this trajectory:

> O truly holy mysteries (ὦ τῶν ἁγίων ὡς ἀληθῶς μυστηρίων)! O incorruptible light! I carry the torches (δᾳδουχοῦμαι)⁴⁷ to heaven to have the vision (ἐποπτεῦσαι)⁴⁸ of God. I become

---

43 So Giulea, "Seeing Christ through the Scriptures," who describes Melito's homily as "a cultic investigation through which the one who does the hermeneutical task undergoes transformation and encounters the concrete manifestations of the Logos. It seems that it played a similar role with the transmission and explication of the ἱεροὶ λόγοι in the mystery cults.... Paschal exegesis was therefore not an abstract ratiocination, but a cultic activity, which should involve Christ's contemplation" (46–47).

44 As Giulea, "Seeing Christ through the Scriptures," notices, Melito's "innovation consists in connecting the old method of reading Scripture as a religious experience with the Christian typological interpretation, Greek mystery terminology, Jewish terms and images, and the Paschal liturgical celebration. Within this complex context of the Paschal feast, viewed as a central Christian mystery, biblical exegesis acquired the character of a special mystery performance or drama" (28).

45 For more on the religious life of Sardis, see George M. A. Hanfmann, *Sardis from Prehistoric to Roman Times: Results of the Archaeological Exploration of Sardis 1958–1975* (Cambridge, MA: Harvard University Press, 1983), esp. 90–96, 128–37; Colin J. Hemer, *The Letters to the Seven Churches of Asia in Their Local Setting* (JSNTSup 11; Sheffield: JSOT Press, 1986), 138–40; and Stephen Mitchell, *Anatolia: Land, Men, and Gods in Asia Minor*, vol. 2, *The Rise of the Church* (Oxford: Clarendon Press, 1993), esp. 11–30. Adolf Hansen, "The 'Sitz im Leben' of the Paschal Homily of Melito of Sardis with Special Reference to the Paschal Festival in Early Christianity," (Ph.D. diss., Northwestern University, 1968), repeatedly emphasizes that "Christianity in Sardis was in some sense quite close to a mystery religion" (123). Hansen even claims that Eusebius' reference to Melito as a eunuch suggests that he had been associated with the Cybele cult, but this is pure speculation.

46 The designation of Christian sacraments as "mysteries" is as early as Tertullian.

47 This verb, and the activity of proceeding with torches, is often used for mystery celebrations.

48 This is the verb used for initiation into to the highest level of the mysteries (the *epopteia*), and it is particularly associated with the Eleusinian cult. See Kevin Clinton, "Stages of Initiation

holy by being initiated (ἅγιος γίνομαι μυούμενος), and the Lord is a hierophant (ἱεροφαντεῖ) as he seals the initiate (τὸν μύστην σφραγίζεται),⁴⁹ providing enlightenment (φωταγωγῶν). And he commends to the Father the one who has trusted, this one being protected for eternity. These are the Bacchic revelries of my mysteries (ταῦτα τῶν ἐμῶν μυστηρίων τὰ βακχεύματα). If you want, be also initiated (μυοῦ), and you will dance with angels around the unbegotten and indestructible and only true God, the Word of God singing with us.⁵⁰

Returning to the juxtapositions in *PP* 2, these contrasts set forth in simple fashion the basic *synkritic* framework that structures Melito's exegesis. He repeatedly maintains that scripture and Israel belong on the "old" side of divide and Christ and the Christian on the "new." He expands the new/old, eternal/temporary, perishable/imperishable, and mortal/immortal contrasts throughout the remainder of the prologue (*PP* 3–10), varying his vocabulary and increasing in specificity. At the heart of these contrasts, however, is the typological concurrence of "the slaughter of the sheep" and "the life of the Lord" (*PP* 3). The former is characterized as "the law," "the type," and "burial in earth," whereas the latter represents "the Word," "grace," and "rising from the dead." An important clarification regarding these juxtapositions is given at the end of *PP* 4–5:

> For the type indeed existed,
> but then the truth was found.
> For instead of a lamb there appeared a Son,
> and instead of a sheep, a man.
> And in the man is Christ, who has extended to all things.
>
> ὁ μὲν γὰρ τύπος ἐγένετο,
> ἡ δὲ ἀλήθεια ηὑρίσκετο.
> ἀντὶ γὰρ τοῦ ἀμνοῦ θεὸς ἐγένετο,
> καὶ ἀντὶ τοῦ προβάτου ἄνθρωπος.
> ἐν δὲ τῷ ἀνθρώπῳ Χριστός, ὃς κεχώρηκεν τὰ πάντα.

This passage further clarifies what Melito means when he defines the Pascha of Exod 12 as a μυστήριον. Such a designation does not deny the literal occurrence

---

in the Eleusinian and Samothracian Mysteries," in *Greek Mysteries: The Archaeology and Ritual of Ancient Greek Secret Cults* (ed. Michael B. Cosmopoulos; London/New York: Routledge, 2003), 50–78, esp. 51–65.
49 The language of sealing also has baptismal overtones in Christianity.
50 *Protr.* 12.120.1–2. Like Clement, many later Christian authors have no qualms about comparing and contrasting Christianity with mystery cults.

of the event – "for the type indeed existed."⁵¹ Rather, it finds in the event a newly discovered meaning. The discovery of this meaning occurs when one reads Exod 12 in light of Christ, whose existence "has extended" to the scriptural events of Exodus and transfigured them. The slaughter of the sheep then becomes, retroactively, a prefiguration of Christ's own death. When newly viewed as prefigurative types, the events of Pascha then themselves "extend" to Christ, the source of their new meaning. Thus Melito states in *PP* 6–7:

> 6 Hence the slaying of the sheep
> and the distribution (πομπή)⁵² of the blood
> and the scripture from the law have extended (κεχώρηκεν) to Christ Jesus,
> on account of whom all things in the ancient law (δι' ὄν τὰ πάντα ἐν τῷ πρεσβυτέρῳ νόμῳ ἐγένετο) happened,
> or rather, in the new word (μᾶλλον δὲ ἐν τῷ νέῳ λόγῳ).⁵³
>
> 7 For indeed the law has become Word (Καὶ γὰρ ὁ νόμος λόγος ἐγένετο),
> and the old new (καὶ ὁ παλαιὸς καινός)—
> "having gone out from Zion and Jerusalem" (συνεξελθὼν ἐκ Σιὼν καὶ Ἰερουσαλήμ)⁵⁴ –
> and the commandment grace (καὶ ἡ ἐντολὴ χάρις),
> and the type truth (καὶ ὁ τύπος ἀλήθεια),
> and the lamb a son (καὶ ὁ ἀμνὸς υἱός),
> and the sheep a man (καὶ τὸ πρόβατον ἄνθρωπος),
> and the man God (καὶ ὁ ἄνθρωπος θεός).⁵⁵

For Melito, Christ is like an ever enlarging hermeneutical spiral, spinning outward and drawing all reality into its vortex. As the one who "has extended (κεχώρηκεν) to all things"⁵⁶ and "is all things,"⁵⁷ Christ becomes the reality to which all existence extends as well. For the story of Pascha, and indeed all scripture, this means that insofar as it "has extended to Christ"⁵⁸ and "has gone out from Zion and Jerusalem"⁵⁹ it has been reconfigured by a new and transformative fact. Absorbed into this new reality, the mystery of the Pascha "becomes" (ἐγένετο) the crucifixion of Christ and the salvation of humanity. It is defined as a

---

51 For more on Melito's typological reasoning, see Jean Daniélou, "Figure et Événement chez Méliton de Sardes," in *Neotestamentica et Patristica: Eine Freundesgabe, Herrn Professor Dr. Oscar Cullmann zu seinem 60. Geburtstag überreicht* (Leiden: Brill, 1962), 282–92.
52 This term is often used to describe various mystery rites.
53 *PP* 6.
54 Cf. Isa 2:3; Mic 4:2.
55 *PP* 7.
56 *PP* 5.
57 *PP* 9.
58 *PP* 6.
59 *PP* 7.

mystery precisely because, when viewed retrospectively through the Christ event, "it has been found" to correspond to that later occurrence.[60] But "correspond" is not quite the correct word. Inasmuch as the mystery of Christ reveals the mystery of scripture, the former "becomes" the latter and the latter "becomes" the former. As the final words of the prologue put it, Christ "is all things…: inasmuch as he suffers, sheep; inasmuch as he is buried, man; inasmuch as he is raised, God. This is Jesus Christ, to whom be glory for ever and ever. Amen."[61] Therefore, again, as Christ extends to Pascha and Pascha then extends to Christ, the two converge, and in this convergence the former event of Pascha is transmuted by the transcendent reality of Christ – "the old becomes new."

7.4.2 Μυστήριον in Peri Pascha 11–45

Immediately following this doxology, Melito begins the first major section (*PP* 11–45), which resumes the principal topics set forth at the very beginning in *PP* 1–2. In *PP* 11 Melito states:

> This is the mystery of the Pascha (τοῦτό ἐστιν τὸ τοῦ πάσχα μυστήριον)
> just as it is written in the law,
> as it has just now been read.
> But I shall describe in detail the words of the scripture,
> how God has given command to Moses in Egypt,
> when he intends to bind Pharaoh under a scourge
> and to free Israel from a scourge by Moses' hand.

Having set forth the various juxtapositions that structure his hermeneutic in *PP* 3–10, in *PP* 11 Melito returns to his original objective, which is to unravel the mystery of Exod 12. And *PP* 12–45 is just that – a point by point rereading of Israel's first Pascha as a prophetic rehearsal of Christ's saving death.[62] The cultic dimension of his rereading is overt at the outset where he describes the rite of

---

[60] Cf. Hainsworth, "The Force of the Mystery," who writes, "Melito's typology is…one of mystery and not mere history, and the Scriptures were the locus of that mystery. This may mean we are encountering a different kind of typology than we are used to dealing with, in that Melito is not playing a literary compare and contrast game. But this recognition might, in reverse, enable us to see a more vital kind of typology at work here, one which takes into account revelation, mystery, and a view of the Scriptures as having literally 'become a recent word'" (133). What Hainsworth is here recognizing is the retrospective character of Melito's typological construals. The type is only recognized to be a type after the later revelation.
[61] *PP* 9–10.
[62] Cf. Justin's reading of the "mystery of the lamb" in *Dial.* 40.1; 111.3.

the Pascha as a mystery, and adds to this other technical terminology from the pagan mysteries such as "performance" and "initiation" (διατελέω; τελέω; ἀμύητος).[63] This terminology also appears alongside ritual language such as "seal" (σφραγίζω) and "anoint" (χρίω):

> 15 Then Moses, when he had slain the sheep,
> and at night performed the mystery with the sons of Israel (καὶ νύκτωρ διατελέσας τὸ μυστήριον μετὰ τῶν υἱῶν Ἰσραήλ),
> marked (ἐσφράγισεν) the doors of the houses
> to protect the people and to win the angel's respect.
>
> 16 But while the sheep is being slain
> and the Pascha is being eaten
> and the mystery is being performed (καὶ τὸ μυστήριον τελεῖται)
> and the people is making merry
> and Israel is being marked (σφραγίζεται),
> then came the angel to strike (πατάσσειν)[64] Egypt,
> the uninitiated in the mystery (τὴν ἀμύητον τοῦ μυστηρίου),[65]
> the non-participating in the Pascha (τὴν ἄμοιρον τοῦ πάσχα),
> the unmarked with the blood (τὴν ἀσφράγιστον τοῦ αἵματος),
> the unguarded by the Spirit (τὴν ἀφρούρητον τοῦ πνεύματος).

In commenting on this passage, Hall writes that "Melito regards the Pascha as an initiatory rite with apotropaic effect, and insinuates into 14–16 the language of Christian baptism and unction."[66] Indeed, the language of "sealing" (σφραγίζω) and "anointing" (χρίω)[67] with the blood of the lamb, when combined with initiatory terminology from mystery cults, certainly invests the passage with ritual overtones, and baptism and unction do appear to be the rites in view.[68] Both σφραγίζω and χρίω are common in Greek scriptural versions but rarely occur to-

---

63 For the association of this verb with pagan mysteries see esp. Philo, *Contempl.* 25; Justin, *2 Apol.* 12.5; Irenaeus, *Haer.* 1.1.8; Clement, *Strom.* 6.2.4; *Protr.* 2.17; 12.18.
64 Cf. Exod 12:12, 23, 27, 29.
65 Cf. the association of these nouns in Philo, *Cher.* 48; Clement, *Protr.* 2.22.3.
66 Hall, *On Pascha*, 9 n. 5. Cf. also the similar language in *PP* 30.
67 See *PP* 14, where the people of Israel are instructed to "anoint" the doors of their houses with the blood.
68 Cf. also Blank, *Vom Passa*, who writes, "Hier schlägt ein christlicher Sprachgebrauch durch, der offensichtlich auf die Taufe, auf die Versiegelung mit dem Heiligen Geist, verweist. Ebenso ist die Wendung vom 'Zeichen des Blutes' (vgl Ex 12,13 vgl. 14) bestimmt keinem aufmerksamen Leser, wie es die altchristlichen Theologen waren, entgangen. Dann ist hier ein Hinweise auf die *Taufe* gegeben und man muss mit der Möglichkeit rechnen, dass auch schon in der Passafeier, deren Typ die Homilie Melitons vertritt, die Taufe gespendet wurde" (56–57).

gether.⁶⁹ They do, however, appear together in Paul, and in a passage that likely refers to baptism (or would likely be read that way in the second century).⁷⁰ In 2 Cor 1:21–22 Paul writes, "The one who secures us with you in Christ, anointing us (χρίσας ἡμᾶς), is God, who also sealed us (ὁ καὶ σφραγισάμενος ἡμᾶς) and gave us the down payment of the Spirit in our hearts." The connection between χρίω, the bestowal of the Spirit, and baptism goes back to traditions about Jesus, whom, according to Acts 10:37–38, God "anointed" (ἔχρισεν) with the Holy Spirit at his baptism (cf. Luke 3:21–22). In scriptural traditions the language of "anointing" is associated with oil consecrations and, at least by the time of Tertullian (*Bapt.* 7),⁷¹ the practice of unction at baptism had become a standard rite.⁷² The language of "sealing" also had baptismal connotations, particularly in the second century.⁷³ As early as the Shepherd of Hermas (*Sim.* 9.16.4) the water of baptism is described as a seal (ἡ σφραγὶς οὖν τὸ ὕδωρ ἐστίν). A nearly identical correlation of "seal" and baptism occurs in *Acts of Paul and Thecla* 25 and also, albeit in a circuitous way, when one compares *2 Clem* 6.9 (τηρήσωμεν τὸ βάπτισμα) with 7.6 (τηρησάντων...τὴν σφραγῖδα) and 8.6 (τηρήσατε...τὴν σφραγῖδα).⁷⁴ Paul also describes the sealing of the Holy Spirit in ways that intimate baptism in Eph 1:13 ("In him you also, when you believed the word of truth, the gospel of your salvation, and trusted in him, you were sealed [ἐσφραγίσθητε] in the Holy Spirit of promise) and 4:30 ("Do not grieve the Holy Spirit of God, in which you were sealed [ἐσφραγίσθητε] for the day of redemption).⁷⁵ Therefore, in his rereading of the Pascha of Exod 12 as an initiation ceremony involving anointing and sealing with the lamb's blood, Melito brings Israel's past into the church's present by reimagining it as prophetic performance of Christ's

---

69 See, however, Dan (Th) 9:24.
70 The classic work on this subject is G.W.H. Lampe, *The Seal of the Spirit: A Study in the Doctrine of Baptism and Confirmation in the New Testament and the Fathers* (London: SPCK, 1951).
71 Tertullian also associates this rite with the biblical practice of anointing priests.
72 For the association of baptism and unction in later writers, see Andrew Radde-Gallwitz, "Gregory of Nyssa's Pneumatology in Context: The Spirit as Anointing and the History of the Trinitarian Controversies," *JECS* 19 (2011): 259–85.
73 For more on the use of this language in relation to baptism in early Christianity, see the excellent study by Karl Olav Sandnes, "Seal and Baptism in Early Christianity," in *Ablution, Initiation, and Baptism: Late Antiquity, Early Judaism, and Early Christianity* (ed. David Hellholm, et al.; BZNW 176.II; Berlin/Boston: de Gruyter, 2011), 1441–81.
74 Irenaeus likewise speaks of baptism as "the seal of eternal life" (*Epid.* 3).
75 Recall that Paul also calls circumcision a σφραγῖδα in Rom 4:11. The association of circumcision and baptism appears in Col 2:11–12.

death and Christian baptism.[76] Just as the people of Israel were sealed and anointed for salvation by the initiatory mystery rite involving the paschal lamb's blood, so also the Christian is sealed and anointed for salvation by the initiatory mystery rite of baptism into Christ's death.[77] Thus once again mystery exegesis and sacramental practice converge.

Melito continues his retelling of the Exod 12 narrative in *PP* 17–30, vividly embellishing the story in a variety of ways. He concludes his renarration in *PP* 31–33 and returns to the mystery motif, stating plainly the meaning of the paschal μυστήριον:

> O new and inexpressible mystery! (ὦ μυστηρίου καινοῦ καὶ ἀνεκδιηγήτου)
> The slaughter of the sheep was found (ηὑρίσκετο) to be Israel's salvation,
> and the death of the sheep became the people's life,
> and the blood won the angel's respect...
> It is clear that your[78] respect was won
> when you saw the mystery of the Lord occurring in the sheep (εἰδὼν τὸ τοῦ κυρίου μυστήριον ἐν τῷ προβάτῳ γινόμενον),
> and the life of the Lord in the slaughter of the lamb,
> the type of the Lord (τὸν τοῦ κυρίου τύπον) in the death of the sheep;
> that is why you did not strike Israel,
> but made only Egypt childless.

The mystery of the Pascha is that the original paschal celebration was simultaneously "the mystery of the Lord" insofar as the death of Christ occurred in the death of the paschal lamb. The angel, recognizing this, passed over those who had been initiated into this mystery by the anointing and sealing with the

---

[76] It should be noted that the comparison requires that the blood of the lamb be the equivalent of the waters of baptism or the oil of anointing. Perhaps Melito would say that Christian baptism is like the anointing and sealing of the lamb's blood in Exod 12 in that it is a baptism into Christ's death (Rom 6:3–4). Cf. also the association of baptism with Christ's death in Mark 10:38 ("But Jesus said to them, 'You do not know what you are asking. Are you able to drink the cup that I drink or be baptized with the baptism that I am baptized with?'").

[77] For more on the relationship between Christian baptism and various water rites within the mystery cults, see esp. Fritz Graf, "Baptism and Graeco-Roman Mystery cults," in *Ablution, Initiation, and Baptism: Late Antiquity, Early Judaism, and Early Christianity* (ed. David Hellholm, et al.; BZNW 176.II; Berlin/Boston: de Gruyter, 2011), 101–18. Graf cautiously, and I believe correctly, concludes that "neither an evolutionary derivation of Christian baptism from specific rituals in the world of early Christianity nor the rejection of any connection between the two worlds are feasible assumptions.... [E]verything suggest that these were independent developments in the common ritual language" (114).

[78] This is now a direct address to the "angel."

lamb's blood.⁷⁹ The Christian who has perceived the mystery of the Lord also now newly recognizes the mystery of the slaughter of the sheep and similarly experiences salvation through rites of baptism and anointing. For both the angel and for the Christian, however, the "new" mystery of Pascha is only "discovered" when viewed through the reality of Christ's death. It is knowledge of this later event that brings to light the mystery of the previous event. Therefore, hermeneutically speaking, it is this new Christian narrative that enables the discovery of the new meaning of Pascha.

Melito continues in *PP* 34 by raising the question that will dominate the remainder of this section (*PP* 35–45):

> What is this new mystery (τί τοῦτο τὸ καινὸν μυστήριον),⁸⁰
> that Egypt was struck for destruction,
> while Israel was protected for salvation?
> Hear the force of the mystery (ἀκούσατε τὴν δύναμιν τοῦ μυστηρίου).

In answering this question and making plain the "force of the mystery" Melito sets forth his most systematic hermeneutical statement in the homily by way of a lengthy *synkrisis* of the old model and the new reality.⁸¹ Although Melito reiterates his *synkrisis* in multiple ways throughout *PP* 35–45, the substance of his understanding is expressed in *PP* 35–37:

> 35 What is said and done is nothing, beloved,
> without a comparison and a preliminary sketch.
> Whatever should be done and said finds a comparison –
> what is said, a comparison,
> what is done, a prototype –
> in order that just as what is done is revealed through the prototype,
> so also what is spoken may be brought to light through the comparison.
>
> 36 This is just what happens in the case of the earlier structure.
> It does not arise as a finished work,
> but on account of what is going to be seen through its typological image.
> For this reason a preliminary sketch is made of the future thing

---

79 Notice that there is no ἄγγελος in Exod 12. Rather it is the Lord who strikes down the first born. For the "angel of the Lord" in Exodus see 3:2; 4:24; 14:19; 23:20, 23; 32:34; 33:2.
80 For the expression τὸ καινὸν μυστήριον see also fragment 9.
81 Stephen G. Wilson, *Related Strangers: Jews and Christians 70–170 C.E.* (Minneapolis: Fortress Press, 1995), describes this passage as "[t]he key to Melito's exposition of the scriptures" and as "a bold and unusually self-conscious statement of hermeneutical principle" (242). Similarly, Manis, "Melito of Sardis: Hermeneutic and Context," brands *PP* 35 "the cornerstone of Melito's hermeneutic" (397).

out of wax or of clay or of wood,
in order that what will arise –
taller in height,
and stronger in force,
and beautiful in form,
and rich in its construction –
may be seen through a small and perishable sketch.

37 But when that of which it is the type should arise,
the thing bearing the image of the future thing
is itself destroyed as growing useless
having yielded its image to the true reality.
And what once was precious becomes worthless
when what is truly precious has been revealed.[82]

35 οὐδέν ἐστιν, ἀγαπητοί, τὸ λεγόμενον καὶ γινόμενον,
δίχα παραβολῆς καὶ προκεντήματος.
πάντα ὅσα ἐὰν γίνεται καὶ λέγεται παραβολῆς τυγχάνε –
τὸ μὲν λεγόμενον παραβολῆς,
τὸ δὲ γινόμενον προτυπώσεως –
ἵνα ὡς ἂν τὸ γινόμενον διὰ τῆς προτυπώσεως δείκνυται,
οὕτως καὶ τὸ λεγόμενον διὰ τῆς παραβολῆς φωτισθῇ.

36 τοῦτο δὴ γίνεται ἐπὶ προκατασκευῆς.
ἔργον οὐκ ἀνίσταται,
διὰ δὲ τὸ μέλλον διὰ τῆς τυπικῆς εἰκόνος ὁρᾶσθαι.
διὰ τοῦτο τοῦ μέλλοντος γίνεται προκέντημα
ἢ ἐκ κηροῦ ἢ ἐκ πηλοῦ ἢ ἐκ ξύλου,
ἵνα τὸ μέλλον ἀνίστασθαι –
ὑψηλότερον ἐν μεγέθει,
καὶ ἰσχυρότερον ἐν δυνάμει,
καὶ καλὸν ἐν σχήματι,
καὶ πλούσιον ἐν τῇ κατασκευῇ
διὰ μικροῦ καὶ φθαρτοῦ προκεντήματος ὁραθῇ.

37 ὁπόταν δὲ ἀναστῇ πρὸς ὃ ὁ τύπος,
τό ποτε τοῦ μέλλοντος τὴν εἰκόνα φέρον,
τοῦτ' ὡς ἄχρηστον γινόμενον λύεται,
παραχωρῆσαν τῷ φύσει ἀληθεῖ τὴν περὶ αὐτοῦ εἰκόνα.
γίνεται δὲ τό ποτε τίμιον ἄτιμον,
τοῦ φύσει τιμίου φανερωθέντος.

This prototype-reality contrast, set in an architectural analogy and assessed in terms of value, encapsulates Melito's hermeneutical procedure. Although this ex-

---

82 For what appears to be the widespread influence of the analogy in this passage on subsequent authors see Hall, *On Pascha*, 19 n. 10.

egetical technique is not without Christian precedent – the most notable being Hebrews and passages such as Col 2:17 – Melito appears to be original in employing it in conjunction with the mystery schema.[83] As Melito goes on to explain, the prototype, like an architect's blueprint, is not entirely without value. Its value, however, is relative and temporally restricted – "For to each belongs a proper season: a proper time for the type...a proper time for the reality" (*PP* 38). When the final structure is completed, the model is no longer needed, and so "what was once precious becomes worthless" (*PP* 37). When the church arose and the gospel was revealed, the preliminary model of Israel "was made void (ἐκενώθη), conceding its power to the gospel" (*PP* 42). Just as a parable is fulfilled "when it is illuminated by an interpretation (ὑπὸ τῆς ἑρμηνείας φωτισθεῖσα), so also the law was fulfilled when it was illuminated by the gospel (τοῦ εὐαγγελίου φωτισθέντος)" (*PP* 43). More than just fulfilled, however, "the type was abolished (ἐλύθη) when the Lord was revealed (φανερωθέντος), and so today, things once precious (ποτε τίμια) have become worthless (ἄτιμα), since the really precious things (τῶν φύσει τιμίων) have been revealed (φανερωθέντων)" (*PP* 43).

In the remainder of this section (*PP* 44–45) Melito presents a series of more specific instances of how what was once of value has lost all worth in light of the corresponding and superseding reality of Christ. For instance, the paschal sheep was once valuable, but now it is worthless because of the life of the Lord. The same is true of the death of the sheep, which is supplanted by the death of the Lord. Likewise the blood of the sheep is void because of the Spirit and the Lord, and the speechless lamb because of the spotless Son, and the temple below because of Christ above, and the Jerusalem below because of the Jerusalem above,[84] and so on (44–45). The point is always the same: the Pascha is a preliminary sketch of a far greater reality. Because this far greater reality has appeared, the sketch is no longer valuable in itself.

What is most interesting about this hermeneutical employment of the mystery schema in conjunction with an exegetical *synkrisis* is the way in which the resultant valuation of Israel and the law differs from previous figures, and most notably Justin. Nowhere does Melito wholly denigrate the law or go so far as to argue that it was given to Israel on account of wickedness. Instead he insists that the people of Israel, their story, their law, and even their temple were all precious in their own time. But that time is over. Therefore, the "force of the mystery" is

---

[83] The contrast in Hebrews is between "sketch" (ὑπόδειγμα) or "shadow" (σκιά) and "reality" (εἰκών) (8:5; 10:1). In Col 2:17 it is "shadow" (σκιά) and "body" (σῶμα). Numerous contrasts with σκιά occur in Philo as well.
[84] Cf. Gal 4:25–26.

that it renders what might remain of Israel's heritage in Judaism powerless. This does not, however, mean the outright abandonment of the old. If this were the case, Melito would not have given a homily on Exod 12, nor would his congregation have memorialized Pascha. Instead it seems that the old model is "useless" and "abolished" and "void" and "worthless" only insofar as it is not reincorporated into the comprehensive reality of the crucified Lord. Thus the old model is worthless when viewed on its own, or apart from the grander reality of which it is a preliminary replica. As Melito will soon explain, when viewed in light of Christ, the old model acquires new value – the value of prophetic prefiguration.[85] Therefore, just as much as the "force of the mystery" renders the old model impotent, it also bestows potency by making it new.[86] In this way Melito's *synkrisis* departs from the usual commendation-through-condemnation *synkritic* procedure.

Daniel Sheerin has pointed out the risks involved with a *synkrisis* that involves deprecating one of the entities in the comparison:[87]

> In rhetoric, as Nicolaus the Sophist and Menander Rhetor warned, destructive invective against one of the *comparanda* of a *synkrisis* ultimately diminishes the subject of praise. Disparaging the types is ἄτεχνον.... At the same time, voiding the types of their proper value, meaning, and significance makes hermeneutic *synkrisis* impossible, for it prevents the types from being propaedeutic, explanatory, and corroborative of their fulfillment. This too, exegetically speaking, is ἄτεχνον.[88]

There is no doubt that Melito voids the types, but it is important to note that he does not leave them this way. Had they remained void for him, then his *synkrisis* would indeed have been potentially compromised, as Nicolaus and Menander warned, and hence ἄτεχνον, or unskillful. But for Melito the types are only annulled when disconnected from the newly revealed reality of Christ. By retrospectively reincorporating the types into the totalizing reality of Christ they become newly "propaedeutic, explanatory, and corroborative of their fulfillment," thus avoiding the hermeneutical risks Sheerin outlined above. Therefore, even though the types are said to be void and worthless for Jews, they are not so for Christians. For the Christian, that which was once precious in its own time and in its own way has now become newly and exceedingly precious as it has

---

[85] As Manis, "Melito of Sardis: Hermeneutic and Context," puts it, "His hermeneutic allows him to straddle this fence: The typological emphasis helps him keep part of his Jewishness, while his analogy of the sculptor's model enables him to relativize severely the claims of Judaism" (398).
[86] See *PP* 7.
[87] Sheerin, "Rhetorical and Hermeneutic *Synkrisis*," describes Melito's *synkrisis* on pp. 36–39.
[88] Sheerin, "Rhetorical and Hermeneutic *Synkrisis*," 39.

been drawn into the reality of Christ. This the point of *PP* 7: "For indeed the law has become (ἐγένετο) word, and the old new,… and the commandment grace, and the model reality, and the lamb a son, and the sheep a man, and the man God." By transforming the old into the new, Melito's paschal *synkrisis* converts and recaptures the mystery of Pascha. When and where this conversion and capture has not occurred, however, Pascha remains rescinded and worthless.

7.4.3 Μυστήριον in Peri Pascha 46–65

Following the brief doxology at the end of *PP* 45, Melito introduces the next major section (*PP* 46–65) and again returns to the subject of mystery: "You have now heard the account (διήγημα)[89] of the type and its correspondence (τῆς ἀνταποδόσεως). Listen also to the construction of the mystery (τὴν κατασκευὴν τοῦ μυστηρίου)."[90] Melito immediately explains what he means by the expression "construction of the mystery":

> What is the Pascha?
> It gets its name from its characteristic:
> from "suffer" comes "suffering" (ἀπὸ τοῦ παθεῖν τὸ πάσχειν).
> Learn therefore who is the suffering one,
> and who shares the suffering of the suffering one,
> and why the Lord is present on the earth
> to clothe himself with the suffering one
> and to carry him off to the heights of heaven.

By the phrase "construction of the mystery" Melito means the salvific story of Christ's incarnation, death, and ascension and the plight this story was meant to address. In treating this topic, Melito begins at the beginning with the creation account (*PP* 47) and ultimate fall of humanity (*PP* 48). Melito soon explains that humanity is the suffering one and Christ the one who, by sharing in the suffering of the suffering one and ascending back to heaven, restores humanity to God. Therefore, since "from 'suffer' comes 'suffering'"[91] (τοῦ παθεῖν τὸ πάσχειν), the suffering of humanity requires the suffering of Christ. And since the salvific suf-

---

[89] Recall the introduction to the previous section, where Melito explains that he will now "relate the words of scripture" (διηγήσομαι τὰ ῥήματα τῆς γραφῆς) (*PP* 11).
[90] *PP* 46.
[91] The fact that this is false etymology, which modern commentators are so quick to point out, is beside the point. For Melito what matters is not the diachronic history of these words but the phonetic likeness of πάσχα, πάσχειν, and παθεῖν.

fering of Christ requires his incarnation and resurrection, the "construction of the mystery" is the basic narrative of Christ's advent, death, and ascent. This narrative is also, in essence, Melito's soteriology.

In *PP* 49–56, Melito elaborates – rather luridly at times – the destructive effects of human sin.[92] Most of these involve relational injustices that create interpersonal suffering – person against person, father against son, mother against child, and so forth. The climax of this self- and socially-inflicted suffering is stated in *PP* 56:

> For the human was being divided by death (ὑπὸ τοῦ θανάτου μεριζόμενος),
> for a new disaster and captivity were enclosing him,
> and he was dragged off a prisoner under the shadows of death,
> and desolate lay the Father's image (ἔκειτο δὲ ἔρημος ἡ τοῦ πατρὸς εἰκών).
> This then is the reason why the mystery of the Pascha (διὰ ταύτην γοῦν τὴν αἰτίαν τὸ τοῦ πάσχα μυστήριον)
> has been fulfilled in the body of the Lord (τετέλεσται ἐν τῷ τοῦ κυρίου σώματι).

Now captive to death, humanity was incapable of its own rehabilitation. On the brink of oblivion, humanity's only possible rescue was for the mystery of Pascha to be performed in the Lord's own body – πάσχειν for παθεῖν. This is just what the mystery of the Lord accomplishes. And so just as the slaughtered lamb proved to be Israel's salvation, so too the crucified Christ proves to be the salvation of all humanity. This is the "construction of the mystery."

Having now explained the construction of the mystery and the reason why it had to occur as it did, Melito concludes this section of the homily by demonstrating that though the revelation of the mystery occurs as a new moment in history, it had been prepared for and prefigured in manifold ways throughout scripture:

> 57 But first the Lord made prior arrangements for his own sufferings (πρότερον δὲ ὁ κύριος προῳκονόμησεν τὰ ἑαυτοῦ πάθη)
> in patriarchs and prophets and in the whole people,
> setting his seal (ἐπισφραγισάμενος) on them through both the law and prophets.
> For the thing which is to be new and great in its realization
> is arranged for well in advance (ἐκ μακροῦ προοικονομεῖται),
> so that when it comes about it may by believed in,
> having been foreseen well in advance (ἐκ μακροῦ προοραθέν).
>
> 58 Just so also the mystery of the Lord (οὕτω δὴ καὶ τὸ τοῦ κυρίου μυστήριον),
> having been prefigured well in advance (ἐκ μακροῦ προτυπωθέν)
> and having been seen through the a type (διὰ δὲ τύπον ὀραθέν),
> is today believed in now that it has been performed (τετελεσμένον),

---

[92] See, for instance, the gruesome depiction of maternal cannibalism in *PP* 52.

though considered new by humanity.
For the mystery of the Lord is new and old (ἔστιν γὰρ παλαιὸν καὶ καινὸν τὸ τοῦ κυρίου μυστήριον):
old according to law,
but new according to grace.
But if you look carefully at the type (ἀλλ' ἐὰν ἀποβλέψῃς εἰς τὸν τύπον),
You will perceive this through the event (τοῦτον ὄψῃ διὰ τῆς ἐκβάσεως).

Returning again to the juxtapositions of the prologue, Melito explains how the mystery of Christ's crucifixion is new as well as old – new according to occurrence, but old according to planning and prefiguration. The idea that God arranged beforehand prefigurations of Christ's death in scripture so that it would be believed in when it finally happened is one we observed in Justin.[93] But it is important to emphasize once again that, as in Justin, this construal of prophetic prefiguration does not operate in the usual prospective manner. In other words, one does not receive the prophecy and then anticipate its promise. Rather, the prophecy becomes prophecy only retrospectively, or after the occurrence of the foretold event. Therefore, though it is "considered new by humanity," it is not in fact new with respect to divine preparation. When one perceives the mystery of the Lord, which is the crucifixion, one then perceives the mystery of the model that prefigures it, which is scripture. This retrospective orientation of the prefiguration and its future analog is most clearly stated in the final words of *PP* 58. When the Christian carefully investigates (ἀποβλέψῃς) the type (or scripture), then the fact that the mystery of the Lord is new and old can be seen (ὄψῃ). But, crucially, this perception is only possible when it occurs "through the event" (διὰ τῆς ἐκβάσεως) of the Lord's death. Thus the mystery of the Lord reveals the mystery of scripture, which itself is then seen to prefigure the mystery of the Lord. In this circular hermeneutical system, the Christ event is the catalyst of the interpretive loop, the initial happening from which the interpretive process flows.[94] Therefore, for Justin as well as Melito, the mystery herme-

---

93 See, for instance, *Dial.* 84.2.
94 The "dynamism" at work in the relationship between the mystery of Christ and the mystery of scripture is reminiscent of Henri de Lubac's characterization of "mystery" in *Corpus Mysticum: The Eucharist and the Church in the Middle Ages* (trans. Gemma Simmonds; London: SCM Press, 2006 [1944]): "[Mystery] conveys dynamism and synthesis. It focuses less on the apparent sign, or rather the hidden reality, than on both at the same time: on their mutual relationship, union and implications, on the way in which one passes into the other, or is penetrated by the other. It focuses on the appeal which the first term makes of the second, or better, on the hidden presence of the second term within the first, already at work secretly but effectively" (51–52). Interestingly, de Lubac further compares this "dynamism" to a *communicatio idiomatum*: "it is the

neutic is one that depends on the *a posteriori* experience of Christ's advent, death, and ascent.

In *PP* 59–60, Melito proceeds to offer some specific instances in which the mystery of the Lord can be "seen" in various scriptural events. His catalogue begins with Abel – "Therefore if you wish to see the mystery of the Lord (εἰ βούλει τὸ τοῦ κυρίου μυστήριον ἰδέσθα), look carefully at Abel who is similarly murdered." To Abel he adds Isaac, who is similarly bound, and Joseph, who is similarly sold, and Moses, who is similarly exposed, and David, who is similarly persecuted, and the prophets, who similarly suffered on account of Christ, and, finally, the paschal sheep that was slain and "which struck Egypt and saved Israel by its blood." In *PP* 61–64 he then shows how "the mystery of the Lord is proclaimed in the prophetic voice as well" (ἔστιν δὲ καὶ διὰ προφητικῆς φωνῆς τὸ τοῦ κυρίου μυστήριον κηρυσσόμενον). He begins with Moses in *PP* 61, citing his own version of Deut 28:66, which evokes the crucifixion.[95] He next in *PP* 62 cites David's words in Ps 2:1–2, which call to mind the crucifixion again.[96] Then in *PP* 63 he quotes Jeremiah and his lament that he is like a harmless lambkin (Jer 11:19), which Melito appears to take as the voice of the soon to be crucified Christ, but uttered first by Jeremiah. Finally he refers to Isaiah and cites the prophecy of Isa 53:7–8, another correlation of Christ and the paschal lamb. He concludes this litany of prophetic witnesses, as well as the entire section, by stating in *PP* 65: "Many other things have been proclaimed by many prophets about the mystery of the Pascha, which is Christ (τὸ τοῦ πάσχα μυστήριον, ὅ ἐστιν Χριστός).[97] To him be glory forever. Amen." The simplicity of these final words is fitting. Throughout this section Melito has shown that the only antidote for human suffering was Christ's suffering – παθεῖν needed πάσχειν – and that this redemptive suffering has been foretold throughout scipture. Therefore, having made clear who "the suffering one" is (humanity), and who the one who "shares the suffering of the suffering one" is (Christ), and how the fact of Christ's suffering has been prophetically announced throughout scripture, Melito returns to what for him is the principal prophetic prototype of the Christ's own suffering: "the mystery of the Pascha, which is Christ."

---

phenomenon of a transfer of attributes, of an exchange or a 'communication of idioms', between the two poles of attraction and location of the '*mystery*', between τύπος and ἀλήθεια" (53).
95 For the use of Melito's version of this verse in later authors, see Hall, *On Pascha*, 33 n. 28.
96 Cf. the same citation in Acts 4:25–26. It is interesting that this psalm, if being read in relation to the crucifixion, implicates the Gentiles, the kings of the earth, and the rulers in Jesus' death, and not the Jews, which is what Melito will later, and viciously, claim.
97 For a similar use of this relative clause, cf. the phrasing of Col 1:27: τὸ πλοῦτος τῆς δόξης τοῦ μυστηρίου τούτου ἐν τοῖς ἔθνεσιν, ὅ ἐστιν Χριστὸς ἐν ὑμῖν.

To conclude: as the prologue makes clear at the outset, the basic structure of Melito's hermeneutic consists of a contrast between the old and the new. By expressing this contrast in terms of a model/reality analogy in which the prototype serves the actuality it prefigures, Melito relativizes Israel in relation to Christ. The value of the old is the value of a preliminary model. With the appearance of the reality, the model loses its independent worth. But this *synkrisis* does not entail the absolute repudiation of the model. For Melito, the old takes on a new existence as it is absorbed into the new reality of Christ. The old, in fact, becomes new as it is seen to prefigure the new revelation. With respect to Pascha, when read through the prism of the mystery of the Lord's death, it becomes a prophetic reenactment of Christ's crucifixion, and in this way it can be said to be "new and old" (*PP* 2). The mystery of the Lord provides the hermeneutical stimulus catalyzing this conversion.

7.5 The Old Model and the Question of Judaism in Peri Pascha 66–105

The final section of this homily (*PP* 66–105) takes on a very different tone and topic, and the use of μυστήριον ceases. The initial portions (*PP* 67–71) summarize the preceding. Melito recalls the event of Pascha, and he directly coordinates it with Christ's death. In *PP* 69, which repeats the catalogue of scriptural prefigurations of *PP* 59, Melito again reminds his audience of how the destiny of Christ has been foreshadowed in the experiences of various scriptural personages.[98] In *PP* 72, however, the timbre turns aggressive as Melito commences a lengthy indictment of "ungrateful Israel" (*PP* 87) as culpable of deicide.[99] This virulent condemnation continues through to the end of the homily and is perhaps deservedly described as "the most prolonged, vitriolic, even violent, attack on Israel in pre-Constintinian Christian writtings."[100]

As previously discussed, one of Melito's apparent innovations is his consolidation of the hidden/revealed mystery schema with a model/reality schema. This merger enables him to preserve – though in a christologically restricted way – the previous worth of the old model of Israel. But by relativizing that

---

[98] This list is almost identical to that of *PP* 59. The only difference is Jacob, who is described as exiled (Gen 29–30), which presumably corresponds to Jesus' sojourn in Egypt (Matt 2:13–23).
[99] See Eric Werner, "Melito of Sardis: The First Poet of Deicide," *Hebrew Union College Annual* 37 (1966): 191–210.
[100] Miriam S. Taylor, *Anti-Judaism and Early Christian Identity: A Critique of the Scholarly Consensus* (StPB 46; Leiden/New York/Köln: Brill, 1995), 55.

worth in relation to the new revelation of Christ, Melito divests ongoing Judaism of any independent value. In the final portions of the homily, this divestiture gives way to denunciation. The Jews become those who murdered God – "you dashed down the Lord, you were dashed to the ground. And you lie dead, but he has risen from the dead and gone up to the heights of heaven"[101] (a statement that feels chilling even to reproduce). Notice, then, the Jewish people for Melito perform a role akin to Paul's "rulers of this age" in 1 Cor 2:6–8. Since the Jews did not "see God" (*PP* 82) when he came to them, the Jesus they executed becomes God's salvation for humanity, but to the Jews he becomes their own ruin. Note the bitter irony here, however. In both the original Pascha and also in Christ's crucifixion, Melito portrays Israel as slaying the lamb. But in the former they do this for deliverance and in the latter unto condemnation. Therefore, though Melito's estimation of old Israel is more positive than other Christian authors, his judgment of contemporary Judaism is as severe as can be imagined.[102] It is worth pointing out, however, that there is nothing about this hermeneutical approach to Israel that necessarily requires or instigates such venomous rhetoric. For this it seems that Melito's personal temperament and perhaps also his social context are to blame.

7.6 Conclusion: Mystery Exegesis, Ritual Practice, and Synkrisis

In this chapter three key features of Melito's use of μυστήριον have emerged, one of which we have observed in previous chapters and two others that appear to be original to Melito. First is Melito's hermeneutical employment of the mystery discourse. As in Justin, Melito's mystery exegesis is an *a posteriori* interpretive technique that transforms previous events and words into prophetic prefigurations and foretellings of Christian realities. It is, however, the Christian realities that supply the initial interpretive energy. The essential premise of Melito's exegetical reasoning is the crucifixion of Christ. Through this christological prism scripture

---

[101] *PP* 99.
[102] Stewart-Sykes, "Melito's Anti-Judaism," *JECS* 5 (1997): 271–83, attributes Melito's bitter polemical posture to his own Jewish heritage. He contends that the rhetoric of *PP* reflects "a personal agenda" and is the result of "personal dissonance" (275). Hence "[t]he vituperation displayed is that of a family argument" (279). This thesis depends in large part on the accuracy of Eusebius' report and thus remains speculative. It is, nonetheless, an intriguing suggestion and, whether or not he was in fact Jewish, some sort of previous intimate affiliation with Judaism is certainly possible.

7.6 Conclusion: Mystery Exegesis, Ritual Practice, and Synkrisis — 219

is newly viewed as a prophetic witness to and rehearsal of the crucifixion. The paschal lamb becomes Christ, the blood of the lamb becomes baptism, the law becomes gospel, and the old becomes new. Thus the mystery of Pascha is that it is not just about Pascha; it is about the cross.

As for the apparent innovations: first is the explicit evocation of ritual practices in Melito's use of μυστήριον and other terminology associated with ancient cultic mysteries. Liturgical gatherings, the exegesis of sacred books (ἱεραὶ βίβλοι) and stories (ἱεροὶ λόγοι),[103] catechetical instruction, the revelation of mysteries, initiation ceremonies, sacramental celebrations and rites of washing: these are all standard features of many of the mystery cults of the ancient Mediterranean world, and the context and content of Melito's paschal homily invokes every one of them.[104] By reading the Pascha of Exod 12 as a mystery performed among initiates, and then by reimagining this event as a prefiguration of Christ's death and Christian sacramental practice, Melito and his congregants exegetically participate in the ritual celebration of the mystery. We can only guess what happened at the homily's end – a paschal or eucharistic meal? a baptism? some other liturgical celebration?[105] – but whatever occurred, Melito's mystery exegesis certainly prompts one to associate Christian rituals, like the Pascha ritual, with mystery rites comparable to those of Cybele, Bacchus, or Isis. This is not to suggest that Melito would have affirmed that Christianity is just another species of the many ancient mysteries. But since comparative evocations of those practices

---

[103] For more on the role of sacred literature in Greek religious life, see the excellent study by Albert Henrichs, "*HIEROI LOGOI* and *HIERAI BIBLOI*: The (Un)Written Margins of the Sacred in Ancient Greece," *HSCP* 101 (2003): 207–66.

[104] Cf. Apuleius' descriptions of the cult Isis and his initiation into it in *Metam.* 11.21–23. For Apuleius' Lucius, the process of initiation included secret instruction, the exposition of sacred books, a cleansing bath and purificatory sprinkling, and the abstention from meat and wine for ten days. It should be noted that Apuleius is a contemporary (and perhaps even predecessor) of Melito.

[105] Consider the reconstruction of Stewart-Sykes, *The Lamb's High Feast*, "From our review of the evidence, and in particular from our reading of *Peri Pascha* we may see that the Quartodecimans at Sardis gathered, fasting in memory of the sufferings of the Lord, before midnight of the fourteenth Nisan/Xanthikos. They heard a reading from *Exodus* 12 with a *diegma*, and kept watch with their lamps lit. Around midnight they broke their fast and joined in a joyous table rite, with music and dancing, as they realized the presence of the risen Lord among them and received his spirit. He became present to them through the medium of the *aphikomen* and of the cup, and most importantly through the liturgy by which they remembered the acts of their salvation" (206).

are patent in his homily, as they are in many other ensuing Christian authors,[106] it is important to acknowledge their role in shaping Christian self-understanding.

Finally there is Melito's innovative combination of the hermeneutical mystery discourse with exegetical *synkrisis*. Both of these interpretive techniques were utilized prior to Melito, but he appears to be the first Christian author to unite them. This unification has two major implications. First, it entails a different understanding of ancient Israel. Since *synkrisis* requires the preliminary praise of the *comparanda*, Melito accordingly characterizes Israel, including her law and temple, as of great value. This value, however, has expired now that Christ, an object of superseding value, has appeared. Therefore, with the advent of Christ, Israel is emptied of any independent worth, and so what was once precious has become worthless. But Melito does not stop here with respect to the heritage of Israel. Had he concluded at this point, with Israel declared defunct, then his understanding of Christianity would have been tantamount to Marcionism. In contrast to such an outright repudiation of Israel, however, Melito reclaims old Israel by resituating it within the now comprehensive reality of Christ. Therefore, following the assertion of rupture between the old and the new comes the hermeneutical recapturing of the old as Melito retells Israel's story as a prophetic anticipation of Christ's story. Through this re-narration Israel acquires new value, although not independent value. Israel's value is instead now contingent on Christ, the new mystery that repossesses and remakes the old mystery of Israel.

---

[106] Again, Clement of Alexandria and other later Alexandrian theologians are probably the best examples. See H.G. Marsh, "The Use of ΜΥΣΤΗΡΙΟΝ in the Writings of Clement of Alexandria with Special Reference to his Sacramental Doctrine," *JTS* 37 (1936): 64–80.

8 Mystery, Scriptural Meaning, and the Unity of God in Tertullian and his *Against Marcion*

8.1 Introduction

Turning now to Tertullian, we enter a very different world. The primary context is Roman North Africa. The language is Latin. And the new problem to which the hidden/revealed mystery discourse is addressed is Marcion's bifurcation of the creator God of Israel and the recently revealed Christ. Although Latin has a cognate for μυστήριον in the word *mysterium*,[1] Tertullian prefers the term *sacramentum*, both in terms of frequency and in his translation of μυστήριον.[2] On the few occasions where Tertullian does use *mysterium*, he employs it exclusively as a technical term for the mystery cults and their ritual objects and practices.[3] *Sacramentum*, by contrast, appears recurrently and has a wide range of functions, translating the Pauline use of μυστήριον being just one of them.[4]

Sacramentum appears some 133 times across Tertullian's corpus. But of these occurrences 41 (or 31%) are in just one work, *Against Marcion*. What is more, 21

---

[1] For an analysis of the word *mysterium* in early Christianity, see Vincenzo Loi, "Il termine 'mysterium' nella letteratura latina christiana prenicena: Parte I," *VC* 19 (1965): 210–32; and "Il termine 'mysterium' nella letteratura latina christiana prenicena: Parte II," *VC* 20 (1966): 25–44.

[2] For more on the use of these two terms in Latin translations of the Bible, see Theodore B. Foster, "'Mysterium' and 'Sacramentum' in the Vulgate and Old Latin Versions," *The American Journal of Theology* 19 (1915): 402–15. Foster demonstrates that although the Vulgate varies in its use of *mysterium* and *sacramentum* to translate μυστήριον in Paul, *sacramentum* alone "was a recognized equivalent of μυστήριον in the North African version before Cyprian, and – if the version then existed – before Tertullian" (415).

[3] See *Apol.* 6.7; 7.6 (recensio vulgata); 39.15 (recensio Fuldensis); *Nat.* 7.68.21; 7.68.26; 7.70.10; *Praescr.* 40.4

[4] This chapter does not present an exhaustive analysis of *sacramentum* in Tertullian since such work already exists. Among the many studies on this topic, see esp. Emile de Backer, *Sacramentum: Le mot et l'idée représentée par lui dans les oeuvres de Tertullien* (Louvain: 1911); and also Backer's "Tertullien," in *Pour L'Histoire du Mot "Sacramentum": I. Les anténicéens* (ed. J. de Ghellinkck et al.; Louvain: 1924), 59–152; Adolf Kolping, *Sacramentum Tertullianeum: Neue Untersuchungen über die Anfänge des christlichen Gebrauchs der Vokabel sacramentum* (Regensberg/Münster: 1948); Christine Mohrmann, "Sacramentum dans le plus Anciens Textes Chrétiens," *HTR* 47 (1954): 141–52; Dimitri Michaélidès, *Sacramentum chez Tertullien* (Études Augustiniennes; Paris: 1970). Michaélidès' monograph, though flawed in terms of semantic theory, is nonetheless still the most comprehensive. The methodological problem with most studies on *sacramentum*, Michaélidès' included, is the mistaken idea that the lexeme has some singular, fundamental sense (such as "oath") from which all other uses of the term derive.

of those 41 (or 16% of the total usage) are in just one section of this work, Book 5, which is Tertullian's letter by letter rereading of Marcion's personally redacted version of the Pauline letter collection against Marcion's own theology. To put these percentages in better perspective, in the 1454 pages of Tertullian's Latin text in the two volumes of *CCSL*, 285 of those are from *Against Marcion*, constituting 20% of his extant writings. Book 5 of *Against Marcion*, however, takes up just 63 pages (or 4%) of the *CCSL* volumes on Tertullian. That over half of the occurrences of *sacramentum* in *Against Marcion* appear in Book 5 and, thus, that 16% of the total occurrences of *sacramentum* appear in just 4% of Tertullian's total corpus is, at least statistically speaking, conspicuous. Though statistically conspicuous, however, these facts should not be surprising. What they reflect is the usefulness of the mystery discourse in Tertullian's dispute with Marcion and the association of mystery with Paul. The notion of the previously hidden but recently revealed Christian mystery provides Tertullian with a crucial schema for defending the union of the Creator and Christ against Marcion's uncoupling of the two. And since the schema is one that Tertullian finds recurrently in Paul, he returns to it regularly in his rereading of Marcion's own "Paul"[5] against Marcion himself.

8.2 Tertullian and His Treatise Against Marcion

The most valuable information about Tertullian's life comes from the man himself, and indeed many important details can be learned or inferred from his vast literary legacy.[6] To illustrate the magnitude of Tertullian's corpus, consider that he is the only author in the *Ante-Nicene Fathers* series to take up a single volume (vol. 3), and even then his works spill over into another (vol. 4). The details that can be gleaned from the over thirty works that are extant and conventionally deemed authentic range, naturally, from the biographically trivial (such as the fact that he probably had a beard and likely did not spend much energy grooming it) to the theologically significant (such as his appreciation for the so-called "New Prophecy" or Montansim).[7] The most basic biographical facts, however, are that he was probably for most of his life a resident of the North African meg-

---

[5] The "Paul" that emerges from Marcion's redaction of his letters, that is.
[6] The most important biographical study of Tertullian is still Timothy David Barnes, *Tertullian: A Historical and Literary Study* (Oxford/New York: Oxford University Press, 1971). See also the more recent summary of Tertullian's life by Geoffrey D. Dunn, *Tertullian* (London/New York: Routledge, 2004).
[7] *Spect.* 23.3; *Cult. fem.* 2.8.2.

alopolis of Carthage;[8] he was a pagan by birth who later converted to Christianity;[9] he was well educated and versed in classical literature;[10] he was a merciless polemicist;[11] he was married but had complicated thoughts on the matter;[12] and his literary career ranged from approximately 196–212 C.E.[13]

As for external evidence, the earliest and most significant data come from Jerome's *On Illustrious Men* (ca. 392 C.E.) wherein we are told, among other things, that Tertullian was one of the most important and prolific Latin theologians, that he was a presbyter of Carthage and son of a centurion, that he flourished during the reigns of Severus and Caracalla (193–217 C.E.), and that he eventually came to sympathize with the teachings of Montanism, even writing several treatises later in life defending and advancing the ideas of that movement.[14] Primarily on the basis of Jerome's account, a conventional narrative of Tertullian's life emerges, and this narrative went mostly unchallenged until well into the 20th century. The basic plot is one of a brilliant theological mind losing its way, slipping from the secure faith of catholic Christianity into the heresy of Montanism. Following the monumental study of Timothy Barnes, this traditional portrait of the "father of Latin Christianity" can no longer be uncritically accepted.[15] Given the specific aims of this chapter, there is no need to rehearse Barnes' investigation. It should be noted, however, that on point after point Barnes weighs Jerome's claims and finds them wanting. In particular, the idea that Tertullian at some point became a schismatic and abandoned the church is no longer defensible.[16]

As for Tertullian's quarrel with Marcion, the principal field upon which this contest occurs is his lengthy five-volume work, *Against Marcion*.[17] The final ver-

---

8 There are several references to Carthage in his works and *The Pallium* is addressed to the men of that city.
9 See, for instance, *Paen.* 1.1.
10 For a description of Tertullian's familiarity with and use of classical sources, see Barnes, *Tertullian*, 196–206.
11 As treatise after treatise shows, Tertullian's literary art was one of rhetorical combat. As Dunn, *Tertullian*, suitably describes him, "He was a pugilist with a pen" (9).
12 See works such as *To His Wife*; *An Exhortation to Chastity*; *Monogamy*.
13 See Barnes, *Tertullian*, 30–56. The so-called "Montanist works" are dated to 206 and after.
14 The most important information on Tertullian is found in *Vir. ill.* 53. Eusebius, *Hist. eccl.* 2.2.4, also reports that he studied law in Rome.
15 See also David I. Rankin, "Was Tertullian a Schismatic?," *Prudentia* 18 (1986): 73–79; and Rankin's *Tertullian and the Church* (Cambridge: Cambridge University Press, 1995).
16 For more on this subject see esp. Rankin, *Tertullian and the Church*, 27–51.
17 For more on Marcion, his theology, and the history of scholarship on this subject, see now Sebastian Moll, *The Arch-Heretic Marcion* (WUNT 250; Tübingen; Mohr Siebeck, 2010).

sion of this treatise can be confidently dated to 207–208 C.E.,[18] a date that places it some sixty years after the height of the Marcionite conflict.[19] As Eric Osborn has described it, this work is "the first extended work of Christian argument,"[20] and it is indeed a sustained exercise in argument, beginning with systematic theological reflection in Books 1 and 2 and then moving on to detailed exegetical demonstration in Books 3, 4, and 5. Energizing the treatise throughout are two integrated questions: who is the creator God of Israel, and what is the relation of this God to the newly revealed Christ? For Marcion a fundamental antithesis exists between the Creator and Christ (*Antitheses* is, in fact, the title of his great work).[21] Tertullian, by contrast, situates all supposed antitheses within the divine economy and an unfolding but unified historical narrative. Therefore, whereas for Marcion an antithesis such as goodness and justice requires rupture between the Creator and the God of Christ, for Tertullian such antitheses are merely expressions of diversity in God and therefore belong together within the unity of the one and only God of Israel. In other words, whereas Marcion views antitheses in the Creator and Christ as reflecting different deities, Tertullian views them as complementary aspects of irreducible diversity within the one God.[22]

In Books 1 and 2 Tertullian argues for the necessity of a single God and also that this God has never been *absolutely* hidden but rather has always been visible throughout creation—both in goodness and in justice. Book 3 turns specifically to Christ, whom Tertullian argues is the true Son of God predicted by the

---

[18] Tertullian himself tells us that it was composed during the fifteenth year of the reign of Severus (1.15.1). Such a date places the work within Tertullian's Montanist era, but hints of Montanism are sparse.

[19] As Judith M. Lieu, "'As much my apostle as Christ is mine': The dispute over Paul between Tertullian and Marcion," *Early Christianity* 1 (2010): 41–59, notes, "[A]lthough Tertullian does, when it suits his polemic, acknowledge the years that separate him from his opponent...he creates the illusion of presence, addressing Marcion directly" (43). Therefore, "by treating Marcion as his contemporary and as perverting the proper understanding of Paul that he himself already possesses, Tertullian conceals Marcion's chronological and logical priority" (44).

[20] Eric Osborn, *Tertullian: First Theologian of the West* (Cambridge: Cambridge University Press, 1997), 90. For more on the theology at work in *Against Marcion*, see 88–115.

[21] For a recent analysis of Marcion's work (about which so little is known with any certainty) and its potential genre, see Eric W. Scherbenske, "Marcion's *Antitheses* and the Isagogic Genre," *VC* 64 (2010): 255–79.

[22] Tertullian even allows for a difference (perhaps even some form of contrariety [*diversitas*]) in time but, unlike Marcion, he does not radicalize it. Thus Lieu, "'As much my apostle'," writes, "Tertullian does allow a 'difference of time', and he is even prepared to describe 'the order of the Creator' as being 'reformed by Christ', although his intention there is to deny its rejection (Adv. Marc. 2.29.2)" (58).

prophets of Israel. Books 4 and 5, the lengthiest in the work, shift into an exclusively exegetical mode as Tertullian embarks on sustained rereadings of Marcion's "mutilated" Luke (Book 4) and then Marcion's heavily edited ten letter version of the Pauline letter collection (Book 5).[23] Tertullian's objective in these final two sections is to prove that even on the field of Marcion's own personally redacted texts the antithesis between the Creator and Christ does not lead to ontological division. Rather, when it is properly viewed within the whole economy of salvation history, the relationship between Christ and the Creator is fundamentally one of harmony and bounded identity. And so how does Tertullian argue this point on the basis on Marcion's own edited Pauline corpus? I contend that Tertullian's key argumentative resource is his ability to discover and develop, even on Marcion's own terms, the previously hidden, but eternally planned, and recently revealed mystery discourse. Tertullian's point throughout is plain: insofar as the Creator and Christ can be shown to have concealed and revealed in concert, then they cannot be sundered. Even when this hidden/revealed mystery schema – or simply the Pauline use of mystery – has probably been redacted from Marcion's Pauline edition, Tertullian often still insinuates it, leading the reader to think in terms of the text she or he knows. And so by a cunning maneuver the temporally ordered schema can still supply the historical architecture for reintegrating the Creator and Christ and so for reinterpreting antitheses in terms of unity.

8.3 Tertullian and Paul

Tertullian's relationship with Paul is, at least on the surface, easy to characterize. Tertullian himself states, "Paul is my apostle, as also Christ is mine" (*Marc.* 5.1.8). The number of references to Paul throughout Tertullian's corpus would seem to confirm this claim. As for the "Paul" who is represented so prominently in Tertullian's writings, many scholars have characterized it as a mistaken one.[24] Beginning with their own construct of a "Pauline theology" and then by comparing this construct with their construct of the "Pauline theology of Tertullian," differences between the two are taken to be departures from the apostle, or

---

[23] For more on Tertullian's own version of the New Testament and his approach to it, see John F. Jansen, "Tertullian and the New Testament," *SecCent* 2 (1982): 191–207.
[24] See esp. Fritz Barth, "Tertullians Auffassung des Apostels Paulus und seines Verhältnisses zu den Uraposteln," *Jahrbuch für Protestantische Theologie* 8 (1882): 706–56; Eva Aleith, *Paulusverständnis in der alten Kirche* (BZNW 18; Berlin: Töppelmann, 1937), 49–61.

at least failures of understanding. Robert Sider has diagnosed the errors of this approach:

> [A]lthough one can hardly dispute the paramount importance in the history of Christianity of the legacy of Paul's teaching as derived from his epistles, it would be a mistake to measure the legacy of Paul in a writer such as Tertullian solely in terms of the representation of the apostle's thought.... He does not offer us a single sustained exposition of a well-reasoned theology in which Paul plays a precisely measurable role, but rather a varied corpus of artful compositions...where both allusions to Paul the man and citations from the epistles as witness to Pauline thought play a part in the orchestration of an argument intended to be immediately persuasive.[25]

Tertullian is his own man with his own aims, his own problems, and his own theological formation. He never set out to write a "theology of Paul," but he did do theology, and Paul is repeatedly appropriated to this end. The more vital question then is not if he understood Paul but how he used Paul.

Identifying the ways in which Tertullian uses Paul is also important for appreciating what Tertullian perceives to be at stake in his rebuttal of Marcion. As Tertullian sees it, not only do Israel's God and her scriptures hang in the balance, but Paul as well, and with him the entire apostolic tradition. As Judith Lieu states, in this "contest over hermeneutical ownership" there appears "a new and enduring facet of Christian self-definition, the struggle over an exclusive right to the specifically Christian tradition and over its textual form and its interpretation – which are here represented by the figure of Paul and by his letters."[26] Therefore, Tertullian's claim on the apostle, though certainly an expression of indebtedness and admiration, is still more than this. In the contest with Marcion, the claim to Paul is a claim to Christianity itself. And as Tertullian sees it, the Christian faith, like the apostle Paul, can either belong to Marcion, or it can belong to Tertullian. It cannot belong to both.

8.4 *Sacramentum* in Tertullian

In turning to Tertullian's use of *sacramentum*, it is first important to recognize that although his application of the word varies widely across his corpus, there are nonetheless three distinguishable categories of usage that emerge:

---

[25] Robert D. Sider, "Literary Artifice and the Figure of Paul in the Writings of Tertullian," in *Paul and the Legacies of Paul* (ed. William S. Babcock; Dallas: Southern Methodist University Press, 1990), 99–120, 100.
[26] Lieu, "'As much my apostle'," 41–42.

(1) *sacramentum* for oaths; (2) *sacramentum* for ritual objects, practices, or liturgical observances; and (3) *sacramentum* for hidden realities, especially hidden scriptural meanings.

8.4.1 *Sacramentum* and Oaths

This first category of usage reflects the common and technical Roman employment of the term: oath.[27] A *sacramentum* could be any type of solemn pledge taken by two or more individuals that joins them in a contractual, and often pecuniary, bond.[28] It was also frequently used for any official vow of allegiance[29] and especially for the official military oath (*sacramentum militiae*).[30] Tertullian only occasionally uses the term in this conventional sense of oath, and usually then in relation to the Roman military oath.[31] For instance, in *Spect.* 24.4 he compares Christians who associate with heathens to professional soldiers who abandon their arms, their standards, and the "oath of the chief" (*sacramentis principis*) by joining enemy ranks. In *Mart.* 3.1 it is the Christian who metaphorically takes on the military oath when "called to the warfare of the living God in response to the words of the oath (*in sacramenti verba respondimus*)." Tertullian goes on in this passage to explain that since Christians accept the oath of soldiers, they should expect no better treatment in life than that of a soldier. A Christian "sealed by such an oath" (*tali sacramento eum consignavit*) is, like the soldier, often fated for death.[32] A similar comparison is made in *Scorp.* 4.5, wherein Tertullian likens the Christian who is challenged by enemies to the soldier committed to his military oath (*sacramento militans*).

8.4.2 *Sacramentum* and Ritual Objects, Practices, or Liturgical Observances

Much more common in Tertullian than oaths is the use of *sacramentum* to designate ritual objects, rites, or observances – whether pagan, Jewish, or Christi-

---

27 Cf. Michaélidès, *Sacramentum*, 41–71.
28 C.f. *Caecin.* 97; *Dom.* 78; *Resp.* 2.60.
29 C.f. Quintilian, *Decl.* 357; Apuleius, *Metam.* 3.3.
30 C.f. Cicero, *Off.* 1.36; Caesar, *Bell. gall.* 6.1.2; Tacitus, *Hist.* 4.21.
31 As for Tertullian's relationship with the Roman army, see John Helgeland, "Christians and the Roman Army A.D. 173–337," *Church History* 42 (1974): 149–63, 200.
32 Cf. also *Scorp.* 8.1; 9.1.

an.³³ In *Apol.* 2.6 Tertullian refers to Pliny's famous letter to Trajan in which the renowned magistrate explains that he found nothing illicit in the Christians' "religious observances" (*sacramentis*).³⁴ The word is used in this instance in a way that suggests an entire way of worshiping, even a whole religious system.³⁵ As for naming specific rites as *sacramenta*, Tertullian refers in *Apol.* 7.1 to a rumor spread by opponents that Christians observe a "rite" (*sacramento*) in which they slaughter and eat a child and then commit incest. He also often refers to rites actually practiced by Christians such as baptism and eucharist as *sacramenta*. The association of baptism with *sacramentum* is especially common in *On Baptism* (1.1; 3.6; 4.4; 5.4; 8.2; 9.1; 12.3; 13.1–2). The word is likewise applied to Christian ritual practices in *Against Marcion* (1.14.3; 1.28.2–3; 4.34.5; 4.38.2; 5.8.3). As for designating pagan ritual practices, Tertullian prefers the term *mysterium*. This distinction between pagan *mysteria* and Christian *sacramenta* can be seen most clearly in *Praesc.* 40.2, as Tertullian differentiates the "divine sacraments" (*sacramentorum divinorum*) of Christianity from the "mysteries of idols" (*idolorum mysteriis*) that belong to the devil.

8.4.3 *Sacramentum* and Hidden Reality or Hidden Scriptural Meaning

On occasion Tertullian refers to unspecified but previously hidden Christian realities or, quite commonly, to the previously hidden "mystery of Christ" (*sacramentum Christi*).³⁶ In his *Prescription against Heretics* Tertullian insists at length that the teachings of Christ and the apostles are plain, have never been concealed, and clearly differ from those of the "heretics" (see *Praescr.* 25–26). In *Praescr.* 26.2 he even explains that Christ always spoke openly and, therefore, "without any suggestion of a hidden mystery" (*sine ulla signficatione alicuius taciti sacramenti*). Although the claim that Christ did not ever speak of a hidden mystery would seem to contradict the Synoptic mystery pericope (Matt 13:11// Mark 4:11//Luke 8:10),³⁷ Tertullian does affirm a few lines later that Christ himself is a mystery. He writes that, given the practice of their Lord, the apostles likewise

---

33 An important introduction to this usage is A.D. Nock, "Hellenistic Mysteries and Christian Sacraments," *Mnemosyne* 5 (1952): 177–213. Cf. also Michaélidès, *Sacramentum*, 165–91, 235–74.
34 Pliny, *Ep.* 10.96.
35 Cf. also *Apol.* 19.2; 47.14; *Test.* 2.2.
36 Cf. Michaélidès, *Sacramentum*, 197–233.
37 It is worth nothing that he never refers to this saying in any of his writings. It does not suit his theological and rhetorical interests.

"did not conceal any portion of the light, that is, of the word of God and of the mystery of Christ" (*non...abscondentes aliquid de lumine, id est, de dei verbo et Christi sacramento*) (26.5). What these statements about the public proclamation of Christ and then the identification of Christ as a mystery underscore is that even though Christ himself is a mystery, he and his followers did not speak about this mystery in a secretive manner. In other words, the mystery was not kept a secret as it has been and still is publically proclaimed.[38]

The much more frequent use of *sacramentum* in Tertullian is for a hidden reality or a hidden meaning now discerned in scripture.[39] The majority of the instances of this usage occur in *Against Marcion*, and so I postpone analysis of those texts until we turn specifically to that treatise. Outside of *Against Marcion*, however, the use of *sacramentum* in relation to scriptural meaning is most widespread in *Against the Jews*. Given the exegetical use of mystery in relation to Christian polemic against Jews in Justin and Melito, this is unsurprising, and Tertullian's own usage is quite similar, and sometimes identical, to his predecessors.[40] Tertullian's use of *sacramentum* in this particular work occurs exclusively in chs. 9–14, chapters that closely resemble sections from Book 3 of *Against Marcion*.[41] The term first appears in 9.22:

> Christ is proclaimed in many modes and figures (*multis modis et figuris praedicatus*), a rock for instance. Therefore, that man who was prepared as an image of this mystery (*sacramenti imagines parabatur*) is also consecrated as a figure of the Lord's name, being named Jesus (i.e. Joshua).

The point here is that scripture announces Christ in various "modes and figures," and so the naming of a biblical *Iesus* (Joshua) signals that he too is a mystery of

---

[38] Notice that this is in direct contrast with the secretive practices that were essential to the pagan mystery cults.
[39] General studies on Tertullian's exegetical approach include Heinrich Karpp, *Schrift und Geist bei Tertullian* (BFCT 47; Gütersloh: Bertelsmann, 1955); R.P.C. Hanson, "Notes on Tertullian's Interpretation of Scripture," *JTS* 12 (1961): 273–79; T.P. O'Malley, *Tertullian and the Bible: Language-Imagery-Exegesis* (Latinitas christianorum primaeva 21; Nijmegen/Utrecht: Dekker and van de Vegt, 1967); J.H. Waszink, "Tertullian's Principles and Methods of Exegesis," in *Early Christian Literature and the Classical Intellectual Tradition: In Honorem Robert M. Grant* (ed. W.R. Schoedel and R.L. Wilken; Paris: Beauchesne, 1979), 17–31; Geoffrey D. Dunn, "Tertullian's Scriptural Exegesis in *de praescriptione haereticorum*," *JECS* 14 (2006): 141–55.
[40] For all issues related to this text, see Geoffrey D. Dunn, *Tertullian's* Aduersus Iudaeos: *A Rhetorical Analysis* (Patristic Monograph Series 19; Washington, D.C.: Catholic University of America Press, 2008).
[41] There is no need to dwell here on the issues surrounding the relationship between these texts. For more on the matter, see Dunn, *Tertullian's* Aduersus Iudaeos, 1–15.

the newly revealed *Iesus* (Jesus).⁴² As previous chapters have shown, this approach to Israel's scripture as christological prophecy is commonplace, as is this particular interpretation of the biblical Joshua.⁴³ Again in 9.25 Tertullian explains that Joshua/Jesus received this name precisely because of "the mystery of his future name" (*nominis sui futuri sacramentum*). The "mystery of the name itself" (*in ipsius nominis sacramento*) is also referred to in 14.7. The surrounding context of these passages describes the various ways in which Joshua's life predicts (*praedicat*) the events of Christ's life. The most notable prediction is the fact that Christ must suffer and be crucified. According to 10.10, "the mystery of the cross" (*crucis...sacramentum*) was also announced in the story of the brazen serpent and other biblical signs of the cross, such as Moses' posture in the battle against Amalek.⁴⁴ As 10.5 explains, it is because of these prophesies and not because of his own wrongdoing that it was necessary for Christ to suffer and thereby accomplish the mystery of salvation which the prophetic prefigurations promised (*et utique sacramentum passionis ipsius figurari in praedicationibus oportuerat*). The mystery of the cross, or "the mystery of the wood" (*ligni sacramentum*), is also mentioned in 13.12, 17, 19. As 13.12 explains, such *sacramenta* were "kept to be perceived in the time of Christ" (*temporibus Christi percipienda servabantur*). Therefore, though these mysteries of Christ were enacted prior to Christ's advent, they are only understood as prophetic after the occurrence of that event. This epistemologically retrospective construal of prophetic foretelling, along with its emphasis on God's foreknowledge and prior planning, agrees exactly with predecessors such as Melito and Justin.

8.5 *Sacramentum* in Against Marcion

As mentioned in the introduction to this chapter, Tertullian uses the term *sacramentum* with noticeable frequency throughout *Against Marcion*, but the occurrences of the term amass most strikingly in the anti-Marcionite rereading of Paul in Book 5. Before considering Book 5 we should first explore the themes of *sacramentum* and revelation in the prior four books of the treatise. What will become clear is that throughout this polemical treatise the discourse of a previously hidden but presently revealed mystery is one of Tertullian's most ef-

---

42 Tertullian interprets both the *Iesus* who succeeded Moses and the *Iesus* who is the high priest described in Zech 3 as *sacramenta*.
43 Much of Tertullian's exegetical argumentation in these sections seems to depend on Justin, or at least a common tradition.
44 Exod 17:8–16.

fective argumentative tactics for recovering the Old Testament as Christian scripture and, in turn, reincorporating the Creator and Christ.[45]

8.5.1 *Sacramentum* in Books 1–4 of Against Marcion

In these sections *sacramentum* is only used once in relation to a non-Christian reality, and there it is applied to the figurative meaning of the lions associated with Mithras (1.13.5).[46] Otherwise in these first four books the term is sometimes applied to Christian sacramental practices such as baptism and eucharist (1.14.3; 1.28.2–3; 3.19.4;[47] 4.34.5; 4.38.2). In 4.34.5 *sacramentum* is applied to both baptism and Eucharist. In 4.38.2 John's baptisms are even designated by *sacramentum*.

The term is also used repeatedly in these sections to refer to some basic aspect of Christian doctrine (1.21.5; 2.27.7; 4.1.11; 4.5.2; 4.3.1; 4.16.12). In 1.21.5, for instance, the *regula sacramenti* seems to refer generally to the "rules" of the churches who abide within the apostolic tradition. Tertullian argues that since these churches universally respect the Creator, then Marcion's repudiation of that God is specious. Similarly in 4.5.2 Tertullian argues that the apostolic churches are "all those that are in alliance in the fellowship of the mystery" (*universas quae illis de societate sacramenti confoederantur*). This "fellowship of the mystery" – like the "rule of the mystery" – appears to refer generally to the theological commitments binding the churches that purport to belong to and to maintain apostolic tradition. According to Tertullian, Marcion's churches, because of their rejection of the Creator and the mysteries of his scriptures, cannot be numbered among these.

As for the use of the term in relation to scriptural meaning, this occurs in Books 3–4, which is where Tertullian begins his exegetical case against Marcion. Tertullian's interpretive arguments in these books are rather predictable and appear to have become customary. Among Tertullian's favorite scriptural mysteries is the *sacramentum* of the name *Iesus* in the Old Testament. In 3.7.6 the *Iesus*

---

[45] For the Latin text of *Against Marcion* I have followed *Tertullien: Contre Marcion* (ed. C. Moreschini and R. Braun; 5 vols.; SC 365, 368, 399, 456, 483; Paris: Éditions de Cerf, 1990–2004). Translations are my own.
[46] All unmarked references in what follows are to *Against Marcion*.
[47] The use of *sacramentum* here is somewhat ambiguous because Jesus is described as interpreting (*interpretaturo*) the *sacramentum* of the eucharistic bread. Therefore, it seems to refer to the hidden meaning of the bread and not the element itself. That the elements have this hidden meaning, however, would seem to be the very reason that they are referred to as *sacramenta*.

under discussion is the high priest mentioned in Zech 3:1. Since that high priest corresponds to Jesus Christ in name, this previous Jesus should be read as a prophetic anticipation of his future namesake. In the case of this Jesus, he is a mystery of Christ in that his filthy garments (Zech 3:3–5) anticipate Christ's first advent, while his pure garments (Zech 3:6) prefigure Christ's second advent. As Erich Auerbach correctly characterizes Tertullian's exegetical approach, "Often vague similarities in the structure of events or in their attendant circumstances suffice to make the *figura* recognizable; to find it, one had to be determined to interpret it in a certain way."[48] The "vague similarity" in this instance is the simple sharing of a name, and the determined way to interpret it is as prefigurative christological prophecy.

Tertullian also explicates the figural mystery that exists between the other biblical *Iesus* (Moses' successor, Joshua) and the newly revealed Jesus a few paragraphs later in 3.16.1–5:

> Why indeed did he choose to be called Jesus, a name for which the Jews had not anticipated? For if we, by God's grace, have gained knowledge of his mysteries (*per dei gratiam intellectum consecuti sacramentorum eius*), and it has been discerned (*agnoscimus*) that this name also was destined for Christ, the Jews, therefore, deprived of this wisdom, were not aware of this fact. In fact, to the present day, they hope for Christ, not for Jesus, and they prefer to interpret Elijah as Christ.... When the successor to Moses was designated as Auses [Oshea] the son of Nave [Nun], he was without doubt transformed from his original name and begins to be called Jesus. Certainly, you say. This previous thing, we say, was to be a figure of the future (*hanc prius dicimus figuram futuri fuiss*). For this reason Jesus Christ was to bring the second people, which we are, who were born in the desert of the world, into the land of promise, flowing with milk and honey, which is the inheritance of eternal life.... For this reason, that man, in whom was prepared the images of this mystery, is consecrated as a figure with the Lord's name, being named Jesus (*ideo is vir, qui in huius sacramenti imagines parabatur, etiam nominis dominici inaugurates est figura, Iesus cognominatus*).... Therefore, he called him Jesus because of the mystery of the future in his own name (*ob nominis sui future sacramentum*).

The first thing to mention here is the emphasis on concealment and the means of disclosure. Tertullian describes the Christian understanding of the mystery of the biblical Jesus' name as a special knowledge that has been given to Christians by God's grace – *per dei gratiam intellectum consecuti sacramentorum* – and this stands in contrast to the Jews who "have been deprived of this wisdom" and "were not aware of this fact." This special epistemological grace is, in Justin's idiolect, the "grace to understand," and it is a grace that the Jews do not possess

---

[48] Erich Auerbach, "Figura," in *Scenes from the Drama of European Literature* (Theory and History of Literature 9; Minneapolis: University of Minnesota Press, 1984), 11–76, 29.

according to Tertullian. Had they possessed it, then they would rightly interpret the *Iesus* of ancient Israel as a mystery of Jesus Christ as opposed to, for instance, Elijah. Nevertheless, because they lack this grace, the mystery of their own biblical Jesus is hidden from them. Notice that this particular concealment schema implies both a chronological and also an interpersonal construal of the hidden/revealed binary. That the revelation of the mystery is new to Christians arises from the fact that Christ's advent is new to the world. Therefore, it is the revelation of Christ himself that makes it possible to see the previous figure of Joshua as a prophetic prefiguration. But just as much as the mystery was once hidden and now revealed, it is also still hidden to those lacking God's "grace to know." Therefore, by arranging the mystery schema both diachronically and synchronically, Tertullian is able to account both for why the mystery of scripture was not known prior to Christ and also why it is not known by some – especially Jews – now after the advent of Christ.[49]

It is also important to stress the historical nature of the *comparanda* in Tertullian's "Jesus" mystery exegesis. This type of interpretation is, in Auerbach's terminology, an instance of "phenomenal prophecy" (*Realprophetie*): "Thus the naming of Joshua-Jesus is a phenomenal prophecy or prefiguration of the future Saviour; *figura* is something real and historical that announces something else that is also real and historical. The relation between the two events is revealed by an accord or similarity."[50] *Realprophetie* is also found in Justin and Melito, who exhibit a very similar (and sometimes identical) exegetical approach that painstakingly exploits prophetic associations between Christ (or Christian realities) and scriptural events, objects, or people. What also unites Justin, Melito, and Tertullian is the belief that *Realprophetie* can only be recognized from a retrospective christological vantage point, or when both the scriptural and the christological *comparanda* are disclosed.

In the remainder of Books 3–4 Tertullian only two other times associates *sacramentum* with scriptural meaning, and in both caes it is with regard to Christ's passion and the alleged biblical prefigurations of that event. In 3.18.2 he explains that there are many good reasons why it was fitting (*oportebat*) for that *sacramentum* to have been predicated beforehand by figures. Within

---

49 It is worth pointing out that the interpersonal arrangement of the schema is not at all prominent in *Against Marcion* (or elsewhere in Tertullian). The primary reason is most likely that Marcion would accept the mystery of Christ. Thus he would not deny that Christ reveals a mystery long ago planned. He would, however, deny that the God associated with that mystery is at all related to the Creator God of Israel. Since Marcion (unlike a Jew such as Trypho) already accepts this, Tertullian does not need to argue (as Justin did) that the cross is a mystery of salvation.
50 Auerbach, "Figura," 29.

the immediate context, the mystery being referred to is the mystery of the cross. Explaining the reasons for anticipating this future mystery in previously obscure figures, Tertullian writes:

> The more incredible it was, the greater the future scandal would be if plainly predicted; the more magnificent it was, the more it needed obscurity, so that the difficulty of understanding would require the grace of God.
>
> Quanto incredibile, tanto magis scandalo futurum si nude praedicaretur; quantoque magnificum, tanto magis obumbrandum, ut difficultas intellectus gratiam dei quaereret.

The point here is that because of the grandeur of the future mystery, it was fitting that its prior prediction be an obscure one. The obscurity of the mystery, however, also has a pedagogical function: it drives the reader of scripture to seek God's grace. Thus Isaac (3.18.2), and Joseph (3.18.3), and various material images of the cross (3.18.4), and Jacob (3.18.5), and Moses (3.18.6), and Moses' successor, Jesus (3.18.7) are all previously obscure predictive prefigurations of Christ. And their previous obscurity, while proportionate to the magnificence of that which they announce, is intended to promote reliance on divine grace.

Finally, in 4.40.1, Tertullian again links Israel's scriptures with Christ's passion, this time by naming Israel's Passover a *sacramentum* of Christ's crucifixion. He writes:

> In the same way [Christ], whose passion the law figures (*lex figurat*), knows also at what time it was necessary for him to suffer. For out of all the Jewish feasts he chose the day of Passover. In reference to this mystery Moses indeed announced (*in hoc enim sacramentum pronuntiarat Moyses*), "It is the Lord's Passover."

The association of Israel's Passover with Christ is, of course, not novel. It was the central topic of Melito's homily, is present in Justin, and is even found in Paul.[51] Throughout 4.40 Tertullian reiterates the various ways in which the Passover prefigures Christ and Christian realities. What again remains clear is that the exegetical discovery of Passover as christological prophecy is necessarily a retrospective one. Thus it is the historical event of Christ that functions as "the illuminator of ancient things" (*illuminator antiquitatum*).[52] Without this *illuminator*, the mysteries of scripture remain hidden.

---

51 1 Cor 5:7.
52 4.40.4.

8.5.2 *Sacramentum* in Book 5 of Against Marcion

In previous chapters I have made the case that Paul has been behind the scenes in various authors' uses of mystery – influential, but seldom overtly so. Here in Book 5, however, Paul and the language of mystery now appear together, front and center in the arena of Tertullian's hermeneutical contest with Marcion.

Although *sacramentum* occurs once in Book 5 in relation to "the mystery of the bread and the cup" (*panis et calicis sacramento*) (5.8.3) and another time in a way that seems to refer to general Christian beliefs (5.5.2), in the nineteen other instances it refers to previously hidden Christian realities. Usually these realities are those that have been hidden in Israel's scriptures but are now made known when those scriptures are examined in light of the fact of Christ. The term first appears in this way at the outset of the book in a demonstration of prophecy that is typical of Book 5. While discussing the biographical origins of Paul, Tertullian argues that the apostle was actually "long ago promised" (*olim repromisit*) in the "figures and prophetical blesssings" (*figuras et propheticas... benedictiones*) offered by Jacob over his son Benjamin (5.1.5). Jacob declared that Benjamin would be a ravening wolf who would devour in the morning and in the evening distribute food (Gen 49:27). As Tertullian reads Jacob's words, they indicate that in his actions Jacob "foresaw" (*providebat*) that Paul himself would arise from the tribe of Benjamin,[53] initially persecute the church, and later feed the Gentiles as Christ's sheep. Also prophetically foreshadowing the biography of Paul is Saul's persecution of David and then his later repentance (5.1.6). Tertullian treats this narrative of the biblical Saul as a prefiguration of Saul/Paul who first persecutes the church and then becomes its faithful apostle. Tertullian describes these prophetic anticipations as "the mysteries of figures" (*figurarum sacramenta*)[54] because, on his reading, they are latent historical figures of a later historical figure – Paul himself. This type of argument is important for Tertullian's cumulative case because in any place that he can demonstrate prophetic harmony between scripture and Christian realities he can insinuate harmony between the God of Israel and Christ. In the case of Paul, if Israel's scriptures provide prophetic mysteries of Paul's own life, then there must be some congruence between the God to whom those scriptures belong and the God proclaimed by Paul and revealed in Christ. Given the fact that Book 5 is about whether or not Paul is on Tertullian's side or Marcion's, this initial argu-

---

[53] See Rom 11:1; Phil 3:5.
[54] 5.1.6.

ment that the Creator himself predicted Paul is an especially important one—even if patently unpersuasive to the Marcionite.

After this introduction, Tertullian commences his letter by letter examination of Marcion's own ten letter version of the Pauline collection (the so-called *Apostolikon*).[55] At the head of this collection is Galatians. Since Tertullian tends to discuss mystery in places where Paul himself does, he does not mobilize the mystery discourse with frequency in this section on Galatians (5.2.1–5.4.15). The term does, however, appear once, and quite fittingly, in relation to Paul's allegory of Hagar and Sarah in Gal 4:22–31. After citing this passage Tertullian comments on it in 5.4.8:

> And therefore [Paul] adds, "So then, brothers, we are not children of the bondwoman, but of the free." Certainly [Paul] was making clear that the excellence of Christianity in the allegory of the son of Abraham born of the free woman also has a mystery (*sacramentum*): just as the legal bondage of Judaism is in the son of the bondwoman, so also, therefore, both dispensations are from God, in whom we have found the sketch of both dispensations.

Tertullian designates Paul's allegory a mystery in order to emphasize that the interpretation of the Sarah and Hagar story is one that necessitates the existence of a subsequently revealed christological (and so historical) correspondence. In other words, Paul's allegory is a mystery precisely because it is not merely a literary trope but an exegetical demonstration of *Realprophetie*. Hence naming the allegory a mystery is to designate it as "something real and historical that announces something else that is also real and historical."[56] As Tertullian reads it, Paul's allegorical exegesis is one that interprets Sarah and Hagar as historical prefigurations of an ensuing historical reality—the freedom of the Christian from bondage. As such, the allegorical mystery of Sarah and Hagar must be one that unites the dispensations of old and new and, consequently, the Creator and Christ. Insofar as the reader accepts these claims, then Tertullian's reading of Marcion's Paul contradicts Marcion's own theology.[57]

After working his way through the rest of Galatians, Tertullian moves on to the second letter in Marcion's *Apostolikon*, 1 Corinthians.[58] *Sacramentum* first ap-

---

[55] For a detailed textual analysis of Marcion's version of the Pauline letters, see John J. Clabeaux, *A Lost Edition of the Letters of Paul: A Reassessment of the Text of the Pauline Corpus Attested by Marcion* (CBQ Monograph Series 21; Washington, DC: The Catholic Biblical Association of America, 1989).

[56] Auerbach, "Figura," 29.

[57] We can only wonder how a Marcionite might respond to this argument.

[58] For a more detailed analysis of Marcion's version of the Corinthian correspondence, see Eve-Marie Becker, "Marcion und die Korintherbriefe nach Tertullian, Adversus Marcionem V," in

pears at the outset of this section in 5.5.2 but, as previously mentioned, it seems here to describe general Christian beliefs about the nature of the relationship between God the Father and Christ. In the next appearance of the term the historically structured hidden/revealed schema reemerges. *Sacramentum* occurs twice in 5.6.2 and fitting in context since this is where Tertullian comments on 1 Cor 2:

> This wisdom, [Paul] says, that was kept in secret (*in occulto fuisse*) is that which was in foolish and in small and in dishonorable things, which lie hidden also under figures, both allegories and enigmas, being revealed afterwards by Christ (*quae latuerit etiam sub figuris, allegoriis et aenigmatibus, revelanda postmodum in Christo*), who was designated the light of the nations by the Creator,[59] who promises through the voice of Isaiah that he will make known treasures invisible and hidden.[60] For that anything should have been concealed by that God who has never done anything at all in which one should suppose he had concealed something, is absurd. He himself, if he existed, could not lie hidden, let alone his mysteries (*ipse se esset, latere non posset, nedum aliqua eius sacramenta*). The Creator, however, is himself as known as his mysteries (*creator autem tam ipse notus quam et sacramenta eius*), which in the presence of Israel flowed openly – though having been concealed according to meaning (*sed de significatiis obumbrata*) – in which he has hidden the wisdom of God, being related to the perfect in his time, having been ordained in reality in the decree of God before the ages. And whose ages, if not the Creator's?

The point of the argument here is clear enough: if the Creator has hidden his mysteries in Israel's scriptures and history, and if those mysteries have now been revealed through Christ, then the relationship between the Creator and Christ cannot be one of division or discord. Rather it must be one of unity. Two other important features in this passage should be mentioned. First is the dual claim that God's mysteries were both plainly performed for Israel ("flowed openly") and yet, at the same time, their meaning was concealed ("though having been concealed according to meaning"). With such a statement Tertullian again reaffirms the retrospective mystery hermeneutic: the mystery of Christ, though previously announced in prophetic scripture is, nonetheless, announced in allegories and enigmas. Therefore, though the mysteries have been declared beforehand by God, their meaning remains veiled (*sed de significatiis obumbrata*) until revealed by Christ. Not only does such exegetical reasoning enable Tertullian to unite the Creator and Christ, it also gives him a way to account for the apparent differences between the two ages—and even the time "before the

---

Marcion und seine kirchengeschichtliche Wirkung: Vorträge der Internationalen Fachkonferenz zu Marcion, gehalten vom 15.–18. August 2001 in Mainz (ed. Gerhard May and Katharina Greschat; TU 150; Berlin/New York: de Gruyter, 2002), 95–109.
59 Isa 42:6.
60 Isa 45:3.

ages." The ages of the Creator are the ages of allegory and, therefore, have a meaning other than their literal one. When viewed through Christ, what otherwise on the literal level appears unrelated (or even contrary) to Christ becomes prefiguratively prophetic. And so, instead of reading scripture independently of Christ, much less contrary to him, Tertullian demands that scripture be interpreted in light of Christ, and in conformity with him. Such a reading is only possible with Christ – the "illuminator of ancient things" – providing the *a posteriori* hermeneutical illumination.

Second, although Tertullian does not tell us exactly how Marcion's text of 1 Cor 2 reads, I see no reason to doubt that Marcion kept the whole of 1 Cor 2. He would, however, have interpreted this passage in a way that accorded with his own theology, and so he would probably have disassociated the God of 1 Cor 2 with the Creator. Notice, however, that in Tertullian's own reading of 1 Cor 2 he makes two key moves that attempt to secure vital tactical advantages against Marcion. Tertullian assumes the Creator is the God in 1 Cor 2:7 who is responsible for hiding the mysteries of Christ in scripture (see also 5.6.5). He also shifts the emphasis from the interpersonal division in 1 Cor 2 to a comprehensive division of history. These two moves are quite cunning, for by altering the accent in that text and by asserting that the "God" of 1 Cor 2 is the God of Israel, Tertullian turns 1 Cor 2 against Marcion. If the Creator is the one who has foretold Christ in scripture, then the Creator and Christ cannot be separated.

As persuasive and plain as Tertullian's reasoning seems, it is important to remember that the Marcionite reader would likely have denied the presupposition that the God of 1 Cor 2 was the Creator and may very well have challenged Tertullian's emphasis on prophecy. Therefore, Tertullian's argument is not without vulnerabilities. Nevertheless, the "once hidden, now revealed" schema in which the Creator conceals and Christ reveals is one that Tertullian repeatedly marshals throughout the treatise to his advantage. In fact, although Tertullian does not elsewhere speak specifically of the previously hidden mystery of Christ in the rest of his exegetical survey of 1 Corinthians,[61] he does emphasize again that Christ is the one who brings to light previously hidden things (5.7.1) and that various events and sayings in Israel's scriptures prefigure Christ (see especially his reading of 1 Cor 9–10 in 5.7.3, 10–14; see also 5.8.4 and 5.10.8).

Moving on to 2 Corinthians, *sacramentum* appears once, and the context of this occurrence is predictable: the veiling of Moses in 2 Cor 3. In 5.11.4–5 Tertullian first attempts to demonstrate that Paul's arguments regarding the old cove-

---

[61] The term *sacramentum* does appear one more time in 5.8.3, but in reference to the eucharistic elements.

nant in 2 Cor 3 are in keeping with Tertullian's own theology. He emphasizes that the creator God is indeed twofold in character: "both judge and also kind" (5.11.4). Therefore, diversity in God need not entail the division of God. Tertullian also argues that Paul's valuation of the new covenant in relation to the old covenant coheres with Tertullian's own teaching, which places gospel above law but does not abrogate law. Indeed, "A new testament will not be other than him who promised it; and if not the letter, but yet his Spirit, this will be newness" (5.11.4). Therefore, while embracing newness, Tertullian does not radicalize it, and instead situates the newness of Christ within the story of the old covenant rather than in opposition to it.

Having emphasized these points, Tertullian next makes a subtle and, to the Marcionite, incendiary comparison between the Jews and Marcion, both of whom Tertullian contends fail to understand the mysteries of their own God. As Tertullian interprets Moses' veiled face in 2 Cor 3, "[Paul] indicates that the veil of the face in Moses was a figure (*figuram*) of the veil of the heart of the people, because still now Moses is not clearly seen with the heart, in the same way as not in the face then" (5.11.6). Therefore, because of the veil over their hearts, "the Jews have failed to understand the mysteries of their own God" (*dei sui sacramenta Iudaei non intellegebant*) (5.11.6).[62] The content of these *sacramenta* that the Jews fail to grasp is clarified in the subsequent claim that "Moses prophesied Christ" (*Moysen...Christo praedicasse*) (5.11.7). Therefore, the Jews' failure of understanding is a hermeneutical failure to discern the christological prophecy of Moses, which has been hidden from them by the veil. The crucial implication for the case against Marcion is that if these mysteries which are now made known to the Christian are the same as those that were hidden from the Jews, then there must be a correspondence between the God who hides and reveals them. Or, as Tertullian poses the question: "How can the Creator's veil be taken away in the Christ of a different God over whose mysteries (*sacramenta*) the Creator has no power to conceal (*velasse*)?" (5.11.7). Tertullian's point here has become routine: Paul's argument in 2 Cor 3 presupposes some sort of cooperation between the God of Israel and the God of Christ when it comes to the veiling and unveiling of God's mysteries, and such cooperation suggests coherence rather than disunion. The irony then is that, just like the Jews, so too Marcion is

---

[62] For examples of similar interpretations of 2 Cor 3 in early Christianity, see Riemer Roukema, "The veil over Moses' face in patristic interpretation," in *The Interpretation of Exodus: Studies in Honor of Cornelius Houtman* (ed. Riemer Roukema; Biblical Exegesis and Theology 44; Leuven/Paris/Dudley, MA: Peeters, 2006), 237–52.

hermeneutically veiled in his inability to recognize the Creator's mysteries of Christ.[63]

After working his way through the rest of 2 Corinthians, Tertullian next analyzes Romans. The subject of prophetic anticipation reappears in 5.13.15 in his comments on Rom 7:12 – "the law is holy, and its commandment just and good." Tertullian writes:

> If [Paul] has such reverence for the Creator's law, I am unable to understand how then he refutes him. What sort of person distinguishes two Gods, one just, the other good, when he whose commandment it is should be considered also both good and just. And so he also confirms that "the law is spiritual" (*spiritualem...legem*),[64] and so prophetic (*utique et propheticam*), and so figurative (*utique et figuratam*). I am obliged to take the position that in the law Christ was predicted figuratively (*Christum in lege figurate praedicatum*), which is why not all the Jews were able to discern (*potuerit agnosci*) him.

Once again Tertullian argues that the law is prophetic of Christ – albeit figuratively prophetic – and that the true referent of the prophecy is only known retrospectively, after the occurrence of the predicted event.

The argument from prophecy reappears again in 5.14.9, and in this instance in relation to *sacramentum*. The context is Tertullian's comments on Paul's appeals to scripture in Rom 9–11. Tertullian claims that Marcion's Pauline text is heavily edited in these sections, and it is likely that Marcion also omitted the mystery passage in 11:25 since Tertullian does not refer to it. Nevertheless, Tertullian and his non-Marcionite readers know this mystery passage, and so Tertullian's own use of *sacramentum* in relation to prophetic scripture is a subtle way of intimating the mystery passage without citing it, leaving the question of its presense in Marcion's version an open one for the reader:

> And now [Paul] cries aloud, "O the depth of the riches and wisdom of God! And his ways unsearchable!" From where does this outburst come? Certainly from his recollection of those scriptures (*ex recordatione scilicet scripturarum*) to which he referred to before, from the contemplation of the mysteries (*ex contemplatione sacramentorum*) which he discussed above in relation to the faith of Christ as coming from the law. If Marcion has erased these diligently, what is his apostle shouting about when he has no riches of [his] God to

---

[63] For more on Marcion's relationship to Judaism, see Stephen G. Wilson, "Marcion and the Jews," in *Anti-Judaism in Early Christianity: Vol 2: Separation and Polemic* (ed. Stephen G. Wilson; Waterloo: Wilfrid Laurier Press, 1986), 45–58. Wilson argues that although both the Marcionite and "Catholic" positions denigrate Judaism, the Marcionite is slightly less hostile; it "was the lesser of two evils" and "left Judaism intact" (58). Even if this is the case, Marcion's posture toward Judaism is still one of opposition.

[64] Rom 7:14.

regard, just a poor and needy one who concealed nothing (*nihil condidit*), predicted nothing (*nihil praedicavit*), indeed possessed nothing, while descending onto foreign land.

Tertullian immediately proceeds to show that even though Marcion has edited his text of Romans to expunge all passages that refer to biblical prophecy and its fulfillment, he cannot erase the fact that the Creator's own scriptures declare that he will hide away and someday reveal hidden treasures; he again cites Isa 45:3 to this effect. Therefore, since even Marcion must admit that the Creator is a God who conceals and reveals, on Tertullian's reading of his own unedited text of Paul, this occurs through scriptural prophecy recounted by Paul in Rom 9 – 11 and the realization of that prophecy in Christ. Paul's doxological outburst in Rom 11:33 then comes from contemplating the mysteries of christological prophecy that are now disclosed through Christ. Marcion, in lacking Paul's citations of scripture, simply cannot account for the apostle's doxological outburst (or so Tertullian submits). Tertullian concludes his analysis of Romans by continuing to press the point that when one considers Paul's arguments from prophecy, the Creator and Christ emerge as unified rather than divided.[65]

Following Romans is 1 Thessalonians. The argument from prophecy appears once in Tertullian's reading of this letter and, once again, the term *sacramentum* with it (5.15.4 – 6). In a bit of a tortured extension (at least to the modern reader), Tertullian connects Paul's teaching on the Parousia in 1 Thess 4:13 – 18 with Isa 60:8 ("Who are these that fly as clouds, as doves with young ones to me?") and Amos 9:6 ("Who builds up his ascent into the heavens"). By taking these passages as prophetic anticipations of the eschatological ascent of Christians, Tertullian finds another occasion to excoriate Marcion for his rejection of scripture's hidden mysteries, explaining that the Christian should challenge Marcion "according to the pattern of spiritual and prophetic grace and power, calling forth on it to predict the future (*futura praenuntiet*), and reveal the secrets of the heart (*occulta cordis revelet*), and explain mysteries (*sacramenta edisserat*)" (5.15.5). Given the usual pattern of usage, the explanation of mysteries in this passage refers to

---

[65] Tertullian does not mention Rom 16:25 – 27. We can presume that whatever Marcion's version of Romans included, it nowhere included the final form of Rom 16:25 – 27, for Tertullian would almost certainly have cited this passage against Marcion. The question of whether Marcion had some alternative form of the doxology – perhaps, for instance, one lacking the reference to the prophetic scriptures – cannot be determined, but it seems unlikely. If Marcion had an abbreviated version of it and Tertullian was aware of the full version as we now known it, then Tertullian would likely have again exploited the occasion to portray Marcion as a mutilator of a Pauline passage that undermines Marcion's own theology. See Origen's accusations regarding Marcion's editorial activity here in *Comm. Rom.* 10.43.2.

the christological interpretation of scripture – in other words, the type of biblical interpretation that understands the prophecies of the Creator as prophecies of Christ. In the immediate context, the mysteries in need of explanation are the prophecies of Christ's coming Parousia – another argument certainly unpersuasive to the Marcionite.

The next major moment in Tertullian's exegetical survey of Marcion's *Apostolikon* is what Marcion has as Paul's letter to the Laodiceans (which, for Tertullian, is Ephesians).[66] Tertullian's use of the hidden/revealed mystery discourse in this section is extensive, and this agrees with the precedent of Ephesians. Tertullian begins by noting that the original addressee of the letter is largely immaterial, for Paul's words address all people. More pressing, Tertullian submits, is the question of the God to whom Paul's Christ belongs. Tertullian poses this question in 5.17.1, and he insinuates his answer by commenting on Paul's statement about God's mystery in Eph 1:9–10:

> Now to whom does it suitably belong – "according to the good pleasure, which he displayed in the mystery of his will for a dispensation of the fullness of the times (that I thus say according to the meaning of the word in Greek) *to recapitulate* (that is, to refer back to the beginning or review from the beginning) all things in Christ which are in heaven and which are in earth" – to whom except him who will be all things from the beginning, even the beginning itself, from whom also are the times, and the dispensation of the fulfilling of the times, from which all things are being reviewed from the beginning in Christ?

> Cui ergo competet – *secundum boni existimationem, quam proposuerit in sacramento voluntatis suae, in dispensationem adimpletionis temporum* (ut ita dixerim, sicut verbum illud in graeco sonat) *recapitulare* (id est ad initium redigere vel ab initio recensere) *omnia in Christum, quae in caelis et quae in terris*, – nisi cuius erunt omnia ab initio, etiam ipsum initium, a quo et tempora et termporum adimpletionis dispensation, ob quam omnia ad initium recensentur in Christo?

Tertullian here contends that the God to whom this mystery mentioned by Paul belongs cannot be Marcion's other God who lacks any relationship to the "beginning" and the "dispensation." Rather, this mystery "for the fullness of times" must belong to the Creator and his times. Thus, as Tertullian reads Paul, it must be the Creator who determined to recapitulate time in Christ, and so it must be the Creator's times that are now "being reviewed from the beginning in Christ." And if this is the case, then the Creator and Christ belong together – the former as prophetic foreteller and the latter as hermeneutical revealer.

---

66 He does discuss 2 Thessalonians prior to Ephesians, but his treatment is brief, and nothing of great consequence emerges.

Tertullian's next use of *sacramentum* occurs again in relation to Paul's own use of the term in Eph 3. Tertullian begins by noting some of the ways that Marcion has edited his text in this section of the letter. First, he reports that Marcion has removed "and the prophets" from Eph 2:20 (5.17.16). The reason for this redaction is obvious: Marcion would not want to admit that the Creator's own prophets are somehow foundational for Christ's church. Tertullian then in 5.18.1 begins to describe another instance of Marcion's editorial trimming. He writes:

> As for the heretic's hand in editing, it is no wonder he subtracts syllables when he has carried off the majority of entire pages. The apostle says that to himself "last of all was given the grace to make all people see what is the dispensation of the mystery which from the ages has been hidden in [or by] the God who created all things (*dispensation sacramenti occulti ab aevis in deo qui omnia condidit*)." The heretic has taken away the preposition "in", and so it is made to read: "hidden from the ages from the God who created all things."[67]

The accusation here is that by deleting the preposition ἐν from his text,[68] Marcion has transformed the statement that the mystery "was hidden *in* [or *by*] the God who created all things"[69] to the statement that it "was hidden *from* the God who created all things." This latter reading is obviously commensurate with Marcion's theology, which would want to disassociate the mystery from the Creator, whereas the former could be problematic. There is, however, perhaps a problem with Tertullian's description of the situation here, and it relates to the long debated question of whether or not Tertullian is reading Marcion and his *Apostolikon* in Greek or Latin.[70] The basic issue is that while *occulti...deo qui*

---

67 Rapuit haereticus "in" praepositionem, et ita legi facit: *occulti ab aevis deo qui omnia condidit*.
68 It would then read: ἀπὸ τῶν αἰώνων τῷ θεῷ τῷ τὰ πάντα κτίσαντι.
69 Either a locative or an instrumental reading of ἐν could be troublesome for a Marcionite.
70 The theory that Tertullian read Marcion's *Apostolikon* in Latin was first put forward by Adolf von Harnack, *Marcion: Das Evangelium vom Fremden Gott: Eine Monographie zur Geschichte der Grundlegung der katholischen Kirche* (TU 45; 2d ed.; Leipzig: J.C. Heinrichs, 1924), 49*, 51*–4*, 178*–81*. Though many scholars after Harnack accepted the hypothesis that Tertullian often, or perhaps exclusively, read Marcion in Latin translation, there have been recent detractors. The first was Gilles Quispel, *De bronnen van Tertullians' Adversus Marcionem* (Leiden: Burgersdijk & Niermans Templum Salomonis, 1943), 104–42. Since Quispel, there is now significant scholarship on both sides of the debate. Many of the challenges to Harnack have come from scholars working primarily on Tertullian's version of the *Apostolikon*. See, i.a., Ulrich Schmid, *Marcion und sein Apostolos: Rekonstruktion und historische Einordnung der marcionitischen Paulusbriefausgabe* (ANTF 25; Berlin: de Gruyter, 1995). For a recent summary of the history of scholarship

omnia condidit can be easily read in Latin as "having been hidden *from* the God who created all things" – with the form *deo* being taken not as a dative but as an ablative – the expression ἀποκεκρυμμένου…τῷ θεῷ τῷ τὰ πάντα κτίσαντι in Greek is not so easily read as Tertullian suggests since the τῷ θεῷ τῷ τὰ πάντα κτίσαντι is still in the dative case. The usual way to express the "hidden from" idea in Greek would be ἀποκρύπτω + genitive (or perhaps κρύπτω + ἀπό).[71] The combination of ἀποκρύπτω + dative can possibly be taken this way, but it is rare.[72] *LSJ* cite only Homer, *Il.* 11.718, as an example of this use of the dative: **ἀπέκρυψεν** δέ **μοι** ἵππους. But the μοι in this passage could just as easily, and perhaps more naturally, be taken as a dative of possession (thus Murray's LCL translation: "hid away my horses"). Another apparent instance of this construction I have found, and closer in time to Tertullian, is from Philo: τὸ δὲ αἴνιγμα οὐ λίαν **τοῖς** ὀξὺ καθορᾶν **δυναμένοις ἀπεκρύπτετο** ("The enigma was not hidden *from those being able* to perceive with great quickness") (*Somn.* 2.3). Even clearer and, importantly, related to the concealment of mysteries is Wis 6:22: τί δέ ἐστιν σοφία καὶ πῶς ἐγένετο ἀπαγγελῶ καὶ οὐκ **ἀποκρύψω ὑμῖν** μυστήρια ("What Wisdom is and how she came about I will declare, and I will not hide mysteries from you"). Therefore, while it is possible to read Marcion's reconstructed Greek text as Tertullian claims, it is probably not the most likely reading, and certainly not a necessary one.[73] Furthermore, the fact that Tertullian's reading works so well in Latin is perhaps evidence that he is in fact, as many have suggested, reading Marcion in Latin.[74] The Latin would then be driving Tertullian's argument and accusations. Although we do not know exactly Marcion's text of Eph 3:9, Tertullian's supposition about the

---

on this subject, see Dieter T. Roth, "Did Tertullian Possess a Greek Copy or Latin Translation of Marcion's Gospel?," *VC* 63 (2009): 429 – 67, esp. 429 – 42, who makes a case for Tertullian reading Marcion's Gospel in Greek.

71 See Isa 2:10 (καὶ νῦν εἰσέλθετε εἰς τὰς πέτρας καὶ **κρύπτεσθε εἰς τὴν γῆν ἀπὸ προσώπου τοῦ φόβου κυρίου καὶ ἀπὸ τῆς δόξης τῆς ἰσχύος αὐτοῦ** ὅταν ἀναστῇ θραῦσαι τὴν γῆν).

72 We would perhaps classify this usage as a dative of respect.

73 Codex Sinaiticus (א) lacks the ἐν as well, though it was added by a later corrector (the fifth to seventh century C^a corrector). Therefore, while this codex apparently agrees with Marcion's text, it does not seem to have been interpreted in this instance as Tertullian interprets Marcion's text (or as Marcion presumably interpreted it). In other words, even without the ἐν, the phrase τῷ θεῷ τῷ τὰ πάντα κτίσαντι is still more likely to be understood in a locative or instrumental sense than in an ablative sense (unless you are a Marcionite, I suppose).

74 In the end, we cannot be certain whether or not Marcion's Greek version of Eph 3:9 just omitted the ἐν or perhaps included other changes as well. That Marcion did omit the ἐν is, however, likely. As Clabeaux, *A Lost Edition*, 32, has noticed, there seems to be a pattern to the removal of ἐν in Marcion's text of Ephesians. It is omitted in Eph 2:15 (5.17.5); 3:9 (5.18.1); 6:14 (3.14.4); and 6:15 (3.15.4).

way in which Marcionite readers would have wanted to interpret the expression seems accurate. And so, setting aside the text critical questions, the allegation as put forth in Tertullian's Latin is clear enough: Marcion has deliberately edited his text to separate the Creator God from Christ and his God.

After noting Marcion's alleged editorial emendation and its alleged exegetical effect, Tertullian proceeds to demonstrate that even on internal grounds Marcion's new reading is contradicted. To make his case he cites the very next verse: "that unto the principalities and powers in the heavenly places the manifold wisdom of God should be made known" (Eph 3:10). Tertullian poses the question: to whom do the principalities and powers in this verse belong? He then immediately suggests that they must be the Creator's. The question then becomes why Marcion's God would want his wisdom to be made known to them but not to the Creator as well. After a bit more complicated, and sometimes not immediately clear, exegetical reasoning, Tertullian finally concludes that Marcion's editorial redaction of Eph 3:9 is inconsistent with the rest of the passage and is, therefore, spurious. The hidden mystery described by Paul was not hidden from the Creator; rather this mystery belongs to the Creator, as does Christ. To conclude his argument, Tertullian again restates his contention in 5.18.4 that even on the basis of Marcion's own text, his redaction and subsequent reading cannot be sustained, and so the "hidden mystery" (*occultum sacramentum*) must belong to the Creator, to whom also belongs Christ.

In 5.18.5 Tertullian begins his next argument which, in his own words, is "to work out my dispute with you with regard to the apostle's allegories" (*tibi de allegoriis apostolic controversiam nectere*). He demonstrates through a litany of biblical citations and references, including those in Ephesians itself, that Marcion's Christ appears to use and to depend on the Creator's biblical models (5.18.8). He presses this point again in his comments on the Eph 5:32 mystery passage in 5.18.9–10:

> Need I labor now to demonstrate that the same God is of the man and of Christ, of the woman and of the church, of the flesh and of the spirit, when the apostle himself applies the expression of the Creator, indeed also explains it: "On behalf of her a man will leave his father and mother, and the two will be one flesh, this is a great mystery (*sacramentum hoc magnum est*)"? It suffices if the Creator's mysteries are great among the apostle (*si creatoris magna sunt apud apostolum sacramenta*), but of low esteem among the heretics. "But I speak moreover," he says, "about Christ and the church." You have an interpretation, not a separation, of the mystery (*habes interpretationem, non separationem, sacramenti*). It demonstrates that the figure of the mystery from him applies to him to whom the mystery certainly will be (*ostendit figuram sacramenti ab eo praeministratam cuius erat utique sacramentum*). What does Marcion think? Certainly the Creator was not able to apply figures to an unknown God who, if known, was also an adversary!

As Tertullian reads it, Paul's citation of Gen 2:24 in Eph 5:31, and then his explanation that it is a mystery of Christ and the church in v. 32, is an instance of biblical interpretation – *habes interpretationem, non separationem, sacramenti*.[75] It is then an occurrence of allegorical exegesis (or, better here, mystery exegesis) in which a scriptural passage is reread to prefigure some consequent Christian reality. In this case, the etiology of marriage in Gen 2 is, according to Tertullian, being reread by Paul as a mystery of Christ's relationship with the church. Once again, therefore, by citing the Creator's scriptures and applying them in a positive way to a Christian reality, Tertullian contends that Paul is uniting rather than dividing the Creator and Christ.

The final use of *sacramentum* in Tertullian's treatment of Ephesians occurs at the conclusion of this section (5.18.14), where he reminds the reader that Paul was in prison for his preaching and his "courage in making known the mystery" (*constantiam manifestandi sacramenti*) (Eph 6:19–20). Although the content of the mystery is undefined here, given the pattern of usage in Book 5, it should be taken as another reference to Paul as a proclaimer of the hidden mystery of Christ which is now found within the Creator's scriptures.

The next letter in Marcion's collection is Colossians. Tertullian's analysis here is brief and, somewhat surprisingly, mystery does not appear in any of his arguments. But this is likely due to the similarities between Colossians and Ephesians, which he has just treated. His most explicit argument for unity between the Creator's scriptures and Christ comes in relation to Col 2:16–17 – "Do not let anyone judge you in meat and drink or in respect of a holy day or the new moon or the Sabbath, which are a shadow of future things, but the body is of Christ." After citing this verse in 5.19.9, Tertullian explains that Paul's contrast of shadow and body must be applied to the law and Christ. Since a shadow must belong to a body, so the law must belong to Christ. He also explains that since we have now moved from shadow to body – and "from figures to truth" (*de figuris ad veritatem*) – then the law "has been canceled" (*exclusa*). Such cancellation does not, however, entail separation. The shadow that is the law and the body that is Christ remain indivisible.

Although he briefly mentions Philemon in his conclusion, the final major letter Tertullian treats is Philippians. At the outset of his examination of this letter he discusses Paul's words in Phil 1:15–18 on the many motivations that drive people to preach. Tertullian explains in 5.20.1 that though Paul permits diverse (and even less noble) motivations for proclaiming the gospel, he does not tolerate disparate expressions of the gospel:

---

75 Notice that this is an early witness to the hermeneutical reading of Eph 5:31–32.

> Though there are unique motivations of mind, there are not [diverse] rules of the mysteries (*regulas sacramentorum*). [Paul] confirms that while presenting in diversity [is permitted], nevertheless there is one Christ, and one God, his God, who is the reason for preaching.

The expression *regulas sacramentorum* should probably be taken as essentially synonymous with Tertullian's other uses of *regula*.[76] In the near context of 5.19.1, which is the introduction to the section on Colossians, Tertullian explains that Paul's statement in Col 1:23 about the gospel having been proclaimed throughout the world proves that "our rule" precedes all heresy (*priorem vindicans regulam nostram omni haeretica posteritate*).[77] The *regula* here is the oft referred to "rule of faith" that derives from Christ and apostolic tradition. Therefore, the *regulas sacramentorum* appear to be another way of describing the rule of faith, but one that places emphasis on the importance of the mysteries within the rule of faith. Marcion's refusal of the Creator's mysteries is one of the primary *regulas* he violates and, consequently, the reason why he remains outside the bounds of the true church as defined by Tertullian.

After briefly noting in 5.21.1 that Philemon has managed "to escape Marcion's falsifying hands," and then admitting that he does not know why Marcion does not include any of the Pastoral epistles,[78] Tertullian offers a short apology for some of the repetition in the treatise as a whole (5.21.2). He then concisely concludes the work, expressing his confidence that the long-deceased Marcion has been sufficiently refuted.

8.6 Conclusion: Mystery, Paul, and Tertullian's Against Marcion

As this chapter has shown, *sacramentum* functions in a variety of ways throughout Tertullian's voluminous corpus, but its use is nowhere more prevalent and more important than in the struggle with Marcion for hermeneutical ownership over Paul. For Tertullian, more than just Paul is at stake in this contest. The identity of the God who Christians worship and, consequently, Christianity itself are equally in question. And so it is to this critical theological challenge that Tertul-

---

[76] For more on the rule of faith in Tertullian, see L. William Countryman, "Tertullian and the Regula Fidei," *SecCent* 2 (1982): 208–27; Bryan M. Litfin, "Tertullian's Use of the *Regula Fidei* as an Interpretive Device in *Adversus Marcionem*," *StPatr* 42 (2003): 405–10.
[77] Cf. also the *regula sacramenti* in 1.21.5.
[78] He does, however, take one final jab here, submitting that the absence of the Pastorals is just one more instance where Marcion is found meddling with Paul's letters.

lian adapts and deploys the hidden/revealed mystery discourse. The fundamental configuration and application of the discourse is just as we have found it in previous authors: Israel's scriptures contain mysteries, and these mysteries constitute prophetic prefigurations of the recently revealed Christ. Though prophetic, however, these biblical mysteries have only recently become knowable, for they were previously concealed under the veil of figures and allegories. When read retrospectively – and so in light of the newly revealed reality that they provide prior witness to – then the veil is removed and the prophetic mysteries are newly seen for what they most truly are. The reality that removes the veil is the Christ of the rule of faith.[79]

When it comes to Marcion, the primary force of Tertullian's argument is that this mystery schema of scriptural prophecy is not Tertullian's own invention, but rather that it is rooted even in the Christian sources that Marcion himself reveres – and especially in the "Paul" of Marcion's personally redacted *Apostolikon*. If, therefore, the mystery schema belongs to Paul, then Marcion's appeal to Paul for his bifurcation of the Creator and Christ has no basis, for the mystery schema is precisely what unites the Creator and Christ. It is unlikely that the committed Marcionite would be persuaded by Tertullian's exegetical reasoning, especially when it comes to Paul. And while Tertullian's attempt to refute Marcion even on the terms of his own texts is an ambitious one – and arguably a necessary one – it is nevertheless the case that the Marcionite can still argue persuasively on the terms of those texts as well. But for those already convinced, Tertullian's cumulative argument would no doubt further confirm what was already accepted: Israel's scriptures are Christian scriptures insofar as they are now retrospectively comprehended as providing prophetic corroboration of the mysteries of Christ. Once again, therefore, the mystery schema of revelation proves to be a resourceful rhetorical tactic for securing a form of Christianity fully committed to a historical consciousness in which Christians are a people both new and old, with a God both known of old in Israel and yet also revealed anew in Christ.

---

[79] The importance of divine grace should be mentioned as well. As with Justin, so with Tertullian, knowledge of Christ and the gift of divine grace coincide in the christological interpretation of scripture.

Conclusion

At the outset of this book I introduced my thesis by quoting a passage from Adolf von Harnak's *The Mission and Expansion of Christianity in the First Three Centuries* in which he describes the formation of a new Christian "political-historical consciousness" (*politisch-historisches Bewusstsein*). What Harnack is attempting to characterize is a particular social and temporal self-perception that enabled Christians to conceive of themselves as genuinely new to the world by virtue of God's recent and definitive revelation in Christ and yet at the same time ancient with respect to God's eternal plans. Harnack goes on to illustrate the rhetorical shape this new self-understanding took:

> Could there be any higher or more comprehensive conception than that of the complex of momenta afforded by the Christians' estimate of themselves as "the true Israel," "the new people," "the original people," and "the people of the future," i.e., of eternity? This estimate of themselves rendered Christians impregnable against all attacks and movements of polemical criticism, while it further enabled them to advance in every direction for a war of conquest. Was the cry raised, "You are renegade Jews"—the answer came, "We are the community of the Messiah, and therefore the true Israelites." If people said, "You are simply Jews," the reply was, "We are a new creation and a new people." If, again, they were taxed with their recent origin and told that they were but of yesterday, they retorted, "We only seem to be the younger People; from the beginning we have been latent; we have always existed, previous to any other people; we are the original people of God."[1]

While it would be wise to relax some of the enthusiasm in Harnack's description, and while the image of a "war of conquest" is regrettable, there is nonetheless something essential in the way Harnack is here depicting how Christians came to account for themselves as both genuinely new to world and yet also ancient according to God's designs. And Harnack is correct in acknowledging that to claim Israel's heritage and Israel's God and, at the same time, to supplement both in ways that entailed their fundamental reconfiguration necessitated something like the reconception of history and social identity he described above.

In this book I have argued that the kind of self-conception that Harnack depicts, while certainly a matter of historical perception, is no less stimulated by a particular commitment to God's definitive revelation in the person of Christ – a revelation eternally planned but previously concealed. I contend that we see this christologically focused conception of divine disclosure, and particularly the his-

---

1 Adolf von Harnack, *The Mission and Expansion of Christianity in the First Three Centuries.* Vol. 1 (trans. James Moffatt; 2d ed; London: Williams and Norgate, 1908), 240–41.

torically structured hidden/revealed dynamic, first in the Pauline letters, and most clearly in what I have identified as the deuteropauline mystery schema of revelation. The structure of this schema is straightforward: God pretemporally established a plan for humanity, but this plan was concealed from humanity. Yet now, through the advent of Christ and Christian proclamation, this eternal arrangement – this mystery – has been disclosed to the world. The cosmic schema thus divides human history into halves: an era of concealment and an era of disclosure. As the investigation of subsequent Christian thinkers has demonstrated, structuring history in such a manner, particularly when coupled with the commitment to the definitiveness of Christian revelation, proved rhetorically potent and theologically adaptable. Whether it be to account for the newness of Christianity – "why did this new race enter the world now and not earlier?" (*Diogn.* 1.1) – as in Ignatius and the *Epistle to Diognetus*, or to systematize and defend revisionary Christian interpretations of Israel's scriptures, as in Justin and Melito, or to repair any alleged rupture between Israel's God and the newly unveiled Christ, as in Tertullian, the appeal to mystery and the historical arrangement of the hidden/revealed binary provided a comprehensive intellectual edifice for promoting and defending these claims.

It is to the success of this theological defense that I turn to briefly in conclusion.

Particularly since Edward Gibbon's famed fifteenth chapter of his *The History of the Decline and Fall of the Roman Empire* (1776) in which he shouldered "the more melancholy duty" of the historian and offered his "candid but rational inquiry into the progress and establishment of Christianity," the social means and material conditions that aided Christianity's eventual domination of the Mediterranean landscape has remained a central question in scholarship on early Christianity.[2] In more recent years scholars such as Rodney Stark[3] and Keith Hopkins[4] have applied the tools of sociological analysis – "the arithmetic of the possible and the plausible"[5] – to the question of Christianity's expansion, shedding interesting light on many matters, particularly those related to Christian population

---

[2] I would say "religious landscape," but this might suggest that the ascendancy of Christianity was not equally political or social, which it most certainly was.
[3] Rodney Stark, *The Rise of Christianity: How the Obscure, Marginal Jesus Movement Became the Dominant Religious Force in the Western World in a Few Centuries* (New York: Harper Collins, 1997). This is the paperback edition. The book was originally published the previous year by Princeton University Press with a more modest subtitle: *A Sociologist Reconsiders History*.
[4] Keith Hopkins, "Christian Number and Its Implications," *JECS* 6 (1998): 185–226.
[5] Stark, *The Rise of Christianity*, 27.

growth in the first four centuries.⁶ But as important as such proposals are for historical reconstructions of the total canvas of Christian origins, it is critical to remember that ideas and the systemic ideologies that sustain them are not necessarily epiphenomenal to material and social factors. This is to say that the analysis of early Christian *theology* need not be subsidiary to the task of reconstructing early Christian *history*. As it persisted as an identifiable social entity that claimed to be the true (or new) people of God, the movement that came to be called "Christianity" naturally generated distinguishable ideas, along with new plausibility structures and conceptual schemes within which to understand and defend them. It is, therefore, worth pointing out in conclusion that the sheer numerical success of Christianity is perhaps less historically impressive than the intellectual transformations of religious identity effected by Christianity and the underlying ideology that enabled them. As J.B. Rives has argued, "The expansion of Christianity is historically significant precisely because it represents something more than a new deity acquiring increasing numbers of adherents: it represents the growth of a new social and conceptual system, a new ideology of religion."⁷ While it is certainly the case that the success of a movement like Christianity, like the success of any individual conversion, cannot be attributed simply to its ability to satisfy intellectual plausibility and to forge new modes of thought – that is, to continue to make sense of the world, to account for ongoing experiences, and to integrate new and existing bodies of knowledge – the fact of its enduring existence indicates that it is certainly no less than this. As Rives goes on to state,

> [T]he Christian ideology...was by no means unique, but instead had significant precedents and/or parallels in Jewish and Graeco-Roman traditions.... It was not these ideas themselves, then, that were distinctive to Christianity, but rather their combination and partic-

---

6 The work of these scholars is anticipated in significant ways by Harnack's *The Mission and Expansion of Christianity*.

7 J.B. Rives, "Christian Expansion and Christian Ideology," in *The Spread of Christianity in the First Four Centuries: Essays in Exploration* (ed. W.V. Harris; Leiden/Boston: Brill, 2005), 15–41, 16. The key aspects in the new Christian ideology are, for Rives, "exclusivity," "homogeneity," and "totalization." The key achievement of this ideology comes in to view vis-à-vis paganism. Rives explains that "the phenomenon of rejecting old practices and beliefs in favor of new ones was something that did not exist within the traditional Graeco-Roman system (except in the context of philosophy), and that consequently the very fact of conversion was an indication of a fundamental systemic change: a system in which choices of religious belief and practice were non-exclusive, open-ended, and virtually limitless was being replaced by one in which choices were exclusive, sharply defined, and relatively restricted. Adherence to the Christian god acquired revolutionary significance...only insofar as it involved participation in this new ideology" (16–17).

ular modulation. Yet in the end we must acknowledge that Christianity represented something genuinely novel, if not absolutely *sui generis*. The expansion of Christianity was not simply an example of another successful cult within the Graeco-Roman world, but a development that ultimately entailed the transformation of that world. In order to understand that development we must explore what there was about Christianity that allowed it to work such a transformation. And this, I would argue, lay in the new ideology, the new conception of religion, that was gradually forged in the ongoing struggles of Christian leaders.[8]

Like Rives, I do not maintain that Christian thinking about mystery and divine revelation was wholly original or even unique in most respects. But I do contend that the creative ways in which various Christians, beginning with Paul, formulated innovative theological arguments by appealing to newly revealed divine mysteries indeed represent something "genuinely novel" that contributed to fundamental transformations in the ancient Mediterranean religious mentality.[9] I offer this book as an exploration of one facet of early Christian thinking that played an essential role in such transformations.

---

[8] Rives, "Christian Expansion and Christian Ideology," 41. In speaking of Christianity as distinctive, if not *sui generis*, Rives rightly distances himself from "theologically-motivated assumptions about Christian uniqueness that for so long dominated the study of early Christianity" (41).
[9] I speak of a single "Mediterranean mentality" cautiously and with reservations, but to qualify this expression sufficiently would take us too far afield.

Bibliography

Abbott, T. K. *The Epistles to the Ephesians and the Colossians.* International Critical Commentary. Edinburgh: T&T Clark, 1897.

Agamben, Giorgio. *The Kingdom and the Glory: For a Theological Genealogy of Economy and Government.* Translated by Lorenzo Chiesa with Matteo Mandarini. Stanford: Stanford University Press, 2011.

Aland, Kurt. "Der Schluss und die ursprüngliche Gestalt des Römerbriefes." Pages 284–301 in *Neutestamentliche Entwürfe.* Theologische Bücherei 63. München: Kaiser,1979.

Aleith, Eva. *Paulusverständnis in der alten Kirche.* Beihefte zur Zeitschrift für die neutestamentliche Wissenschaft 18. Berlin: Töppelmann, 1937.

Aletti, Jean-Noël. *Saint Paul: Épitre aux Colossiens. Etudes bibliques* 20. Paris: Gabalda, 1993.

Allert, Craig D. *Revelation, Truth, Canon and Interpretation: Studies in Justin Martyr's Dialogue with Trypho.* Vigiliae Christianae Supplements 64. Leiden/Boston: Brill, 2002.

Allo, E.-B. *Saint Paul. Première Épître aux Corinthiens.* Paris: Gabalda, 1934.

Anrich, Gustav. *Das antike Mysterienwesen in seinem Einfluss auf das Christentum.* Göttingen: Vandenhoeck & Ruprecht, 1894.

Arnold, Clinton E. *The Colossian Syncretism: The Interface between Christianity and Folk Belief at Colossae.* Wissenschaftliche Untersuchungen zum Neuen Testament 2/77. Tübingen: Mohr Siebeck, 1995.

Auerbach, Erich. "Figura." Pages 11–76 in *Scenes from the Drama of European Literature.* Theory and History of Literature 9. Minneapolis: University of Minnesota Press, 1984.

Aune, David E. "Charismatic Exegesis in Early Judaism and Early Christianity." Pages 126–50 in *The Pseudepigrapha and Early Biblical Interpretation.* Edited by James H. Charlesworth, and Craig A. Evans. Journal for the Study of the Old Testament: Supplement Series 14. Sheffield: JSOT Press, 1993.

—. "Justin Martyr's Use of the Old Testament." *Bulletin of the Evangelical Theological Society* 9 (1966): 179–97.

—. *Prophecy in Early Christianity and the Ancient Mediterranean World.* Grand Rapids: Eerdmans, 1983.

—. *Revelation 17–22.* Word Biblical Commentary 52C. Nashville: Thomas Nelson, 1998.

Backer, Emile de. *Sacramentum: Le mot et l'idée représentée par lui dans les œuvres de Tertullien.* Louvain: 1911.

—. "Tertullien." Pages 59–152 in *Pour L'Histoire du Mot "Sacramentum": I. Les anténicéens.* Edited by J. de Ghellinkck et al. Louvain: 1924.

Baird, William. "Among the Mature: The Idea of Wisdom in I Corinthians 2:6." *Interpretation* 13 (1959): 425–32.

Barclay, John M. G. "Πνευματικός in the Social Dialect of Pauline Christianity." Pages 205–15 in *Pauline Churches and Diaspora Jews.* Wissenschaftliche Untersuchungen zum Neuen Testament 275. Tübingen: Mohr Siebeck, 2011.

Barnard, L. W. "The Epistle Ad Diognetum: Two Units from One Author." *Zeitschrift für die neutestamentliche Wissenschaft und die Kunde der älteren Kirche* 56 (1965): 130–37.

Barnes, Timothy D. *Tertullian: A Historical and Literary Study.* Oxford/New York: Oxford University Press, 1971.

—. "The Date of Ignatius." *Expository Times* 120 (2008): 119–130.

Barnett, Albert E. *Paul Becomes a Literary Influence*. Chicago: The University of Chicago Press, 1941.
Barr, James. *The Semantics of Biblical Language*. London: Oxford University Press, 1961.
Barrett, C. K. *A Commentary on the Epistle to the Romans*. Harper's New Testament Commentaries. New York: Harper & Brothers, 1957.
——. *A Commentary on the First Epistle to the Corinthians*. London: Black, 1968.
Barth, Fritz. "Tertullians Auffassung des Apostels Paulus und seines Verhältnisses zu den Uraposteln." *Jahrbuch für Protestantische Theologie* 8 (1882): 706–56.
Barth, Markus, and Helmut Blanke. *Colossians: A New Translation with Introduction and Commentary*. Anchor Bible 34B. New York: Doubleday, 1994.
Bates, Matthew W. "Justin Martyr's Logocentric Hermeneutical Transformation of Isaiah's Vision of the Nations," *Journal of Theological Studies* 60 (2009): 538–55.
Baur, F. C. *Paulus, der Apostel Jesu Christi, sein Leben und Wirken, seine Briefe und seine Lehre*. Stuttgart: Becher and Müller, 1845.
Beck, Hans. "Interne *Synkrisis* bei Plutarch." *Hermes* 130 (2002): 467–89.
Becker, Eve-Marie. "Marcion und die Korintherbriefe nach Tertullian, Adversus Marcionem V." Pages 95–109 in *Marcion und seine kirchengeschichtliche Wirkung: Vorträge der Internationalen Fachkonferenz zu Marcion, gehalten vom 15.–18. August 2001 in Mainz*. Edited by Gerhard May, and Katharina Greschat. Texte und Untersuchungen 150. Berlin/New York: de Gruyter, 2002.
Beet, Joseph Agar. *A Commentary on St. Paul's Epistles to the Corinthians*. New York: Thomas Whittaker, 1883.
Bell, Richard H. *Provoked to Jealousy: The Origin and Purpose of the Jealousy Motif in Romans 9–11*. Wissenschaftliche Untersuchungen zum Neuen Testament 2/63. Tübingen: Mohr Siebeck, 1994.
Berrin, Shani. "Qumran Pesharim." Pages 110–33 in *Biblical Interpretation at Qumran*. Edited by Matthias Henze. Grand Rapids: Eerdmans, 2005.
Best, E. *A Critical and Exegetical Commentary on Ephesians*. International Critical Commentary. London/New York: T&T Clark, 1998.
——. "The Revelation to Evangelize the Gentiles." *Journal of Theological Studies* 35 (1984): 1–30.
——. "Who Used Whom? The Relationship of Ephesians and Colossians." *New Testament Studies* 43 (1997): 72–96.
Bieder, Werner. "Das Geheimnis des Christus nach dem Epheserbrief." *Theologische Zeitschrift* 11 (1955): 329–43.
Bird, Michael F. "The Reception of Paul in the *Epistle to Diognetus*." Pages 70–90 in *Paul and the Second Century*. Edited by Michael F. Bird, and Joseph R. Dodson. Library of New Testament Studies 412. London/New York: T&T Clark, 2011.
Birdsall, J. N. "Melito of Sardis, Περὶ τοῦ Πάσχα in a Georgian version." *Le Muséon* 80 (1967): 121–38.
Blank, Josef. *Vom Passa: Die älteste christliche Osterpredigt*. Freiburg: Lambertus, 1963.
Bloom, Harold. *The Anxiety of Influence: A Theory of Poetry*. New York: Oxford University Press, 1973.
Bobichon, Philippe. *Justin Martyr: Dialogue avec Tryphon*. Paradosis 47/1–2. Fribourg: Academic Press Fribourg, 2003.
Bockmuehl, Markus N. A. "A Note on the Text of Colossians 4:3." *Journal of Theological Studies* 39 (1988): 489–94.

—. *Revelation and Mystery in Ancient Judaism and Pauline Christianity.* Wissenschaftliche Untersuchungen zum Neuen Testament 2/36. Tübingen: Mohr Siebeck, 1990.

Boersma, Hans. *Heavenly Participation: The Weaving of a Sacramental Tapestry.* Grand Rapids: Eerdmans, 2011.

Bonner, Campbell. *The Homily on the Passion by Melito Bishop of Sardis with some Fragments of the Apocryphal Ezekiel.* Studies and Documents 12. Philadelphia: University of Philadelphia Press, 1940.

Bourgeois, Daniel. *La sagesse des anciens dans le mystère du verbe: évangile et philosophie chez saint Justin, philosophe et martyr.* Paris: Téqui, 1981.

Bousset, Wilhelm. "Christentum und Mysterienreligionen." *Theologische Rundschau* 15 (1912): 41–61.

—. "Die Religionsgeschichte und das Neue Testament." *Theologische Rundschau* 15 (1912): 251–78.

—. *Kyrios Christos: Geschichte des Christusglaubens von den Anfängen des Christentums bis Irenaeus.* Göttingen: Vandenhoeck & Ruprecht, 1916.

Boyarin, Daniel. *Border Lines: The Partition of Judaeo-Christianity.* Philadelphia: University of Pennsylvania Press, 2004.

Boyer, Steven D. "The Logic of Mystery." *Religious Studies* 43 (2007): 89–102.

Brändle, Rudolf. *Die Ethik der "Schrift an Diognet": Eine Wiederaufnahme paulinischer und johanneischer Theologie am Ausgang des zweiten Jahrhunderts.* Abhandlungen zur Theologie des Alten und Neuen Testaments 64. Zürich: Theologischer Verlag Zürich, 1975.

Brent, Allen. "Ignatius and Polycarp: The Transformation of New Testament Traditions in the Context of Mystery Cults." Pages 325–49 in *Trajectories through the New Testament and the Apostolic Fathers.* Edited by Andrew Gregory, and Christopher Tuckett. Oxford/New York: Oxford University Press, 2005.

—. *Ignatius of Antioch and the Second Sophistic Movement: A Study of an Early Christian Transformation of Pagan Culture.* Studies and Texts in Antiquity and Christianity 36. Tübingen: Mohr Siebeck, 2006.

Brown, Raymond E. "The Pre-Christian Semitic Concept of 'Mystery'." *Catholic Biblical Quarterly* 20 (1958): 417–43.

—. "The Semitic Background of the New Testament *Mystêrion* (I)." *Biblica* 39 (1958): 426–48.

—. "The Semitic Background of the New Testament *Mystêrion* (II)." *Biblica* 40 (1959): 70–87.

—. *The Semitic Background of the Term "Mystery" in the New Testament.* Philadelphia: Fortress Press, 1968.

Buell, Denise Kimber. *Why this New Race: Ethnic Reasoning in Early Christianity.* New York: Columbia University Press, 2005.

Bull, Christian H., Liv Ingeborg Lied, and John D. Turner, eds. *Mystery and Secrecy in the Nag Hammadi Collection and Other Ancient Literature: Ideas and Practices.* Nag Hammadi and Manichaean Studies 76. Leiden/Boston: Brill, 2012.

Burkert, Walter. *Ancient Mystery Cults.* Cambridge: Harvard University Press, 1987.

Cacciarai, A. "In margine a Giustino, *dial.* vii, 3, le porte della luce." Pages 101–34 in *In Verbis verum amare.* Edited by P. Serra Zanetti. Florence: La Nuova Italia, 1980.

Cameron, Averil. *Christianity and the Rhetoric of Empire: The Development of Christian Discourse.* Sather Classical Lectures 55. Berkeley: University of California Press, 1991.

Campbell, Douglas A. "Galatians 5.11: Evidence of an Early Law-observant Mission by Paul?" *New Testament Studies* 57 (2011): 325–47.

—. *The Deliverance of God: An Apocalyptic Rereading of Justification in Paul*. Grand Rapids: Eerdmans, 2009.

Caragounis, Chrys C. *The Ephesian* Mysterion: *Meaning and Content*. Coniectanea neotestamentica or Coniectanea biblica: New Testament Series 8. Lund: CWK Gleerup, 1977.

Cheetham, Samuel. *The Mysteries, Pagan and Christian*. London: Macmillan, 1897.

Childs, Brevard. *The New Testament as Canon: An Introduction*. Philadelphia: Fortress Press, 1984.

Chilton, Bruce. "Justin and Israelite Prophecy." Pages 77–87 in *Justin Martyr and his Worlds*. Edited by Sara Parvis, and Paul Foster. Minneapolis: Fortress Press, 2007.

Ciampa, Roy E., and Brian S. Rosner. *The First Letter to the Corinthians*. Pillar New Testament Commentary. Grand Rapids: Eerdmans, 2010.

Clabeaux, John J. *A Lost Edition of the Letters of Paul: A Reassessment of the Text of the Pauline Corpus Attested by Marcion*. Catholic Biblical Quarterly Monograph Series 21. Washington, DC: The Catholic Biblical Association of America, 1989.

Clinton, Kevin. "Stages of Initiation in the Eleusinian and Samothracian Mysteries." Pages 50–78 in *Greek Mysteries: The Archaeology and Ritual of Ancient Greek Secret Cults*. Edited by Michael B. Cosmopoulos. London/New York: Routledge, 2003.

Cohen, Shaye J. D. "Judaism without Circumcision and 'Judaism' without 'Circumcision' in Ignatius." *Harvard Theological Review* 95 (2002): 395–415.

Cohick, Lynn. *The* Peri Pascha *Attributed to Melito of Sardis: Setting, Purpose, and Sources*. Brown Judaic Studies 327. Providence: Brown Judaic Studies, 2000.

Collins, John J. *Daniel*. Hermeneia. Minneapolis: Fortress Press, 1993.

Collins, John N. "A Monocultural Usage: διακον- words in Classical, Hellenistic, and Patristic Sources." *Vigiliae Christianae* 66 (2012): 287–309.

—. *Diakonia: Re-interpreting the Ancient Sources*. New York: Oxford University Press, 1990.

Collins, Raymond F. *First Corinthians*. Sacra pagina 7. Collegeville, MN: The Liturgical Press, 1991.

—. "The Case of a Wandering Doxology: Rom 16,25–27." Pages 293–303 in *New Testament Textual Criticism and Exegesis: Festschrift J. Delobel*. Edited by A. Denaux. Bibliotheca ephemeridum theologicarum lovaniensium 161. Leuven: Leuven University Press, 2002.

Conzelmann, Hans. *1 Corinthians*. Translated by James W. Leitch. Hemeneia. Philadelphia: Fortress Press, 1975 [1969].

Coppens, Joseph. "'Mystery' in the Theology of Saint Paul and its Parallels at Qumran." Pages 132–58 in *Paul and Qumran: Studies in New Testament Exegesis*. Edited by Jerome Murphy-O'Connor. Chicago: Priory Press, 1968.

Countryman, L. William. "Tertullian and the Regula Fidei." *Second Century* 2 (1982): 208–27.

Cranfield, C. E. B. *A Critical and Exegetical Commentary on the Epistle to the Romans*. International Critical Commentary. Edinburgh: T&T Clark, 1979.

Croissant, Jeanne. *Aristote et les Mystères*. Liège: Faculté de philosophie et lettres. Paris: E. Droz, 1932.

Crook, Zeba A. *Reconceptualising Conversion: Patronage, Loyalty, and Conversion in the Religions of the Ancient Mediterranean*. Beihefte zur Zeitschrift für die neutestamentliche Wissenschaft 130. Berlin/New York: de Gruyter, 2004.

Cross, F. L. *The Early Christian Fathers*. London: Gerald Duckworth and Co., 1960.

Dahl, Nils Alstrup. "Formgeschichtliche Beobachtungen zur Christusverkündigung in der Gemeindepredigt." Pages 309 in *Neutestamentliche Studien für Rudolf Bultmann*. Beihefte zur Zeitschrift für die neutestamentliche Wissenschaft 21. Berlin: Alfred Töpelmann, 1957.

D'Angelo, Mary R. "Εὐσέβεια: Roman Imperial Family Values and the Sexual Politics of 4 Maccabees and the Pastorals." *Biblical Interpretation* 11 (2003): 139–65.

Daniélou, Jean. "Figure et Événement chez Méliton de Sardes." Pages 282–92 in *Neotestamentica et Patristica: Eine Freundesgabe, Herrn Professor Dr. Oscar Cullmann zu seinem 60. Geburtstag überreicht*. Novum Testamentum Supplements 6. Leiden: Brill, 1962.

Dassmann, Ernst. *Der Stachel im Fleisch: Paulus in der frühchristlichen Literatur bis Irenäus*. Münster: Aschendorff, 1979.

Daube, David. "Τρία μυστήρια κραυγῆς: Ignatius, *Ephesians*, XIX. I." *Journal of Theological Studies* 16 (1965): 128–29.

Dautzenberg, Gerhard. *Urchristliche Prophetie: Ihre Erforschung, ihre Voraussetzung im Judentum und ihre Struktur im ersten Korintherbrief*. Beiträge zur Wissenschaft vom Alten und Neuen Testament 6/4. Stuttgart: W. Kohlhammer, 1975.

Deden, D. "Le 'Mystère' Paulinien." *Ephemerides theologicae lovanienses* 13 (1936): 405–42.

Deissmann, Adolf. *Paulus: Eine kultur- und religionsgeschichtliche Skizze*. Tübingen: Mohr Siebeck, 1911.

Dibelius, Martin, and Hans Conzelmann. *The Pastoral Epistles*. Translated by Philip Buttolph, and Adela Yarbro. Hermeneia. Philadelphia: Fortress Press, 1972 [1955].

Donfried, Karl P. "The Cults of Thessalonica and the Thessalonian Correspondence." *New Testament Studies* 31 (1985): 336–56.

Dunn, Geoffrey D. *Tertullian*. London/New York: Routledge, 2004.

———. *Tertullian's Aduersus Iudaeos: A Rhetorical Analysis*. Patristic Monograph Series 19. Washington, D.C.: Catholic University of America Press, 2008.

———. "Tertullian's Scriptural Exegesis in *de praescriptione haereticorum*." *Journal of Early Christian Studies* 14 (2006): 141–55.

Dunn, James D. G. *The Epistles to Colossians and to Philemon*. New International Greek Text Commentary. Grand Rapids: Eerdmans, 1996.

Edwards, M. J. "Ignatius and the Second Century: An Answer to R. Hübner." *Zeitschrift für Antikes Christentum* 2 (1998): 214–26.

Ehrman, Bart D. *Apostolic Fathers*. 2 vols. Loeb Classical Library. Cambridge: Harvard University Press, 2003.

Elliott, J. K. "The Language and Style of the Concluding Doxology of the Epistle to the Romans." *Zeitschrift für die neutestamentliche Wissenschaft und die Kunde der älteren Kirche* 72 (1981): 124–30.

Ellis, E. Earle. "Traditions in 1 Corinthians." *NewTestament Studies* 32 (1986): 481–502.

Eltester, Walther. "Das Mysterium des Christentums: Anmerkungen zum Diognethrief." *Zeitschrift für die neutestamentliche Wissenschaft und die Kunde der älteren Kirche* 61 (1970): 278–93.

Engberg-Pedersen, Troels, ed. *Paul Beyond the Judaism/Hellenism Divide*. Louisville: Westminster/John Knox Press, 2001.

Erbse, Hartmut. "Die Bedeutung der Synkrisis in den Parallelbiographien Plutarchs." *Hermes* 84 (1956): 398–424.

Fee, Gordon D. "Textual-Exegetical Observations on 1 Corinthians 1:2, 2:1, and 2:10." Pages 1–15 in *Scribes and Scriptures: New Testament Essays in Honor of J. Harold Greenlee*. Edited by David Alan Black. Winona Lake, IN: Eisenbrauns, 1992.
—. *The First and Second Letters to the Thessalonians*. New International Commentary on the New Testament. Grand Rapids: Eerdmans, 2009.
—. *The First Epistle to the Corinthians*. New International Commentary on the New Testament. Grand Rapids: Eerdmans, 1987.
Fitzmyer, Joseph A. *First Corinthians: A New Translation with Introduction and Commentary*. Anchor Bible 32. New Haven: Yale University Press, 2008.
Focke, Friedrich. "Synkrisis." *Hermes* 58 (1923): 327–68.
Forbes, Christopher. *Prophecy and Inspired Speech in Early Christianity and its Hellenistic Environment*. Wissenschaftliche Untersuchungen zum Neuen Testament 2/75. Tübingen: Mohr Siebeck, 1995.
Foster, Paul. "The *Epistle to Diognetus*." Pages 147–56 in *The Writings of the Apostolic Fathers*. Edited by Paul Foster. London/New York: T&T Clark, 2007.
Foster, Theodore B. "'Mysterium' and 'Sacramentum' in the Vulgate and Old Latin Versions." *The American Journal of Theology* 19 (1915): 402–15.
Foucault, Michel. *Archaeology of Knowledge and the Discourse on Language*. Translated by A.M. Sheridan Smith. New York: Pantheon, 1972.
Fraade, Steven D. "Interpretive Authority in the Studying Community at Qumran." *Journal of Jewish Studies* 44 (1993): 46–69.
Frid, Bo. "The Enigmatic ΑΛΛΑ in 1 Corinthians 2.9." *New Testament Studies* 31 (1985): 603–11.
Furfey, Paul Hanly. "'The Mystery of Lawlessness'." *Catholic Biblical Quarterly* 8 (1946): 179–91.
Gadenz, Pablo T. *Called from the Jews and from the Gentiles*. Wissenschaftliche Untersuchungen zum Neuen Testament 2/267. Tübingen: Mohr Siebeck, 2009.
Gamble, Harry. *The Textual History of the Letter to the Romans: A Study in Textual and Literary Criticism*. Studies and Documents 42. Grand Rapids: Eerdmans, 1977.
García Martínez, Florentino. *The Dead Sea Scrolls Translated: The Qumran Texts in English*. Translated by Wilfred G.E. Watson. Leiden: Brill; Grand Rapids: Eerdmans, 1996.
Gardner, Percy. *The Growth of Christianity*. London: Adam and Charles Black, 1907.
—. *The Religious Experience of St. Paul*. London: Williams & Norgate, 1911.
Garland, David E. *1 Corinthians*. Baker Exegetical Commentary on the New Testament. Grand Rapids: Baker, 2003.
Gerlach, Karl. *The Antenicene Pascha: A Rhetorical History*. Liturgia condenda. Leuven: Peeters, 1998.
Gese, Michael. *Das Vermächtnis des Apostels: Die Rezeption der paulinischen Theologie im Epheserbrief*. Wissenschaftliche Untersuchungen zum Neuen Testament 2/99. Tübingen: Mohr Siebeck, 1997.
Giulea, Dragoș-Andrei. "Seeing Christ through the Scriptures at the Paschal Celebration: Exegesis as Mystery Performance in the Paschal Writings of Melito, Pseudo Hippolytus, and Origen." *Orientalia Christiana Periodica* 74 (2008): 27–47.
Gladd, Benjamin L. *Revealing the* Mysterion: *The Use of* Mystery *in Daniel and Second Temple Judaism with Its Bearing on First Corinthians*. Beihefte zur Zeitschrift für die neutestamentliche Wissenschaft 160. Berlin/New York: Walter de Gruyter, 2008.

Gnilka, Joachim. *Der Kolosserbrief.* Herders theologischer Kommentar zum Neuen Testament 10/1. Freiburg: Herder, 1980.

Godet, Frédéric. *Commentaire sur la première épître aux Corinthiens, t. 2.* Neuchâtel: l'Imprimerie Nouvelle L.-A. Monnier, 1965 [1865].

Goodenough, Erwin R. "Literal Mystery in Hellenistic Judaism." Pages 227–41 in *Quantulacumque: Studies Presented to Kirsopp Lake.* Edited by Robert P. Casey, Silva Lake, and Agnes K. Lake. London: Christophers, 1937.

Goodenough, Erwin R. *The Theology of Justin Martyr.* Jena: Frommannsche Buchhandlung, 1923.

Goodrich, John K. *Paul as an Administrator of God in 1 Corinthians.* Society for New Testament Studies Monograph Series 152. Cambridge: Cambridge University Press, 2012.

Graf, Fritz. "Baptism and Graeco-Roman Mystery cults." Pages 101–18 in *Ablution, Initiation, and Baptism: Late Antiquity, Early Judaism, and Early Christianity.* Edited by David Hellholm, et al. Beihefte zur Zeitschrift für die neutestamentliche Wissenschaft 176.II. Berlin/Boston: de Gruyter, 2011.

Grant, R. M. *The Letter and the Spirit.* London: SPCK, 1957.

Greer, Rowan A., trans. *Theodore of Mopsuestia: The Commentaries on the Minor Epistles of Paul.* Society of Biblical Literature Writings from the Greco-Roman World 26. Atlanta: Society of Biblical Literature, 2010.

Grindheim, Sigurd. "What the OT Prophets Did Not Know: The Mystery of the Church in Eph 3,2–13." *Biblica* 84 (2003): 531–53.

——. "Wisdom for the Perfect: Paul's Challenge to the Corinthian Church (1 Corinthians 2:6–16)." *Journal of Biblical Literature* 121 (2002): 689–709.

Gundry, Robert H. "The Form, Meaning and Background of the Hymn Quoted in Timothy 3:16." Pages 203–22 in *Apostolic History and the Gospel: Biblical and Historical Essays presented to F.F. Bruce on his 60th Birthday.* Edited by W. Ward Gasque, and Ralph P. Martin. Grand Rapids: Eerdmans, 1970.

Hainsworth, John. "The Force of the Mystery: Anamnesis and Exegesis in Melito's *Peri Pascha*." *St. Vladimir's Theological Quarterly* 46 (2002): 107–46.

Hall, Stuart G. "Melito in the Light of the Passover Haggadah." *Journal of Theological Studies* 22 (1971): 29–46.

——. *Melito of Sardis On Pascha and Fragments.* Oxford: Clarendon Press, 1979.

——. "Melito *Peri Pascha* 1 and 2. Text and Interpretation." Pages 238–48 in *Kyriakon: Festschrift Johannes Quasten.* Edited by Patrick Granfield, and Josef A. Jungmann. Münster: Aschendorff, 1970.

——. "Melito *Peri Pascha*: Corrections and Revisions." *Journal of Theological Studies* 64 (2013): 105–10.

Hamilton, J. D. B. "The Church and the Language of Mystery: The First Four Centuries." *Ephemerides theologicae lovanienses* 53 (1977): 479–94.

Hanfmann, George M. A. *Sardis from Prehistoric to Roman Times: Results of the Archaeological Exploration of Sardis 1958–1975.* Cambridge, MA: Harvard University Press, 1983.

Hansen, Adolf. "The 'Sitz im Leben' of the Paschal Homily of Melito of Sardis with Special Reference to the Paschal Festival in Early Christianity." Ph.D. diss., Northwestern University, 1968.

Hanson, R. P. C. "Notes on Tertullian's Interpretation of Scripture." *Journal of Theological Studies* 12 (1961): 273–79.

Harnack, Adolf von. *Die Zeit des Ignatius*. Leipzig: J.C. Hinrischs'sche Buchhandlung, 1878.
—. *Marcion: Das Evangelium vom Fremden Gott: Eine Monographie zur Geschichte der Grundlegung der katholischen Kirche*. 2d ed. Texte und Untersuchungen 45. Leipzig: J.C. Heinrichs, 1924.
—. *The Mission and Expansion of Christianity in the First Three Centuries. Vol. 1*. Translated by James Moffatt. 2d ed. London: Williams and Norgate, 1908.
Harrison, James R. *Paul's Language of Grace in its Graeco-Roman Context*. Wissenschaftliche Untersuchungen zum Neuen Testament 2/172. Tübingen: Mohr Siebeck, 2003.
—. "The 'grace' of Augustus paves a Street at Ephesus." *New Documents Illustrating Early Christianity* 10 (2012): 59–63.
Hatch, Edwin. *The Influence of Greek Ideas and Usages upon the Christian Church*. Edited by A.M. Fairbairn. London/Edinburgh: Williams and Norgate, 1891.
Hays, Richard B. *First Corinthians*. Interpretation: A Bible Commentary for Teaching and Preaching. Louisville: John Knox Press, 1997.
Heil, John Paul. *Colossians: Encouragement to Walk in All Wisdom as Holy Ones in Christ*. Society of Biblical Literature Early Christianity and its Literature 4. Atlanta: Society of Biblical Literature, 2010.
Heine, Ronald E. "Gregory of Nyssa's Apology for Allegory." *Vigiliae Christianae* 38 (1984): 360–70.
—. "Recovering Origen's Commentary on Ephesians from Jerome." *Journal of Theological Studies* 51 (2000): 478–514.
Heintz, Michael. "Μιμητὴς θεοῦ in the *Epistle to Diognetus*." *Journal of Early Christian Studies* 12 (2004): 107–19.
Helgeland, John. "Christians and the Roman Army A.D. 173–337." *Church History* 42 (1974): 149–63, 200.
Hemer, Colin J. *The Letters to the Seven Churches of Asia in Their Local Setting*. Journal for the Study of the New Testament: Supplement Series 11. Sheffield: JSOT Press, 1986.
Henrichs, Albert. "*HIEROI LOGOI* and *HIERAI BIBLOI*: The (Un)Written Margins of the Sacred in Ancient Greece." *Harvard Studies in Classical Philology* 101 (2003): 207–66.
Héring, Jean. *The First Epistle of Saint Paul to the Corinthians*. Translated by A. W. Heathcote, and P. J. Allcock. London: Epworth Press, 1962.
Hill, Charles E. *From the Lost Teaching of Polycarp: Identifying Irenaeus' Apostolic Presbyter and the Author of* Ad Diognetum. Wissenschaftliche Untersuchungen zum Neuen Testament 186. Tübingen: Mohr Siebeck, 2006.
Hock, Ronald F. *The Infancy Gospels of James and Thomas*. The Scholars Bible 2. Santa Rosa, CA: Polebridge Press, 1995.
Hooker, M. D. "Hard Sayings: 1 Corinthians 3:2." *Theology* 69 (1966): 19–22.
Hopkins, Keith. "Christian Number and Its Implications." *Journal of Early Christian Studies* 6 (1998): 185–226.
Hübner, Reinhard M. "Thesen zur Echtheit und Datierung der sieben Briefe des Ignatius von Antiochien." *Zeitschrift für Antikes Christentum* 1 (1997): 44–72.
Jansen, John F. "Tertullian and the New Testament." *Second Century* 2 (1982): 191–207.
Jefford, Clayton N. *The Epistle to Diognetus (with the Fragment of Quadratus): Introduction, Text, and Commentary*. Oxford: Oxford University Press, 2013.
Jervis, L. Ann. "Paul the Poet in First Timothy 1:11–17; 2:3b–7; 3:14–16." *Catholic Biblical Quarterly* 61 (1999): 695–712.
Jewett, Robert. *Romans*. Hermeneia. Minneapolis: Fortress Press, 2007.

Johnson, Luke Timothy. *The First and Second Letters to Timothy: A New Translation with Introduction and Commentary.* Anchor Bible 35 A. New York: Doubleday, 2001.
Joly, Robert. *Christianisme et Philosophie: Études sur Justin et les Apologistes grecs du deuxième siècle.* Bruxelles: l'Université de Bruxelles, 1973.
Karpp, Heinrich. *Schrift und Geist bei Tertullian.* Beiträge zur Förderung christlicher Theologie 47. Gütersloh: Bertelsmann, 1955.
Kennedy, George A., ed. *Progymnasmata: Greek Textbooks of Prose Composition and Rhetoric.* Society of Biblical Literature Writings from the Greco-Roman World 10. Atlanta: Society of Biblical Literature, 2003.
Kenyon, Frederick G. "The Chester Beatty Biblical Papyri." *Gnomon* 8 (1932): 46–49.
Kim, Seyoon. "The 'Mystery' of Rom 11.25–6 Once More." *New Testament Studies* 43 (1997): 412–29.
Kittel, G., and G. Friedrich, eds. *Theological Dictionary of the New Testament.* Translated by G. W. Bromiley. 10 vols. Grand Rapids: Eerdmans, 1964–1976.
Knapp, Henry. "Melito's Use of Scripture in *Peri Pascha:* Second Century Typology." *Vigiliae Christianae* 54 (2000): 343–74.
Koester, Helmut. *History, Culture, and Religion of the Hellenistic Age.* 2d ed. New York/Berlin: de Gruyter, 1995.
Kolping, Adolf. *Sacramentum Tertullianeum: Neue Untersuchungen über die Anfänge des christlichen Gebrauchs der Vokabel sacramentum.* Regensburg/Münster: 1948.
Koltun-Fromm, Naomi. "Psalm 22's Christological Interpretive Tradition in Light of Christian Anti-Jewish Polemic." *Journal of Early Christian Studies* 6 (1998): 37–58.
Koperski, V. "'Mystery of God' or 'Testimony of God' in 1 Cor 2,1: Textual and Exegetical Considerations." Pages 305–15 in *New Testament Textual Criticism and Exegesis.* Edited by A. Denaux. Bibliotheca ephemeridum theologicarum lovaniensium 161. Leuven: Leuven University Press, 2002.
Kremer, Jacob. *Was an den Leiden Christi noch mangelt: Eine interpretationsgeschichtliche und exegetische Untersuchung zu Kol. 1,24b.* Bonner biblische Beiträge 12. Bonn: Peter Hanstein, 1956.
Kwon, Yon-Gyong. "Ἀρραβών as Pledge in Second Corinthians." *New Testament Studies* 54 (2008): 525–41.
Lampe, G. W. H. *The Seal of the Spirit: A Study in the Doctrine of Baptism and Confirmation in the New Testament and the Fathers.* London: SPCK, 1951.
Lampe, Peter. "Theological Wisdom and the 'Word About the Cross': The Rhetorical Scheme in 1 Corinthians 1–4." *Interpretation* 44 (1990): 117–31.
—. "Zur Textgeschichte des Römerbriefes." *Novum Testamentum* 27 (1985): 273–77.
Landvogt, Peter. *Epigraphische Untersuchung über den Oikonomos: Ein Beitrag zum hellenistischen Beamtenwesen.* Strasbourg: M. Dumont Schauberg, 1908.
Lang, T. J. "Spectres of the Real Paul and the Prospect of Pauline Scholarship." On Benjamin L. White's *Remembering Paul: Ancient and Modern Contests over the Image of the Apostle. Marginalia Review of Books,* 26 May 2015: http://marginalia.lareviewofbooks.org/spectres-of-the-real-paul-and-the-prospect-of-pauline-scholarship-by-t-j-lang/.
Lau, Andrew Y. *Manifest in Flesh: The Epiphany Christology of the Pastoral Epistles.* Wissenschaftliche Untersuchungen zum Neuen Testament 2/86. Tübingen: Mohr Siebeck, 1996.

Lawson, Jack N. "'The God Who Reveals Secrets': The Mesopotamian Background to Daniel 2.47." *Journal for the Study of the Old Testament* 74 (1997): 61–76.
Lechner, Thomas. *Ignatius adversus Valentinianos? Chronologische und theologiegeschichtliche Studien zu den Briefen des Ignatius von Antiochen.* Leiden: Brill, 1999.
Légasse, Simon. *L'Épître de Paul aux Romains.* Lectio divina 10. Paris: Cerf, 2002.
Leppä, Outi. *The Making of Colossians: A Study on the Formation and Purpose of a Deutero-Pauline Letter.* Publications of the Finnish Exegetical Society 86. Göttingen: Vandenhoeck & Ruprecht, 2003.
Lienhard, Joseph T. "The Christology of the Epistle to Diognetus." *Vigiliae Christianae* 24 (1970): 280–89.
Lieu, Judith M. "'As much my apostle as Christ is mine': The dispute over Paul between Tertullian and Marcion." *Early Christianity* 1 (2010): 41–59.
—. *Image & Reality: The Jews in the World of the Christians in the SecondCentury.* Edinburgh: T&T Clark, 1996.
—. "The Battle for Paul in the Second Century." *Irish Theological Quarterly* 75 (2010): 3–14.
Lightfoot, J. B. *Apostolic Fathers Part II, Ignatius and Polycarp: Volume 2.* London/New York: Macmillan, 1889.
—. *Saint Paul's Epistles to the Colossians and to Philemon.* London/New York: Macmillan, 1904.
Lincoln, Andrew T. *Ephesians.* Word Biblical Commentary 42. Dallas: Word Books, 1990.
Lindemann, Andreas. "Antwort auf die 'Thesen zur Echtheit und Datierung der sieben Briefe des Ignatius von Antiochien'." *Zeitschrift für Antikes Christentum* 1 (1997): 185–94.
—. *Der Erste Korintherbrief.* Handbuch zum Neuen Testament 9/1. Tübingen: Mohr Siebeck, 2000.
—. "Die Sammlung der Paulusbriefe im 1. und 2. Jahrhundert." Pages 321–51 in *The Biblical Canons.* Edited by J.-M. Auwers, and H.J. DeJonge. Lueven: University Press, 2003.
—. "Paulinische Theologie im Brief an Diognet." Pages 337–50 in *Kerygma und Logos: Beiträge zu den geistesgeschichtlichen Beziehungen zwischen Antike und Christentum.* Göttingen: Vandenhoeck & Ruprecht, 1979.
—. "Paul in the Writings of the Apostolic Fathers." Pages 25–45 in *Paul and the Legacies of Paul.* Edited by William S. Babcock. Dallas: Southern Methodist University Press, 1990.
—. "Paul's Influence on 'Clement' and Ignatius." Pages 9–24 in *Trajectories through the New Testament and the Apostolic Fathers.* Edited by Andrew F. Gregory, and Christopher M. Tuckett. Oxford/New York: Oxford University Press, 2005.
—. *Paulus im ältesten Christentum: Das Bild des Apostels und die Rezeption der paulinischen Theologie in der frühchristlichen Literatur bis Marcion.* Beiträge zur historischen Theologie 58. Tübingen: J.C.B. Mohr (Paul Siebeck), 1979.
Litfin, Bryan M. "Tertullian's Use of the *Regula Fidei* as an Interpretive Device in *Adversus Marcionem.*" *Studia patristica* 42 (2003): 405–10.
Livesey, Nina E. "Theological Identity Making: Justin's Use of Circumcision to Create Jews and Christians." *Journal of Early Christian Studies* 18 (2010): 51–79.
Löhr, Hermut. "The Epistles of Ignatius of Antioch." Pages 91–115 in *The Apostolic Fathers: An Introduction.* Edited by Wilhelm Pratscher. Waco: Baylor University Press, 2010.
Lohse, Eduard. *Colossians and Philemon.* Translated by W. R. Poehlmann, and R. J. Karris. Hermeneia. Philadelphia: Fortress Press, 1971.

Loi, Vincenzo. "Il termine 'mysterium' nella letteratura latina christiana prenicena: Parte I." *Vigiliae Christianae* 19 (1965): 210–32.

—. "Il termine 'mysterium' nella letteratura latina christiana prenicena: Parte II." *Vigiliae Christianae* 20 (1966): 25–44.

Loisy, Alfred. *Les mystères païens et le mystère Chrétien*. Paris: Nourry, 1914.

—. "The Christian Mystery." *Hibbert Journal* 10 (1911): 45–64.

Lona, Horacio E. *An Diognet: Übersetzt und erklärt*. Kommentar zu frühchristlichen Apologeten 8. Freiburg: Herder, 2001.

—. "Diognetus." Pages 197–213 in *The Apostolic Fathers: An Introduction*. Edited by Wilhelm Pratscher. Waco: Baylor University Press, 2010.

Lubac, Henri de. *Corpus Mysticum: The Eucharist and the Church in the Middle Ages*. Translated by Gemma Simmonds. London: SCM Press, 2006 [1944].

—. *History and Spirit: The Understanding of Scripture According to Origen*. Translated by Anne Englund Nash. San Francisco: Ignatius Press, 2007 [1950].

—. *Medieval Exegesis: Volume 1 The Four Senses of Scripture*. Translatd by Mark Sebanc. Grand Rapids: Eerdmans, 1998 [1959].

—. *Medieval Exegesis: Volume 2 The Four Senses of Scripture*. Translated by E.M. Macierowski. Grand Rapids: Eerdmans, 2000 [1959]).

Lührmann, Dieter. *Das Offenbarungsverständnis bei Paulus und in paulinischen Gemeinden*. Wissenschaftliche Monographien zum Alten und Neuen Testament 16. Neukirchen-Vluyn: Neukirchener Verlag, 1965.

Maier, Adalbert. *Commentar über den ersten Brief Pauli an die Korinther*. Freiburg im Breisgau: Friedrich Wagner, 1857.

Manis, Andrew Michael. "Melito of Sardis: Hermeneutic and Context." *Greek Orthodox Theological Review* 32 (1987): 387–401.

Marcovich, Miroslav. *Iustini Martyris: Dialogus cum Tryphone*. Patristische Texte und Studien 47. Berlin/New York: Walter de Gruyter, 1997.

Marcus, Joel. "Mark 4:10–12 and Marcan Epistemology." *Journal of Biblical Literature* 103 (1984): 557–74.

—. "Mark – Interpreter of Paul." *New Testament Studies* 46 (2000): 473–87.

—. "The *Testaments of the Twelve Patriarchs* and the *Didascalia Apostolorum*: A Common Jewish Christian Milieu?" *Journal of Theological Studies* 61 (2010): 596–626.

Marrou, Henri Irénée. *A Diognète: Introduction, édition critique, traduction et commentaire*. Sources chrétiennes 33. Paris: Cerf, 1951.

Marsh, H. G. "The Use of ΜΥΣΤΗΡΙΟΝ in the Writings of Clement of Alexandria with Special Reference to his Sacramental Doctrine." *Journal of Theological Studies* 37 (1936): 64–80.

Marshall, I. Howard. *A Critical and Exegetical Commentary on the Pastoral Epistles*. International Critical Commentary. Edinburgh: T&T Clark, 1999.

Martens, Peter. "Revisiting the Allegory/Typology Distinction: The Case of Origen." *Journal of Early Christian Studies* 16 (2008): 283–317.

Martin, Dale B. *Slavery as Salvation: The Metaphor of Slavery in Pauline Christianity*. New Haven: Yale University Press, 1990.

McVee, Mary B., Kailonnie Dunsmore, and James R. Gavelek. "Schema Theory Revisited." *Review of Educational Research* 75 (2005): 531–66.

Meecham, Henry G. *The Epistle to Diognetus: The Greek Text with Introduction, Translation and Notes*. Manchester: Manchester University Press, 1949.

Meinhold, Peter. "Die geschichtstheologischen Konzeptionen des Ignatius von Antiochien." Pages 37–47 in *Studien zu Ignatius von Antiochien*. Wiesbaden: Franz Steiner, 1979.

Merklein, Helmut. *Das kirchliche Amt nach dem Epheserbrief.* Studien zum Alten und Neuen Testaments 33. Munich: Kösel, 1973.

——. *Der erste Brief an die Korinther: Kapitel 1–4*. Ökumenischer Taschenbuchkommentar zum Neuen Testament. Gütersloher: Gütersloher Verlaghaus Mohn and Würzburg: Echter, 1992.

Metzger, Bruce M. "Considerations of Methodology in the Study of the Mystery Religions and Early Christianity." *Harvard Theological Review* 48 (1955): 1–20.

Metzger, Paul. *Katechon: II Thess 2,1–12 im Horizont apokalyptischen Denkens*. Beihefte zur Zeitschrift für die neutestamentliche Wissenschaft 135. Berlin/New York: de Gruyter, 2005.

Metzger, Wolfgang. *Der Christushymnus 1. Timotheus 3,16: Fragment einer Homologie der paulinischen Gemeinden*. Arbeiten zur Theologie 62. Stuttgart: Calwer, 1979.

Meyer, H. A. W. *Critical and Exegetical Handbook to the Epistles to the Corinthians*. Translated by W. P. Dickson. New York: Funk & Wagnalls, 1884 [1870].

Meyer, Marvin W. *The Ancient Mysteries: A Sourcebook of Sacred Texts*. Philadelphia: University of Pennsylvania Press, 1999.

Michaélidès, Dimitri. *Sacramentum chez Tertullien*. Études Augustiniennes. Paris: 1970.

Micou, R. W. "On ὤφθη ἀγγέλοις, I Tim. iii. 16." *Journal of Biblical Literature* 11 (1892): 201–5.

Minear, Paul. "Historical Consciousness vs. Historical Knowledge." *Journal of Bible and Religion* 8 (1940): 72–76.

Minns, Denis, and Paul Parvis. *Justin, Philosopher and Martyr: Apologies*. Oxford Early Christian Texts. Oxford/New York: Oxford University Press, 2009.

Mitchell, Margaret M. *Paul and the Rhetoric of Reconciliation: An Exegetical Investigation of the Language and Composition of 1 Corinthians*. Hermeneutische Untersuchungen zur Theologie. Tübingen: J.C.B Mohr (Paul Siebeck), 1992.

Mitchell, Matthew W. "In the Footsteps of Paul: Scriptural and Apostolic Authority in Ignatius of Antioch." *Journal of Early Christian Studies* 14 (2006): 27–45.

Mitchell, Stephen. *Anatolia: Land, Men, and Gods in Asia Minor, vol. 2, The Rise of the Church*. Oxford: Clarendon Press, 1993.

Mitton, C. Leslie. *The Epistle to the Ephesians: Its Authorship, Origin and Purpose*. Oxford: Clarendon Press, 1951.

Mohrmann, Christine. "Sacramentum dans le plus Anciens Textes Chrétiens." *Harvard Theological Review* 47 (1954): 141–52.

Moll, Sebastian. *The Arch-Heretic Marcion*. Wissenschaftliche Untersuchungen zum Neuen Testament 250. Tübingen: Mohr Siebeck, 2010.

Molland, Einar. "Die literatur- und dogmengeschichtliche Stellung des Diognetbriefes." *Zeitschrift für die neutestamentliche Wissenschaft und die Kunde der älteren Kirche* 33 (1934): 308–10.

Moreschini, C., and R. Braun, eds. *Tertullien: Contre Marcion*. 5 vols. Sources chrétiennes 365, 368, 399, 456, 483. Paris: Cerf, 1990–2004.

Mussner, F. "'Ganz Israel wird gerettet werden' (Rom 11,26)." *Kairos* 18 (1976): 241–55.

Nasrallah, Laura. *An Ecstasy of Folly: Prophecy and Authority in Early Christianity*. Harvard Theological Studies 52. Cambridge: Harvard University Press, 2003.

Nautin, P. "L'homélie de 'Méliton' sur la passion." *Revue d'histoire ecclésiastique* 44 (1949): 429–38.
Nicholl, Colin. "Michael, the Restrainer Removed (2 Thess. 2:6–7)." *Journal of Theological Studies* 51 (2000): 27–53.
Niebuhr, Karl-Wilhelm. "'Judentum' und 'Christentum' bei Paulus und Ignatius von Antiochien." *Zeitschrift für die neutestamentliche Wissenschaft und die Kunde der älteren Kirche* 85 (1994): 218–33.
Niederwimmer, Kurt. *The Didache*. Translated by Linda M. Maloney. Hermeneia. Minneapolis: Fortress Press, 1998.
Nielsen, Charles M. "The Epistle to Diognetus: Its Date and Relationship to Marcion." *Anglican Theological Review* 52 (1970): 77–91.
Nickelsburg, George W. E. *1 Enoch 1: A Commentary on the Book of 1 Enoch, Chapters 1–36; 81–108*. Hermeneia. Minneapolis: Fortress Press, 2001.
Nock, Arthur Darby. *Early Gentile Christianity and Its Hellenistic Background*. New York: Harper & Row, 1964.
—. "Hellenistic Mysteries and Christian Sacraments." *Mnemosyne* 5 (1952): 177–213.
—. "Mysterion." *Harvard Studies in Classical Philology* 60 (1951): 201–4.
—. "The Vocabulary of the New Testament." *Journal of Biblical Literature* 52 (1933): 131–39.
Nongbri, Brent. *Before Religion: A History of a Modern Concept*. New Haven: Yale University Press, 2013
Norden, Eduard. *Agnostos Theos: Untersuchungen zur Formengeschichte religiöser Rede*. Leipzig/Berlin:Teubner, 1913.
O'Brien, Peter T. *The Letter to the Ephesians*. Pillar New Testament Commentary. Grand Rapids: Eerdmans, 1999.
O'Malley, T. P. *Tertullian and the Bible: Language-Imagery-Exegesis*. Latinitas christianorum primaeva 21. Nijmegen/Utrecht: Dekker and van de Vegt, 1967.
Osborn, Eric. *Tertullian: First Theologian of the West*. Cambridge: Cambridge University Press, 1997.
Otranto, Giorgio. "La terminologia esegetica in Giustino." *Vetera Christianorum* 24 (1987): 23–41.
Pahl, Michael W. *Discerning the 'Word of the Lord': The 'Word of the Lord' in 1 Thessalonians 4:15*. Library of New Testament Studies 389. London/New York: T&T Clark, 2009.
Passaro, Angelo. "The secrets of God. Investigation into Sir 3:21–24." Pages 155–71 in *The Wisdom of Ben Sira: Studies in Tradition, Redaction, and Theology*. Edited by Angelo Passaro, and Giuseppe Bellia. Deuterocanonical and Cognate Literature Studies 1. Berlin/New York: Walter de Gruyter, 2008.
Paulsen, Henning. *Die Briefe des Ignatius von Antiochia und der Briefe des Polykarp von Smyrna: zweite, neubearbeitete Auflage der Auslegung von Walter Bauer*. Handbuch zum Neuen Testament 18. Tübingen: Mohr Siebeck, 1985.
—. *Studien zur Theologie des Ignatius von Antiochien*. Göttingen: Vandenhoeck & Ruprecht, 1978.
Perriman, Andrew. "The Pattern of Christ's Sufferings: Colossians 1:24 and Philippians 3:10–11." *Tyndale Bulletin* 42 (1991): 62–79.
Pervo, Richard I. *The Making of Paul: Constructions of the Apostle in Early Christianity*. Minneapolis: Fortress Press, 2010.
Places, Édouard des. "Platon et la Langue des Mystères." *Annales de la Faculté des Lettres d'Aix* 38 (1964): 9–23.

Pokorný, Petr. *Der Brief des Paulus an die Kolosser.* Theologischer Handkommentar zum Neuen Testament 10/1. Berlin: Evangelische Verlagsanstalt, 1987.

Prümm, K. "Mystères." Pages 10–225 in vol. 6 of *Dictionnaire de la Bible: Supplément.* Edited by L. Pirot, A. Robert, and A. Feuillet. 12 vols. Paris: 1928–1960.

———. "'Mysterion' von Paulus bis Origenes." *Zeitschrift für katholische Theologie* 61 (1937): 391–425.

———. "Zur Phänomenologie des paulinischen Mysteriums und dessen seelischer Aufnahme: Eine Übersicht." *Biblica* 37 (1956): 135–61.

Pycke, Nestor. "Connaissance rationnelle et connaissance de grace chez saint Justin." *Ephemerides theologicae lovanienses* 37 (1961): 52–85.

Quispel, Gilles. *De bronnen van Tertullians' Adversus Marcionem.* Leiden: Burgersdijk & Niermans Templum Salomonis, 1943.

Radde-Gallwitz, Andrew. "Gregory of Nyssa's Pneumatology in Context: The Spirit as Anointing and the History of the Trinitarian Controversies." *Journal of Early Christian Studies* 19 (2011): 259–85.

Rathke, Heinrich. *Ignatius von Antiochien und die Paulusbriefe.* Texte und Untersuchungen 99. Berlin: Akademie, 1967.

Rankin, David I. *Tertullian and the Church.* Cambridge: Cambridge University Press, 1995.

———. "Was Tertullian a Schismatic?" *Prudentia* 18 (1986): 73–79.

Reis, David M. "Following in Paul's Footsteps: *Mimēsis* and Power in Ignatius of Antioch." Pages 287–305 in *Trajectories through the New Testament and the Apostolic Fathers.* Edited by Andrew Gregory, and Christopher Tuckett. Oxford/New York: Oxford University Press, 2005.

Reitzenstein, Richard. *Die Hellenistischen Mysterienreligionen nach ihren Grundgedanken und Wirkungen.* Leipzig: Tübner, 1910.

Rensberger, David K. "As the Apostle Teaches: The Development of the Use of Paul's Letters in Second-Century Christianity." Ph.D. diss., Yale University, 1981.

Reumann, John. "Colossians 1:24 ('What is Lacking in the Afflictions of Christ'): History of Exegesis and Ecumenical Advance." *Currents in Theology and Mission* 17 (1990): 454–61.

———. "'Stewards of God' – Pre-Christian Religious Application of OIKONOMOS in Greek." *Journal of Biblical Literature* 77 (1958): 339–49.

Reynier, Chantal. *Évangile et Mystère: Les enjeux théologiques de l'épître aux Éphésiens.* Lectio divina 149. Paris: Cerf, 1992.

Richter, Gerhard. *Oikonomia: Der Gebrauch des Wortes Oikonomia im Neuen Testament, bei den Kirchenvätern und in der theologischen Literatur bis ins 20. Jahrhundert.* Arbeiten zur Kirchengeschichte 90. Berlin/New York: de Gruyter, 2005.

Riedweg, Christoph. *Mysterienterminologie bei Platon, Philon und Klemens von Alexandrien.* Texte und Untersuchungen zur antiken Literatur und Geschichte 26. Berlin/New York: de Gruyter, 1987.

Rives, J. B. "Christian Expansion and Christian Ideology." Pages 15–41 in *The Spread of Christianity in the First Four Centuries: Essays in Exploration.* Edited by W. V. Harris. Leiden/Boston: Brill, 2005.

Robertson, Archibald, and Alfred Plummer. *A Critical and Exegetical Commentary on the First Epistle of St. Paul to the Corinthians.* 2d ed. International Critical Commentary. Edinburgh: T&T Clark, 1929.

Robinson, J. Armitage. *St Paul's Epistle to the Ephesians*. 2d ed. London/New York: Macmillan, 1904.
Rokéah, David. *Justin Martyr and the Jews*. Leiden/Boston/Köln: Brill, 2002.
Roth, Dieter T. "Did Tertullian Possess a Greek Copy or Latin Translation of Marcion's Gospel?" *Vigiliae Christianae* 63 (2009): 429–67.
Roukema, Riemer. "The veil over Moses' face in patristic interpretation." Pages 237–52 in *The Interpretation of Exodus: Studies in Honor of Cornelius Houtman*. Edited by Riemer Roukema. Biblical Exegesis and Theology 44. Leuven/Paris/Dudley, MA: Peeters, 2006.
Sandnes, Karl Olav. *Paul – One of the Prophets?: A Contribution to the Apostle's Self-Understanding*. Wissenschaftliche Untersuchungen zum Neuen Testament 2/43. Tübingen: Mohr Siebeck, 1991.
—. "Seal and Baptism in Early Christianity." Pages 1441–81 in *Ablution, Initiation, and Baptism: Late Antiquity, Early Judaism, and Early Christianity*. Edited by David Hellholm, et al. Beihefte zur Zeitschrift für die neutestamentliche Wissenschaft 176.II. Berlin/Boston: de Gruyter, 2011.
Sanders, E. P. *Paul, the Law, and the Jewish People*. Minneapolis: Fortress, 1983.
Scarpat, Giuseppe. *Libro della Sapienza. Vol. 1*. Brescia: Paideia, 1989.
Scherbenske, Eric W. "Marcion's *Antitheses* and the Isagogic Genre." *Vigiliae Christianae* 64 (2010): 255–79.
Schlier, Heinrich. *Der Brief an die Epheser: Ein Kommentar*. Düsseldorf: Patmos, 1957.
Schoedel, William R. "Ignatius and the Archives." *Harvard Theological Review* 71 (1978): 97–106.
—. *Ignatius of Antioch*. Hermeneia. Philadelphia: Fortress Press, 1985.
—. "Polycarp of Smyrna and Ignatius of Antioch." *ANRW* 27.1: 272–358. Part 2, *Principat*, 27.1. Edited by W. Haase. New York/Berlin: de Gruyter, 1992.
Schöllgen, Georg. "Die Ignatianen als pseudepigraphisches Briefcorpus: Anmerkung zu den Thesen von Reinhard M. Hübner." *Zeitschrift für Antikes Christentum* 2 (1998): 16–25.
Schmid, Ulrich. *Marcion und sein Apostolos: Rekonstruktion und historische Einordnung der marcionitischen Paulusbriefausgabe*. Arbeiten zur neutestamentlichen Textforschung 25. Berlin: de Gruyter, 1995.
Schmithals, Walter. *Der Römerbrief: Ein Kommentar*. Gütersloh: Gütersloher Verlagshaus Gerd Mohn, 1988.
Schrage, Wolfgang. *Der erste Brief an die Korinther (1 Kor 11,17–14:40)*. Evangelisch-katholischer Kommentar zum Neuen Testament VII/3. Zürich: Benziger and Neukirchen-Vluyn: Neukirchener Verlag, 1999.
Schweizer, Eduard. *The Letter to the Colossians: A Commentary*. Translated by Andrew Chester. Minneapolis: Augsburg Publishing House, 1982 [1976].
Selby, Gary S. "Paul, the Seer: The Rhetorical Persona in 1 Corinthians 2.1–16." Pages 351–73 in *The Rhetorical Analysis of Scripture: Essays from the 1995 London Conference*. Edited by Stanley E. Porter, and Thomas H. Olbricht. Journal for the Study of the New Testament: Supplement Series 146. Sheffield: Sheffield Academic Press, 1997.
Setzer, Claudia J. *Jewish Responses to Early Christians: History and Polemics, 30–150 C.E.* Minneapolis: Fortress Press, 1994.
Sheerin, Daniel. "Rhetorical and Hermeneutic *Synkrisis* in Patristic Typology." Pages 22–39 in *Nova et Vetera: Patristic Studies in Honor of Thomas Patrick Halton*. Edited by John Petruccione. Washington, D.C.: Catholic University of America Press, 1998.

Sherwood, Aaron. "Paul's Imprisonment as the Glory of the *Ethnē:* A Discourse Analysis of Ephesians 3:1–13." *Bulletin for Biblical Research* 22 (2012): 97–112.
Shotwell, Willis A. *The Biblical Exegesis of Justin Martyr.* London: SPCK, 1965.
Sider, Robert D. "Literary Artifice and the Figure of Paul in the Writings of Tertullian." Pages 99–120 in *Paul and the Legacies of Paul.* Edited by William S. Babcock. Dallas: Southern Methodist University Press, 1990.
Silva, Moisés. *Biblical Words and Their Meaning: An Introduction to Lexical Semantics.* Grand Rapids: Zondervan, 1983.
Simon, Marcel. "The *religionsgeschichtliche Schule*, Fifty Years Later." *Religious Studies* 11 (1975): 135–44.
Skarsaune, Oskar. "Justin and His Bible." Pages 53–76 in *Justin Martyr and His Worlds.* Edited by Sara Parvis and Paul Foster. Minneapolis: Fortress Press, 2007.
—. *The Proof from Prophecy: A Study in Justin Martyr's Proof-Text Tradition Text-Type, Provenance, Theological Profile.* Novum Testamentum Supplements 56. Leiden: Brill, 1987.
Smith, Carl B. "Ministry, Martyrdom, and Other Mysteries: Pauline Influence on Ignatius of Antioch." Pages 37–56 in *Paul and the Second Century.* Edited by Michael F. Bird, and Joseph R. Dodson. Library of New Testament Studies 412. London/New York: T&T Clark, 2011.
Smith, Jonathan Z. *Drudgery Divine: On the Comparison of Early Christianities and the Religions of Late Antiquity.* Chicago: University of Chicago Press, 1990.
—. "Dying and Rising Gods." Pages 2535–40 in vol. 4 of *The Encyclopedia of Religion.* Edited by Mircea Eliade. 15 vols. New York: Macmillan, 1987.
—. "What A Difference A Difference Makes." Pages 3–48 in *"To See Ourselves as Others See us": Christians, Jews, "Others" in Late Antiquity.* Edited by Jacob Neusner, and Ernest S. Frerichs. Chico, CA: Scholars Press, 1985.
Smith, Morton. "On the History of ΑΠΟΚΑΛΥΠΤΩ and ΑΠΟΚΑΛΥΨΙΣ." Pages 9–20 in *Apocalypticism in the Mediterranean World and the Near East: Proceedings of the International Colloquium on Apocalypticism, Uppsala, August 12–17, 1979.* Edited by David Hellholm. Tübingen: Mohr Siebeck, 1983.
Soden, Hans von. "ΜΥΣΤΗΡΙΟΝ und *sacramentum* in den ersten zwei Jahrhunderten der Kirche." *Zeitschrift für die neutestamentliche Wissenschaft und die Kunde der älteren Kirche* 12 (1911): 188–227.
Spicq, Ceslas. *Theological Lexicon on the New Testament.* Translated and edited by James D. Ernest. 3 vols. Peabody, MA: Hendrickson, 1994.
Standhartinger, Angela. "*Eusebeia* in den Pastoralbriefen: Ein Beitrag zum Einfluss römischen Denkens auf das Entstehende Christentum." *Novum Testamentum* 48 (2006): 51–82.
Staples, Jason A. "What Do the Gentiles Have to Do with 'All Israel'? A Fresh Look at Romans 11:25–27." *Journal of Biblical Literature* 130 (2011): 371–90.
Stark, Rodney. *The Rise of Christianity: How the Obscure, Marginal Jesus Movement Became the Dominant Religious Force in the Western World in a Few Centuries.* New York: Harper Collins, 1997.
Stewart-Sykes, Alistair. "Melito's Anti-Judaism." *Journal of Early Christian Studies* 5 (1997): 271–83.
—. *The Lamb's High Feast: Melito, Peri Pascha and the Quartodeciman Paschal Liturgy at Sardis.* Supplements to Vigiliae Christianae 42. Leiden/Boston: Brill, 1998.

Stroumsa, Guy. *Hidden Wisdom: Esoteric Wisdom and the Roots of Christian Mysticism.* Leiden/New York: Brill, 1996.
Stuhlmacher, Peter. "The Hermeneutical Significance of 1 Cor 2:6–16." Pages 328–47 in *Tradition and Interpretation in the New Testament: Essays in Honor of E. Earl Ellis.* Edited by Gerald F. Hawthorne, and Otto Betz. Grand Rapids: Eerdmans, 1987.
Stylianopoulos, Theodore. *Justin Martyr and the Mosaic Law.* Society of Biblical Literature Dissertation Series 20. Missoula, MT: Society of Biblical Literature and Scholars Press, 1975.
Sumney, Jerry L. "'I Fill Up What Is Lacking in the Afflictions of Christ'." *Catholic Biblical Quarterly* 68 (2006): 664–80.
Taylor, Miriam S. *Anti-Judaism and Early Christian Identity: A Critique of the Scholarly Consensus.* Studia post-biblica 46. Leiden/New York/Köln: Brill, 1995.
Testuz, M. *Papyrus Bodmer XIII, Méliton de Sardes Homélie sur la Pâque.* Geneva: Bodner, 1960.
Theissen, Gerd. *Psychological Aspects of Pauline Theology.* Translated by John Galvin. Philadelphia: Fortress, 1987 [1983].
Thielman, Frank. *Ephesians.* Baker Exegetical Commentary on the New Testament. Grand Rapids: Baker, 2010.
Thiselton, Anthony C. *The First Epistle to the Corinthians.* New International Greek Text Commentary. Grand Rapids: Eerdmans, 2000.
Thomas, Samuel I. *The "Mysteries" of Qumran: Mystery, Secrecy, and Esotericism in the Dead Sea Scrolls.* Society of Biblical Literature Early Judaism and Its Literature 25. Leiden/Boston: Brill, 2009.
Tibbs, Clint. *Religious Experience of the Pneuma: Communication with the Spirit World in 1 Corinthians 12 and 14.* Wissenschaftliche Untersuchungen zum Neuen Testament 2/230. Tübingen: Mohr Siebeck, 2007.
Towner, Philip H. *The Letters to Timothy and Titus.* New International Commentary on the New Testament. Grand Rapids: Eerdmans, 2006.
Tsouna, Voula, ed. *Philodemus, On Property Management.* Society of Biblical Literature Writings from the Greco-Roman World 33. Atlanta: Society of Biblical Literature, 2012.
Trobisch, David. *Die Entstehung der Paulusbriefsammlung: Studien zu den Anfängen christlicher Publizistik.* Novum Testamentum et Orbis Antiquus 10. Göttingen: Vandenhoeck & Ruprecht, 1989.
Turner, John D. "I Tell You a Mystery: From Hidden to Revealed in Sethian Revelation, Ritual, and Protology." Pages 161–201 in *Mystery and Secrecy in the Nag Hammadi Collection and Other Ancient Literature: Ideas and Practices: Studies for Einar Thomassen at Sixty.* Edited by Christian H. Bull, Liv Ingeborg Lied, and John D. Turner. Nag Hammadi and Manichaean Studies 76. Leiden/Boston: Brill: 2012.
—. "From hidden to revealed in Sethian revelation, ritual, and protology." Pages 149–74 in *Histories of the Hidden God: Concealment and Revelation in Western Gnostic, Esoteric, and Mystical Traditions.* Edited by April D. DeConick, and Grant Adamson. Gnostica. Durham: Acumen, 2013.
Van Esbroeck, M. "Le traité sur la Pâque de Méliton de Sardes en georgien." *Le Muséon* 84 (1971): 373–94.
Vielhauer, Philipp. *Geschichte der urchristlichen Literatur: Einleitung in das Neue Testament, die Apokryphen und die Apostolischen Väter.* Berlin/New York: de Gruyter, 1975.

Vinzent, Markus. "'Ich bin kein körperloses Geistwesen': Zum Verhältnis von κήρυγμα Πέτρου, 'Doctrina Petri', διδασκαλία Πέτρου und IgnSm3." Pages 241–86 in *Der Paradox Eine: Antignostischer Monarchianismus im zweiten Jahrhundert*. Edited by Reinhard M. Hübner. Leiden/Boston: Brill, 1999.

Walker, William O. Jr. "1 Corinthians 2.6–16: A Non-Pauline Interpolation?" *Journal for the Study of the New Testament* 47 (1992): 75–94.

Watson, Francis. *Text and Truth: Redefining Biblical Theology*. Grand Rapids: Eerdmans, 1997.

Waszink, J. H. "Tertullian's Principles and Methods of Exegesis." Pages 17–31 in *Early Christian Literature and the Classical Intellectual Tradition: In Honorem Robert M. Grant*. Edited by W.R. Schoedel, and R.L. Wilken. Paris: Beauchesne, 1979.

Weima, Jeffery A. D. *Neglected Endings: The Significance of the Pauline Letter Closings*. Journal for the Study of the New Testament: Supplement Series 101. Sheffield: JSOT Press, 1994.

Weiss, Johannes. *Der erste Korintherbrief*. Meyer, Kommentar über das Neue Testament. Göttingen: Vandenhoeck & Ruprecht, 1910.

Wengst, Klaus. "'Paulinismus' und 'Gnosis' in der Schrift an Diognet." *Zeitschrift für Kirchengeschichte* 90 (1979): 41–62.

——. *Schriften des Urchristentums: 2 Didache (Apostellehre), Barnabasbrief. Zweiter Clemensbrief, Schrift an Diognet*. Darmstadt: Wissenschaftliche Buchgesellschaft, 1984.

Wendel, Susan. *Scriptural Interpretation and Community Self-Definition in Luke-Acts and the Writings of Justin Martyr*. Novum Testamentum Supplements 139. Leiden/Boston: Brill, 2011.

Werline, Rodney. "The Transformation of Pauline Arguments in Justin Martyr's Dialogue with Trypho." *Harvard Theological Review* 92 (1999): 79–93.

Werner, Eric. "Melito of Sardis: The First Poet of Deicide." *Hebrew Union College Annual* 37 (1966): 191–210.

White, Benjamin L. *Remembering Paul: Ancient and Modern Contests over the Image of the Apostle*. Oxford: Oxford University Press, 2014.

Widmann, Martin. "1 Kor 2 6–16: Ein Einspruch gegen Paulus." *Zeitschrift für die neutestamentliche Wissenschaft und die Kunde der älteren Kirche* 70 (1979): 44–53.

Wilckens, Ulrich. *Der Brief an die Römer (Röm 12–16)*. Evangelisch-katholischer Kommentar zum Neuen Testament VI/3. Zürich/Neukirchener-Vluyn: Benziger/Neukirchener, 1989.

Wilson, Stephen. "Marcion and the Jews." Pages 45–58 in *Anti-Judaism in Early Christianity: Vol 2: Separation and Polemic*. Edited by Stephen G. Wilson. Waterloo: Wilfrid Laurier Press, 1986.

——. *Related Strangers: Jews and Christians 70–170 C.E.* Minneapolis: Fortress Press, 1995.

Wilson, R. McL. *A Critical and Exegetical Commentary on Colossians and Philemon*. International Critical Commentary. London/New York: T&T Clark, 2005.

Wittgenstein, Ludwig. *Philosophical Investigations: The German Text with a Revised English Translation*. Translated by G.E.M. Anscombe. 3d ed. Oxford: Blackwell, 2001 [1953].

Wobbermin, Georg. *Religionsgeschichtliche Studien zur Frage der Beeinflussung des Urchristentums durch das antike Mysterienwesen*. Berlin: E. Ebering, 1896.

Wolter, Michael. "Verborgene Weisheit und Heil für die Heiden: Zur Traditionsgeschichte und Intention des "Revelationsschemas"." *Zeitschrift für Theologie und Kirche* 84 (1987): 297–319.

Wrede, William. *Paul*. Translated by Edward Lummis. Eugene, OR: Wipf and Stock, 2001 [1904].

Yarbrough, Mark M. *Paul's Utilization of Preformed Traditions in 1 Timothy: An Evaluation of the Apostle's Literary, Rhetorical, and Theological Tactics.* Library of New Testament Studies 417. New York/London: T&T Clark, 2009.
Zahn, Theodor. *Ignatius von Antiochien.* Gotha: Perthes, 1873.
Zeller, Dieter. *Der erste Brief an die Korinther. Kritisch-exegetischer Kommentar über das Neue Testament.* Meyer-Kommentar 5. Göttingen: Vandenhoeck & Ruprecht, 2010.
Zuntz, G. "On the Opening Sentence of Melito's Paschal Homily." *Harvard Theological Review* 36 (1943): 298–315.

Index of names

Abbott, T. K.   71, 77, 101
Agamben, Giorgio   74–75, 100
Aland, Kurt   112
Aleith, Eva   225
Aletti, Jean-Noël   70, 72
Allert, Craig D.   168
Allo, E. -B.   39, 55
Anrich, Gustav   20
Arnold, Clinton E.   79
Auerbach, Erich   179, 232–233, 236
Aune, David E.   9, 15, 19, 189

Backer, Emile de   221
Baird, William   61
Barclay, John M. G.   64
Barnard, L. W.   149
Barnes, Timothy D.   131–132, 222–223
Barnett, Albert E.   133, 136, 144
Barr, James   8
Barrett, C. K.   40, 55, 110–111
Barth, Fritz   225
Barth, Markus   72–73
Bates, Matthew W.   174
Baur, F. C.   31
Beck, Hans   193
Becker, Eve-Marie   236
Beet, Joseph Agar   56
Bell, Richard H.   45, 227
Berrin, Shani   16
Best, E.   86–87, 90, 93, 94, 104
Bieder, Werner   106
Bird, Michael F.   133, 152
Birdsall, J. N.   197
Blank, Josef   73, 201, 206
Blanke, Helmut   72
Bloom, Harold   169
Bobichon, Philippe   165, 174, 181, 183
Bockmuehl, Markus N. A.   3–5, 14–16, 22, 23, 42, 44–46, 76, 77, 80, 82–83, 90, 108, 160, 164
Boersma, Hans   2
Bonner, Campbell   194–195, 198, 201
Bornkamm, Günther   9, 10, 22, 149
Bourgeois, Daniel   178, 179

Bousset, Wilhelm   21
Boyarin, Daniel   165, 166
Boyer, Steven D.   69, 84
Brändle, Rudolf   151–154
Braun, R.   231
Brent, Allen   132 f., 143
Brown, Raymond E.   12, 14–15, 21–22, 42, 78, 81, 105–106
Buell, Denise Kimber   150, 165–166, 173
Burkert, Walter   9–10, 120–121

Cacciarai, A.   185
Cameron, Averil   7
Campbell, Douglas A.   94
Caragounis, Chrys C.   102
Cheetham, Samuel   20
Childs, Brevard   3
Chilton, Bruce   188
Ciampa, Roy E.   55
Clabeaux, John J.   236, 244
Clinton, Kevin   202
Cohen, Shaye J. D.   137
Cohick, Lynn   195–197, 201
Collins, John J.   4, 52, 56, 250
Collins, John N.   74
Collins, Raymond F.   39, 111
Conzelmann, Hans   18, 36, 55, 61
Coppens, Joseph   25
Countryman, L. William   247
Cranfield, C. E. B.   114
Croissant, Jeanne   11
Crook, Zeba A.   98–99
Cross, F. L.   196

Dahl, Nils Alstrup   3–5, 117–118, 125
D'Angelo, Mary R.   120
Daniélou, Jean   204
Dassmann, Ernst   133, 151
Daube, David   143
Dautzenberg, Gerhard   40
Deden, D.   22
Deissmann, Adolf   72
Dibelius, Martin   127
Donfried, Karl P.   122

Dunn, Geoffrey D. 222, 223, 229
Dunn, James D. G. 72, 81
Dunsmore, Kailonnie 5

Edwards, M. J. 131
Ehrman, Bart D. 148–149
Elliott, J. K. 111
Ellis, E. Earle 53, 67
Eltester, Walther 153–154
Engberg-Pedersen, Troels 22
Erbse, Hartmut 193

Fee, Gordon D. 39, 41–42, 49, 52, 55–56
Fitzmyer, Joseph A. 38–39, 56
Focke, Friedrich 193
Forbes, Christopher 37, 40
Foster, Paul 147
Foster, Theodore B. 221
Foucault, Michel 7
Fraade, Steven D. 15, 16
Frid, Bo 60, 62
Furfey, Paul Hanly 42

Gadenz, Pablo T. 45
Gamble, Harry 111
García Martínez, Florentino 16
Gardner, Percy 21
Garland, David E. 55–56, 63
Gavelek, James R. 5
Gerlach, Karl 198
Gese, Michael 86
Giulea, Dragoş-Andrei 193, 201–202
Gladd, Benjamin L. 15, 22–23, 34–35, 48, 52
Gnilka, Joachim 81
Godet, Frédéric 38
Goodenough, Erwin R. 10–11, 170
Graf, Fritz 208
Grant, R. M. 178, 184
Greer, Rowan A. 74, 101
Grindheim, Sigurd 66, 96
Gundry, Robert H. 123–124

Hainsworth, John 200, 205
Hall, Stuart G. 194–196, 201, 206, 210, 216
Hamilton, J. D. B. 5, 10
Hanfmann, George M. A. 202

Hansen, Adolf 202
Hanson, R. P. C. 229
Harnack, Adolf von 6, 132, 243, 249, 251
Harrison, James R. 98–99
Hatch, Edwin 20
Hays, Richard B. 36, 48, 53–54, 63
Heil, John Paul 70–71, 78
Heine, Ronald E. 95, 176
Heintz, Michael. 157
Helgeland, John 227
Hemer, Colin J. 202
Henrichs, Albert 120, 124, 219
Héring, Jean 38
Hill, Charles E. 148, 150
Hock, Ronald F. 141
Hooker, M. D. 65
Hopkins, Keith 250
Hübner, Reinhard M. 131

Jansen, John F. 225
Jefford, Clayton N. 147
Jervis, L. Ann 120–122
Jewett, Robert 111–112, 114
Johnson, Luke Timothy 120
Joly, Robert 189

Karpp, Heinrich 229
Kennedy George A. 193
Kenyon, Frederick G. 194
Kim, Seyoon 45
Knapp, Henry 200
Koester, Helmut 121, 124
Kolping, Adolf 221
Koltun-Fromm, Naomi 172
Koperski, V. 49
Kremer, Jacob 71–72
Kwon, Yon-Gyong 90

Lampe, G. W. H. 207
Lampe, Peter 66, 111–12,
Landvogt, Peter 34
Lang, T. J. 31
Lau, Andrew Y. 13–15, 17
Lawson, Jack N. 14
Lechner, Thomas 143
Légasse, Simon 116
Leppä, Outi 70

Lied, Liv Ingeborg 20
Lienhard, Joseph T. 155, 157
Lieu, Judith M. 136, 140, 165–167, 224, 226
Lightfoot, J. B. 71, 134–136, 141–142, 145
Lincoln, Andrew T. 86, 96–97, 104–105
Lindemann, Andreas 31, 37, 39, 55, 62–63, 65, 131, 133, 151–152, 167
Litfin, Bryan M. 247
Livesey, Nina E. 165–166
Löhr, Hermut 131
Lohse, Eduard 78, 80
Loi, Vincenzo 221
Loisy, Alfred 21
Lona, Horacio E. 147, 155, 161
Lubac, Henri de 1–2, 5, 215
Lührmann, Dieter 4, 93

Maier, Adalbert 59
Manis, Andrew Michael 200, 209, 212
Marcovich, Miroslav 165
Marcus, Joel 17, 31, 57
Marrou, Henri Irénée 147
Marsh, H. G. 220
Marshall, I. Howard 119, 123
Martens, Peter 1–2
Martin, Dale B. 34
McVee, Mary B. 5
Meecham, Henry G. 147–148, 151–153, 156–157, 161
Meinhold, Peter 145
Merklein, Helmut 55, 93, 95
Metzger, Bruce M. 21
Metzger, Paul 41
Metzger, Wolfgang 123
Meyer, H. A. W. 55
Meyer, Marvin W. 9
Michaélidès, Dimitri 221, 227–228
Micou, R. W. 123
Minear, Paul 6
Minns, Denis 171
Mitchell, Margaret M. 65
Mitchell, Matthew W. 145, 146
Mitchell, Stephen 202
Mitton, C. Leslie 85–86
Mohrmann, Christine 221
Moll, Sebastian 132, 223
Molland, Einar 151

Moreschini, C. 231
Mussner, F. 45

Nasrallah, Laura 7
Nautin, P. 195
Nicholl, Colin 42
Nickelsburg, George W. E. 57
Niebuhr, Karl-Wilhelm 135
Niederwimmer, Kurt 134
Nielsen, Charles M. 148–149
Nock, Arthur Darby 22, 228
Nongbri, Brent 10
Norden, Eduard 86

O'Brien, Peter T. 102
O'Malley, T. P. 229
Osborn, Eric 224
Otranto, Giorgio 178, 181

Pahl, Michael W. 47
Parvis, Paul 168, 171, 188
Passaro, Angelo 12
Paulsen, Henning 134, 136, 138, 141–142
Perriman, Andrew 72
Pervo, Richard I. 31
Places, Édouard des 10
Plummer, Alfred 39, 52, 55, 59, 63
Pokorný, Petr 73
Prümm, K. 5, 22
Pycke, Nestor 189

Quispel, Gilles 243

Radde-Gallwitz, Andrew 207
Rankin, David I. 223
Rathke, Heinrich 132
Reis, David M. 133
Reitzenstein, Richard 21
Rensberger, David K. 133, 151, 166–168
Reumann, John 34–35, 72, 74
Reynier, Chantal 91
Richter, Gerhard 34
Riedweg, Christoph 10
Rives, J. B. 251f.
Robertson, Archibald 39, 52, 55, 59, 63
Robinson, J. Armitage 105
Rokéah, David 165, 170

Rosner, Brian S. 55
Roth, Dieter T. 244
Roukema, Riemer 239

Sanders, E. P. 44
Sandnes, Karl Olav 46, 207
Scarpat, Giuseppe 13
Scherbenske, Eric W. 224
Schlier, Heinrich 104, 106
Schmid, Ulrich 243
Schmithals, Walter 111
Schoedel, William R. 131, 134–136, 138–139, 143–144, 146, 229
Schöllgen, Georg 131
Schrage, Wolfgang 40, 55, 63
Schweizer, Eduard 73, 81
Selby, Gary S. 51–53
Setzer, Claudia J. 165
Sheerin, Daniel 193, 212
Sherwood, Aaron 91
Shotwell, Willis A. 170, 178–179
Sider, Robert D. 226
Silva, Moisés 8
Simon, Marcel 79
Skarsaune, Oskar 163, 168, 189
Smith, Carl B. 133
Smith, Jonathan Z. 11–13, 20–23, 79, 166
Smith, Morton 93
Soden, Hans von 5
Spicq, Ceslas 34
Standhartinger, Angela 11
Staples, Jason A. 44
Stark, Rodney 250
Stewart-Sykes, Alistair 192, 196–197, 201, 218–219
Stroumsa, Guy 143
Stuhlmacher, Peter 67
Stylianopoulos, Theodore 165
Sumney, Jerry L. 72

Taylor, Miriam S. 217
Testuz, M. 195
Theissen, Gerd 66–68
Thielman, Frank 104
Thiselton, Anthony C. 38–39, 46, 54–55, 62
Thomas, Samuel I. 51, 56, 141, 193
Tibbs, Clint 37
Towner, Philip H. 119, 128
Trobisch, David 112
Tsouna, Voula 99
Turner, John D. 20

Van Esbroeck, M. 197
Vielhauer, Philipp 71
Vinzent, Markus 132

Walker, William O. Jr. 53
Waszink, J. H. 229
Watson, Francis 163–164, 183
Weima, Jeffery A. D. 117
Weiss, Johannes 37, 39, 47, 52, 59
Wendel, Susan 188–189
Wengst, Klaus 148, 151
Werline, Rodney 169, 173–174
Werner, Eric 217
White, Benjamin L. 31
Widmann, Martin 53
Wilkens, Ulrich 114
Wilson, R. McL. 73
Wilson, Stephen 165, 209, 240
Wittgenstein, Ludwig 9
Wobbermin, Georg 20
Wolter, Michael 25, 27, 60, 67
Wrede, William 93

Yarbrough, Mark M. 122

Zahn, Theodor 131
Zeller, Dieter 55
Zuntz, G. 201

Index of Ancient Sources

Old Testament and Deuterocanonical

Genesis
2:24   103–105, 246
12:3   173
15:6   173
17:24   173
29–30   217
40:8   64
40:16   64
40:22   64
41:12   64
41:13   64
41:15   64
49   182
49:27   235

Exodus
3:2   209
4:24   209
12   28–29, 197–198, 201–212, 219
12:9   180
12:12   206
12:23   206
12:27   206
12:29   206
14:19   209
15:16   51
17   174
17:8–16   230
23:20   209
23:23   209
28:17–21   180
28:33–34   180
32:34   209
33:2   209

Leviticus
14:10   179

Deuteronomy
11:25   51
28:66   216

1 Samuel
20:30   93

Job
15:8   12

Psalms
2:1–2   216
2:11   51
22 (21 LXX)   172, 182
78:2   58
96 (95 LXX)   171–172

Proverbs
2:3–6   80
3:7   44
3:34   145
8   2
16:23   95
18:17   145

Isaiah
1:13   140
2:3   204
2:10   244
7:14   176
8:4   176
19:16   51
24:16   11
25:8   47
27:9   45

33:6   80
42:6   237
45:3   237, 241, 80
52:5   145
52:15 (LXX)   62
53:7–8   216
53:7   2
59:20–21   45
60:8   241
64:3 (LXX)   62

Jeremiah
11:19   216

Daniel
1:17   92
1:20   92
2   13–14
2:4   14
2:5   14
2:6   14
2:7   14
2:9   14
2:12   14
2:16   14
2:18–47   14
2:18   13
2:19   13
2:21   92
2:26   14
2:27–30   13
2:31–35   14
2:34   57
2:36–45   14
2:36   14
2:45   14
2:47   13–14
4:8–9 (Th)   96
4:9 (Th)   13, 36–37, 63
4:19   51
5:7   64
5:11–14 (Th)   92
5:12 (Th)   64
5:16   64
7:15 (Th)   51

8:15   92
8:27   51
9:22   92
9:24 (Th)   13, 207
10:1   92
10:7–9   51
10:17   51
12:2–3   47
12:7   18

Hosea
13:14   47

Amos
3:7   18–19
9:6   241

Zechariah
3   230
3:1   232
3:3–5   232
3:6   232
9:9   180

Baruch
3:15   80

Judith
2:2   12

2 Maccabees
13:21   12

Sirach
1:24–25   80
1:30   12
3:19   12
3:22   12
4:11–19   12
4:18   12
8:18   12
11:4   12

14:21   12
16:21   12
22:22   12, 93
27:16   12
27:17   12
27:21   12
39:3   12
39:6–7   12
42:19   12
43:32   12
48:25   12

Tobit
12:7   12
12:11   12

Wisdom
2:21   13

2:22   13
6:22   13, 60, 80, 244
7:13–14   80
7:17   155
7:21   13
8:4   13
8:8   13
8:17–22   13
9:9–18   13
9:13–17   63
12:4–5   12
14:15   12
14:23   12
18:13   138
18:14–15   138
19:18   155

Ancient Jewish

1 Enoch
8.3   14
9.6   14
10.7   14
14:13–14   51
16.3   14
41.1–7   80
46.3   80
60.3–4   50
62.15–16   47
96.2   14
97.12   14

2 Baruch
44:14   80
50:1–51:6   47
54:13   80

4 Ezra
5.13–15   51–52

Dead Sea Scrolls
1QapGen 1:2   42
1QH 5:36   42
1QH 50:5 (frg.)   42
1QpHab 7:1–8   15–17, 19, 46, 105, 114, 116
1Q27 1:2–4   42

Josephus
Jewish War
1.470   42

Mishnah
Pesahim
10:5   196

Philo
On Agriculture
9   65
On the Contemplative Life
25   206
On Dreams

2.3   244

Testament of Abraham
3.4   14
3.12   14
6.13   14

Testament of Gad
6.5   14

Testament of Judah
12.6   14
16.3–4   14

Testament of Levi
2.10   14

Testament of Zebulun
1.6   14

New Testament

Matthew
2:1–12   144
2:13–23   217
5:22   104
5:28   104
5:32   104
5:34   104
5:39   104
5:44   104
10:27   58
13:10–13   17
13:11   58, 228
13:35   58
19:5–6   103

Mark
4:10–12   17
4:10   17
4:11   17, 58, 228
10:7–8   103
10:38   208
11:22–23   36

Luke
1:42   143
2:7   173
2:32   93
3:21–22   207
8:9–10   17
8:10   58, 228
10:21   60

12:42   34
16:1–8   34
24   188
24:44–48   114
24:45–46   184

John
9:32   76

Acts
2   37
4:25–26   216
4:28   61
9:27   106
9:28   106
10:37–38   207
10:46   37
13:7   196
13:46   106
14:3   106
16:11   121
19:6   37
19:8   106
26:26   106

Romans
1:1–2   115–116
1:5   116–117
1:11   113
1:13   44
3:21–26   156

3:21   76, 95, 115–116
3:25   88
4   173
4:9–10   190
4:11   207
5:9   88
5:14   176
5:15–21   157
6:3–4   208
6:4   136
6:17–18   7
6:19   50
7:1   64
7:6   136
7:12   240
7:14   240
8:12   152
8:13   152
8:17   97, 173
8:23   87
8:26   50
8:29   61, 173, 198
8:30   61
9–11   46, 240–241
9:23   77, 88
11:1   235
11:12   88
11:16–24   43
11:23–24   43
11:25–27   105
11:25–26   32, 43–46, 116
11:25   36–37, 40, 43–47, 69, 84, 240
11:26–27   45, 47
11:33   80, 88, 98, 241
14:23   111
15:1–16:24   112
15:33   111
16:23   33–34, 111
16:24   111
16:25–27   24–25, 32, 67, 110–117, 128–129, 241
16:25–26   3, 18, 89, 101, 105, 123, 138–140, 143, 175, 183
16:25   60, 68, 93, 126, 128
16:26   45, 68, 93, 115, 117, 126, 128, 140

1 Corinthians

1–2   53
1:1–9   65
1:6   48–49
1:10–17   65
1:17–31   172
1:18–2:16   65, 67
1:18–2:5   36, 53–54, 61
1:18–31   50, 53
1:18–26   64
1:18   50
1:19   142
1:20   142
1:23   142
1:24   60–61
1:30   60–61
2   238
2:1–5   53, 83
2:1–2   35
2:1   18, 32, 36, 40, 48–53, 59, 64, 82, 118
2:2   50
2:3   50, 52
2:4–5   53
2:4   52–53
2:5   53
2:6–16   3, 4, 37, 53–68, 76
2:6–8   156, 172, 218
2:6–7   67, 78, 85
2:6   54, 59, 67–68, 78, 145
2:7–8   54, 60, 76, 102, 142
2:7   32, 36, 40, 48–49, 53–68, 76, 82, 100, 108, 118, 126, 170–171, 199, 238
2:8   61–63, 67, 76, 123, 143–144
2:9   61–63, 67
2:10–16   37, 63
2:10–13   38
2:10–12   67
2:10   45, 64, 67
2:11   38
2:12   64
2:13   59, 63–64
2:14   64–65, 67
2:15   64, 67
2:16   64, 67
3   35
3:1–5   64–65
3:1–4   66

3:1–2   145
3:1   64–65, 67–68
3:2   65
3:3–4   65
3:4   66
3:5   33
4:1–2   118
4:1   32–36, 75, 84, 134, 154
4:2   33
4:12   152
4:21   38
5:3–4   38
5:7–8   198
5:7   136, 198, 234
6:11   38
6:16   103
7:34   38
8:1   151
9–10   238
9:8   64
9:9–10   176
9:17   33, 35, 154
9:19–22   22
9:33   47
10:1–11   176
10:1   44
10:6   176
10:16
11:25–27   88
12–14   37–38
12:1   44
12:3   38
12:8–9   38
12:8   36–37
12:9   36, 38
12:10–11   37–38
12:10   36
12:13   38
12:30   38
13:1   37
13:2   33, 36–37
13:9–12   36
14:1   38
14:2   32–33, 37–40, 49–50, 59, 82, 96, 157
14:3–5   40
14:4   38
14:5   38
14:13   38
14:14–15   38
14:18   38
14:26–28   38
14:35   59
14:37   66
15:35   47
15:36–50   47
15:36–44   47
15:43   50
15:45–50   47
15:51–57   105
15:51–54   47
15:51–52   32, 46–48
15:51   13, 36–37, 40, 46–50, 59, 82
15:54–55   47
16:3   99

2 Corinthians

1:8   44
1:12   120
1:21–22   207
2:17   59
3   238–240
3:7–18   176
4:7–12   73
4:7–10   53
5:20   107
6:2   47
6:4–6   53
6:9–10   152
6:9   47
7:11   47
7:15   50
8–9   99
8:1   99
8:4   99
8:6–7   99
8:9   99
8:19   99
9:8   99
9:14   99
10:3   152
10:10   52
10:12   64

11:17   64
11:23–12:12   53
11:23   64
11:30   50
12:1–4   145
12:4   47
12:5   50
12:9   50
12:10   50
12:19   59
13:4   50

Galatians
1:12   108
1:15   108
1:20   47
2   96
2:2   93
3:7   173
3:23–25   7
4:2   33–34
4:3   50, 155
4:5   87
4:9   155
4:13–14   52–53
4:22–31   176, 236
4:25–26   198, 211
6:9   127
6:17   53

Ephesians
1:3–14   86
1:3–8   88
1:3   86–87, 89
1:4   76, 87, 89, 126
1:5   61, 86–87, 89–90
1:6   86–87, 126
1:7   87–88, 98, 126, 198
1:8   88
1:9–10   85, 87–90, 92, 102, 107, 109, 242
1:9   45, 86–90, 92–93, 95, 101, 105, 115
1:10   33, 87–88, 100–101, 126, 154
1:11   61, 89–90, 103, 126
1:12   86, 90
1:13   90, 97, 207
1:14   86, 90, 97
1:17–18   88
1:17   93, 96
1:18   77, 88, 97, 100
1:20–23   90
1:21   100
2:1–9   156
2:3   120
2:7   88, 98, 100
2:11–22   97
2:11–12   92
2:12   97
2:13–16   97
2:13   88
2:15   244
2:20   96, 243
2:22   96
3   243
3:1   90–92, 107, 126
3:2–13   90–103, 107
3:2–12   85
3:2–9   102
3:2–8   68, 105
3:2–7   90–92, 94–95, 100
3:2–4   91–92
3:2   33, 35, 89, 97–98, 100, 126, 154
3:3–9   118
3:3–5   96
3:3   45, 89, 93–94, 101, 113, 115
3:4–7   3
3:4–5   4
3:4   82, 106–107, 172
3:5–10   109
3:5   76, 89, 91, 93–95, 100–101, 107–108, 115, 126, 136
3:6   94–96, 101, 106, 108, 114, 126, 173
3:7–8   126
3:7   74, 94, 98, 126
3:8–13   90–91, 98
3:8–11   3
3:8–9   96
3:8   35, 88, 91, 97–98, 101–102, 126
3:9   33, 35, 60, 89, 91, 94–95, 100–102, 108, 126, 154, 243–245
3:10   89, 91, 93, 100–102, 108, 115, 123, 126, 245
3:11   100–103, 126

3:13   91–92, 107, 126
3:14–21   91
3:16   88
3:21   100
4:7   98
4:17   103
4:21   92
4:30   207
5:19   59
5:22–33   103
5:25–27   104–105
5:31–32   85, 103–105, 108–109, 176, 246
5:31   103, 246
5:32   40, 103–105, 115, 119, 174, 245–246
6:5   50
6:14   244
6:15   98, 244
6:19–20   82, 85, 106, 108, 126, 246
6:19   49–50, 93, 97–98, 101, 106–107, 114–115, 118, 126

Philippians
1:12–14   83
1:15–18   246
2:12   50
3:5   235
3:20   152

Colossians
1:2   76
1:4   76
1:7   77–78
1:11–12   77
1:12   76
1:13–22   71
1:14   88, 198
1:15–20   80, 107
1:15   155, 173, 198
1:16   145
1:18   77, 173, 198
1:20   88
1:22   76
1:23–26   118
1:23   74, 92, 247
1:24–2:5   70–81, 82, 84
1:24–29   70
1:24–26   76, 107
1:24–25   99
1:24   71–74, 126
1:25–27   77, 109
1:25–26   92
1:25   33, 35, 74–75, 77–78, 82, 84, 89, 100, 126, 154
1:26–2:2   79
1:26–27   95
1:26–28   78
1:26   3, 4, 60, 75–77, 82, 85, 94, 100–101, 115, 123, 126
1:27   35, 72–78, 80, 82, 88–89, 92–93, 101, 115, 124, 216
1:28   68, 72–73, 78–79, 85, 100, 126
1:29–2:1   80
2   80
2:1–5   70
2:2–3   73, 80
2:2   18, 35, 74, 79–80, 92, 172
2:3   74, 82
2:4–5   81
2:5–8   77
2:8–23   81
2:8   155
2:10   80
2:11–13   79
2:11–12   207
2:13–14   71
2:16–17   246
2:16   135
2:17   211
2:20   155
2:22   88
3:7–8   77
3:12   76
4:3–4   81–83, 106, 108, 123
4:3   49–50, 81–84, 92, 126, 171–172
4:12   79

1 Thessalonians
1:5   52
1:6   72
4:13–17   46
4:13–16   44
4:13   44

4:15–18   47

2 Thessalonians
1:10   48
2:1   41
2:2   41, 106
2:3–12   41, 120
2:3   41
2:4   41–42
2:5   41
2:6–7   41
2:6   41
2:7   32, 40–43, 46, 120
2:8   41
2:9   42

1 Timothy
1:2   118
1:3   137
1:4   33, 137
1:9–11   3
1:15   125
1:17   155
1:19   118
2:6   48, 127
2:7   124, 158
3:9   117–125, 134, 153
3:14–15   120
3:16   105, 117–126, 153, 159
4:1   118
4:6–7   125
4:6   118
4:7   137
4:13–18   241
5:8   118
5:23   50
6:3   125, 137
6:10   118
6:14   122
6:15   127
6:20   118
6:21   118

2 Timothy
1:8   48

1:9–11   117
1:9–10   76, 125–128
1:9   103, 115, 127
1:10   114–115, 122
1:11   68, 158
2:9   83
3:3–7   156
4:1   122
4:8   122

Titus
1:1   128
1:2–3   3, 76, 117, 127–128, 139
1:2   115, 128
1:3   114
1:7   33–34
1:14   137
2:3   122
3:6–7   128

Hebrews
1:6   173, 198
5:12–14   65
8:5   211
10:1   211
11:9   173
11:28   173
12:23   178

James
3:15   65
4:6   145

1 Peter
1:10–12   76
1:11–12   136
1:18   21   3
2:1–2   65
2:5   190
2:9   90
3:7   173
4:10   34
5:5   145

2 Peter
3:10   155
3:12   155
3:15–16   31
3:16   115

1 John
1:1–3

Jude
6   123
19   65
24–25   111

Revelation
1:5   173
1:10   135
1:20   17–18
2:14   18
8:20   18
10:7   17–19
11:7   18
11:8   18
15:1   18
15:8   18
17:5   17–18
17:7   17–18
17:17   18
20:3   18
20:5   18
20:7   18

Early Christian

1 Clement
5.5   31
30.2   145
47.1   31

2 Clement
6.9   207
7.6   207
8.6   207

Acts of Andrew
16   154

Acts of John
106   154

Acts of Paul and Thecla
25   207

Acts of Peter
38   57

Ascension of Isaiah
11.16   142

Barnabas
1.2   186
1.7   185
5.6   183
6.10   181
6.11   179
7.3   179
7.7   179
7.10   179
7.11   179
8.1   179
8.2   179
12.2   179
12.5   179
12.6   179
12.9   179
13.5   179
15.8   140
17.2   181
19.7   179

Chrysostom
Homilies on 1 Corinthians
7 (PG 61:55–56)   58

Clement of Alexandria
Excerpts from Theodotus
69–75   144
Protrepticus
1.10.1   139
2.17   206
12.18   206
12.119–120   125
12.120.1–2   202–203
Stromata
2.11   31
5.12.80.7   58
6.2.4   206
6.15.124.5–6   58

Didache
11.11   134, 170
14.1   135

Epistle to Diognetus
1–10   149–151, 158–160, 162
1.1   26, 130, 250
2–4   150
2.1   26
2.2–20   153
3.1–4.5   153
3.1   162
3.2   162
4.1   150
4.6   26–27, 119, 151, 153–154, 159, 170
5–10   150
5–6   150, 153
5.1–17   153
5.3   153–154
5.4   122
5.8–16   152
5.8   152
5.9   152
5.10–11   152
5.12–13   152
5.15   152
5.16   152
6   154
6.1–10   154
7–9   154
7–8   150
7.1–2   27, 158
7.1   34, 151, 154, 170
7.2   151, 154–155, 170
7.3   155
7.6   149
8.1   155, 162
8.2–4   144
8.4   155
8.5–11   155–156
8.6   159
8.7–8   155
8.9–11   27, 155
8.10   151, 170
9   150, 156
9.1   157
9.2–6   157
9.2   157
9.5   157
9.6   157
10   149–150
10.1   159
10.6   157
10.7   151,157, 170
10.8   158
11–12   149, 151, 161–162
11   149, 151, 158, 160
11.1–2   158
11.1   149, 158
11.2–3   119, 158
11.2   151, 170
11.3   124, 158, 161
11.4–5   159
11.5   151, 159, 170
11.6   162
12   151, 162
12.5   151

Eusebius
Ecclesiastical History
2.2.4   223

3.36.2–4   131
4.18.2–6   164
4.18.6   165
4.26   194–195
4.26.3   196
4.26.4   196
5.24   194

Gospel of Thomas
17   62

Gregory of Nyssa
De Anima
PG 46:132a

Hippolytus
Commentary on Daniel
4.48.1   49

Ignatius
Ephesians
1.1   143
5.3   145
8.1   143
11.1   141
12.2   133
14.1   142
15.2   143
15.3   142
17.1   142
18.1–19.3   142
18.1–2   142
18.1   142
19.1   26, 102, 114, 134, 138, 141–144, 170–171
19.2–3   26, 143–144, 176
19.2   143
19.3   144
Magnesians
6.1   3
7.2   138
8.1–9.2   26, 135, 138, 140–141
8.1–2   137
8.1   136, 137
8.2–9.1   26
8.2   114, 137–139, 142, 145
9.1–2   135
9.1   134, 137, 140, 144, 170
9.2   136, 139, 145
10.1–3   135, 137
10.2   136
12   145
Philadelphians
5–9   135
5.2   145–146
6.1   137
8.2   146
9.1   145
9.2   145
11.1   134
Polycarp
2.2   145
3.2   132
Romans
2.2   131
8.2   139
Smyrnaeans
5.1   145
7.2   145–146
Trallians
2.3   134–135, 170
5.1–2   145
8.2   145

Irenaeus
Against Heresies
1.1.1   132
1.1.1.43   114
1.1.8   206
4.6.2   168
5.26.2   168
Demonstration of the Apostolic Preaching
3   207

Jerome
On Illustrious Men
53   223
Preface to the Commentary on Titus   31

Justin
First Apology
13.4   171
25.1   171
27.4   171
29.2   171
49.5   188
50.12   188
54.5–6   171
65.7   135
66.4   171
67.5   135
Second Apology
12.5   171, 206
Dialogue with Trypho
3–4   185
3.7   185
4.1   185
7.1   182–183, 185
7.3   185
9.3   165
10.3   190
11–22   190
11   173
11.5   190
14.2   180, 186
16.2   164, 180
17.3–4   167
18.1   167
21.1   180
23   172
23.4   180
23.5   180
24.1   174
28.4   180
29.2   186, 190
30.1   186–187
31.7   184
35.6   167
36.2   182
38.2   187
39.2   186
40   198, 201
40.1   174–175, 179, 205
40.3   180
41.1   179
42.4   180
43.1   180
43.3   171
44.2   171–172
47   166, 191
48.1   187–188
48.2   187
49.6   187
52.1   182
53.4   180
53.5   188
58.1   186
63.2   182
68.6   176, 180, 182
68.7   176
69.2   171, 178
70.1   171, 178
74.3   171–172
75.1   57, 176
76.1   57
76.2   176
76.6   28, 184, 188
77.4   181
78.6   171, 178, 180
78.8–10   182
78.9   176
78.10   186–187
81.3   176–177
82.1   187
84.1   173
84.2   173, 185, 215
85.2   173
86.1   180
86.6   174
88.8   180
90.2   179, 181, 184
90.3–5   180
90.5   180
91.1   173
91.2   179
91.4   179–180
92.1   187
93.5   180, 187
94.1–5   180
97.3–4   172
97.3   182
100.1   58, 177
100.2   173, 186

106.1	172
107.1	180
108.1	180
109.2	186
111.1	180
111.2	174
111.3	205
111.4	180
112.1	180, 186
112.2	180
112.3	174
112.4	186
114.2	182
114.4	186
115.1	182
115.3	184
116.3	173
119	173
119.1	186
120.2	180
120.5	174
120.6	165
122.1–5	186
123.4	186
123.8	182
125.3	173–174
130.2	173
131.2	172–173
131.4	175, 179–180
131.5	180
133.1	187
134.2	154, 175
134.3	179
134.5	172–173
138.1	174–175, 180
138.2	172–173, 175, 180
138.3	180
139.1	175
140.1	179
141.4	154, 175

Melito
Peri Pascha

1–65	198–205
1–45	197
1–10	197, 200–205
1–2	205
2	29, 203, 217
3–10	203, 205
3	203
4–5	29, 203
5	204
6–7	204
6	204
7	204, 212–213
9–10	205
9	204
11–45	197, 205–213
11	205, 213
12–45	205
14–16	206
14	206
15–17	201
15–16	206
17–30	208
30	206
31–33	208
31	199
34	199, 209
35–45	209
35–37	209–210
37	211
38	211
42	211
43	211
44–45	211
45	198, 213
46–105	197
46–65	197, 213–217
46	213
47	213
48	213
49–56	214
52	214
56	214
57–58	214–215
58	215
59–60	216
59	217
61–64	216
61	216
62	216
63	216

65 216	1.13.5 231
66–105 197–198, 217–218	1.14.3 228, 231
67–71 217	1.15.1 224
68 196	1.21.5 231, 247
69 217	1.28.2–3 228, 231
72 217	2.21 31
82 198, 218	2.27.7 231
87 217	2.29.2 224
99 218	3.7.6 231–232
103 198	3.14.4 244
Fragments	3.15.4 244
9 199, 209	3.16.1–5 232–233
13 199	3.18.2 233–234
	3.18.3 234
	3.18.5 234

Origen

Commentary on Matthew
17.2.12   56
13.3   56
15.28   56

Homilies on Luke
10   49

Commentary on John
10.15.85   56
10.41.286   56

Commentary on Romans
Fragment 11, Line 7   56
8.6   95
10.43   95
10.43.2   112, 241

Protoevangelium of James

11.5–8   141
12.6–9   141
12.6   141
19.2   144

Shepherd of Hermas

Similitude
9.12   3
9.16.4   207

Tertullian

Adversus Marcionem

3.18.6   234
3.18.7   234
3.19.4   231
4.1.11   231
4.3.1   231
4.5.2   231
4.16.12   231
4.34.5   228, 231
4.38.2   228, 231
4.40   234
4.40.1   234
4.40.4   234
5.1.5   235
5.1.6   235
5.1.8   225
5.4.8   236
5.5.2   235, 237
5.6.2   237
5.6.5   238
5.7.1   238
5.7.3   238
5.7.10–14   238
5.8.3   228, 235
5.8.4   238
5.10.8   238
5.11.4–5   238–240
5.11.6   239
5.11.7   239
5.13.5   240
5.14.9   240–241
5.15.4–6   241–242
5.15.5   241

5.17.1   242
5.17.5   244
5.17.16   243
5.18.1   243–244
5.18.4   245
5.18.5   245
5.18.8   245
5.18.9–10   245–246
5.18.14   246
5.19.1   247
5.19.9   246
5.20.1   246–247
5.21.1   247
5.21.2   247
Adversus Valentinianos
5.1   168
Apologeticus
2.6   228
6.7   221
7.1   228
7.6   221
19.2   228
39.15   221
47.14   228
De baptismo
228
3.6   228
4.4   228
5.4   228
7   201, 207
8.2   228
9.1   228
12.3   228
13.1–2   228
De cultu feminarum
2.8.2   221
Adversus Judaeos

9.22   229–230
9.25   230
10.5   230
10.10   230
13.12   230
13.17   230
13.19   230
14.7   230
Ad martyras
3.1   227
Ad nationes
7.68.21   221
7.68.26   221
7.70.10   221
De paenitentia
1.1   223
De praescriptione haereticorum
25–26   228
26.2   228
26.5   228–229
40.2   228
40.4   221
Scorpiace
4.5   227
8.1   227
9.1   227
De spectaculis
23.3   221
24.4   227
De testimonio animae
2.2   228

Theodoret
Interpretation of 1 and 2 Corinthians
PG 82:241b   58

Greco-Roman

Apuleius
Metamorphoses
3.3   227
11.21–24   79
11.21–23   219

Aristotle
Rhetoric
1368 A   193
Rhetoric to Alexander
1441 A   193

Index of Ancient Sources — 293

Caesar
Gallic War
6.1.2   227

Cicero
Pro Caecina
97   227
De domo suo
78   227
De offici
1.36   227
De republica
2.60   227

Diodorus Siculus
The Library of History
5.49.6   121, 125

Epictetus
Dissertations
2.16.39–41   65

Heraclitus
Fragment 14 (DK)   9

Herodotus
Histories
2.171   10

Homer
Illiad
11.718   244

Marcus Aurelius
Meditations
1.6   150

Philodemus
On Property Management
19.34–36   99

Plato
Euthydemus
277D   10
Gorgias
497C   10
Meno
76E   10
Phaedo
97C-98B   185
98C-99D   185
Phaedrus
249C-250C   10
Philebus
30C   185
Symposium
209E-210 A   10
Theatetus
155C   11
155E   11
156 A   11

Pliny the Younger
Epistles
10.96   228

Plutarch
De garrulitate
504 A   138
505F   138

Quintilian
Declamations
357   227
Institutio oratoria
2.4.21   193

Tacitus
History
4.21   227

www.ingramcontent.com/pod-product-compliance
Lightning Source LLC
Chambersburg PA
CBHW050103170426
43198CB00014B/2442